THE ECONOMICS OF NATURAL ENVIRONMENTS

JOHN V. KRUTILLA

ANTHONY C. FISHER

The Economics of Natural Environments

STUDIES IN THE VALUATION

OF COMMODITY AND AMENITY

RESOURCES

RESOURCES FOR THE FUTURE / WASHINGTON, D.C.

Copyright © 1975, 1985 by Resources for the Future, Inc.

All rights reserved

Manufactured in the United States of America

Published by Resources for the Future, Inc.
1616 P Street, N.W., Washington, D.C. 20036

Resources for the Future books are distributed worldwide by
The Johns Hopkins University Press, Baltimore, Maryland.

Library of Congress Cataloging in Publication Data

Krutilla, John V.
  The economics of natural environments.

  Includes bibliographies and index.
    1. Natural resources—United States. 2. Natural resources—Valuation—United States.
  3. United States—Public lands. I. Fisher, Anthony C. II. Title.
  HC103.7.K78 1985   333.7'0973   85-42949
  ISBN 0-915707-19-5

Originally published, 1975

Second printing, 1976

Revised edition, 1985

Resources for the Future is a nonprofit organization for research and education in the development, conservation, and use of natural resources, including the quality of the environment. It was established in 1952 with the cooperation of the Ford Foundation. Grants for research are accepted from government and private sources only on the condition that RFF shall be solely responsible for the conduct of the research and free to make its results available to the public. Most of the work of Resources for the Future is carried out by its resident staff; part is supported by grants to universities and other nonprofit organizations. Unless otherwise stated, interpretations and conclusions in RFF publications are those of the authors; the organization takes responsibility for the selection of significant subjects for study, the competence of the researchers, and their freedom of inquiry.

This book was edited by Ruth Haas. Charts and maps were drawn by Clare and Frank Ford. John V. Krutilla is a senior fellow in the Renewable Resources Division of Resources for the Future; Anthony C. Fisher is a professor of Energy and Resources and of Economics and Agricultural and Resource Economics, at the University of California at Berkeley.

CONTENTS

LIST OF TABLES

LIST OF FIGURES

PREFACE

This volume represents a synthesis of selected work undertaken in the Natural Environments Program at Resources for the Future. It addresses the valuation, allocation, and management of the resources—commercial and otherwise—of natural environments. In particular it seeks to engage the range of amenity resources that, while long recognized in public policies providing, for example, for National Parks, Wildlife Refuges, and Wilderness Areas, have not been explicitly included in economic analyses. In this respect then, the present work represents a "first generation" effort to incorporate the noncommercial, or amenity, resources of natural environments into the body of economic theory and application. At the same time, the analysis of the more conventional, commercial uses of natural environments has been extended to deal with such important issues as how progress in thermal electric power technology will affect the valuation of a site for hydroelectric power production.

An institutional point worth noting here is that observations and remarks in the text generally apply to the management of public lands in the United States. This is because, as suggested by the empirical cases considered in chapters 5 through 10, most of the remaining natural and scenic areas of any great extent, and related resources, are in fact found on the public lands. It hardly needs to be added that most theorems about resource valuation and allocation are not dependent on the ownership status—public or private—of the resource in question, so that most of our results apply to the socially efficient use of any substantial wilderness area currently in private ownership as well.

As an early effort, this volume doubtless raises more issues than it is capable of resolving satisfactorily. Nevertheless, since the value of the resources it addresses is of considerable magnitude, it is hoped that the effort will stimulate others to a wider and more intensive application of analytical inclinations and talent. With this in mind, both theoretical and practical issues are raised and addressed in this volume. The theoretical apparatus has been presented and advanced as far as our capabilities permitted in the time available. There is, nonetheless, much theoretical work remaining to be done. We have not on that account, however, avoided confronting urgent practical problems of national significance in the applied portions of the study. As a matter of fact, there is scarcely an applied study in any scientific area to which some theoretical objection cannot be interposed at some level. Specific objections to some of our operational procedures are therefore to be anticipated, but should be regarded more as within the tradition of applied analysis than as an exception to it. Moreover, the approaches adopted in these studies, although within the format laid out in the theoretical sections, and drawing on the theory to organize and interpret the available data to the extent permissible, do represent in most instances the type of analysis that might be expected of conscientious resource managers addressing a real and significant resource allocation issue in a relevant time context.

None of the foregoing is to be interpreted as suggesting that the most sophisticated analytical techniques that may ultimately prove useful in problems of this sort are presented in this volume. The authors are the first to concede that much remains to be done on a much wider scale than permitted within the short period and limited resources available thus far. But while we await the desirable advances in methodology and standardization of practices and conventions in applied analysis, we present this volume as a recommended point of departure for site evaluations when the issue of allocating natural environments among incompatible uses needs to be faced.

One other point, and a very important one, deserves mention here. Doubtless it will occur to some, on the basis of certain themes that run through the book, that we have a point of view. This is quite correct. As was stated earlier, our purpose has been to bring the amenity resources of natural environments into an analytical valuation framework comparable to that for the extractive resources. We have sought to do this by applying tools and concepts of conventional economic theory in somewhat unconventional situations. A relevant special feature of a situation, for example, the irreproducibility of amenity resources, is first introduced and explored in detail. It is then set in an appropriate management decision framework and its implications for efficient use of the environment are derived. The empirical studies are loosely tied to the theory in that the theory indicates what data are relevant and how they are to be processed and interpreted.

Where considerations involving amenity resources are put forward with unusual emphasis, the reason is not that we are advocates for one side or the other in a debate over the use of a particular environment. Rather, we are trying to compensate for a history of analytical neglect. In fact, we could turn the argument around and observe that only by proceeding as we have to build the unconventional special features of natural environments into our economic models can we as economists hope to contribute to the policy debate.

It is hoped that the volume will prove useful to resource managers and related administrative personnel in the field. Indeed, it is intended to be of utility to decision makers since several of the empirical studies have been prepared specifically in response to requests from public officials for assistance in presenting analyses of relative benefits of alternative uses of natural environments. At the same time it is hoped that the format, the level of both theoretical and empirical inquiry, and the relevance of the issues addressed will commend themselves to economists interested in problems of natural and environmental resource use, benefit–cost analysis, and price and welfare theory generally, and to graduate students and upper division undergraduates in these areas. We want to emphasize the accessibility of virtually all of the material presented here to students, including undergraduates. In a few places material is indented to indicate that the discussion becomes more technical. This material may be quickly skimmed, or even skipped without interrupting the flow of the discussion.

John Krutilla is responsible for the outline and general content of the volume, and is primarily responsible for chapters 1, 2, 5, 6, 7, 10, and 11. Anthony Fisher is primarily responsible for chapters 3, 4, 8, and 9. Finally, each has reviewed and participated in the revision of the parts of the manuscript for which the other has been primarily responsible.

Resources for the Future J. V. K.
January 1975 A. C. F.

PREFACE TO THE SECOND EDITION

The objectives that motivated the first edition of this volume were first of all to show how economic analysis can be used to address certain vital issues in an area that had been notably neglected by economics; and second, in doing so, to introduce relevant economic information into the debate over how the issues should be resolved. The effort, we believe, has been largely successful. Although all of the issues that were addressed in the first edition have by now been resolved, the tack taken in some cases was sufficiently novel and approach to the problems sufficiently distinctive to continue to serve students in natural resources and environmental economics courses. With a new printing required to keep the volume in print, we felt certain things should be done to bring the volume up to date. Hence, this revised edition.

One matter deals with the theoretical developments that have occurred over the many years since the Arrow-Fisher paper on environmental preservation, uncertainty, and irreversibility—on which chapter 4 of the first edition was partially based—was originally published. Thus, section 3 of chapter 4 has been completely reworked to include these developments.

Another area demanding attention, as suggested by calls from teaching faculty, was: "So what happened next?—The students want to know." This is understandable, given the celebrated set of cases we worked with. It, therefore, seemed a good idea to summarize briefly the outcomes. This we have done in an afterword.

Another reason for providing such a summary is to underscore the fact that a set of studies which meets the standards for use in academic curricula, ought not to be dismissed out of hand as "ivory tower" by program officers who have lost the inclination to read. We are convinced that high quality analysis can also affect the outcome of policy debate. Indeed, it is the only kind that should.

April 1985

J.V.K.
A.C.F.

ACKNOWLEDGMENTS

The research reported in this volume has been undertaken over several years by members of the Natural Environments Program staff of Resources for the Future. We should first of all like to acknowledge with appreciation the general contribution of our former colleagues, Charles J. Cicchetti and V. Kerry Smith, which goes quite beyond the reference in the text to specific debts of gratitude associated with the writing of this volume. Charles Cicchetti also reviewed chapter 10, which is based on his *Alaskan Oil: Alternative Routes and Markets.* Similarly, chapter 9 has been reviewed by Judd Hammack, co-author with Gardner Brown of the study, *Waterfowl and Wetlands: Toward Bioeconomic Analysis,* on which it is based.

A first draft of the manuscript was reviewed by our program colleagues Talbot Page and Kerry Smith, and by Mancur Olson, Anthony Scott, and Vernon Smith. We are most grateful for their perceptive comments and constructive suggestions on both matters of substance and style. We are also grateful to Henry Jarrett and Irving Fox for their valuable comments on a later version of the study. A debt of gratitude is also due Adrian Gilbert and John Butt of the U.S. Forest Service for careful review and detailed comments, particularly regarding chapter 8, which deals with the Mineral King Valley project.

Many individuals have contributed in one way or another to the material presented in the separate chapters. We are indebted to Marion Clawson for a review of chapter 1, and to him and Robert Dorfman for suggestions concerning revision of the content of chapter 2, appearing in *The Governance of Common Property Resources,* edited by Edwin Haefele.

Chapters 3 and 4, as indicated by a number of references, owe much to the work of Kenneth Arrow. Beyond this, the treatment of uncertainty and information is based on collaboration between Arrow and Anthony Fisher. Helpful suggestions by John Brown and Harl Ryder regarding the formulation and solution of the optimal control problem are gratefully acknowledged, as are editorial suggestions by George Borts on an earlier version of some of this material, published in the *American Economic Review.*

The discussion of the intergenerational problem in chapter 4 has been importantly affected by the ongoing work of Talbot Page.

Chapters 5 and 6, the Hells Canyon studies, have benefited from many constructive suggestions by Darwin Nelson, Arnold Quint, and Donald Sander of the Federal Power Commission, and from students and staff of the Natural Resources Institute held at Oregon State University during the summer of 1969. We are also grateful for input to the study by Charles Cicchetti and Clifford Russell, and for comments on drafts of an earlier version by Gardner Brown, Ronald Cummings, Myrick Freeman, and Richard Judy.

Chapter 7 was undertaken in part using information supplied by members of the staff of Region 4 of the U.S. Forest Service. Particular mention needs to be made of the assistance of Fred Wagstaff, regional economist of the U.S. Forest Service, Ogden, in preparing a report with John Krutilla from which this chapter is abstracted. We are also indebted to Don T. Nebeker, study coordinator, White Cloud–Boulder–Pioneer Mountain Area investigations for making numerous arrangements to obtain data and for access to study reports. Acknowledgment of assistance is also due Frank Gunnell, wildlife biologist, U.S. Forest Service; and to William Mellick, Clayton District, and Dan Pence, Clayton District ranger, for much assistance in connection with data and analysis of grazing on the district. To Richard Carter, White Cloud patrolman, we are indebted for testing impressions gained in the field, particularly in connection with estimates of recreational carrying capacity and to Ed Schlatterer, ecologist, U.S. Forest Service, for information regarding ecological carrying capacity in connection with recreational uses. Robert Williams was very helpful, along with Delworth Gardner and Darwin Nielson of Utah State University in assisting with the unit value of grazing permits. To Kenji Shiozawa, staff assistant for landscape architecture and perhaps others in the field of recreation planning at the Ogden office of the Forest Service, we are most grateful for the information on trails, developmental and maintenance costs, and related information on recreational facilities. Acknowledgment is also due Les Pengelly, of the Department of Wildlife Management, School of Forestry, University of Montana, and to Keith Whiting of the American Smelting and Refining Company for information supplied in connection with the study.

Additionally we are indebted to John Merriam, Idaho State University, for a "guided packtrip for John Krutilla through the White Cloud Mountains, and for much on-the-spot information regarding local conditions, as well as for a careful review of an earlier draft of this study. A very special debt of gratitude is due Kerry Smith and Charles Cicchetti for their contribution in adapting for application to the White Cloud Peaks, models developed for their study of the Spanish Peaks Primitive Area.

Chapter 8, as noted in the text, draws on a study by Charles Cicchetti, Kerry Smith, and Anthony Fisher. Comments and suggestions by Anthony Scott and Joseph Seneca on a draft of the study are gratefully acknowledged. Generous assistance in obtaining and interpreting the data on the use of California ski sites, and much information about Mineral King, has been provided by Craig Stanley, and through Stanley, by the U.S. Forest Service, in particular Pete Wyckoff. Programming assistance has been provided by Joseph Tu.

Chapters 9 and 10, as noted above, represent our condensed versions of work done by others (Charles Cicchetti, Gardner Brown, and Judd Hammack) in the Natural Environments Program at RFF, and graciously made available to us for inclusion here.

In revising and editing this volume, it has been our good fortune to work with Ruth Haas of the RFF editorial staff. Although her contributions are too many and varied to list here, much of the credit for the readability of the final product is due to her.

The list of those to whom acknowledgment is due grows long, but it cannot be terminated without reflecting our appreciation for the even-tempered toleration, patience, and perseverance of Rita Gromacki in typing and retyping the manuscript.

Needless to say, while assistance has been rendered by many individuals and organizations, the responsibility for the material included, analysis, and conclusions remain solely with the authors.

Resources for the Future   John V. Krutilla
December 1974   Anthony C. Fisher

PART I

INSTITUTIONAL AND THEORETICAL CONSIDERATIONS

CHAPTER 1

MANAGING NATURAL ENVIRONMENTS

1. INTRODUCTION

There are many dimensions to environmental quality and, thus, many dimensions to the threats to this quality. These may range from minor local disturbances causing physical or psychic discomfort, to large-scale ecological upsets that may affect the length of time man can occupy the earth (Brubaker, 1972). In this study we address issues that cover the entire range of environmental threats.

The theoretical portions of this book are devoted to an abstract, and therefore widely applicable, treatment of the side effects, or externalities, associated with human economic behavior. These range from minor spillovers that impinge on the amenities of life, to major results of irreversible decisions. The problems taken up in the applied studies, while specific, are important in the models they offer for dealing with environmental considerations that have mostly been neglected in the decision-making process. That is, our empirical work is concerned with the valuation of the opportunity costs of economic activities that can be expressed as loss of amenities otherwise available from a natural environment. It consists of explorations in the relative valuation of amenity and commodity resources.

While the empirical portion of the study does not deal with the gravest environmental threats, it should not be inferred that the problems addressed are of minor significance or little economic consequence. Indeed, the aesthetic dimensions of the environment have been of such profound and persevering concern to the American people that they have occupied an important position in conservation and environmental legislation and policy. It is interesting to note, for example, that the Wild and Scenic Rivers Act preceded the National Environmental Policy Act (NEPA) by a year and the Wilderness Act by several years. In a decade that witnessed the commissioning of a national outdoor recreation resources review, we also saw passage of the Classification and Multiple Use Act of 1964, which required the Department of the Interior to recognize the

3

amenity aspects of the environment in its management of the public domain. In addition, there was the Multiple Use and Sustained Yield Act of 1960, which required that the amenity services of the national forests be recognized equally with more conventional forest products as valuable and deserving of managerial attention.

The passage of this legislation, which expresses the importance of amenities in the public mind, does not mean that there is no concern for the graver environmental insults. The Federal Water Pollution Control Act and the Clean Air Act obviously reflect a concern about health as well as the aesthetic dimensions of the environment. But it may not be amiss to note that public action taken to preserve the amenities of Yellowstone National Park, for example, predates the establishment of the Food and Drug Administration. America's pioneering role in establishing national parks, a wilderness preservation system, and wildlife refuges, and similar evidences of concern for preserving natural environments attest to the status of these values in the American psyche.

Much of the new legislation seeks to achieve amenity-oriented environmental goals through changes in practices and policies in management of the public lands, and regulation of the nation's use of streams and other bodies of water in which the federal government has a paramount interest. Now, while these policies may be limited largely to actions taken in connection with public lands and waters under federal control, the impact of the new legislation is nonetheless very extensive because of the vast extent of the public lands and the resources represented by them.

In summary, this study seeks to develop and apply some of the theoretical concepts and measurement techniques relevant to the valuation of natural environments. Although the analytical propositions about socially efficient resource use clearly have applications to privately owned natural environments, most of the remaining natural areas of any great extent in the United States appear on the public lands. This chapter is mainly devoted to exploring the association between natural environments and public lands, with particular attention to the problems posed for public land management (and incidentally for research as well).

2. THE PUBLIC LANDS AND COMMODITY AND AMENITY RESOURCES IN THE UNITED STATES

While the United States stands in the forefront among economies that are oriented toward private enterprise and the vestment of property rights in private parties, the federal government simultaneously has vast holdings of public lands and related resources. Indeed, after the Soviet Union, China, and possibly Canada, the U.S. Bureau of Land Management and the U.S. Forest Service administer perhaps the fourth and fifth largest land holdings in the world. The combined holdings of the two agencies amount to about 650 million acres. This is roughly comparable in area to the eastern European socialist states and equal, similarly, to the combined area of the Common Market countries of western Europe, excluding the United Kingdom. In short, these agencies would rank near the top of the world's largest public enterprises. However, although these lands are publicly owned, their use is often designed to meet the demands of private parties.

A substantial portion of the government-owned land consists of public lands in Alaska, where the settlement of claims in connection with the transition from territorial status to statehood has not yet been completed. Even excepting Alaska, however, the public lands in the coterminous United States represent about a fifth of the total land area, and among some of the western states, where the bulk of the public lands are concentrated, the share is more than half.

While the amount of the land held by the public is relatively large, the share of the total land and land-related resource value may not be proportionate. More precisely, the distribution of resources among these lands differs in character from that among lands in general. Much of the land administered by the Bureau of Land Management is located in the arid West and represents, along with the bulk of the federally owned lands in the Rocky Mountains, Cascades, and Sierra Nevadas, land not suitable for agriculture. Indeed, much of the land remaining in the public domain escaped appropriation by private parties under the Homestead Act and similar land disposal programs because of its unsuitability for agriculture. While National Forest lands are much less the result of neglected private appropriation, having been explicitly reserved under numerous acts of legislation over the years (beginning with the 1891 Act), it is nonetheless true that much if not most of the best timber areas are to be found among the private lands outside the national forests. Many vast areas within the national forests, because of elevation and terrain, in fact do not support stands of merchantable timber. In spite of their immense extent, the public lands thus fall far short of supporting potential silvicultural and agricultural activities at anything approaching the levels that might be obtained from equivalent acreage in private holdings.

The public lands that are the most inhospitable to agriculture and silviculture in many instances are lands valued for their desert or mountain scenery and the wildlife and fish that they support. They may, however, also contain mineral deposits, sites for hydroelectric and other water development, and related extractive industries. It is here that we often find a conflict between exploitation of commodity resources and use of the areas for their recreational amenities.

In recognition of the amenities that natural and scenic environments provide, the U.S. Congress has over the years reserved nearly 50 million acres to establish national parks (26.6 million acres) and the National Wildlife Refuge System (23.3 million acres). Approximately half of this total, however, consists of the vast Arctic National Wildlife Range of about 9 million acres in the northeast corner of Alaska along with another 9 million in 17 other Alaskan refuges, and the land associated with McKinley National Park. The bulk of the remaining 24 million acres are distributed among the various national parks and wildlife refuges in the coterminous United States.[1] Along with the refuge system and the national parks, the Wilderness System (11 million acres), established pursuant to the Wilderness Act of 1964, represents a "primary purpose" category of land with Congressional intent to exclude uses not compatible with nature preservation and recreation. In addition, but representing a much smaller area in the aggregate are Wild and Scenic Rivers, National Recreation Areas, National Trails, Scenic, Geological, and Research Areas, among the more specialized primary purpose areas.

No specific primary purpose has been designated for the remaining federally owned lands administered by the Bureau of Land Management and the Forest Service.

3. A CRITIQUE OF EXISTING APPROACHES TO PUBLIC LAND MANAGEMENT

The Public Land Law Review Commission, established in 1964 to help resolve the conflicting demands being made on the public lands, after a comprehensive examination of their resources, and the present and potential uses of the lands, had the following to report:

Although Congress has established goals in the statutes setting aside and providing for the administration of national parks, wilderness areas, and wildlife refuges, it has not provided adequate goals for lands not having a clearly defined primary purpose. It is on these lands, primarily those managed by the Forest Service and the Bureau of Land Management, that the absence of goals has led to major problems. (1970, p. 42)

It is most likely not the "absence of goals" that represents the problem here but rather the absence of a method of evaluating the relative worth of alternative goals, or combinations of goals, to which a given river or tract of wild land can be dedicated.

Since the Wilderness Act requires, among other things, that all roadless areas of 5,000 acres or more on select public lands be reviewed for possible inclusion in the Wilderness Preservation System, the problem of estimating the relative value of such areas when dedicated to alternative pur-

---

[1] There is also an inconsequential part of this total (220,000 acres) in Hawaii.

poses is quite important. Moreover, a related problem arises in connection with any adequate environmental impact statement (EIS) required under NEPA for any action on the public lands, among others, resulting in a significant modification of the environment.

The problems of multiple uses of an area, particularly where such uses are mutually incompatible, or where one use may be irreparably destructive for another, have been frequently underscored by the controversies, both in the political arena and in the courts, from the time of Hetch Hetchy to the more recent legal maneuvers over the Trans-Alaska pipeline. In recent years, under provisions of NEPA, conservation organizations such as the Sierra Club and the Wilderness Society, among others, have compelled the land management agencies to detail the environmental impacts of their decisions in a manner wholly unanticipated a few years ago. The basis of the challenges has been that many of the unique values of the public lands—the visual or aesthetic character of landscapes, the freedom to float an untrammeled river or enjoy the seclusion of wild places—are not properly safeguarded by the decisions of field level public land managers. This does not necessarily mean that the deficiencies are to be found in the competence of the field level resource manager. The Public Land Law Review Commission makes it clear that while multiple-use authority has been granted by the Congress to the public land management agencies, the guidelines in the statutes have been so ambiguous as to provide no adequate basis for guidance (1970, pp. 44, 48).

The 1960 Multiple Use and Sustained Yield Act for the national forests provides that the relative values of various resources and their uses, and not just the private market values, be taken into account so as to maximize the annual flow of benefits without impairing the basic productivity of the land. The Act is clear that noncommercial as well as commercial values are to be incorporated, and furthermore, that a proper concern for the future—particularly in connection with decisions having irreversible and potentially adverse consequences (impairment of the productivity of land)— be reflected in the actions taken. This legislation, of course, simply reflects the intent of the Congress, and enunciates broad policies. The operational criteria for their implementation, as is inevitably the case, are left to be developed, but somehow seem not to have received the necessary attention.

Similarly in the Classification and Multiple Use Act of 1964, the secretary of the interior was directed to develop criteria to give consideration to all pertinent factors including "ecology, priorities of use and the relative values of the various resources in particular areas." The secretary has published the "criteria," and the Bureau of Land Management has issued instructions to its field personnel. Nonetheless, in the judgment of the Public Land Law Review Commission, which considers the maximization of net social benefits an appropriate objective of public land management, federal lands are not being administered in a manner consistent with this objective (1970, p. 46).

In addition to the problem of clear criteria for choice in decisions affecting the public lands, the Public Land Law Review Commission has confronted the problem of obtaining data that are relevant to the various choices being made. For example, they note that it is difficult to get information that is truly of value in making many kinds of decisions. They have found it especially difficult to obtain information for use in weighing choices between economic uses of the public land such as timber and forage, and other uses, or protection of environmental values (1970, p. 46).

While the commission's observations are doubtless correct, there appears to run through the report a somewhat naive belief that there are, or ought to be, data which *in general* can be consulted to answer specific questions regarding the relative value of alternative uses of particular tracts of wild land. The problem, however, is not simply one of elusive data. It is rather one of developing adequate and correct procedures of analysis to ensure that welfare maximizing criteria are applied.

There are many facets to the task of expressing the relationship between, say, the value of mineral output from a particular location and the value of recreation in a pristine environment that may be destroyed by such mining activities. For example, how rich is the mineral deposit and how near to developed transport facilities? Or more properly, how much does it cost to mine and refine per unit and thus, what is the net value of the mineral deposit on exploitation? This will vary from one area to another, depending on grades of ore, location, and similarly related conditions. Moreover, the relationship will vary from one allocation problem to another, depending on the significance of the area for the amenity services it otherwise would provide. Are there some highly unusual, if not unique, natural characteristics which are threatened with destruction by the mining operation? If so, are these irretrievably lost if there are no alternative options available? Are there anticipated changes over time in the relative value of the goods or services to be offered by two incompatible uses of the area, and precisely how does this affect the optimal choice between them?

In short, any important decision concerning allocation between incompatible purposes, particularly where one choice would be inconsistent with retention of some valuable attributes of a given natural environment, calls for careful analysis and specific site evaluation using operational criteria for determining "relative preferredness." It is not likely to be usefully addressed by broad "planning criteria" which are ambiguous, if not inconsistent, if their implications are pursued to any length. Nor can we expect that the land management agencies, making records for administrative purposes, will be generating data which are specifically and directly useful for addressing the question: "What is the relative value of hydro power versus preservation in this particular canyon?" That question is both too technical and too specific for the Public Land Law Review Commission to answer, despite the fact that in its charge it was requested to provide the answer to the aggregate of all of such questions affecting the use of the public lands (1970, p. 19).

What then might we learn from land economics in addressing the problems of allocation, management, and administration of public lands? Unfortunately, at the moment, we cannot learn a great deal in the conventional presentations of land economics. In the general American view no less than among land economists, the belief has persisted until recently that the wilderness, wildlands, and "unimproved resources" had no value. Nash (1967, pp. 40–43) indicates that wilderness represented a negative value in the minds of Americans in the seventeenth and eighteenth centuries and the concept of the "valueless character of land in nature" has persisted into the present and even exists to some extent among resource managers charged with responsibility for the preservation of wildlands and related resources.[2] Among leading contributors to the field of land economics, such as Ely and Wehrwein (1940, p. 144), one may find the statement, "while land as nature has no cost of production, land is *not* a factor of production, or even a consumption good until it has been modified or 'produced'."

Consistent with the belief that land in its natural state has no value, nowhere in the literature on land development costs is there recognition of opportunity costs in the form of the amenity services precluded by improvement or development of wildlands. This is in spite of the fact that in the better textbooks there is a chapter or more on outdoor recreation and the national parks.[3] Several possible reasons can be suggested for this omission. Earlier in the nation's development the wilderness areas and their wildlife populations were vast in relation to the lands under cultivation and the populations of domesticated stock. Under these circumstances, the reduction of the size of wildlands and their wildlife populations represented a transformation of resources that were abundant, and hence of no value *at the margin,* into goods and services of high marginal value in a

---

[2] An example is the case of the Assistant Chief Park Ranger (a forester by professional training) who, while commenting on the proposed Redwoods National Park in personal conversation with one of the authors, mused that the redwoods were, however, "a resource that should be put to use."

[3] See the detailed and otherwise most complete discussion of the costs of land development in Barlowe (1958), p. 228 ff. The discussion in Ely and Wehrwein of the "Environment and Recreation Land" is fundamentally descriptive rather than analytical and affords no criteria for choice in allocating "land in nature," Chapter X, pp. 315–350.

developing economy. With the wilderness reduced to only about 2 percent of its original extent, and a highly advanced technology that can utilize substitute sources of raw materials, there is no longer any reason wildlands should not be valued.[4]

The puritan ethic impeded the perception of recreational use of leisure time as the consumption of highly valued services of natural resources. Perhaps as much as anything, however, such perception was hindered by the general difficulty in coming to grips with the measurement of values involving preservation of the attributes of natural environments, from genetic stocks to research materials on which advances in the earth and life sciences might depend.[5] It is perhaps for the latter reason that not only have land economists failed to address the question of opportunity costs arising out of the transformation of natural environments by land and extractive resource development, but also those who over the decades of the 1950s and 1960s addressed themselves to the methodology of benefit–cost analysis in resources. While references are made to the values associated with wilderness, parks, cultural heritage and the like, these are treated as intangible values requiring "high policy," rather than analysis for their resolution. In short, they are regarded in the literature as "extraeconomic," albeit recognition is given to their reality even if it is not explicitly measurable as opportunity costs.[6]

A seminal work by Clawson (1959) and an equally imaginative, but less well-known effort by Davis (1963) provided the means for estimating the value of at least a significant part of the amenity service flow, namely that connected with recreational use of the natural environment. Estimates of the recreational value of a site can now be obtained in the same terms and with perhaps equivalent precision as the power values derived from developing a site for electricity generation, or the damage reduction from flood control storage. There is, of course, much room for refinement and improvement in the methodology of recreation resources valuation, just as there is in the development of the hydrology of extreme events in estimates of flood damage reduction, and estimates of firm energy from hydropower resources. While excellent and imaginative work on the estimation of the demand for, and value of, outdoor recreation resources has been done, the history of work in the field is quite recent, and the extent of the work has been limited both by length of time and the restricted auspices under which

[4] For a fuller treatment of these points see Krutilla (1967a, b).

[5] For a discussion of the economic value of natural environments, see Krutilla (1967a); also Gannon (1969) and Smith and Krutilla (1972).

[6] See for example, Subcommittee on Evaluation Standards (1958), p. 44; Krutilla and Eckstein (1958), p. 265, McKean (1958), p. 61, and Hufschmidt, Krutilla and Margolis, with Marglin (1961), pp. 52–53. A possible exception may be found in the unpublished papers of Mason Gaffney.

it has been undertaken.[7] Under different institutional auspices, as we shall suggest in detail in chapter 11, these limitations on the capacity to make evaluations in the area which the Public Land Law Review Commission finds so deficient could be readily removed.

4. A NEW DEPARTURE: VALUING AMENITY RESOURCES OF NATURAL ENVIRONMENTS

As a good example of the sort of management decision this volume addresses, consider the allocation of a *de facto* wilderness area which is also known, or believed, to contain valuable mineral deposits. Should the area be set aside as a park or wilderness preserve or should mining or other extractive activities be permitted?

The question posed here goes to the heart of the analytical issue. In the extractive industries—forestry, agriculture, minerals—there are specialized branches of economics that can provide professionally competent estimates of the economic value of services provided by the extractive output. The present value of service flows will give the resource value of a tract of land when it is used for commercial extractive activities. The costs of the extractive activities today, of course, include the opportunity returns lost in transforming the tract of wildland (and/or reach of stream) into the developmental alternative. And what is the opportunity cost of this land transformed from its natural state? It is the value of the service flows that the public would derive from the land in its natural state.

Because wildlands are natural environments, they are gifts of nature not producible by man. Increases in the demand for the services of natural environments cannot be met by increases in the supply. The total stock of such environments cannot be increased and the previous reduction of the stock in the past is virtually irreversible. For example, the creation of a municipal water supply storage reservoir in Hetch Hetchy Valley has irretrievably reduced the amenity resources of Yosemite National Park.[8]

---

[7] Consider for example, the support for the estimation of demand for agricultural commodities over the past several decades. Here, both through the U.S. Department of Agriculture, and the United Nations Special agency, the Food and Agricultural Organization, the estimation of demand, with both price and income elasticities, cross elasticities, etc., has been carried to a fine art. An effort considerably less extensive, but many times the present level of work supported in the analysis of demand for outdoor recreation resources, could move a long way toward achieving the necessary advances and extensions.

[8] We should acknowledge that every decision, once implemented, is irreversible. What is important, however, is the distinction between cases in which the consequences of a decision (i.e., its opportunity costs) are permanent and those in which they are ephemeral; and between those that are significant and those that are inconsequential. A decision, for example, to use a commercially produced stock of leather

Under conditions of uncertainty regarding future circumstances, it is, of course, very difficult to make decisions that may result in significantly adverse and irreversible consequences. Perhaps knowledge of the implications of assumed continued advances in technology may be of assistance in dealing with this problem. We know that advances in the technology of extractive and logistic support industries have both reduced the costs of extraction and enlarged the economic range of resources amenable to economic exploitation. The history of resource extraction costs suggests that the products of extractive industries generally, "exhaustible" minerals in particular, have been forthcoming at constant or falling supply prices relative to the prices of goods and services generally.[9] Advances in manufacturing similarly have resulted in increases in output per unit of total inputs, in turn resulting in increases in income per capita over the entire course of the nation's industrial history. This experience is likely to be perpetuated under a regime of institutionalized research and development. The results of technological advance, however, are asymmetric for development compared with the alternative of preserving a natural environment.

The value of the services that natural areas provide enters directly into the utility functions of final consumers. There is no intervening production technology. True, with advances in transportation, areas that were too distant for some individuals to visit have now become accessible. But this has another aspect. The areas previously enjoyed by these individuals because of their proximity become accessible to others from more distant locations. No new areas have been "produced." Advances in transportation technology simply increase the cross traveling. Moreover, the general

---

in some proportion between handbags and belts, once implemented, is irreversible. But should hindsight reveal the decision to have been faulty, the proportions can be altered in the next production cycle using a newly supplied (produced) stock of leather. Through periodic batch adjustments in response to changes in relative demand, the consequences of faulty decisions will be ephemeral and thus of minor significance. Actually the cost of a faulty decision in this example can be represented by the cost of maintaining a small inventory to absorb fluctuations in accumulated deviations of actual sales from expected sales of each item.

On the other hand, a decision leading to disfigurement of an unusually scenic area by open-pit mineral extraction, for example, while no more irreversible, will have consequences that can be of near infinite duration; hence it is potentially very significant. There is no known technology for the production of a new natural environment, which is the accident of geomorphology, weathering, and biological processes involving a time span far exceeding human planning horizons. Since a new stock of natural scenery cannot be produced, the destruction of a part of the original represents an opportunity cost that continues in perpetuity. This point will be developed in greater detail in chapter 3.

[9] See Barnett and Morse (1963, chapter 8) and Potter and Christy (1962, pp. 18–52). Although the historical trend appears to continue, broadly speaking, through 1972, it should be noted that casual observation suggests a possibility of at least a short-run reversal more recently.

advances in technology have resulted in increased incomes, allowing more persons to visit the same number of natural areas. The increased per capita demand, along with increases in population, results in growing aggregate demand for the nonaugmentable services of fixed natural assets. Advances in technology in this case simply compound the fixity in supply and create growing relative scarcity.

What is needed for resource valuation is a dynamic model that reflects the growth in demand and the appreciating nature of the value of the service flow from such resources. This is a problem to which we give detailed, rigorous attention in chapter 3. Here we simply note that the implications of technical change are asymmetric for the value of natural areas used for extractive purposes, on the one hand, and for the amenity services they render in their natural state, on the other. The relative value of the alternative uses is likely to change, tending to favor the retention of the area in its "unimproved" state. The quantitative significance of this observation is decisive in important cases, as illustrated in detail in chapters 5 and 6.[10]

In considering the problem of growing demand for services of irreplaceable assets in fixed supply, attention must be given to potential congestion and the risk of degradation in product or service quality which this growth implies for such assets. How many visitors can be admitted to a wilderness area during a given period without altering the characteristics of the wilderness (solitude, absence of evidence of human occupation)? How large a multitude can be accommodated at a national park originally established to preserve unique natural features, including fragile ecosystems, before these are eroded in quality, if not irretrievably lost through intensity of use?

The first question perhaps deals only with the tolerance which those users of the wilderness who share the values reflected in the Wilderness Act have for encountering other parties, or evidence of their use, in the wilderness. This is a social–psychological phenomenon that may lead to a capacity constraint more restrictive than one that considers only the damage to the ecological environment.[11] Here we recognize the disutility inflicted on others by the admission of an additional party to an area during a given period of time. The problem is to identify the intensity of use that will maximize the value of the resource when dedicated to a wilderness purpose. This will occur at the point at which the disutility inflicted on others by the addition of a party will just cancel the utility gained by the additional party. Information of this nature, of course, is not to be found

---

[10] See also Krutilla et al. (1972). For a rigorous statement specifying the conditions which are necessary for the above conclusions to hold see also Smith (1972), and further discussion in chapters 5 and 6.

[11] For a treatment of this question see Stankey (1972, pp. 88–114).

in agency files, but must be developed by appropriate analysis addressed to the specific area under review.[12]

The second question is related more directly to the potentially deleterious effects of use on the wilderness ecology. In some instances, in very fragile ecosystems, a limit derived from this consideration may be more restrictive than one derived from taking into account only the disutility of encountering other parties in the wilderness. More generally, however, protection of the wilderness ecology is likely to be accomplished by limits on use set to avoid the erosive effects of human interaction on the satisfaction obtained from a wilderness recreational experience. In any event, the problem of discovering how to preserve the ecological integrity of an area falls largely outside the research of social or behavioral scientists, and is being given some attention through the efforts of applied ecologists.[13]

A major element neglected in the decision criteria for allocating uses of natural environments is consideration of capacity limits along with dynamic demand functions. There is in addition a problem in evaluating amenity resources that is not present in evaluating producible assets or other resources for which substitute sources exist. Decisions taken by man which affect irreproducible gifts of nature for which there are no satisfactory substitutes (for at least some segments of the population) differ from decisions which can be undone if the consequences are deemed undesirable on hindsight. In an uncertain economic environment there is a value in the retention of an option which would be otherwise foreclosed.[14]

In what ways may we conceive the values of retaining options to enjoy wildlands and rivers in their natural state? From a purely scientific point of view, much is yet to be learned in the earth and life sciences; preservation of the objects of study may be defended on these grounds, given the serendipity value of basic research. We know also that the natural biota represent our reservoir of genetic information, which has economic value. For example, modern agriculture in developed economies represents cultivation figuratively in a hot-house environment in which crops are protected against disease, pests, and drought by a variety of agricultural practices. The energy released from some of the genetic characteristics, redundant for growth under cultivated conditions, is redirected toward greater productivity. Yet, because of the monocultural reduction of biological diver-

---

[12] For a discussion of this problem and a suggestion for a method of dealing with it, see Fisher and Krutilla (1972, pp. 115–141), Cicchetti and Smith (1973), and the discussion in chapter 7.

[13] See, for example, Wagar (1964).

[14] This proposition was first introduced into the literature by Weisbrod (1964). The existence of option value as separate from consumer surplus was more rigorously established by Cicchetti and Freeman (1971) after it had come under question. More recently a conceptually similar proposition has been established by Arrow and Fisher (1974). Uncertainty and option value are discussed in more detail in chapter 4.

sity, need occasionally arises for the reintroduction of some genetic information lost in the domestication of modern crop varieties. It is from the diversified natural biota that this information can still be obtained.

The value of botanical specimens for medicinal purposes also has been long, if not widely, recognized. Approximately half of the new drugs currently being developed are obtained from this source.[15] Commerce in medicinal plants approximates a third of a billion dollars annually. Cortisone, digitalis, and heparin are among the better known of the myriad drugs which are derived from natural vegetation or zoological sources. Since only a small fraction of the potential medicinal value of biological specimens has yet been realized, preserving the option to examine all species among the natural biota represents a value of some consequence for human welfare.

Option value may have only a psychic basis in some instances. There are many persons who obtain satisfaction from the mere knowledge that part of wilderness North America exists even though they might be appalled by the prospect of being exposed to it. An option demand may exist, therefore, not only among persons currently or prospectively in the market, but among others who place a value on the mere existence of biological diversity and natural landscape variety.

When a tract of wildland is being considered for a use that irreversibly changes the landscape or ecology, the values which are lost by foreclosing future options must be taken into account in the decision. Neither traditional land economics nor the standard benefit–cost approach to resource management problems have done so. The practical conclusion of recent theoretical work on this issue, discussed in detail in chapter 4, is that where the choice is between preservation and development, and there are some uncertainties with respect to the future demand for the service flows from either alternative, there may be an additional cost attributable to the alternative that forecloses future options, because of the irreversibility of miscalculation. Accordingly, even when the expected value of the preservation alternative is estimated, and appreciating benefits derived from the asymmetric results of technological progress are taken into account, the asymmetric consequences of irreversibility under uncertainty also may have to be considered.

5. SUMMARY AND CONCLUSIONS

In this chapter we have referred to the awakening of environmental awareness in the United States and indicated that it had its earliest expression in the concerns about the aesthetic dimensions of the environment. Much of the early legislation on wildlands, wildlife, and scenic resources relates to lands held by the public. Indeed, it is on the hundreds

---

[15] For a discussion of this point see Kreig (1964, p. 8).

of millions of acres of public lands that we find most of the remaining wilderness areas and the remnant wildlife populations. These make up the unique larger ecosystems requiring vast areas of undisturbed natural environments. Some of these areas are protected under legislation that has established the National Wilderness System, the National Parks, National Wildlife Refuges, and some Natural Research Areas. There remain as many as 50 million acres of *de facto* wilderness—roadless wildland areas—which are not under statutory protection. These are the lands on which may be found also, in places, merchantable timber, hydroelectric power, reservoir sites, and mineral deposits. Exploitation of such resources on these lands would be incompatible with retaining the natural environment.

Many of the resource exploitation proposals that are undertaken are inherently uneconomic judged by established efficiency criteria, but may be privately profitable because of governmental policies favoring exploitation. Among these are the "deficit sales" of the Forest Service, i.e., timber sales the proceeds from which do not cover the costs of the sale; provisions of the Internal Revenue acts that permit the expensing of capital expenditures by the mineral industry; and the subsidization of investment in water resource projects. Under strict efficiency criteria, these activities modifying the natural environment would not be undertaken whether or not there were adverse environmental side effects.[16] There are some, though fewer, possibilities to exploit the conventional commodity resources in *de facto* wilderness areas, which would provide a positive net return when the environmental costs are ignored, as for the most part they have been.

There are no adequate guidelines in the legislation or in the administrative practices governing the management of such public lands, nor in the conventional theory and practice of benefit–cost analysis, that provide decision criteria for addressing the problems we have exposed as relevant in valuing and allocating the resources of natural environments: asymmetric technical change, congestion of wilderness areas, and irreversibility under uncertainty. These and related conceptual problems are explored from a primarily theoretical point of view in the next three chapters and then applied to a number of empirical cases. We begin in chapter 2 with a discussion of common property resources, public goods, and externalities on the public lands, and the relation between assignment of property rights and resource valuation.

REFERENCES

Arrow, K. J. and Fisher, A. C. 1974. "Environmental Preservation, Uncertainty and Irreversibility," *Quarterly Journal of Economics,* vol. LXXXVIII, no. 2.

[16] Efficiency criteria and their relation to distributional issues are discussed in chapters 2 and 4.

Barlowe, Raleigh. 1958. *Land Resource Economics: The Political Economy of Rural and Urban Land Resource Use* (Englewood Cliffs, N.J.: Prentice-Hall).

Barnett, H. J. and Morse, Chandler. 1963. *Scarcity and Growth: The Economics of Natural Resource Availability* (Baltimore: Johns Hopkins Press).

Brubaker, Sterling. 1972. *To Live on Earth: Man and His Environment in Perspective* (Baltimore: Johns Hopkins Press).

Cicchetti, C. J. and Freeman, A. M., III. 1971. "Option Demand and Consumer Surplus: Further Comments," *Quarterly Journal of Economics,* vol. LXXXV, no. 3.

———— and Smith, V. K. 1973. "Congestion, Quality Deterioration and Optimal Use: Wilderness Recreation in the Spanish Peaks Primitive Area," *Social Science Research,* vol. 2, no. 1.

———— and Smith, V. K. 1974. "An Econometric Analysis of Congestion Effects in Wilderness Recreation," manuscript in preparation.

Clawson, Marion. 1959. "Methods of Measuring the Demand for and Value of Outdoor Recreation," Resources for the Future Reprint No. 10.

Davis, R. K. 1963. "The Demand for Outdoor Recreation: An Economic Study of the Maine Woods," unpublished Ph.D. dissertation, Harvard University.

Eckstein, Otto. 1968. *Economic Analysis of Public Investment Decisions: Interest Rate Policy and Discounting Analysis,* Hearings before the Joint Economic Committee, 90 Cong. 2 sess.

Ely, R. T. and Wehrwein, G. S. 1940. *Land Economics* (New York: Macmillan).

Fisher, A. C. and Krutilla, J. V. 1972. "Determination of Optimal Capacity of Resource-Based Recreation Facilities," *Natural Resources Journal,* vol. 12, no. 3.

————. 1973. "Environmental Externalities and the Arrow–Lind Public Investment Theorem," *American Economic Review,* vol. LXIII, no. 4.

Gannon, C. A. 1969. "Towards a Strategy for Conservation in A World of Technological Change," *Socio-Economic Planning Sciences,* vol. 3, pp. 159–178.

Hufschmidt, M. M., Krutilla, J. V., Margolis, Julius, with Marglin, Stephen. 1961. *Standards and Criteria for Formulating and Evaluating Federal Water Resources Developments.* Report to the Bureau of the Budget (Washington, D.C.).

Kreig, M. B. 1964. *Green Medicine, The Search for Plants that Heal* (New York: Rand McNally).

Krutilla, J. V. 1968. "Balancing Extractive Industries with Wildlife Habitat," *Transactions of the Thirty-third North American Wildlife and Natural Resources Conference,* Wildlife Management Institute, Washington, D.C.

————. 1967a. "Conservation Reconsidered," *American Economic Review,* vol. LVII, no. 4.

————. 1967b. "Some Environmental Effects of Economic Development," *Daedalus,* vol. 96 (Fall).

————, Cicchetti, C. J., Freeman, A. M., III, and Russell, C. S. 1972. "Observations on the Economics of Irreplaceable Assets," in *Environmental Quality Analysis: Theory and Method in the Social Sciences,* Allen Kneese and Blair T. Bower, eds. (Baltimore: Johns Hopkins Press).

———— and Eckstein, Otto. 1958. *Multiple Purpose River Development: Studies in Applied Economic Analysis* (Baltimore: Johns Hopkins Press).

McKean, R. N. 1958. *Efficiency in Government Through Systems Analysis* (New York: Wiley).

Nash, Roderick. 1967. *Wilderness and the American Mind* (New Haven: Yale University Press).

Potter, Neal and Christy, F. T., Jr. 1962. *Trends in Natural Resource Commodities* (Baltimore: Johns Hopkins Press).

Public Land Law Review Commission. 1970. *One-Third of the Nation's Land.* Report to the President and the Congress by the Public Land Law Review Commission (Washington, D.C.: Government Printing Office).

Smith, V. K. 1972. "The Incidence of Technological Progress on Different Uses of Environmental Resources," in *Natural Environments: Studies in Theoretical and Applied Analysis,* John V. Krutilla, ed. (Baltimore: Johns Hopkins Press).

———— and Krutilla, J. V. 1972. "Technical Change and Environmental Resources," *Socio-Economic Planning Sciences,* vol. 6, pp. 125–132.

Stankey, G. H. 1972. "A Strategy for the Definition and Management of Wilderness Quality," in *Natural Environments: Studies in Theoretical and Applied Analysis,* John V. Krutilla, ed. (Baltimore: Johns Hopkins Press).

Subcommittee on Evaluation Standards. 1958. *Proposed Practices for Economic Analysis of River Basin Projects.* Report to the Inter-Agency Committee on Water Resources (Washington, D.C.).

Timmons, J. F. and Murray, W. G. 1950. *Land Problems and Policies* (Ames: Iowa State College Press).

Water Resources Council. 1962. *Policies, Standards and Procedures in the Formulation, Evaluation, and Review of Plans for Use and Development of Water and Related Land Resources.* Prepared under the direction of the President's Water Resources Council, S. Doc. 97, 87 Cong. 2 sess.

————. 1964. *Policies, Standards and Procedures in the Formulation, Evaluation, and Review of Plans for Use and Development of Water and Related Land Resources,* Supplement no. 1. Evaluation Standards for Primary Outdoor Recreation Benefits, Ad Hoc Water Resources Council (Washington, D.C.).

Wagar, A. J. 1964. *The Carrying Capacity of Wildlands for Recreation,* Forest Science Monograph 7 (Washington, D.C.: Society of Foresters).

Weisbrod, B. A. 1964. "Collective Consumption Services of Individual Consumption Goods," *Quarterly Journal of Economics,* vol. LXXVIII, no. 3.

CHAPTER 2

EXTERNALITIES, PROPERTY RIGHTS, AND VALUATION OF RESOURCES ON THE PUBLIC LANDS

1. INTRODUCTION

It has been noted in the report of the Public Land Law Review Commission (1970) cited in chapter 1 that the public lands have not been particularly well managed precisely in the area where there is a conflict between the production of commodity compared with amenity resources, i.e., where the production of the former is incompatible with the simultaneous production, or supply of, the latter. While the Public Land Law Review Commission's survey of the problem has been the most systematic and comprehensive to date, perhaps the activities of conservation and environmental organizations have been the more publicized. Court actions brought by such groups as the Audubon Society, the Environmental Defense Fund, the Sierra Club, and the Wilderness Society are mostly of recent origin and of considerable interest. The ability of the citizens' groups to obtain injunctions (irrespective of the Environmental Policy Act of 1969) which in effect challenge administrative decisions of such land management agencies as the Forest Service represents a remarkable change in the ground rules, first, for citizens dealing with their government, and second, for what is admissible as providing standing in damage suits. That is, the courts appear to be saying that individuals who do not have vested *private* property rights may be regarded as suffering damage incurred from losses through abridgement of continued use of *common* property resources.

The recognition that individuals or groups without vested rights can have standing in damage suits on these matters leads us to consider in more detail the question of property rights on the public lands and the related question of resource valuation. More specifically, we consider the effect of different assignments of property rights on the valuation of natural areas and related resources in alternative uses. Our results here might be characterized briefly and somewhat paradoxically as follows: although

19

the valuation problem could be uniquely resolved by the creation of a market, the implied allocation would not likely be socially efficient.

Before developing this point, though, we inquire more closely into the nature of rights to different types of resources on the public lands. A general theme that emerges from the discussion here is the failure of the market to allocate efficiently the resources of natural environments. The market failure dealt with here is generally due to the presence of what Bator (1958) has termed ownership and public goods externalities in a static or timeless context. As suggested in the preceding chapter, there are additional problems for efficient market and nonmarket allocation where the resources in question are natural endowments not producible by man. We reserve discussion of these problems to the next chapter.

2. PUBLIC LANDS AND COMMON AND PRIVATE PROPERTY RESOURCES

The public lands, of course, are owned by the public and are public property in the conventional sense of the term. In law and economics, however, public ownership need not imply that access rights are obtained or enjoyed in any sense differently from the way they are on private lands. To some extent (depending on technical conditions and policy) public lands are in fact treated as, and reflect the characteristics of, private property resources.

In what sense are public lands managed as private property resources? In the case of the latter, ownership is vested in an identifiable entity that possesses rights of exclusion, or rights to set the conditions and terms of access to the property or its services. A common property resource, on the other hand, is a resource used, if not necessarily owned, in common by all of the members of the community.[1] Neither exclusion nor discrimination is permitted with respect to its access. It is, therefore, often referred to as an "open access" resource.

Public lands are not in all cases treated under law and policy as common property resources. Use of the services to which they give rise, or access to the land for the purpose of exploiting its associated resources are subject to exclusion in some cases. Access to the timber on a national forest for logging, or receipt of a grazing permit, are privileges that are

---

[1] The original analyses of the allocation of common property resources (of a fishery) are by Gordon (1954) and Scott (1955). More recently the analysis has been extended by Smith (1968) and others. For an informative review, see Haveman (1973). The major finding of these studies is essentially that open access leads to overuse of the common property resource. As this is by now well understood, we shall not dwell on it, rather concentrating on other aspects of public land management, including the conflicts that may arise between competing common property uses such as certain kinds of extractive and recreation activities.

obtained only for a consideration, much as in the case of private lands and other private property resources. (Though often, especially in the past, for less than their market value.[2])

Under the law (Mining Act of 1872), however, the public lands, with the exception of "primary use" reservations such as parks and wilderness areas, are open to the public for certain types of mineral exploration (the "hardrock" minerals). The availability of these lands for mineral exploration represents a common property attribute. If the exploration is sufficiently successful to enable establishing a valid claim that is "patented," the title to the minerals and to all resources on the land overlying the claim is transferred in fee simple to the private party holding the patent. By this means public lands have under the mineral acts been transferred to private ownership in a manner not unlike the transfer of ownership under the operation of the Homestead Act and other means of alienating public lands.

There are certain other common property attributes of resources that occur on public lands. Somewhat similarly to the marine fisheries (which are the primary example of common property resources), fish and wildlife in the United States are publicly owned. Fish and game were originally viewed as common property in the common law, and under our federal system responsibility for regulating game cropping was reserved to the states, except for the migratory species covered under international treaty. Ownership by the individual states tends to be regarded as a stewardship of the wildlife held in trust for the people. In this sense, wildlife tends to be a common property resource subject to the right of capture under terms and conditions specified by the state. While the search and pursuit of wildlife on federal lands are subject to regulation by the state, access to the land is open; thus both the game and its habitat represent common property features of public lands. This is a condition that most frequently is not found in connection with private lands.

Do other recreational resources partake of common property attributes? That is, are the resources that give rise to various types of environmental amenity services on public lands common property resources? The answer would seem to be yes, at least in part. To the extent that sunlight and air, and meteorological phenomena are part of the recreational experience, we do have open access or common property resources associated with recreational use of public lands. But these common property features are not exclusively associated with public ownership. They are also found in association with private land—indeed, this is equally true of the distribution

---

[2] By the same token, it should be noted that private property has at certain times and places been open access, or overexploited, or both. Here, however, we are concerned with management of the *public* lands, and how this is appropriately affected by the presence of common property resources.

of fish and wildlife. And, access to developed recreation areas on public lands *is* subject to user charges (though they are often nominal, as in the case of admission fees to the national parks), and indeed, to exclusion, as when a campground is closed to further use.

In some instances, however, the administration of admissions reflects an open access character. For example, charges are not typically made, nor fees collected, from visitors to the wilderness areas in the national forests. The reason for this, it would appear, is not necessarily because exclusion is impossible, but rather is partly because it is assumed that the capacity of these facilities is (has been) large in relation to the demand, and that efficient use requires a zero admission fee until such time as capacity limitations justify price rationing.

Beyond this, a preserved natural environment may be regarded as an open access resource for those who benefit from its existence without necessarily appearing on site to claim their rights or benefits. In this category are:

1. vicarious consumers; those who derive satisfaction simply from knowing that certain rare or remarkable species and environments still exist, and indeed are willing to pay something for their preservation
2. option demanders; those who value the option of experiencing some time in the future a particular environment, perhaps for their children and grandchildren, if not for themselves; and
3. those who may benefit from advances in medicine, agriculture, and so on, made possible by the preservation of genetic information in the more numerous wild species

Of course, not all of these intangible benefits will be significant in any given natural area, but then neither will mineral deposits, or merchantable timber.[3]

To summarize the discussion of this section, we can say that the way a publicly owned natural asset is managed depends on how the rights to the services of the asset are assigned. At one pole, the asset may be managed as a private property resource, with access limited by rights which are bought and sold, as, for example, logging rights. At the other, it may be managed as a common property resource with open access; for example, hardrock mineral exploration, some wilderness recreation, and, of course, the "nonuser" uses indicated above. There is also the possibility of some intermediate solution involving mixed, or partly private, management of the asset, as for example with private riparian rights on a publicly owned natural asset. The definition of use or access rights is in turn determined by certain attributes of the asset, or perhaps in some cases just tradition,

---

[3] For a fuller discussion of the various types of nonuser benefits that may be provided by a preserved natural environment, see Krutilla (1967).

embodied in law and institution. The attributes that are particularly important in this connection, at least for the various amenity services, include nonexcludability, absence of congestion, and something that might be termed "renewability" (i.e., the asset "recovers" so that use by one individual does not impair the asset for use by others). As these are variously taken to be defining characteristics of what are known, following Samuelson (1954), as "public goods," it may be appropriate to look more closely at the relationship between the public lands, common property, and public goods.

3. PUBLIC LANDS AND PUBLIC AND PRIVATE GOODS

A public good, as Samuelson defined it, is one in which each individual's consumption leads to no subtraction from any other individual's consumption of that good. In symbols, a pure public good is one for which the total output $X = X_A = X_B = \ldots$, where $X_A =$ the amount of the good going to individual A, and so on. The classic example is national defense. Police protection serves almost as well; street lighting and flood hazard reduction provided through storage reservoirs are readily seen to meet this definition. The receipt of protection by one occupant of a floodplain does not reduce the amount of similar protection enjoyed by his neighbor. There naturally are public bads as well as goods; air and water pollution, landscape disfigurement—or general environmental degradation —are examples of public bads. The smelling of malodorous pulp mill fumes by one individual does not reduce the intensity of the odor for another. Conversely, the elimination or prevention of a public bad is a public good. How do these considerations relate to the question of public lands and common property? We shall get to this presently, but first we need to investigate further some characteristics and qualifications attaching to public goods.

Although the Samuelsonian definition of the public good (bad) opens a way to investigate a previously neglected area, it was in retrospect discovered to be somewhat simplistic. Margolis (1955), Davis and Whinston (1967), and Mishan (1971b), among others, perceived that the characteristic that consumption of a service by one person does not reduce the quantity available to another did not hold in general for many publicly provided services such as education (especially when facilities are inadequate), service from insufficiently staffed police forces and crowded court calendars, and highways. In these cases we have what might be characterized as partly public goods, for which individual consumption $X_A = aX$, $0 \leqslant a \leqslant 1$, $X_B = bX, 0 \leqslant b \leqslant 1$ .... In the special case of the pure public good defined above, the fraction a of total output X going to individual A, the fraction b of total output X going to individual B, and so on, are all equal to unity. Similarly, it was noted that the condition of "publicness" (if a good is available to one individual, it is indivisibly available to all) was not necessarily a technical condition of supply that made it difficult or impossible to exclude any individual if a good was made available to any other. While it may not be feasible to deny the occupant of a floodplain the benefits of flood control storage upstream, it is physically possible to exclude a student from a school, or a motorist from a freeway—or a backpacker from a wilderness—even if these facilities are provided or made available for another's use. Finally, it was recognized that even if a facility is privately provided, such as a television antenna atop an apartment building (Minasian, 1964), efficient allocation might require that other parties have free connections, since no additional cost would be attributable to the additional connections. This rule of course is also applicable to private theatres, stadia, and similar facilities that may have excess capacity in that the amount of the services received by one will not reduce the amount available to another.[4]

Accordingly, we have noted some difficulties with the original definition of public goods of the following nature:

1. Conventional public services may be provided under conditions in which one person's availing himself of the service *will* diminish the amount available to another.
2. Conventional private services may be provided under conditions in which one person's availing himself of the service will *not* diminish the amount available to another.
3. Both public and private services may be provided under conditions which may or may not be subject to exclusion, depending not only on *technical conditions* of production and consumption, but also on the assignments of ownership rights in law.

What then is the relationship between public goods and public lands and common property resources? First, it may be desirable, following Mishan (1971b, p. 10 ff.), to avoid characterizing goods as public or private in light of the inescapable confusion with lay terminology and understanding involving public services. It is, for example, quite possible to develop a theory of public budgeting and expenditures without relying on the notion of public goods as discussed in the theoretical literature.[5]

---

[4] For this to hold strictly, the seats would have to be subject to random selection rather than a first-come first-served basis because the quality (quantity?) of the service for spectator events may be a function of the seat location of the observer, and other observers, and their numbers.

[5] If not a theory of public expenditure, an adequate rationale for public intervention is presented in Bator (1958), Krutilla and Eckstein (1958) chapters 2 and 3, and Musgrave (1959) chapter 1.

When we look at goods and services without having to consider their degree of "publicness," the indicated analysis can be performed with conventional concepts of market allocation criteria, supplemented by the necessary adjustments for externalities which, in fact, justify making provision for collective wants due to market failure. One can even make the case that each of the conditions mentioned above gives rise to goods that not only vary in degrees of "publicness," but also change between their public and private character as capacity constraints (1) become effective with sufficient growth in demand, and (2) are relaxed as additional investment is made in capacity to relieve excess demand—where the facilities *are not irreproducible assets.*

Given these relationships, there is no purpose in attempting to detail a relationship between public lands and public goods. There is no *necessary* relationship, and certainly no simple, straightforward one. Relationships arise more naturally between public lands and common property resources, as suggested in the preceding section, and between common property resources and public goods. The latter is the service provided by the former under conditions of no exclusion and demand insufficient to generate congestion or marginal resource costs, as for example with wilderness recreation (up to a point) and the nonuser activities. What might be said more properly in connection with public lands and public goods is that we have here both private and collective consumption services of both private and common property resources, in numerous mixes and blends. Indeed, it is on the public lands that we can find almost every example of property right, class of good, and type of market failure. These, however, may all be discussed as particular types of externalities or indivisibilities on either the factor service or product side, and a number of examples will be given in the following section.

4. PUBLIC LANDS, OWNERSHIP, AND OTHER EXTERNALITIES

The remaining public domain, the national forests, parks, wildlife refuges, and research natural areas, along with some special classes of land, are managed as public properties by the major land management agencies. Forest land, waters of the national forests, and portions of the public domain offer perhaps the widest ranges of joint products or jointly supplied services. Because of the richness of the resource associations, these jointly supplied services are not only numerous, but also can be supplied in varying proportions (unlike the classical case of "beef and hides").

The scenery within a tract of wildlands, for example, may represent on the one hand a common property resource, a source of a private ownership externality as seen from a point outside the boundary of the tract, and on the other a good without attributable marginal resource costs, as viewed from within. In the first instance, access to the tract can be denied, yet the grosser visual attributes of the landscape can, in many instances, be viewed from without the boundaries, and this represents a limitation on the power of the management agency to regulate access (and therefore extract payment for the benefits) through the extent of its ownership. On the other hand, while access to the forest land may be controlled, viewing the landscape from within the boundaries of the national forest does not incur, up to a point, either resource or congestion costs attributable to the viewer. If the area, moreover, is jointly supplied with campsites essential to viewing the scenery, but these are primitive, undeveloped sites not involving resource costs (including appreciable damage to the ecological environment), there would be no warrant to impose fees on visitation, as there would be no costs associated with the viewing. Thus, all the services of the landscape, both visual attributes and congenial undeveloped sites on which to make camp, should be supplied without marginal user charges, since no marginal resource costs have been incurred.[6]

If the "open access" policy coupled with the demand for the services of this area result in reaching a capacity restriction, charges then could be employed to ration capacity when it is exceeded by demand at a zero price. This is, of course, the classic common property management problem referred to in footnote 1. Note, however, that the capacity limitation relates to only one of the jointly supplied complementary services—the campsites. Access to the latter is subject to regulation or exclusion *as a matter of policy since it is technically feasible.* There are some attributes of the landscape that are jointly consumed (scenery and campsites used in reaching a vantage point for viewing) where one attribute is technically not subject to exclusion (visual stimuli) or diminution by use, and consumption of the other, though subject to exclusion, also has no attributable costs until a point is reached where congestion sets in.

This illustration presents an example of jointly supplied services which provide positive utility to the consumers. There is, of course, a somewhat different case where joint production results in a positive good and a negative good, or bad, which inflicts uncompensated costs, or externalities, on others who would use the services of an unimpaired environment.

Before proceeding with some examples, it might be helpful to define precisely what is meant by "externality," and show how it is distinguished from the related concepts of jointness in supply and Samuelsonian public-

---

[6] There *is* a case for lump-sum payment to capture the (external) site rent. We shall omit for the moment the case where returns from exploitation of associated resources are precluded by retention of the area in its natural state. This relates to evaluation for a specific allocation decision, as contrasted with admissions policy after the allocation decision has been made.

ness. An externality is said to exist "whenever an output of one economic agent appears as an input in the consumption or production vector of another," without accompanying payment (Holtermann, 1972). This can be represented symbolically as $A = (X_{1A}, -X_{1A}^E, X_{2A})$, $B = (X_{1B}, X_{1A \cdot B}^E, X_{2B})$, where A and B are activity vectors (consumption or production) of agents (consumers or firms) A and B respectively; X_{ij} is the input of good i to agent j, $i = 1, 2, j = A, B$; $-X_{1A}^E$ is an (unpriced) output associated with A's use of 1; and $X_{1A \cdot B}^E$ is an (unpriced) input to B from A's use of 1.[7] $X_{1A \cdot B}^E$ is the externality in this framework, which is easily extended from the two goods–two persons case represented here for simplicity.

Now suppose there is a third agent, C, who also receives an (unpriced) input $X_{1A \cdot C}^E$ from A's use of 1. If the externality is a public good, then $X_{1A \cdot B}^E = X_{1A \cdot C}^E$, from the definition of a public good given earlier.

Jointness in supply of what has been called a mixed good (Cicchetti and Smith, 1970) can also be represented in this framework. A mixed good is a good, such as a scenic natural area, having both a public (scenery) and a private (campsites) component. If we designate this good as X_3, then consumption of its public aspect, X_3', is $X_3' = X_{3A}' = X_{3B}' = X_{3C}' = \ldots$, and of its private, X_3'', is $X_3'' = X_{3A}'' + X_{3B}'' + X_{3C}'' + \ldots$.

Now let us imagine a setting similar to our previous example in which people visit an area in order to enjoy the scenery, remoteness from industrial–urban activity, and solitude. Imagine further the discovery of mineral deposits, leading to establishment of a valid mineral claim on this setting, followed by patent. Assume that the working of the deposit requires removal of substantial overburden and related landscape modification for ore beneficiation, tailing ponds, and other facilities that are significant in relation to the total scenic area. Recall that in the first example the use of the area by any viewer did not reduce the aesthetic stimuli that were available to any other. Moreover, to the extent that any costs imposed by the viewers arose as the result of congestion, they were *reciprocal without* real income or utility *redistribution*.[8]

The nature of the externalities occasioned by the mining in the second illustration, however, is different in that there is a *unidirectional* rather than a reciprocal relationship between competing uses of the visual environment, *with attendant utility redistributive effects*.[9] Rothenberg (1970) has used these distinctions to characterize the essential difference between

---

[7] Our notation here is adopted from Holtermann, and is also consistent with Meade (1952), and Buchanan and Stubblebine (1962), the classic references.

[8] This is a little too strong. The negative externality need not be equally valued by all those who impose it on each other.

[9] Mining is only given as an example of a class of uses covered by developmental or extractive activities such as road building and logging in *de facto* wilderness, construction of roads along, or dams across wild rivers, etc., where physical aspects of natural environments are irreversibly altered.

congestion and *pollution*. The former is the identical use of the environment by all parties who suffer reciprocally inflicted costs, but, within limits, do not inflict damage to the environment (Rothenberg's constructive use of the environment). *Pollution* is a competing and dissimilar use of the environment which alters the characteristics of the environmental resources in a way that is in some sense destructive, and in which there is a unidirectional flow of the costs associated with resource exploitation.[10] In the context of a discussion of common property resources, the situation described above might be characterized as one of between-group as well as within-group competition for a resource by two (or more) different common property uses.

5. DISTRIBUTION, PROPERTY RIGHTS, AND VALUES ON THE PUBLIC LANDS

If we accept, at least tentatively, the Rothenberg distinctions [with some support from Mishan (1971b)], we now come to what is a very significant aspect relating to the matter of evaluating the relative worth of alternative incompatible uses to which given natural areas, or public wildlands, may be put. In confronting the choice between incompatible alternative uses of natural environments, as will be the case in allocating *de facto* wilderness and wild and scenic rivers under the current legislation[11] (and in considering management of these and other multiple-use areas), the redistributive aspects enter directly into the evaluation of opportunity costs.

The problem here is an old one in welfare economics. It is, how is a project or land use policy which results in gains to some individuals and losses to others properly evaluated? In particular, can the gains and losses be algebraically added over all affected individuals to determine the net gain (from each of the alternative uses of an area's resources)? Underlying any policy prescription from a benefit–cost analysis of a resource use project is the potential Pareto, or Kaldor (1939)–Hicks (1939) criterion, according to which the project is efficient, and presumably therefore de-

---

[10] Nelson (1970), commenting on the Rothenberg characterization, observed a qualification in connection with the use of automobiles in which there may be not only the reciprocal externalities of congestion, but also an environmentally destructive deterioration of air quality. In some cases, where there are multiple-source noxious effluents of a mobile character, there will be competition for the resource (clean air, a common property resource technically given) as well as for use of the travel route (technically a private property resource, used under open access conditions given by law or policy). In this instance it reflects characteristics of both cases discussed here. Unless unregulated use of trails and campsites has an ecologically damaging effect on the environment, the Nelson criticism would not apply to the examples presented here.

[11] This is a task implicit in the Wilderness Act of 1964, the Wild and Scenic Rivers Act of 1968, and the National Environmental Policy Act of 1969.

sirable, if the gains exceed the losses, so that the gainers could compensate the losers and retain a residual gain. This was amended by Scitovsky (1941), who demonstrated that no unambiguous improvement in welfare is associated with undertaking a project that is efficient in the sense of Kaldor and Hicks unless, at the same time, it is possible to show that the prospective losers could not bribe the gainers to forgo the project, or return to the *status quo ante*. Of course, even this is not satisfactory to one who is concerned about the actual distribution of gains and losses from alternative uses of an environment (or any other resource endowment).[12]

Perhaps the only sensible way to proceed here is to follow Harberger (1971), who argues that the unweighted aggregation underlying estimation of net benefits and costs of a project is simply the best we can hope for in applied welfare analysis, and that this information ought to be one component, but not necessarily the only one, in a decision as to its desirability. In the empirical cases we review in part II, moreover, it seems that prospective gainers and losers are likely to be drawn, with minor exceptions, from the same (middle to upper) income classes—where they are not in fact the same individuals. Even should a planner wish to attach some sort of welfare "weight" to the gains and losses from a project, we assume that the weights in these cases would be about the same. Those who disagree are of course free to substitute their own weights, or to emphasize the redistributional effects of the project.

Measurement of the gains and losses associated with a change in the allocation of resources, however, is not entirely a straightforward exercise, even conceptually, when resources with ambiguously defined use rights are at issue. How can this be when the by-now well-known Coase (1960) theorem states that resource allocation, explicitly, and resource valuation, implicitly, are invariant with respect to the assignment of property rights? The explicit part of the theorem states that a resource such as a piece of land subject to competing uses will be put to its optimal, or highest valued use regardless of the initial assignment of the rights to it. In the example given above, if the site in question is worth more to a wealthy environmentalist, say, than to the holder of a patented mining claim, the environmentalist simply buys out the miner, and the site is left undisturbed. If it is worth more to the miner, he refuses the bid, and develops the site for minerals production. The analysis is symmetric if rights to use of the site initially lie with the environmentalist, only now the roles are reversed. The environmentalist refuses the miner's offer if the site is worth more to him undisturbed, and accepts it, and the resulting disfigurement of the landscape, if it is not. In each case, the land and related resources are put to

---

[12] For a careful and rigorous, though not very encouraging discussion of this point in the larger context of evaluating changes in real national income, see Samuelson (1950).

their highest valued use, which is clearly the same regardless of who has to compensate whom. Implicit in the theorem is the assumption that evaluations of the alternatives are not affected by the prior distribution of property rights. In our example the land is worth a certain amount to the environmentalist. He is willing to pay this amount in the event that the miner has title, and will accept it in the event that the land is his to dispose of.

If the explicit and implicit statements of the Coase theorem are valid, then it seems that, contrary to the assertion made at the start of the preceding paragraph, measurement of the gains and losses from a project is in fact straightforward and unambiguous. There are, however, a couple of problems—not with the logic of the theorem, but with its application in typical environmental externality situations, as pointed out perhaps most clearly by Mishan (1971a)—which further consideration of our example can bring out.

Recall that on one side of the bargaining table is a wealthy environmentalist. Now, if instead of this single individual there were a great many, thousands, or even millions of consumers who would in one way or another suffer a welfare loss from conversion of a particular scenic natural area into a mining operation, it could be very costly to evaluate and represent the interest of each. The costs of negotiation, or more generally, the transaction costs, in this situation could be so high that even though the value of the site to all consumers of its amenity services exceeds the value to the mining firm, assignment of property rights to the firm, as under current mining law, would result in use of the site for mining.

A second problem with application of the theorem, and one that bears directly on the evaluations of alternatives under differing property regimes, is indicated by the assumption that the environmentalist is "wealthy." The problem is very simply that the amount a consumer would be willing to pay for a given natural environment will generally be less than the amount he would accept to part with it, owing to the income constraint on the former. Perhaps a better illustration of the significance of this point is the selective process in kidnapping. Wealthy families are the universal victims for ransom purposes, presumably because of their greater ability to pay, and not because poor folks are less attached to (would accept less for) their offspring. Although this is admittedly an extreme case, it emphasizes the potential range of values given by measures of consumer's surplus that are respectively constrained and unconstrained by income. Similarly, many people who are not particularly wealthy feel that only with reluctance would they accept the loss of a natural area important to them or as part of a national heritage to their children and grandchildren, and so on. This is not to suggest that the implied reservation prices would be easy to determine (any more than the amounts people would be "will-

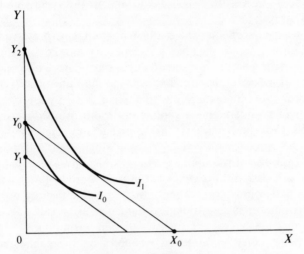

*Figure 2-1. Property rights
and consumer's surplus.*

ing to pay" under an alternative property regime), or even that this is
necessarily the appropriate regime. Again, the point is simply that valuation of a common property environmental resource is, as suggested, not
entirely straightforward.

The variation in value corresponding in general to different assignments
of property rights can be demonstrated with the aid of a diagram. In figure
2-1, Y represents the (aggregate) market good, let us say the output of
the mine, and X the environmental amenity. If the miner has the initial
property right, then the consumer with budget line OY_0 would be willing
to pay an amount (compensating variation) equal to $Y_0 - Y_1$, which
would leave him just as well off as before the transaction (on his original
indifference curve I_0) for the right to use (part of) the site for its amenity
services.[13] Note that he could not in any case pay more than Y_0; his willingness to pay is bounded by his income.

Now suppose property rights to the environment are vested in the consumer. Assuming his consumption opportunities are described by line
Y_0X_0, the amount he would accept in return for his right to consume X is
given by the intersection of indifference curve I_1 with the Y axis, Y_2 in the
diagram. By keeping him on the same indifference curve, we again ensure
that he is just as well off after the transaction as before, but note that this
requires following the curve I_1 until it reaches the Y axis—independently

[13] See Mishan (1971a) for a detailed discussion of the compensating and equivalent variation concepts of consumer's surplus, and the sufficiency of the former for
our purposes.

of initial income Y_0. Clearly, $Y_2 - Y_0$ can, and in the typical case will, exceed $Y_0 - Y_1$.[14]

In order to determine whether the net benefit from, say, preservation of the environmental resource is positive, it is necessary to take the difference between the aggregate over all consumer–environmentalists, of one of the consumer's surplus measures described above, and the value of the resource to the mining firm. Note that where the competing use is by a profit-maximizing producer of an intermediate good traded on a competitive market, and with access to capital markets (as is presumably the case for the mining firm), the two measures collapse to a single figure. This is the excess revenue from use of the site in question, which gives its value to the firm. In defense of Coase, his examples are primarily producer-to-producer externalities, so that neither transaction costs nor the ambiguity produced by consumer income effects legitimately influence his results. It is our view, however, that the typical externality situation arising out of competing claims to the use of environmental resources on the public lands is better represented in our example, in which both effects are likely to be significant.[15]

If it is accepted that there are in theory two (potentially significantly different) measures of the value of any environmental amenity services provided by a tract of public land, the question of which is appropriate naturally arises. Can the difference perhaps be resolved? Consideration of the valuation by the mining firm suggests an appealing market solution to the latter question. Suppose a private firm is given the right, perhaps as a result of a competitive bid, to sell the camping and related recreational services of a wild tract of land. Then we are back in a Coasian world of (at most) two-party negotiation, based on unique valuation of each of the alternatives by private profit-maximizing producers with access to capital markets (and a determinate optimal solution). This idea has been advanced, but we foresee at least two difficulties. First, the land in part may necessarily be common property, or open access, due to the public good nature of some of the services it provides—the nonuser uses touched upon in the discussion of common property resources in section 2. In other words, as suggested in the introduction, although a market solution could uniquely determine value, the resulting allocation would probably not be optimal due to the lack of incentive to take account of all of the benefits

[14] This follows from the assumption that the income, or welfare, effect is positive. See Mishan (1971a), p. 127.

[15] It may not be too much to suggest that one's position on the "Coase controversy" is determined by one's model of externality. If so, this would be a good example of Milton Friedman's proposition that differences in positions taken by economists on various issues result not so much from differences in theory as from differences in (sometimes implicit) empirical judgments, which may, however, be resolved by further empirical work.

of nonextractive use—or for that matter, all of the costs of extractive use, including perhaps too-rapid exploitation due to a private discount rate that is above the social rate.[16] Second, a market solution may be politically infeasible since many persons appear to regard "free" access to wilderness on the public lands as a part of their inalienable heritage.[17]

In the event that market resolution of the difference is not feasible, then which measure is appropriate? The answer to this question is neither obvious nor entirely satisfactory. While an open-pit mine will reduce the benefits of the scenic and related aesthetic attributes of a landscape for some, thereby effectively restricting their rights to enjoy an undisturbed natural environment, denial of mining rights is also a restriction on the rights of the mining enterprise. The same observation, of course, is applicable to logging a tract of land, which results in landscape degradation, or altering the characteristics of a scenic or wild river. The question is, who should have to buy out whom? Who has the original rights? If the position of "ethical neutrality" advanced by Coase (1960) and further elaborated by Demsetz (1964, 1966) is accepted, then those who would infringe the rights of the mining enterprise, for example, by denying access, would have an obligation to compensate the mining company that is as justifiable as the obligation of the mining enterprise to compensate the losers for disfiguring the landscape. Indeed, the strict Coasian would presumably reject the notion of unidirectional externality and the Rothenberg distinctions based upon it.

A variation of no prior assignment of rights, or the case of ethical neutrality, has recently been advanced by Mohring and Boyd (1971). All open access rights are required to be withdrawn in this case and all formerly common property resources are to be converted to private property resources. Access to any resource under this doctrine would involve allocation to the highest bid, whether by prospective final or intermediate service users. Here willingness to pay, based on the measure of consumer surplus bounded by relevant income constraints, would be the indicated criterion of value. All parties have equal access in return for a consideration, as all are excluded in the absence of payments to the agency managing a restricted access resource. Alternatively, symmetry could be preserved by giving rights to all, and requiring compensation for any infringement.

Another method of assignment of rights has been that of prior appropriation, or prior use. This is the basic legal doctrine, with numerous

---

[16] Although the discussion here is in the context of *static* externality, especially challenging problems of market failure on the public lands arise in a dynamic setting, as the mention of option value and discounting would indicate. These problems are treated at length in chapters 1, 3, and 4.

[17] For example, this attitude filters through responses of recreationists to survey questions about their values and preferences in regard to wilderness management. See Hammack and Brown (1974).

variations, attaching to the allocation of water rights in western regions of the United States, and is basically the method of assigning rights among different contenders for mineral rights on public lands. Also it might be noted, it seems to be consistent with a pure Pareto criterion in that it implicitly requires anyone wanting a change from the status quo to *actually* compensate those who would lose thereby (the "squatters"). While the establishment of valid claims to mineral resources has not been without its ambiguities in western history, these difficulties appear to be trivial compared to determining the priority of use between recreationists and prospectors in today's controversies over allocation of public lands.

An alternative water rights doctrine relates to the accessibility of water to riparian owners, to the extent that the users do not diminish the supply in quantity or quality. While the use of water under the riparian doctrine has not observed the provision of water quality maintenance, it introduces the elements of the rights to the usufruct of common property resources. Consumer sovereignty is partially constrained; property rights are vested in private parties only in part. Here the services can be utilized provided that the substance of the resource is left intact. This doctrine provides a link to the Rothenberg distinction between the "constructive" and "destructive" uses of the environment.

It is obvious that pursuing this distinction much further would lead us out of economics and into ethics. There are deep philosophical issues involved, which have been raised also by conservationists and environmentalists, and on which we do not feel particularly qualified to pronounce.[18] Nevertheless, as they have been raised here, and are so interesting, we will offer just a few observations. An argument has been advanced by Page (1973) for justifying a hierarchy of rights based on the difference between rights to the use of the services of a common property resource which does not impair the substance, and rights to the consumption, preemption, or destruction of the resource itself. Is there a basis for making a valid ethical distinction? It appears that an argument of some persuasiveness can be advanced, depending on the nature of the destructive use: namely, the severity and duration of its detrimental effect, and their implications for human welfare.

The gravity of the threat to human welfare stemming from a destructive use of the environment may well evoke a valid moral judgment. Where health and life itself are jeopardized by pollution, the law is quite clear. The law regulating emission of noxious substances into environmental media represents a clear assignment of priority in which matters of "will-

---

[18] These are basically issues involving the ethical base of the doctrine of consumer sovereignty. See Rawls (1971) for discussion in a much more general context, and Leopold (1949) for an application of ethical arguments specifically to problems of land and other environmental resource use.

ingness to pay" are regarded as irrelevant.[19] But where the infringement of rights to the usufruct of common property resources involves only convenience or a consideration of aesthetics, the courts have not yet rendered a conclusive judgment.

The matter of the duration of the damages, or rights infringement, has drawn attention in the debate over the responsibility for compensation. Mishan (1971b) has argued that if a destructive use of environmental resources involves a welfare loss in perpetuity, irrespective of its implications for the more basic constituents of human welfare, a case can be made for giving different weights or priority to the rights based on the constructive–destructive distinction made in the use of the environment. But bringing time explicitly into the analysis makes it properly dynamic, and the subject of the following chapter.

To summarize the discussion of this section, in cases where the resource services in question represent a significant part of the real income of final consumers, the outcome could turn on the issue of who is liable for the opportunity returns foreclosed by the preclusion of one of two (or more) incompatible alternative allocations of common property resources. The willingness to pay on the part of nondestructive users represents the lower bound value of the resource when allocated to such a purpose. It is, moreover, based on a polar interpretation of priority in a possible hierarchy of rights. If the destructive use is one of sufficient gravity to elicit valid moral judgments, the correct measure of the environmental degradation may require priority in the consideration of rights, with the responsibility for compensation assigned to the destructive use. Compensation in such cases may well be substantially greater than the sum which the losers would be willing (or able) to pay to avoid the losses. In cases of health, life, and survival of the species, absolute prohibition—the practical equivalent of infinite compensation—may be justified, and has been as a matter of law and policy, in recognition of the irrelevance of market-determined distribution of income.

6. SUMMARY AND CONCLUSIONS

The major points of this chapter can be summarized as follows. For many, though not all uses, the public lands are managed as common property resources, for both technical and institutional reasons. Although management of common property resources is now fairly well understood, at least in theory, more difficult issues arise on the public lands as a result of competing claims of dissimilar common property uses, such as mining and recreation.

---

[19] See, for example, the Clean Air Act of 1967.

Where values of these competing uses must be weighed, as in a benefit–cost analysis for a public decision on allocation, a problem arises. The value of the resource in an important class of uses, namely those such as recreation in which the resource service enters directly the utility functions of consumers, is not uniquely determined. Rather, contrary to the Coasian presumption, it will vary with the assignment of property rights. Where a competing use (say mining) has the initial rights, value to the recreationist is determined by his income-constrained maximum willingness to pay to buy out the miner. Where the recreationist has the initial rights, value is determined by the unconstrained minimum amount he will accept in exchange for his rights. Since these two measures of value are in general not the same, assignment of property rights could determine the outcome of a decision to allocate a resource to its optimal, or highest valued, use in an appreciable proportion of the cases.

This suggests the questions: Which measure is appropriate? Who should have the initial rights? The answer is not obvious, though a better case can perhaps be made for assigning priority to the nondestructive use. A result that has similar allocative implications also emerges from analysis of the effect of irreversibility in an uncertain economic environment, as established in chapter 4.

REFERENCES

Arrow, K. J. and Fisher, A. C. 1974. "Environmental Preservation, Uncertainty, and Irreversibility," *Quarterly Journal of Economics,* vol. LXXXVIII, no. 2.

Bator, F. M. 1958. "The Anatomy of Market Failure," *Quarterly Journal of Economics,* vol. LXXII, no. 3.

Buchanan, J. M. and Stubblebine, W. C. 1962. "Externality," *Economica,* N.S., vol. 29, no. 116.

Cicchetti, C. J. and Smith, V. K. 1970. "A Note on Jointly Supplied Mixed Goods," *Quarterly Review of Economics and Business,* vol. 10, no. 3.

Coase, R. H. 1960. "The Problem of Social Cost," *Journal of Law and Economics,* vol. 3 (October).

Davis, O. A. and Whinston, A. B. 1967. "On the Distinction Between Public and Private Goods," *American Economic Review,* vol. LVII, no. 2.

Demsetz, Harold. 1964. "The Exchange and Enforcement of Property Rights," *Journal of Law and Economics,* vol. 7 (October).

————. 1966. "Some Aspects of Property Rights," *Journal of Law and Economics,* vol. 9 (October).

Fisher, A. C., Krutilla, J. V., and Cicchetti, C. J. 1972. "The Economics of Environmental Preservation," *American Economic Review,* vol. LXII, no. 4.

Gordon, H. S. 1954. "The Economic Theory of a Common Property Resource: The Fishery," *Journal of Political Economy,* vol. 62, no. 2.

Hammack, Judd and Brown, G. M., Jr. 1974. *Waterfowl and Wetlands: Toward Bioeconomic Analysis* (Baltimore: Johns Hopkins Press).

Harberger, A. C. 1971. "Three Basic Postulates for Applied Welfare Economics: An Interpretive Essay," *Journal of Economic Literature*, vol. IX, no. 3.

Haveman, R. H. 1973. "Common Property, Congestion, and Environmental Pollution," *Quarterly Journal of Economics*, vol. LXXXVII, no. 3.

Hicks, J. R. 1939. "Foundations of Welfare Economics," *Economic Journal*, vol. 49, no. 196.

Holtermann, S. E. 1972. "Externalities and Public Goods," *Economica*, N.S., vol. 39, no. 153.

Kaldor, Nicholas. 1939. "Welfare Propositions of Economics and Interpersonal Comparisons of Utility," *Economic Journal*, vol. 49, no. 195.

Krutilla, J. V. 1967. "Conservation Reconsidered," *American Economic Review*, vol. LVII, no. 4.

———— and Eckstein, Otto. 1958. *Multiple Purpose River Development: Studies in Applied Economic Analysis* (Baltimore: Johns Hopkins Press).

Leopold, Aldo. 1949. *A Sand County Almanac* (London: Oxford University Press).

Margolis, Julius. 1955. "A Comment on the Pure Theory of Public Expenditure," *Review of Economics and Statistics*, vol. 37, no. 4.

Meade, J. E. 1952. "External Economies and Diseconomies in a Competitive Situation," *Economic Journal*, vol. 62, no. 245.

Minasian, J. R. 1964. "Television Pricing and the Theory of Public Goods," *Journal of Law and Economics*, vol. 7 (October).

Mishan, E. J. 1969, "The Relationship Between Joint Products, Collective Goods, and External Effects," *Journal of Political Economy*, vol. LXXVII, no. 3.

————. 1971a. *Cost–Benefit Analysis* (New York: Praeger).

————. 1971b. "The Postwar Literature on Externalities: An Interpretive Essay," *Journal of Economic Literature*, vol. IX, no. 1.

Mohring, Herbert and Boyd, J. H. 1971. "Analyzing Externalities: Direct Interaction vs. Asset Utilization Frameworks," *Economica*, vol. 38, no. 152.

Musgrave, R. A. 1959. *The Theory of Public Finance: A Study in Public Economy* (New York: McGraw-Hill).

Nelson, Richard. 1970. "Discussion," *American Economic Review*, vol. LX, no. 2.

Nickel, W. F., III. 1971. "The Current Legal Status of Ownership and Management of Fish and Wildlife on the Public Lands." Paper prepared as part of the Clinical Program in Environmental Law, the National Law Center, George Washington Univ., Washington, D.C.

Page, Talbot. 1973. *Economics of Involuntary Transfers: A Unified Approach to Pollution and Congestion Externalities* (New York: Springer-Verlag).

Rawls, John. 1971. *A Theory of Justice* (Cambridge: Harvard University Press).

Rothenberg, Jerome. 1970. "The Economics of Congestion and Pollution: An Integrated View," *American Economic Review*, vol. LX, no. 2.

Samuelson, P. A. 1950. "Evaluation of Real National Income," *Oxford Economic Papers*, N.S., vol. 2, no. 1.

————. 1954. "The Pure Theory of Public Expenditure," *Review of Economics and Statistics*, vol. 36, no. 4.

Scitovsky, T. S. 1941. "A Note on Welfare Propositions in Economics," *Review of Economic Studies*, vol. 9.

Scott, Anthony. 1955. "The Fishery: The Objectives of Sole Ownership," *Journal of Political Economy*, vol. 63, no. 2.

Smith, V. L. 1968. "Economics of Production from Natural Resources," *American Economic Review*, vol. LVIII, no. 3.

Weisbrod, B. A. 1964. "Collective-Consumption Services of Individual-Consumption Goods," *Quarterly Journal of Economics*, vol. LXXVIII, no. 3.

CHAPTER 3

IRREVERSIBILITY AND THE OPTIMAL USE OF NATURAL ENVIRONMENTS

1. INTRODUCTION

Previously we have suggested that some of the distinctive and challenging problems for valuation and allocation of the resources of natural environments are dynamic. Clearly, if decisions with respect to the use of these resources are impossible to reverse in a way that ordinary economic decisions are not, effects over long periods of time must be considered. This in turn raises the question of discounting, or more generally, of the efficiency and equity of resource use in the very long run. Moreover, where information about the costs and gains of alternative uses is particularly poor, due to the long period to which it must apply and the nonmarket character of some of the uses, decisions should take account of this uncertainty. For example, what is the appropriate social attitude toward the risk associated with the (irreversible) conversion of a natural environment to developmental purposes? What are the implications for option value?

In this and the following chapter we address these issues primarily from a theoretical point of view. We begin with a discussion of irreversibility in economic processes, with particular reference to the conversion of natural environments. The remainder of the chapter is devoted to a model of irreversible investment in a resource development project in a natural environment. The model assumes a planning authority whose objective is to maximize the present value of net social returns from use of the environment, taking account of the opportunity returns forgone. That is, it is explicitly concerned with the sacrifice in value derived from the amenity resources of the environment that accompanies the project.

As noted in chapter 2, it is not claimed that a social choice concerning the desirability of a project should be made solely on the basis of aggregate benefit, even net of environmental costs, i.e., on the basis of Kaldor–Hicks efficiency. We do feel that information about these magnitudes is relevant to a public decision. (Recall the even stronger statement by the Public Land Law Review Commission that maximization of net social benefits is an appropriate objective for public land management.) The model then describes how the resources of a natural environment would be allocated *if* the criterion were to maximize net benefits over time. Even where other considerations (for example, the distribution of benefits and costs) are important, the model provides a useful framework for organizing and interpreting the data in empirical investigation of the sort undertaken in later chapters.

This approach differs from what we referred to (chapter 1) as conventional benefit–cost analysis in at least two ways. First, as we have emphasized, the environmental opportunity costs are reckoned into the net present value of a project. Second, as described in detail in the fourth section, the valuation problem is formulated most generally as one of assessing a whole time path of (irreversible) investments in expanding development at a site. This contrasts with the standard analysis of a one-time investment at the site. Interestingly, it turns out that there are plausible circumstances in which the optimal time path is, in fact, a one-time investment. In this case the standard computational format may be applied, as in several of our empirical studies, but as a special case of a more general approach to valuation. More importantly, the general approach suggests conditions under which the standard format is *not* appropriate, and suggests how it should be amended. Simple comparison of present values, say of the alternatives to develop an area for minerals production, or preserve it for wilderness recreation, can be misleading.

In chapter 4 we consider the choice of discount rate, broader problems of efficiency and equity in resource allocation over generations, and the implications of uncertainty for irreversible investment.

2. IRREVERSIBILITY IN ECONOMIC PROCESSES

We recognize that for some of our readers, everything is irreversible in the sense that time does not move backward. For others, perhaps including many of our fellow economists, the consequences of any decision (e.g., to develop a natural environment) are reversible given sufficient application of technique and conventional resource inputs.

We suggest that neither of these views is particularly helpful in determining how best to use the resources of a natural environment. On the contrary, meaningful distinctions can be made between uses that are reversible and those that, for all practical purposes, are not. In the next section it will be shown that the computational format of the standard benefit–cost analysis in fact assumes that a development project in a natural environment is not reversible.

In the field of economics, a fairly easily made distinction with respect to reversibility is that between production and investment. Consider the problem facing a farm operator in determining whether to allocate his stock of land between the production of carrots or beets. After exercising his best judgment, taking into account such relevant factors as anticipated future prices of associated inputs and the products he wishes to market, he will opt for the crop that appears to be most profitable. Assuming that this does not have implications for long-lived equipment that is specialized for one or another root crop, he can review his decision at the beginning of the next planting period. If his judgment regarding the relative profitability of the two alternatives was faulty, and he has good reason to suspect a change in production plans is called for, he can adjust his plans after only one production cycle.

If the problem that a decision maker faces is not that of a choice between two different root crops, or different mixes of products in a production batch—either of which is possible with land, plant, and equipment needed for production, the problem takes on consequences of longer duration. Assume that an individual wishes to consider two possible extractive pursuits, one involving truck gardening and the other ranching. A choice here will involve the commitment of resources to more or less specialized land, plant, and equipment. A faulty decision, with benefit of hindsight, could not be as readily adjusted to the changes that would be desired in some future period. So long as receipts cover variable production costs, the decision maker would be "locked in" to his decision at least over the period required to depreciate his specialized equipment.[1]

From the individual's point of view, the consequences of his decision might not be trivial, but from the standpoint of society at large, the particular decision impinges only at the margin of the total production of beef, truck, and specialized capital equipment. The consequences are neither ephemeral nor trivial for the decision maker, but to society the irreversible consequences of the particular decision are of no great moment. This is probably true of all such marginal investment decisions.

There are, however, long-run effects of individual actions that may be anything but trivial for society as a whole. Consider, for example, the allocation of resources that represent an accident of geological processes—the geysers in Yellowstone National Park. This unusual phenomenon has at least two possible uses. It can serve as a source of geothermal energy for the production of electricity, or it can be reserved as a unique natural phenomenon serving as the basis for viewing and related recreational activities. A decision to reserve the area for nature appreciation and related recreation, and/or scientific interests, is a decision that has been made, but is not, of course, immutable. It is true that Yellowstone National Park, being established by legislation, represents a serious commitment to preserving

---

[1] This, of course, would not be true if there were a ready market for the specialized resources no longer capable of profitable employment in the chosen pursuit.

the natural features, but should the continued existence of humanity depend on its being rededicated to another use, no *technical* constraint would prevent a reversal of the decision and termination of the consequences of the initial decision.

If the geothermal resources of the Yellowstone National Park were allocated to energy production, on the other hand, there would be a set of consequences stemming from this decision that would have more permanent and therefore more significant implications. Construction of steam electric power plants, switchyards, transmission towers, and so on, would result in an adverse modification of the visual environment in the park for a considerable period of time, if not permanently. The mining of the superheated water would, in sufficient time, reduce subsurface pressures, eliminate the geyser action, and thus remove the primary basis that induced the establishment of the area as a national park. A decision to "restore" the area following depletion of the geothermal resources would be technically impossible to implement.[2] The consequence of the decision to use the geothermal resources for energy production, in terms of the opportunity returns forgone from the alternative aesthetic and scientific uses, would be experienced in perpetuity. On the other hand, we have the forgone energy opportunity returns which are limited both by the availability of economical substitutes for generating electrical energy, and by the duration of the effects of the decision, i.e., legislation can be repealed when desired. In the alternative allocation, the decision will involve precluded opportunity returns in perpetuity. There are no known technical means of restoring the original character of a natural environment that includes the periodic eruption of Old Faithful.

The matter of irreversibility seems simple enough, yet it is elusive for some. It may be well to devote some additional discussion to this matter at the outset. The investment in specialized plant and equipment will, in a sense, represent an irreversible commitment of capital to an undertaking, and for an individual making the decision, it is not to be taken lightly. But in some sense, from society's viewpoint it is not unlike the irreversibility

---

[2] The withdrawal of the steam for electric power production implies a withdrawal rate of superheated water exceeding the natural discharge, and hence the aquifer's recharge rate. This results in mining of the heated waters, which causes the geyser action to stop. Cessation of the geothermal energy operations would not automatically restore the geyser action. Many years would be required to replenish the water in the reservoir and to restore the heat energy of the system. Reestablishment or replacement of the geyser and spring vents would probably require hundreds of years. Many hundreds or thousands of years were required to form the vents and cones in the first instance; they disintegrate rapidly when exposed to steam and acid gases, if not maintained by continuous deposition of silica from flowing springs and geysers. (The technical information regarding effects of geothermal operations on geyser action was supplied in personal correspondence with Dr. Donald E. White, Branch of Field Geochemistry, United States Geological Survey, March 30, 1973.)

that attends the death of any single member of a population. There does not appear to be overwhelming concern, except for the individuals directly involved, for the demise of a member of a species, provided that the reproductive capability is retained within the population. The risk of the loss of the last viable mating pair, hence the genetic information that it possesses essential to survival of the species, however, is a matter of much greater moment. Reverting to the example of the investment decision, the loss of capital value of a misjudged investment, for society, is not unlike the loss of a member of a given, viable population.

The loss of the scientific–technological information necessary to meet future demand for capital goods would be a matter of greater gravity, and may be likened to the loss of genetic information. This irreversibility is the basis for the concern that society exhibits for the losses associated with dying arts and crafts. The extinction of these reduces cultural diversity. While there may be different implications for system stability (cultural or ecological homeostasis), the loss of either cultural or genetic information reduces the options available, and thus illustrates a central postulate of welfare economics, i.e., an expansion of choice represents a welfare gain; reduction of options, a welfare loss.

Although irreversibility represents an extreme case, like the economist's "public good," or "perfect competition," it similarly captures an important feature of some real situations. But what of the possible objection that a natural environment, once developed and used for extractive purposes, can be restored? We have already observed that this would not be technically feasible for the geysers of Yellowstone, but perhaps this is an exception. Problems more generally associated with restoration are discussed below. There are two important considerations that require attention. One involves the time during which the adverse consequences of an investment decision must be suffered. The other involves the fidelity of the reproduction or restoration, and perhaps more importantly, its acceptability.

Duration of Welfare Loss

Consider the conversion of a wilderness ecosystem to meet the demands for the output of extractive industries. If the environmental modification results in the elimination of essential habitat for a given species, e.g., the passenger pigeon or the grizzly bear, restoration is impossible—or at least incomplete without the fauna dependent on the original plant associations. But, even if the survival of a species is not at issue, restoration is not a simple remedy for redressing the impact of an inappropriate decision that disturbed the original ecological system.

The clear-cutting of a climax species is equivalent to removing the results of an ecological succession that represents in many cases centuries of natural processes.[3] The removed climax species would be succeeded by various seral species in a procession of changing plant and animal communities, culminating in the original ecological relationships only after a lapse of much time. In tropical climates this restoration under natural processes, of course, might take less time. In subhumid climes typical of some parts of the eastern United States, restoration over several generations might be sufficient to produce at least a superficial resemblance to the original conditions. But it is unlikely that even here the original faunal communities will be reestablished in their original associations. The woods bison, the eastern race of elk, and the caribou, for example, along with the predator populations that made up in part the wilderness ecosystems, are doubtless features of the original wilderness that are permanently lost from society's options in modern times. In the arid and semiarid west, in the higher elevations in alpine settings in western mountains of the United States, and in much of Alaskan subarctic and arctic life zones, perturbations to the ecology would take centuries to correct.

Environmental modifications that affect the abiotic base are even more difficult to contend with. If the basic geological and soil conditions are adversely affected, replacement by perhaps more primitive biotic communities might occur eventually, but restoration of the original biological environment will not be possible in anything like a time span that is meaningful for human societies. Vast open-pit mining operations and transportation facilities in ecologically fragile environments such as high mountain areas or the Arctic, and some water resource developments, are among the activities that have a potential for affecting the abiotic base in a manner that is irreversible for all practical purposes in terms of human time spans.

Consider some of the complications that attend the development of a water storage reservoir in an ecologically fragile area. Correcting a faulty decision to construct a dam involves more than dismantling the structure when its existence begins to incur environmental opportunity costs exceeding the returns from development. Supersaturation of reservoir banks at full pool elevations may result in sloughing and landslides into the reservoir on drawdowns. An example of this condition is found in the Brownlee Reservoir in the upper reaches of the Hells Canyon. Moreover, if streams of high turbidity are impounded, some storage space must be reserved in the reservoir to trap the sediments. Dismantling the structure at some future time will, in many instances, leave the impoundment area with an abiotic base entirely different from that which existed under original conditions.

---

[3] This, of course, assumes that the clear-cutting does not involve critical modifications of the abiotic base, such as soil erosion, siltation of spawning beds for salmon and trout fisheries, and other similar processes that would permanently foreclose the restoration of original ecological relationships.

As a consequence, an entirely different ecological system is likely, even if the dam is removed and natural restorative processes are permitted.

In arctic regions, removal of the primitive vegetal cover to expose mineral earth has long-run disruptive effects. The increased absorption of solar heat may affect the unstable soil relationships in areas of permafrost, with thawing, erosion, and gullying that leave the landscape permanently and seriously disfigured.

Artificial Restoration and the
Significance of Authenticity

A question can be raised, however, whether it is not possible, by mobilizing the scientific–technological knowledge that also accumulates with time, to short-circuit the time element in restoration. This is doubtless a possibility in many cases involving rather ordinary landscapes, particularly in the more rapid restoration areas of subhumid and humid climatic zones. But when we consider the extraordinary natural environments that are prized for their scientific research materials or their unusual scenic features, the problems are more difficult. If the objective is simply to restore some type of outdoor recreational facility in place of the original, it is doubtless possible to replicate in some particulars the original features that would satisfy the bulk of the demands of those seeking outdoor recreation.[4] But, there is a legitimate question whether undisturbed natural environments should be allocated to extractive industrial activities on the supposition that they can be eventually restored. Even the most painstaking application of modern scientific–technological resources would provide replicas of the original that would satisfy the recreational interests of only the less discriminating clientele. The matter turns on the importance of authenticity as an attribute of the recreational experience, quite apart from the matter of preserving relevant research materials for advancing knowledge in the life and earth sciences.

The demand for authenticity as an attribute of undisturbed natural areas may be likened to the demand for authenticity in the visual arts. For the bulk of the art museum clientele, the difference between an original work of art of one of the masters and a copy by one of his protegés, or a contemporary artist or student, may be undetectable, and may well satisfy their tastes. But to a connoisseur of the arts, the mere suspicion of a forgery, even one so expert that art critics will differ in their opinions of its authen-

---

[4] On the other hand, of the 186 million acres of land administered by the Forest Service, for example, only some 56 million remain in a relatively undisturbed natural state and are suitable for reservation for the national wilderness system. The remaining 130 million acres that have been modified in some particular, perhaps by roads, are available for the type of recreation that is serviced by facilities consistent with artificial restoration of original environmental characteristics.

ticity, will result in a drastic reduction in the market value of the *objet d'art,* as many museum curators have been embarrassed to discover. The question then turns on what is the clientele, or market, that a particular amenity resource is to satisfy.

The outdoor recreation market is a vast and complicated structure of numerous submarkets. A developed campground in an attractive roadside location may be all that the "typical" family car-camper desires. A more developed campground with electrical outlets for portable television sets, however, also seems to be favored by many, and a primitive undeveloped (natural) site in some primeval setting that would require a day of strenuous backpacking to reach is likely to hold no attraction for this clientele. For the accommodation of these submarkets there are state, regional, and National Park and Forest Service areas totaling upwards of 150 million acres. But there are types of users, and growing numbers of them,[5] who seek solitude and primeval settings for the gratification of their recreational tastes. This group represents a distinct submarket among outdoor recreation enthusiasts. Even within the ranks of wilderness users there appears to be a bimodal distribution among "purists" and "nonpurists."[6] In the important work of Stankey (1972), an analysis was made of the values reflected in the Wilderness Act and its legislative history as a basis for distinguishing among wilderness users those whose preferences should be taken into account in the administration of the system. A bimodal distribution along a purist–nonpurist scale was apparent, with the preference for authenticity markedly exhibited by the group that had values corresponding to those reflected in the Wilderness Act.[7] To members of this puristic submarket, no less than to the life and earth scientist, an artificial replica, no matter how "exact," is as unsatisfying a remedy for a disturbed natural environment as is the replica of a work of art to a connoisseur, no matter how difficult detection of the reproduction may be for the bulk of the less sophisticated consumers.

The reason for the unsatisfying nature of even relatively accurate, or expert, replicas for the purist is not, of course, a matter of economic knowledge, and perhaps not even of scientific knowledge generally. There may be an aura about the work of creative genius that the most gifted imitator cannot provide. There may be even a cult composed of those who

---

[5] Wilderness recreation and recreation in undeveloped natural areas is the most rapidly growing outdoor recreational activity. It has been increasing at the rate of approximately 10 percent per year over the past several decades without evidence of slackening. It seems to be a result of changing tastes in addition to elasticity of demand with respect to income and educational achievement. See George Stankey (1972) for a discussion of this phenomenon.

[6] Stankey (1972) and V. Kerry Smith, unpublished analysis, Resources for the Future (1971).

[7] Purism as measured by Stankey was positively related to educational attainment, and interestingly to urban rather than rural origin among wilderness users.

revere the works of nature in a sense similar to that in which Buddhists revere it, which may not itself be dissimilar from the reverence that many primitive societies confer on nature in their religious observances. To those who number among the purists, preservation of the biosphere in precisely the way it has evolved, without disturbances from postindustrial man, is a matter of great significance in a profound personal sense. Such feelings, in fact, have been captured in the works of Wordsworth, Emerson, and Thoreau in very moving fashion. Whatever the reasons may be, whether mystical or religious, they are felt with great intensity. For analytical purposes this translates into a highly inelastic demand for the "originals." This clientele represents, currently, a significant market that appears to be recruiting members rapidly as the income, education, and urban composition of American society change (see Stankey, 1972). Moreover, this is a market for which refinements in restorative technology will do little by way of recreating "undisturbed" natural environments. Accordingly, the argument for irreversibility is a powerful one where the user group places a high value on the attribute of authenticity in the amenity services yielded by given natural environmental resources.

3. IRREVERSIBLE DECISIONS AND EXHAUSTIBLE RESOURCES

Before proceeding with the formal model, we should say something about the relationship between conversion of a natural environment, the problem we have been discussing, and the depletion of an exhaustible extractive resource, such as a mineral deposit. The problem of the optimal rate of depletion has been extensively studied by economists: first perhaps by Gray (1914); elegantly, using the calculus of variations, by Hotelling (1931); with special reference to a mineral deposit by Scott (1967), among others; and most recently from a pure theoretical point of view that extends Hotelling, by several, including Gordon (1967), Cummings and Burt (1969), Peterson (1973), and Solow (1974). Common to all of these studies is the assumption that the resource has value only when extracted, or regarded as a store of future extractions. A general theme of this volume is that the resource may have another value, realized only if it is *not* extracted. Extraction, then, is irreversible in two senses. It gives rise to a "user cost," the forgone future extractive output, and also to a loss (in perpetuity) in value from the undisturbed environment.

There are reasons for believing that the second type of irreversibility may be more important in certain cases. A development project may not involve the use of an exhaustible extractive resource. It may, like a high-density recreation facility, be capable of operation over an indefinitely long period. Loss of the amenity resources of the original environment could, however, be regarded as irreversible, for the reasons indicated earlier in this chapter. Or, suppose the open pit mining in a scenic area of an exhaustible extractive resource, such as an energy commodity, is being considered. The consumer of electrical energy is presumably indifferent (at a given price per kilowatt hour) to the type and source of the fuel used to produce the energy. Technical change can find ways to extract usable energy from other sources, and so on. Although depletion of a particular deposit is irreversible, this may not matter very much if substitute fuel materials are likely to be available. In fact, as we have seen already in chapter 1, technical change in the extractive and logistic support industries has made possible the production of minerals commodities at generally declining relative supply prices (Potter and Christy, 1962; Barnett and Morse, 1963). But, as also noted in chapter 1, technology can do little to produce the results of the particular patterns of geomorphology, weathering, and ecological succession found in the scenic environment in which the fuel deposit also occurs. Amenity services of the environment tend to enter directly the utility functions of consumers, with no intervening production technology. Where there are perceived differences between this environment and others, as in general there will be, perfect substitution (in consumption) is not possible, and loss of a particular environment may matter, at least to some.

4. IRREVERSIBLE INVESTMENT AND
PROJECT EVALUATION

In this section we present a model of irreversible investment in a resource development project in a natural environment. A planner is assumed to maximize the present value of net social returns from use of the environment, the project site. The decision or control variable at his disposal is the amount of investment (in expanding development) to be made at each point in time. Each increment in investment then adds something to the stream of discounted future benefits from the project, at the same time using up current investment funds and perhaps diminishing the stream of discounted future benefits obtainable from the amenity resources of the environment. It is further assumed that the site is characterized by some initial level of development. For example, suppose we are considering the development of additional hydroelectric capacity along the Hells Canyon reach of the Snake River. The Snake is a part of the larger Columbia River system of the Pacific Northwest, which has been considerably developed for power production—though part of the Hells Canyon still retains its wilderness character. Additional doses of investment in power and related facilities, as well as some current expenditure here can increase capacity—at the cost of reduced opportunities for hunting and fishing recreation in a wilderness environment.

The major result derived from the model is that, if returns from development of a site are decreasing over time relative to returns from preservation (as would result, for example, from the former decreasing and the latter increasing), it will suffice for the choice of the optimal policy, or time path of investment, to consider the present values of only (1) an immediate, once-and-for-all investment, and (2) no further investment, i.e., preservation. A particular project or scale of development is selected and evaluated, and then compared with value of the services otherwise provided by the environment. This is what we have referred to as the standard benefit–cost format: computation of the net present value of a single investment. This very useful result emerges as a special case of a more general theorem. If there exists some interval of time over which development benefits are decreasing relative to preservation-related benefits, so that the instantaneous optimal scale of development is decreasing, then the net present value of the project site, the natural environment, will be maximized by stopping investment at some point before the start of the interval, i.e., while it is still profitable to expand development. The sacrifice of some near-term gains is a consequence of the restriction on reversibility, required to avoid greater future losses from too much development.

These results are obtained by optimal control theory. This is a technique for finding the solution to certain dynamic optimization problems in economics. An example of the type of problem to which it has been applied is that of the firm seeking the time path of investment that maximizes its value, the stream of discounted net revenues. Another example would be that of the planner seeking a savings policy that minimizes the time required to reach a target level of output, subject of course to some minimum constraint on intervening consumption. Optimal control theory may be regarded as an extension of the classical calculus of variations. Its advantages, for economists, appear to lie in (1) its greater flexibility with respect to the type of constraints it can accommodate—for example, inequality constraints on the control variables—and (2) the very natural economic interpretation that can be given to the variables.[8]

The interested reader may wish to refer to the discussions of optimal control theory listed in footnote 8, prior to working through the remainder of this section. Alternatively, the major results having been presented, it is possible to merely skim the material and move rather quickly to the next section, which offers some concluding remarks.

[8] There are a number of good introductions to optimal control theory and in particular to its applications in economics. The interested reader is referred to Dorfman (1969) for a very clear discussion assuming a relatively elementary background in mathematics. Other somewhat more advanced treatments are found in Arrow (1968b), Shell (1969), and Intriligator (1971), to suggest a few.

The Model

We begin discussion of the formal material by introducing some notation and related assumptions. The size of project, or scale of development, at any time t is represented by $S(t)$. $S(t)$ is measured in physical units, as, for example, kilowatts of installed capacity for a hydroelectric project. The (flow of) benefits from the project net of operating costs is represented by $b^d[S(t), t]$, i.e., benefits are a function of project size. For the type of project we shall be considering, this seems appropriate. Assuming for the moment stable demand and technology (shifts in either of which could affect the benefit function), benefits should be related to scale, as measured, for instance, by installed capacity for a hydroelectric project, by the area taken for development of a high-density recreation complex, by the number of waterfowl-producing ponds drained for conversion to cropland, and so on.

What this formulation does not explicitly capture, however, is the relationship of the benefits to the rate of extraction of a resource such as a commercial mineral deposit (as opposed to the scale of the environmental modification). Were we primarily concerned with the rate-of-extraction problem, this relationship would probably have to be explicit. As it is, in the one case of this type we do study (possible future molybdenum mining in the White Cloud Peaks area near Sun Valley, Idaho), any shifts over time in benefits from a given scale of operations can be attributed to changes in the (assumed optimal) rate of extraction, as well as in resource prices.

More can be said about the relationship between benefits and project size. Clearly, benefits are positively related to size. But we shall assume that marginal benefits are diminishing, i.e., that the benefit function is concave. It is conceivable that initial stages of water resource development in an area would exhibit increasing returns. This will not, however, be true of a river system in advanced stages of development, such as the Columbia River system. Further, what really matters, as we shall see, is the behavior of benefits net of environmental opportunity costs, the latter being plausibly assumed to increase at an increasing rate with development.

The environmental costs are just the forgone benefits from preservation. To emphasize this point, we shall represent these benefits explicitly as a function of scale and time; in symbols, as $b^p[S(t), t]$. Note that the relationship between b^p and S is then negative. b^p decreases with increase in S, and as noted above, at an increasing rate.

Before the problem is stated formally, a few other symbols can be defined. In addition to the flow of operating costs associated with a project, already netted out of the b^d term, there will be at any time a flow of capital, or investment costs. These are assumed to be positively related to the level of investment: $C = C[I(t)]$, where C is cost and $I(t)$ is investment at time t.[9] Investment is defined as the time rate of change in project scale, i.e., $I = dS/dt$, and is accordingly in physical units. It is further assumed that the cost–investment relationship is linear, i.e., $C = I/\sigma$, or $I = \sigma C$. In other words, the dollar cost of each unit of investment is $1/\sigma$. Alternatively, the amount of investment produced by each dollar is just σ. A substantial portion of this chapter has been devoted to establishing the proposition that this investment is irreversible. In symbols, we shall require now that $I \geqslant 0$.

One final point: As noted earlier, discussions of discounting and uncertainty are reserved for the next chapter. For now we assume an appropriately chosen rate, ρ, to discount future benefits and costs, which in turn are just those expected to prevail by the planning authority.

The planning problem can now be stated as:[10]

$$(3\text{-}1) \qquad \int_0^\infty e^{-\rho t}[b^d(S(t), t) + b^p(S(t), t) - C(I(t))]\, dt$$

subject to

$$(3\text{-}2) \qquad \frac{dS}{dt} = I,$$

$$(3\text{-}3) \qquad I \geqslant 0,$$

and

$$(3\text{-}4) \qquad S(0) = \bar{S}(0)$$

Expression (3-1) is the integral of discounted net benefits and investment costs. Expressions (3-2) and (3-3) have already been described, and represent respectively the dynamic constraint on development and the restriction on reversibility. Equation (3-4) says that the state of the system, as indicated by the level of development S, is known at the beginning of the planning period and is equal to $\bar{S}(0)$.

Formally, the model given by expressions (3-1)–(3-4) is very

[9] Especially in discussion of business investment, these costs are also known as cost of adjustment (of the capital stock). See Eisner and Strotz (1963).

[10] We shall generally omit the arguments of functions in order to avoid cumbersome notation. $b^d(S(t), t)$ will be written b^d, and so on.

similar to models of the firm's or the economy's optimal accumulation of capital, and we shall exploit the similarity. Recall that in models of the economy, the fundamental differential equation for the growth of the capital stock typically takes the form[11]

$$(3\text{-}5) \quad \frac{dk}{dt} = f(k) - c - (n + \delta)k$$

where k is capital, $f(k)$ is output, c is consumption, n is the rate of growth of population, and δ is the rate of depreciation. Since it is ordinarily assumed that c cannot exceed $f(k)$, dk/dt can be negative only if $(n + \delta)$ is sufficiently large, and in any case the rate of decumulation cannot exceed $(n + \delta)$. Recently in the work of Arrow (1968) and Arrow and Kurz (1970), the stronger assumption of irreversible investment has been made, for the firm and the economy respectively. We shall proceed to the solution of (3-1)–(3-4) by adapting some of Arrow's results.

From expression (3-1), the current-value Hamiltonian equation is written as

$$(3\text{-}6) \quad H = e^{-\rho t}[b^d + b^p - C] + p\sigma C$$

where p is an auxiliary variable, the discounted shadow price (value of future benefits) of investment. The first term on the right-hand side is the discounted flow of net benefits at time t and the second term is the discounted future value of investment at time t.

According to the theory of optimal control, due to Pontryagin et al. (1962), evolution of the shadow price satisfies the equation

$$(3\text{-}7) \quad \frac{dp}{dt} = -\frac{\partial H_{\max}}{\partial S}$$
$$= -e^{-\rho t}(b_S^d + b_S^p)$$

where b_S^d is the first partial derivative of b^d with respect to S, and similarly for b_S^p. $H_{\max}$ in equation (3-7) indicates that H is evaluated at the point at which it is maximum with respect to the control variable I. This "maximum principle" enables us to begin determination of the optimal level of I at each moment in time. First rewrite H as

$$(3\text{-}8) \quad H = e^{-\rho t}[b^d + b^p] + \frac{q}{\sigma}I$$

[11] See, for example, the discussion of optimal capital accumulation in Dorfman (1969).

where $q = p\sigma - e^{-\rho t}$. Now it is clear that H is maximized by

(3-9) $\quad I = 0 \qquad\qquad q < 0$

$\qquad\quad\; I \geqslant 0 \qquad\qquad q = 0$

If q were positive, there would be no solution to the maximization problem, as it would pay to increase I indefinitely. Now, from the point of view of the firm, an infinite rate of investment at a moment in time is perfectly possible. This would represent the purchase of a block of capital, as opposed to gradual accumulation at some finite rate over an interval. It is not clear, however, that there is an analog in our problem to block acquisition by the firm. Presumably some time is required to develop a site for power production, or mining operations, for example—though a discrete-time version of the model could allow for an investment period of sufficient length. But even accepting the notion of development virtually "overnight," i.e., approximately at a moment in time, we know it cannot be optimal except possibly at the initial moment, from Arrow's proof that a discontinuous jump in the firm's capital stock, or block acquisition, is not optimal, except possibly initially (1968a, p. 8). Accordingly, we have an initial condition on p, namely, $p(0)$ must be sufficiently small that $q(t) \leqslant 0$.

From (3-9) we know that some amount of investment in expanding the scale of development will be indicated when $q = 0$, and also that no expansion is warranted when $q < 0$. What remains to be determined are the bounds of the no-expansion intervals (called "blocked intervals" by Arrow) and the precise levels of expansion that will be optimal at other times (nonblocked, or "free intervals"). We begin by deriving an expression for dq/dt, namely

(3-10) $\quad \dfrac{dq}{dt} = \sigma \dfrac{dp}{dt} + \rho e^{-\rho t}$

or from equation (3-7), following some rearrangement,

(3-11) $\quad \dfrac{dq}{dt} = e^{-\rho t}[\rho - \sigma(b_S^d + b_S^p)]$

and

(3-12) $\quad q(t_1) - q(t_0) = \displaystyle\int_{t_0}^{t_1} e^{-\rho t}[\rho - \sigma(b_S^d + b_S^p)]\, dt$

Over a free interval defined by the condition that $q = 0$, $dq/dt = 0$, so that

(3-13) $\quad \rho - \sigma(b_S^d + b_S^p) = 0$

Now suppose investment were reversible, that some or all of a natural environment developed, say as the site of a hydroelectric power project, could be restored to its predevelopment state. This would be equivalent to the rental of a block of capital goods by a firm for some period, in the Arrow problem. In our case, reversibility could result either from costless restoration of the environment, as would be accomplished, for example, by the wave of a wand, instantly eliminating all traces of the project, or by a restoration involving costs, which may be both direct (ripping out the installed capacity) and opportunity (continuing losses from the inability to restore some attributes of the natural environment, as discussed earlier), but which are just balanced by the scrap value of the no longer wanted project materials. It is intuitively plausible, and has been shown in another, earlier work of Arrow (1964), that a firm's optimal investment policy in these circumstances would be "myopic" in the sense that it would be determined solely by current profitability and not at all by anticipations of future demand, technology, and so on, because instantaneous adjustment of the capital stock is possible in any direction. In other words, the firm ought to hold, at each instant, the stock of capital for which the marginal return just equals the cost in interest charges. For our problem this can be expressed as

$$(3\text{-}14) \quad b_S^d(S^*) + b_S^p(S^*) = \frac{\rho}{\sigma}$$

where S^* is the instantaneous optimum scale of project, $b_S^d(S^*)$ is the benefit from an increment to the project, $b_S^p(S^*)$ is the disbenefit, or loss in preservation-related benefit, from the increment, and ρ/σ is the direct investment cost.

Comparing (3-13) and (3-14), we have determined precisely the level of project development that will be optimal when investment is not blocked, i.e., when q is not negative. The solution in this case is that I should be chosen such that $S(t) = S^*(t)$ over a free interval, i.e., for $q = 0$. In other words, the optimum size of project $S(t)$ coincides with the instantaneous optimum $S^*(t)$, for all t within a free interval.

The next question is obviously, how are the bounds of the alternating blocked and free intervals determined? Consider some properties of the state and auxiliary variables, S and q respectively, on these intervals. On a blocked interval (t_0, t_1), $S(t_0) = S^*(t_0)$ and $q(t_0) = 0$, since t_0 is also the end of a free interval. Moreover, since $I = 0$, $S(t) = S^*(t_0)$, and also $S(t) = S^*(t_1)$, $t_0 \leqslant t \leqslant t_1$ since t_1 is the end of a blocked interval, and

$q(t_1) = 0$ since t_1 is also the start of a free interval. The bounds of the blocked interval (t_0, t_1) are then defined by the following conditions, in conjunction with equation (3-12):

(3-15) $S^*(t_0) = S^*(t_1)$

(3-16) $\displaystyle\int_{t_0}^{t_1} e^{-\rho t}\{\rho - \sigma[b_S^d(S^*(t_0)) + b_S^p(S^*(t_0))]\}\, dt = 0,$

(3-17) $\displaystyle\int_{t_0}^{t} e^{-\rho t}\{\rho - \sigma[b_S^d(S^*(t_0)) + b_S^p(S^*(t_0))]\}\, dt < 0,$
$$t_0 < t < t_1$$

and

(3-18) $\displaystyle\int_{t}^{t_1} e^{-\rho t}\{\rho - \sigma[b_S^d(S^*(t_0)) + b_S^p(S^*(t_0))]\}\, dt > 0,$
$$t_0 < t < t_1$$

These expressions can be given economic interpretations. If $S(t)$ is held equal to $S^*(t_0)$, net marginal benefits $\sigma(b_S^d + b_S^p)$ first exceed constant marginal costs ρ, since investment is not pushed all the way to the point at which they would be equal. As the instantaneous optimum $S^*(t)$ begins to fall, however, beyond some point there is too much development, i.e., $S(t) = S^*(t_0) > S^*(t)$, $t_0 < t < t_1$. From this point, marginal benefits are less than marginal costs. Equation (3-16) states that over the full interval (t_0, t_1) the sum of (discounted) marginal costs just equals the sum of (discounted) marginal benefits. Equation (3-17) states that over an interval starting at t_0 and ending at any time t short of t_1, accumulated marginal costs are less than benefits. Expression (3-18) is of course not independent of (3-16) and (3-17) and states that over an interval starting at any time t beyond t_0 and ending at t_1, costs exceed benefits.

The two paths, $S^*(t)$ and $S(t)$, might be characterized respectively as "myopic" and "corrected" optima. What has been shown is that the corrected path will at times diverge from the myopic. In particular, it will generally be optimal to refrain from investment warranted by current benefits and costs, i.e., to take short-term losses, if in the not too distant future a lesser level of development would be desired.

Having derived this quite general theorem about scheduling of investment subject to a restriction on reversibility, it remains only to consider the implications of the special case, referred to earlier, in which benefits from development are decreasing over time relative to benefits from preservation. We first obtain the result that in order to determine optimal use it will suffice to evaluate a project or scale of development produced by an immediate one-time investment, and then compare this value with that of the services otherwise provided by the environment. We then, in concluding remarks, suggest why this result is likely to be applicable in empirical situations.

Suppose benefits from development at a site are decreasing at rate r, and benefits from preservation are increasing at rate α. Then the flow of benefits (net of investment costs) from the site at any time t is given by

$$(3\text{-}19) \quad b = b_0^d e^{-rt} + b_0^p e^{\alpha t} - C$$

In a small change in notation, the subscripts indicate not first partial derivatives, as before, but rather benefits b^d and b^p at time $t = 0$ (as a function of scale, S). The instantaneous optimum scale, S^*, is found by differentiating (3-19) with respect to S and setting the result equal to zero, as in

$$(3\text{-}20) \quad b_S = \frac{db_0^d}{dS} e^{-rt} + \frac{db_0^p}{dS} e^{\alpha t}$$

and

$$(3\text{-}21) \quad \frac{db_0^d}{dS} = -\frac{db_0^p}{dS} e^{(r+\alpha)t}$$

Since db_0^p/dS is negative, the right-hand side of (3-21) is positive. As t increases, $e^{(r+\alpha)t}$ increases, so that db_0^p/dS must decrease, or db_0^d/dS increase, or both, to maintain the equality. Recalling the concavity of both benefit functions in S, this in turn implies that S^* must decrease as t increases.

Now consider the implications of S^* always decreasing. Since a free interval must be within an increasing segment of S^*, there is in effect an infinite blocked interval. However, since the start of a blocked interval is a boundary point of a free interval, investment at the initial moment, $t = 0$, is possible. In other words, value will be maximized only by investing immediately, or not at all. Furthermore, from the general theorem we know that any investment should be less than what appears profitable at the time it is made. The present value of a one-time investment

$$(3\text{-}22a) \quad \int_0^\infty e^{-\rho t}[b_0^d(\bar{S})e^{-rt} + b_0^p(\bar{S})e^{\alpha t} - C]\, dt,$$

where $\bar{S}$ is the scale resulting from the investment, is compared with the present value of no further investment

(3-22b) $\displaystyle\int_0^\infty e^{-\rho t}[b_0^d(\bar{S}(0))e^{-rt} + b_0^p(\bar{S}(0))e^{\alpha t}]\,dt,$

where $\bar{S}(0)$ is the initial scale, as defined earlier.

There remains of course the difficult empirical problem of determination of $\bar{S}$, the development project to be compared with the preservation alternative. We have no general method for doing this. Rather, a selected project will be evaluated, as in the studies reported beginning in chapter 5. Knowledge of the benefit functions in the actual case suggests the scale of the project to be evaluated.

5. CONCLUDING REMARKS

We have seen that where benefits from development of a natural environment are decreasing over time relative to benefits from preservation, the instantaneous optimum level of development is also decreasing. If the development is not reversible, this poses a problem: Should the planner seeking to maximize the value of the environment's resources invest in development that is currently profitable, but will not be in the future? The analytical solution to the problem, as given in the preceding section, indicates that he should not, at least beyond some point.

An obvious question that might now be asked is, how realistic is the assumed time path of relative benefits? That is, are there likely to be empirical cases for which it holds—and in particular, over the entire planning period, in which case the standard benefit–cost format is applicable? Reasons for thinking this to be so have in fact been suggested in the discussion in chapter 1 of the asymmetric implications of technical change for the values of commodity and amenity resources.

The services of amenity resources generally enter directly the utility functions of consumers. Since there is no production technology other than natural processes, we cannot look for advances in the "state of the art" to augment the supply and reduce the scarcity value of these resources. The value of an environment's commodity resources, on the other hand, may well be reduced through technical progress which makes substitutes (in production) increasingly abundant. In this simple two-sector model, an increase in the supply of material commodities must result in a decrease in unit value, relative to that of a fixed stock of amenity resources, as long as preferences do not change sufficiently in favor of commodities to compensate.[12] Behavior of relative values is considered more specifically in the empirical studies in part II.

[12] See Smith (1972) for a rigorous derivation of this proposition and others in both two- and three-sector models.

REFERENCES

Arrow, K. J. 1964. "Optimal Capital Policy, the Cost of Capital, and Myopic Decision Rules," *Annals of the Institute of Statistical Mathematics,* vol. 16.
———. 1968a. "Optimal Capital Policy with Irreversible Investment," in *Value, Capital and Growth,* J. N. Wolfe, ed. (Chicago: Aldine-Atherton).
———. 1968b. "Application of Control Theory to Economic Growth," in *Lectures in Applied Mathematics,* vol. 12, *Mathematics of the Decision Sciences*—Part 2 (Providence, R.I.: American Mathematical Society).
——— and Kurz, Mordecai. 1970. *Public Investment, The Rate of Return, and Optimal Fiscal Policy* (Baltimore: Johns Hopkins Press).
Barlowe, Raleigh. 1972. *Land Resource Economics: The Economics of Real Property,* 2nd ed. (Englewood Cliffs, N.J.: Prentice-Hall).
Barnett, H. J. and Morse, Chandler. 1963. *Scarcity and Growth: The Economics of Natural Resource Availability* (Baltimore: Johns Hopkins Press).
Cummings, Ronald and Burt, O. R. 1969. "The Economics of Production from Natural Resources: Note," *American Economic Review,* vol. LIX, no. 5.
Dorfman, Robert. 1969. "An Economic Interpretation of Optimal Control Theory," *American Economic Review,* vol. LIX, no. 5.
Eisner, Robert and Strotz, Robert. 1963. "Determinants of Business Investment," in *Impacts of Monetary Policy,* prepared for the Commission on Money and Credit (Englewood Cliffs, N.J.: Prentice-Hall).
Ely, R. T. and Wehrwein, G. S. 1940. *Land Economics* (New York: Macmillan).
Gordon, R. L. 1967. "A Reinterpretation of the Pure Theory of Exhaustion," *Journal of Political Economy,* vol. 75, no. 3.
Gray, L. C. 1914. "Rent Under the Assumption of Exhaustibility," *Quarterly Journal of Economics,* vol. XXVIII, no. 2.
Hotelling, Harold. 1931. "The Economics of Exhaustible Resources," *Journal of Political Economy,* vol. 39, no. 2.
Intriligator, M. D. 1971. *Mathematical Optimization and Economic Theory* (Englewood Cliffs, N.J.: Prentice-Hall).
Peterson, Frederick. 1973. "A Variational Model of Mining and Exploration," mimeo.
Pontryagin, L. S., *et al.* 1962. *The Mathematical Theory of Optimal Processes* (New York: Interscience).
Potter, Neal and Christy, F. T., Jr. 1962. *Trends in Natural Resource Commodities* (Baltimore: Johns Hopkins Press).
Scott, Anthony. 1967. "The Theory of the Mine Under Conditions of Certainty," in *Extractive Resources and Taxation,* Mason Gaffney, ed. (Madison, Wis.: University of Wisconsin Press).
Shell, Karl. 1969. "Applications of Pontryagin's Maximum Principle to Economics," in *Mathematical Systems Theory and Economics,* H. W. Kuhn and G. P. Szego, eds. (Berlin: Springer-Verlag).
Smith, V. K. 1972. "The Effect of Technological Change on Different Uses of Environmental Resources," in *Natural Environments: Studies in Theoreti-*

cal and Applied Analysis, John V. Krutilla, ed. (Baltimore: Johns Hopkins Press).

Solow, R. M. 1974. "The Economics of Resources or Resources of Economics," *American Economic Review,* vol. LXIV, no. 2.

Stankey, G. H. 1972. "A Strategy for the Definition and Management of Wilderness Quality," in *Natural Environments: Studies in Theoretical and Applied Analysis,* John V. Krutilla, ed. (Baltimore: Johns Hopkins Press).

CHAPTER 4

FURTHER ANALYSIS OF IRREVERSIBILITY: DISCOUNTING, INTERGENERATIONAL TRANSFERS, AND UNCERTAINTY

In chapter 3 it was suggested that problems posed by the irreversibility of a decision to develop a natural environment, along with the unusual degree of uncertainty surrounding evaluation of the alternatives, deserve additional attention. While these problems are profoundly difficult and are at best only partially resolved, in this chapter we shall address the relevant issues to which they give rise.

1. DETERMINING THE DISCOUNT RATE

In its simplest expression, a dollar currently in hand has a higher present worth than one promised to be available only after a time lapse. Similarly, the present value of benefits today is greater than equivalent benefits, reckoned in constant dollars, expected to be received in the future. The recognized method of obtaining the present value at any moment in time is to weight the net returns from an investment by a discount factor. The discounted value per dollar should ordinarily be larger for near term returns and smaller for those more distant. That is, it is a decreasing function of time such as $e^{-\rho t}$, where ρ is some positive number, the discount rate. Clearly the discount factor weight, and hence the relative importance of a future benefit or cost, will be determined by the rate ρ. There is a substantial literature on the determination of the discount rate for public projects. Moreover, it has been suggested that the conservation of exhaustible natural resources might be achieved through lowering the discount rate (Pigou, 1932). While it is possible to review the relevant discussion in only the sketchiest manner here, we do so in this section in order to provide both the background to understand this problem and some explanation for the choice of discount rates in our empirical procedures. In section 2 we enter more deeply into the intergenerational distributional issues, and in section 3 we consider the issues involving uncertainty associated with irreversibilities, and the value of preserving options under such circumstances.

In the simplified neoclassical world of Irving Fisher (1907), the discount rate was determined in the market by the interplay between individual time preferences and the productivity of investment. Individuals making their decisions regarding present consumption and savings would be governed by their time preferences regarding consumption, i.e., their marginal rates of substitution between present and deferred consumption. The aggregate of savings would provide the schedule or supply of loanable funds in the market, while the schedule of the marginal productivity of capital would provide the opportunity for returns, or increases in future income, through deferral of consumption. The intersection of the two schedules, of savings and investment, respectively, would determine uniquely the equilibrium marginal productivity of capital and marginal time preference rates. That is, the marginal rate of return and the marginal time preference were coincidentally one and the same—the results of the operation of perfectly competitive financial markets. This rather neat solution is the result of an idealized abstraction from the real world, even in Irving Fisher's day. There are some difficulties with this prescription for determining the discount rate that are of both a theoretical and a practical nature.

One early theoretical and fundamental question about the normative significance, i.e., the significance for public policy decisions, of the market-determined rate of discount is that it is partially determined by the private time preferences of the present generation of individuals. In the next section we consider some implications of the fact that only the present generation participates in the decision as to what proportion of the natural endowment will be preserved for the future. But aside from the question of legitimacy of the participants in the intergenerational distribution decision, individuals with finite life expectancies, among other things, are likely to be guided in their private consumption decisions in a manner that is not necessarily optimal for a society that has a collective commitment to life in perpetuity. Accordingly, the supply of funds available for investment is at least influenced by private time preferences that depart from what might be a collectively determined rate of social time preference. The rate of discount will be too high and the level of investment too low to make adequate provision for future generations (Ramsey, 1928; Pigou, 1932, p. 27).[1]

---

[1] The fact that it has been observed that individuals are also motivated to leave their heirs an estate (Modigliani and Brumberg, 1954; Chase, 1963), while in part offsetting the "myopia" argument, does not go directly to the issue of the optimal intertemporal distribution of welfare. It should be noted that private estates involve

The argument that the private market results generally in a rate of consumption that is too high, and makes too little provision for the future, has been directed also specifically to the consumption of exhaustible resources (Pigou, 1932, p. 29). Pigou argued that investment in resource conservation should be undertaken by the state even though the yield may be less than that necessary to attract private investment; namely, a lower discount rate than the market-determined rate in the private sector is appropriate for resource conservation programs. This prescription, of course, would lead to productive resources being diverted from higher yield investment opportunities in the private sector to lower yielding opportunities in the public resource development sector. This is felt by many economists to be a dubious proposition at best, and has been a source of continuing controversy.

Here one might argue, as have Krutilla and Eckstein (1958, pp. 126–127) and Hirshliefer (1961, p. 120), that if providing for the future is the objective, the level of investment generally should be increased (the level of current consumption reduced) throughout the economy. Hence, if the market rate of discount (however determined) is too high, government monetary and fiscal policy should stimulate the appropriate level of investment by a general reduction in the rate of interest, consistent with the correction implied by Pigou's diagnosis of myopia. Since, however, Pigou's prescription at one point, at least, was directed to the investment in the natural resource sector, and the objectives of monetary and fiscal policy at any moment in time are not restricted to determining a long-run normative discount rate for resource conservation, the prescription is not practicable.

In answer to the need that then arises for a "second best" solution, Eckstein (1958, p. 101) has suggested that if a lower rate of discount is to be used for evaluating public projects in the resource sector, the identical rate should be used for discounting the opportunity returns in the private sector. The resulting difference in the present-value sums obtained by using the market, as compared with the social, rate of discount in the opportunity sector should be reflected in the investment criterion governing the resource conservation program.[2] This procedure would avoid the

only private property resources and goods. It follows therefore that the composition, if not the level, of bequests is likely to depart from bequests under a collectively determined "estate" policy. Moreover, Marglin, for example, argues that consumption by future generations is a public good externality. Individuals making up the present generation can be made better off by a collective choice to save and invest more of their income than each, acting individually, would have done (Marglin, 1963).

[2] An example might be useful to illustrate the operation of the Eckstein prescription. Assume that the opportunity returns in the private sector can be represented by a perpetuity of ten cents per dollar of investment. If the prescribed social rate of discount were to be 5 percent, then the present value of the opportunity returns would be two dollars per dollar diverted from the private sector to the resource

inefficiencies inherent in the two-tier discount rate and perhaps meet the conservation objectives sought by Pigou, by favoring alternatives with a higher futurity of yield.

The differences in the clearing rates for funds in financial markets that occur independently of government policies that may affect such markets differentially[3] relates to the riskiness of investments in an uncertain world. There appear to be two issues here. With risk differences being reflected in different interest and expected yield rates for funds within, as well as between, markets for investment funds on the one hand, and consumption on the other, there is the practical question of how to distill *the* appropriate rate from among the rates in the markets from which funds would be withdrawn to support resource conservation programs. This problem was dealt with in a practical manner by Krutilla and Eckstein (1958) by determining the likely mix of opportunity uses of project funds, whether within the investment or consumption area, and constructing a weighted average opportunity cost of capital used in the resource development sector. A less detailed alternative method of estimating the opportunity discount rate has been proposed by Baumol (1968, 1969).

A second issue to which the risk and uncertainty give rise involves the possible difference in the treatment of risk, and hence the magnitude of the discount rate, between public and private investments. Most students of the discounting problem tend to feel the opportunity cost principle implies that private preferences regarding risk are relevant since these preferences are reflected in behavior in the private opportunity sector. However, this view has been challenged by prominent theorists. Samuelson (1964) has suggested that the government should be risk neutral, i.e., should not include a premium for risk in its discount rate, because of the diversity of investments. There are so many public projects that a loss in one will be canceled by a gain in others. The probability of a net loss in the aggregate is vanishingly small (assuming that returns to different projects are uncorrelated) and can be neglected. Arrow and Lind (1970) have taken a different approach, demonstrating that the spreading of risk associated with a single public project over a large number of taxpayer-beneficiaries, each having a small share in the net returns, can also result in the disappearance of a (social) risk premium. Where there are irreversibilities

---

conservation sector. Accordingly, the marginal benefit-to-cost ratio in the conservation investment program would need to be 2:1, i.e., two dollars in present value of benefits discounted at 5 percent, per dollar invested so as not to withdraw resources from a higher, for investment in a lower, yield opportunity.

[3] A particularly relevant example for our later analyses is the preferential tax treatment accorded under the doctrine of intergovernmental tax immunity to holders of bonds for state and local governments and quasi-public bodies such as public utility districts. Here exemption from income taxation of interest earnings on such bonds results in preferential terms on which financial resources can be obtained by such entities.

involved, however, the matter of uncertainty and how it should affect a public decision on development of a natural environment deserves specific consideration, and is taken up in detail in section 3.

To summarize, there appears to be general agreement that a uniform rate of discount should be applied to all investment opportunities, public and private (with possible adjustment for the treatment of risk) to avoid reallocation of resources from higher to lower yield alternatives. There is less agreement, however, on the question of what should determine this rate, much less its precise numerical value.[4] Of course, the selection of a numerical value for the discount rate is required only in application. Chapter 3's theoretical discussion was able to proceed adequately on the basis of the symbolic value of ρ. Accordingly, it seems to us that the sensible way to handle the choice of discount rate is to recognize that it has not yet been completely resolved on the theoretical level, and defer further discussion to the empirical studies of part II. There, a first approach will be to use the prevailing market opportunity cost of capital to reflect the general agreement that the project in question not displace higher yielding alternative uses of funds. For purposes of sensitivity analysis, we shall try other rates to bracket the results. But several points should be borne in mind with respect to the use of these other rates. Where a lower rate is used, the present value of the project would have to be correspondingly higher to pass the Eckstein test. Of course, this would not apply if one accepts some version of the Samuelson–Arrow–Lind argument that the lower rate appropriately reflects government neutrality toward risk. But in any case, discounting at a lower rate is likely to discriminate *against* a resource development project rather than in favor of it. This is because the environmental opportunity costs, i.e., the forgone benefits from use of the site in its natural condition, usually neglected, must also be discounted at a lower rate. If, as suggested previously, there are likely cases in which costs can be expected to grow relative to development project benefits, they are given greater weight by a low discount rate. Preservation is in such cases the alternative with the higher futurity of yield.

Anticipated changes over time in relative values of the alternative uses of a natural environment are also, in our judgment, one explanation for the view that the choice of a discount rate should somehow be affected by conservation considerations. Recall that Pigou felt the state should take some action, perhaps lower the discount rate, to remedy our "defective telescopic faculty" (1932, pp. 24–27), i.e., to foster conservation. Yet as Scott (1955) has shown, such a policy would stimulate investment gen-

---

[4] For a review of the views expressed on this matter in hearings before the Joint Economic Committee of the U.S. Congress (1969), see Seagraves (1970).

erally, which would tend in turn to lead to more rapid exploitation of exhaustible resources.

Consider now the situation in which benefits from development of a site are falling relative to benefits from its preservation. In particular, consider the (sufficient but not necessary) case described in chapter 3, in which the benefits from development are falling at the rate r, and those from preservation are rising at the rate α. Another way of putting this might be that the initial benefit flows are discounted at the different effective rates $(\rho + r)$ and $(\rho - \alpha)$. The difference in rates is arrived at, not through any arbitrary manipulation of the discount rate ρ, but rather through changes over time in relative values. It may be this result that Pigou sought in his concern for the protection of exhaustible resources of increasing scarcity value.[5]

The "defective telescopic faculty" as a metaphor for the irrationality of discounting, from a social point of view, has occurred to others besides Pigou.[6] In section 2 we present a version of the argument which applies with a special force to the model developed in chapter 3.

2. THE "INTERTEMPORAL TUSSLE": WHOSE CONSUMER SOVEREIGNTY?

The concern over discounting expressed by Pigou and Ramsey (and others) seems to be an ethical one. All effects on welfare are evaluated from the point of view of present consumers. But what is the ethical basis for this discrimination against future generations? In the model in chapter 3 we do make an effort to take account of changing values, including those of future consumers of the services provided by natural environments. These values are, however, discounted back to the present. The problem arises in this context because the criterion of present-value maximization may yield inconsistent implications for investment policy when applied at different times.

In this section we show how the inconsistency comes about, and how it leads to a kind of intertemporal inefficiency. Policy implications of the results for the management of natural environments are also suggested. The discussion is developed first in the context of a model originally due to Strotz (1956), and then applied to the discussion of chapter 3.

Strotz's problem can be described as follows. Suppose a decision maker is choosing a consumption plan to maximize the utility or other measure of its contribution to his welfare, as evaluated at the present moment ($t = 0$). If he reconsiders the plan at a later date ($t = t_1$), will he abide

---

[5] This point is explored further in Fisher and Krutilla (1975).
[6] See, for example, the influential work of Ramsey (1928) on this point.

by it or disobey it, even assuming his expectations for $0 < t < t_1$ have been realized, and those for $t_1 < t < T$, where T is the planning horizon, have not changed? The answer, as demonstrated by Strotz, is that in general the decision maker would want to revise his "optimal" plan.

A simple example can illustrate this result, and then be extended to show the relationship between inconsistency and inefficiency. Assume three nonoverlapping generations, each taking a decision as to how much of a fixed resource stock to extract and consume, and how much to pass on to succeeding generations. Each generation's utility is a function of its own consumption, and that of each succeeding generation. In symbols

(4-1) $U^1 = U^1(X_1, X_2, X_3)$ and $U^2 = U^2(X_2, X_3)$

where U^i = utility of generation i and X_i = consumption of generation i. More specifically, assume

(4-2) $U^1 = U(X_1) + \gamma_2 U(X_2) + \gamma_3 U(X_3)$

and

$$U^2 = U(X_2) + \gamma_2 U(X_3)$$

The $U(X_i)$ are identical utility functions, and the γ_i are discount factors where, following Phelps and Pollak (1968), $\gamma_2 = \beta\delta$ and $\gamma_3 = \beta^2\delta$, $0 < \beta < 1$, $0 < \delta \leqslant 1$. β represents ordinary time preference and δ is a constant factor, applied *equally* to all future generations, reflecting the preference of the present generation for its own consumption relative to that of others.

The problem, for each generation, is then to choose a consumption plan which maximizes its utility subject to the constraint

(4-3) $X_1 + X_2 + X_3 = X$

where X is the total amount of the resource available initially. First-order conditions for generations 1 and 2 respectively include, on rearrangement,

(4-4) $\dfrac{\partial U}{\partial X_2} = \dfrac{\beta}{} \dfrac{\partial U}{\partial X_3}$ (generation 1)

and

$\dfrac{\partial U}{\partial X_2} = \dfrac{\beta\delta}{} \dfrac{\partial U}{\partial X_3}$ (generation 2)

On the further assumption of diminishing marginal utility, these conditions together imply that generation 2 will want to consume more, relative to generation 3, than generation 1 would have it consume, hence will revise the consumption plan handed down to it by generation 1. This is Strotz's problem of inconsistent planning, or "inconsistency in dynamic utility maximization" (p. 165). It is also easy to see how the plans can be brought into harmony. All that is required is that $\delta = 1$, the case of "perfect altruism" in the terminology of Phelps and Pollak. The discount factor then becomes the declining geometric sequence β^0, β^1, β^2, or in other words, the discount rate must be constant over time, or generations, as Strotz demonstrates.

One reaction to all this might be, so what? Let each generation revise the consumption plan where this is indicated in the case of imperfect altruism, or other deviation from a constant rate of discount, in order to maximize its utility. But this misses an important point. The inconsistency is interesting because of its implications for efficiency. From (4-4) it is clear that generation 1 would like generation 2 to consume less, relative to generation 3, and presumably therefore would be willing to offer something in exchange for this reduction in consumption. What it has to offer is of course a larger inheritance, $X - X_1$, through reducing its own consumption, X_1. Generation 2, in turn, presumably would be willing to consume less relative to generation 3 in exchange for a greater absolute level of consumption (for both) made possible by the larger inheritance from generation 1. The problem is that the indicated exchange is not possible because the generations cannot bargain. One interpretation of the inability to realize the gains from trade is that the criterion of present-value maximization leads to inefficiency. Another is that since it is in any case not possible to exploit them, the statement that there are potential gains from trade is meaningless. The resulting allocation is efficient subject to the constraint on trade imposed by infinite transaction costs.

We would like to propose an intermediate position here. Clearly, both theoretical models of dynamic optimization of resource use, such as the one in chapter 3, and empirical benefit–cost analyses, are based on the sovereignty of present consumers. This point is so fundamental that it has received little discussion in the literature on these topics.[7] There may be no practical alternative. But if we have any sympathy for the concern of Ramsey and Pigou that the welfare of future generations is not adequately protected under this arrangement, we might look for compensating policy adjustments. Recall the discussion of the effect that assigning liability for externalities has on resource valuation. If individuals affected by a firm's pollution cannot get together to bargain with the firm for a reduction, the resulting level of externality is not necessarily the most efficient. Rather, the point is to look for an institutional arrangement, such as an appropriately designed tax on pollution, which can increase efficiency by reducing the transaction costs. In the intertemporal case, perhaps something like a

[7] An exception is Marglin, who considers it "axiomatic that a democratic government reflects only the preferences of the individuals who are presently members of the body politic" (1963, p. 97).

severance tax on the extraction and consumption of the fixed resource stock could serve the same purpose.

The point about intertemporal inefficiency has an obvious application to chapter 3's discussion of irreversible investment in the development of a natural environment. Consider the effects of a change in the vantage point from which the present worths of the two alternative uses, development and preservation, are evaluated, moving forward from time 0 to time t_1. Two things change: (1) the discount factors are shifted, from $e^{-\rho t}$ to $e^{-\rho(t-t_1)}$; and (2) past benefits, from 0 to t_1, are dropped from consideration. Now, as demonstrated in the simple model of intergenerational consumption and saving presented above, translation of the discount factor in this fashion has no effect where the discount rate is constant, here equal to ρ. In this case it is easy to see that the translation factor is also constant, $e^{\rho t_1}$, and drops out of the expressions for the present values of both alternatives [expressions (3-22a) and (3-22b)]. But dropping past benefits does have an effect, particularly where there is some systematic relationship between the two benefit streams. For the case in which benefits from development are falling relative to benefits from preservation, as the vantage point shifts from 0 to t_1, the earlier years in which a development project is relatively highly valued are dropped. Even supposing that the present value of the project at time 0 is greater than the present value of no project at that time, the fall in relative project value makes it likely that, at some point, this inequality will be reversed.

Here again we are confronted with something that might be interpreted as intertemporal inefficiency. As the present-value criterion slides through time, future generations are increasingly less likely to want development. Were bargaining possible, conceivably a future generation could compensate the present for not building a project which would otherwise provide net benefits, especially in the period from 0 to t_1. At $t = 0$, net gains from the project (let us say) exceed the costs, so that according to the Kaldor–Hicks, or potential Pareto criterion, it ought to be undertaken. The gainers could compensate the losers and still have something left over, or in other words, there exists some reallocation of goods with the project that would make everyone better off. Now suppose that at $t = t_1$, benefits from the project are less than benefits from preservation. Then the gainers from not having the project could compensate the losers, all those who would benefit from having the project, possibly even including those in the period before t_1. As before, there exists some reallocation of goods that would make everyone better off, but in this case without the project. The project does not pass the second part of an intertemporal Scitovsky test, and could therefore be judged not to represent an unambiguous improvement in welfare.[8]

[8] The second part of the Scitovsky test checks whether it is possible, starting from

Consideration of a concrete example, the construction of a dam and reservoir in the Hetch Hetchy Valley in Yosemite National Park, back in 1914, may clarify this point. Hetch Hetchy, which was considered by John Muir and others to be fully as remarkable a natural phenomenon as the lower Yosemite Valley, was flooded to provide a reservoir to supply water for the city of San Francisco. Given the dwindling supply of unspoiled environment, particularly environment as remarkable as Hetch Hetchy, it is not surprising that many people now wish it were possible to have the valley back in its natural state. They might indeed be willing to give some of their (greater) material wealth in exchange for a preserved Hetch Hetchy. Were it possible for them to compensate the water users of San Francisco in 1914, in addition to any who would prefer the dam today, they might choose to do so.

What sort of policy instrument might play the role of the pollution or severance tax in this situation? If the objective is to bind present and future in some mutually advantageous course of action, legislative zoning as under the Wilderness Act of 1964 might do. Future reversal of a decision by the present generation to preserve, say, a virgin redwood forest, is made more difficult. And if the present generation believes there is a reduced probability of the next generation's clear-cutting the forest, it will in turn be more likely to vote for preservation. Of course it is still true that the decision to clear-cut is technically irreversible, whereas to refrain from clear-cutting is not. Legislative classification of wilderness areas, perhaps with provisions to make reclassification more difficult, could then be viewed as a partial compensation for the asymmetry.

Whether inefficiency can be said to result from dynamically inconsistent planning is probably a matter of interpretation. We have indicated why there may be something to the view that it can. In the next section a more clear-cut finding (of inefficiency in conventional benefit–cost criteria) emerges from an analysis of the consequences of failure to take proper account of uncertainty in planning investment at a site.

3. UNCERTAINTY, IRREVERSIBILITY, AND OPTION VALUE

Uncertainty has already played a considerable role in our discussions. Earlier in this chapter we saw how the discount rate for public projects may not appropriately include a premium for risk, even though

the initial situation, which would be no project at $t = 0$, to make everyone better off without the project by some reallocation of goods, or redistribution of income. This is not the same as making the check at $t = t_1$, when preferences and technology have changed. Nevertheless, we feel this latter version of the test, though weaker than the original, is not without interest.

rates of return in the private opportunity sector do. In chapter 1 we introduced the notion of option value. This is the value, in addition to consumers' surplus, that arises from retaining an option to a good or service for which future demand is uncertain. It has been suggested that the option value of preserving a natural environment could be significant. This is further explored here.

Our model is based on the original contributions of Arrow and Fisher (1974) and Henry (1974), but we adopt the more transparent approach of Hanemann (1983), and Fisher and Hanemann (1984). Following these authors a two-period discrete-time formulation is employed. The decision problem is: How much of a tract of wild land should be developed in each of the two periods? We choose units of measurement such that the maximum level of development (or preservation) is just unity. Then, there are three substantive assumptions. First, development in any period is irreversible. Second, the benefits of development in the first period are known, those of development in the second period are not. These assumptions capture the essential features of our problem. A third, made more for ease in obtaining unambiguous results, is that benefits are a linear function of the level of development. Later we consider what happens when this assumption is relaxed.

Let us interpret the assumed structure a bit to indicate both its rationale and its limits. The benefits associated with a given level of development are the benefits of development *and* the benefits of preservation. Let the former be given, for the first period, as

$$(4.5) \qquad B_{1d}(d_1) = \alpha d_1$$

where d indicates development; d_1, the level of development in period 1; and α, a positive constant. Note that $0 \leqq d_1 \leqq 1$.

Let the benefits of preservation be

$$(4.6) \qquad B_{1p}(d_1) = \beta - \gamma d_1$$

where p indicates preservation and β and γ are positive constants. Then, benefits in period 1 are

$$(4.7) \qquad B_1(d_1) = B_{1d}(d_1) + B_{1p}(d_1)$$
$$= \beta + (\alpha - \gamma) d_1$$

The relationship between B_1 and d_1 is clearly linear, implying that first-period benefits will be maximized by choosing either $d_1 = 0$ (if $\alpha < \gamma$), or $d_1 = 1$ (if $\alpha > \gamma$). Thus, the problem is restricted to a choice of corner solutions. The argument would be more complicated were we to consider uncertain second-period benefits as well, but this key restriction carries over.

Second-period (discounted) benefits are $B_2 (d_1 + d_2, \theta)$ where d_2 is the amount of land developed in period 2 and θ is a random variable. Thus, second-period benefits depend on development in periods 1 and 2 and are uncertain. Note that $d_2 \geqq 0$, and $d_1 + d_2 \leqq 1$. We shall assume that the problem is to maximize *expected* benefits over both periods. This is one particular way of dealing with the uncertainty. It is not, however, as restrictive as it may seem since we have not specified that benefits are measured in money units. If, for example, benefits are measured in utility units, then our formulation is equivalent to the quite general expected utility maximization. The important point is: the results we shall obtain *do not depend on risk aversion*.

The remaining structural element of the problem involves the behavior of uncertainty over time. More specifically, we consider two possible cases. In the first, nothing further is learned about the value of θ by period 2 so that d_1 and d_2 are chosen in period 1. In the second, the value of θ is learned by period 2, so that it makes sense to defer a decision on d_2 to period 2. Now comes a very important assumption. It is that the learning, in case 2, does not depend on first-period development, d_1. For the kind of uncertainty we are trying to capture, this seems appropriate. Uncertainty is largely about the future (period 2) benefits of preservation—the value that may be discovered in some indigenous species, for example. This will be determined *not* by developing its habitat but by undertaking research into its medicinal or other properties. The research is not endogenous to our problem, but we do asume that the answer it yields, concerning the value of θ, does not depend on the development of the tract in question. Not surprisingly, this assumption importantly affects the results we shall obtain. At that point, we shall have more to say about the alternative assumption and its consequences.

Now let us write down expressions for the value to be maximized under each information structure. Where no new information is forthcoming by the second period, define $V^*(d_1)$ by

$$(4.8) \qquad V^*(d_1) = B_1 (d_1) + \max_{\substack{d_2 \\ 0 \leqq d_1 + d_2 \leqq 1 \\ 0 \leqq d_2}} \{E[B_2 (d_1 + d_2, \theta)]\}.$$

Then, the maximum value is $V^* = V^*(d_1^*)$, where d_1^* maximizes $V^*(d_1)$ subject to $0 \leqq d_1 \leqq 1$.

Where new information is forthcoming, define $\hat{V}(d_1)$ by

$$(4.9) \qquad \hat{V}(d_1) = B_1 (d_1) + E[\max_{\substack{d_2 \\ 0 \leqq d_1 + d_2 \leqq 1 \\ 0 \leqq d_2}} \{B_2 (d_1 + d_2, \theta)\}].$$

The maximum value in this case is $\hat{V} = \hat{V}(\hat{d}_1)$ where $\hat{d}_1$ maximizes $\hat{V}(\hat{d}_1)$ subject to $0 \le d_l \le 1$.

What can we say about value-maximizing, or optimal, development in the first period in each case? Clearly, since $V^*(d_1)$ and $\hat{V}(d_1)$ are different, d_1^* and $\hat{d}_1$ will be different. A natural hypothesis is that $\hat{d}_1 \le d_1^*$ since it would seem to make sense to put off development, which is irreversible, if there is a prospect of better information about the benefits it will preclude. Put differently, if the decisionmaker ignores the prospect of better information, first-period development will be too great. We can prove this result, not in general, but where the choice is between no development $(d_t = 0)$ and full development $(d_t = 1)$. Recall that this is precisely the choice implied by our linearity assumption.

We wish, then, to compare the alternatives of developing and preserving in each information setting. Where no information is forthcoming, we have

(4.10) $V^*(0) = B_1(0) + \max\{E[B_2(0, \theta)], E[B_2(1, \theta)]\}$

and

(4.11) $V^*(1) = B_1(1) + E[B_2(1, \theta)]$

Then

(4.12)
$$d_1^* = \begin{cases} 0 \text{ if } V^*(0) - V^*(1) \ge 0 \\ \\ 1 \text{ if } V^*(0) - V^*(1) < 0 \end{cases}$$

Where new information is forthcoming, we have

(4.13) $\hat{V}(0) = B_1(0) + E[\max\{B_2(0, \theta), B_2(1, \theta)\}]$

and

(4.14) $\hat{V}(1) = B_1(1) + E[B_2(1, \theta)]$

Then

(4.15)
$$\hat{d}_1 = \begin{cases} 0 \text{ if } \hat{V}(0) - \hat{V}(1) \ge 0 \\ \\ 1 \text{ if } \hat{V}(0) - \hat{V}(1) < 0 \end{cases}$$

Notice that $V^*(1) = \hat{V}(1)$. With full development in the first period, total value over both periods must be the same since the development is locked in for the second period regardless of what is learned about the random variable θ in the first.

We have still not shown the relationship of d_1^* to $\hat{d}_1$. For this, just one more step is needed. From the convexity of the maximum operator, and Jensen's Inequality, it follows that

(4.16) $\quad \hat{V}(0) - V^*(0) = E[\max\{B_2(0, \theta), B_2(1, \theta)\}]$

$$- \max\{E[B_2(0, \theta)], E[B_2(1, \theta)]\} \geqq 0$$

Since $\hat{V}(0) \geqq V^*(0)$ and $\hat{V}(1) = V^*(1)$, $\hat{d}_1 \leqq d_1^*$. In practice, what this means is that optimal first-period use of the area is less likely to be full development ($d_1 = 1$) where it is possible to learn about the benefits precluded than where it is not.

To produce this result, we made two assumptions that deserve further comment. First, we assumed the benefit functions are linear. This allowed us to consider development as a binary choice: to develop or not to develop. In fact, a related theorem shows that, in our terminology, $\hat{d}_1 \leqq d_1^*$ as long as the benefit functions are concave (see Freixas and Laffont (1984), and Jones and Ostroy (1984)). Unfortunately, as Hanemann shows, option value is not well defined when development is not a binary choice. Given our subsequent focus on option value, we shall restrict ourselves to the binary choice scenario, but note that a fundamental result does not depend on this.

The second key assumption was that resolution of the uncertainty is independent of development in the first period. We have argued that this is plausible; but the judgment is an empirical one. It is fairly obvious that, if resolution depends on development, and, in particular, on a positive level of development, then (some) development may be optimal to provide information even where this involves an irreversible commitment of resources that turns out to be a mistake. Such a result is obtained in a recent study by Miller and Lad (1984). Similarly, development for the purpose of providing information about whether the development is, in fact, irreversible may be optimal, as has been shown by Viscusi and Zeckhauser (1976). The reader is free to choose among these alternative assumptions about the structure of information, but we continue to feel that ours is most plausible *for our problem*, i.e., relevant information about the properties of indigenous species will come not from developing their habitat but rather from research that, if anything, depends on preserving habitat.

*Option Value and the
Value of Information*

Beginning with the article by Weisbrod (1964), there has been a notion—advanced by some, including Weisbrod, disputed by others—that preservation carries with it a value (option value) above and beyond conventional consumer's surplus. A number of articles following Weisbrod established that option value could be identified with a risk premium: the difference between what a risk-averse consumer is willing to pay for the option of consuming (wilderness recreation, say), at a predetermined nondiscriminatory price, and his expected consumer's surplus (Zeckhauser (1969), Cicchetti and Freeman (1971)). These and other studies also exposed a difficulty; namely, that preservation, as well as development, can bring risks, e.g., floods or power failures (Schmalensee, 1971, Bohm, 1975). The net option value of preserving a wilderness environment could then be negative. And, in any case, option value in this interpretation depends on risk aversion.[9]

A different interpretation has been put forward by Arrow and Fisher (1974) and Henry (1974) and, more recently, by Conrad (1980) and Hanemann (1983). Unlike the first, it does not depend on risk aversion. Also, unlike the first, it is explicitly dynamic. In fact, it falls out quite naturally from the model presented in the preceding section. Option value, in this interpretation, is the gain from being able to learn about future benefits that would be precluded by development if one does not develop initially—the gain from retaining the option to preserve or develop in the future. In our terminology, this is

(4.17) $OV = \hat{V}(0) - V^*(0)$

From equation (4.16), option value, OV, is nonnegative.

We can obtain this result in a somewhat different fashion following Arrow and Fisher's original presentation. Suppose the decisionmaker ignores the prospect of new information. Then he will compare $V^*(0)$ and $V^*(1)$. A correct decision—one that takes account of this prospect—can be induced, in principle, by a subsidy to preservation. The optimal subsidy will clearly be one which leads the decisionmaker to compare $\hat{V}(0)$ and $\hat{V}(1)$. To solve for the subsidy, S, write

(4.18) $[V^*(0) + S] - V^*(1) = \hat{V}(0) - \hat{V}(1);$

so that

(4.19) $S = [\hat{V}(0) - \hat{V}(1)] - [V^*(0) - V^*(1)]$

From equations (4.11) and (4.14), $V^*(1) = \hat{V}(1)$, and equation (4.19) reduces to equation (4.17). The subsidy, S, is just what we mean by option

[9] Strictly speaking, it can also be produced by a non-zero covariance between a measure of the value of the environmental good and the marginal utility of income (Mäler, 1985).

value—the extra value attaching to the preservation option that would be overlooked in a conventional decision, a decision that did not take account of the prospective gains from information.

It is tempting to identify this concept of option value with another one familiar in decision theory: the value of information, or more precisely, the expected value of perfect information. However, the identification is not quite correct. Option value in this interpretation is a *conditional* value of information, conditioned on $d_1 = 0$.

The *unconditional* value of information is $\hat{V}(\hat{d}_1) - V^*(d_1^*)$ or, in other words, the gain from being able to learn about future benefits provided d_1 is optimally chosen in each case. This may mean $\hat{d}_1 = d_1^* = 0$ or it may not. In fact, two other outcomes are possible: $\hat{d}_1 = d_1^* = 1$ and $\hat{d}_1 = 0$, $d_1^* = 1$. (Note that $\hat{d}_1 = 1$, $d_1^* = 0$ is ruled out by the result that $\hat{d}_1 \leq d_1^*$.) If $\hat{d}_1 = d_1^* = 1$, the value of information is $\hat{V}(1) - V^*(1) = 0$, whereas option value is still $\hat{V}(0) - V^*(0) \geq 0$. If $\hat{d}_1 = 0$ and $d_1^* = 1$, the value of information is $\hat{V}(0) - V^*(1)$. Notice that option value is once again greater than the value of information since $\hat{V}(0) \geq \hat{V}(1) = V^*(1) \geq V^*(0)$.

To summarize, then, option value is not identical to the value of information in the development decision problem. Option value is instead a conditional value of information, conditional on a particular choice of first-period development ($d_1 = 0$) and, moreover, is equal to or greater than the (unconditional) value of information.

4. CONCLUDING REMARKS

In chapter 2 we suggested, following Mishan (1971) and others, that priority in use of the resources of a natural environment on the public lands might appropriately be assigned to nondestructive pursuits. Their value would then be determined by the amount required to compensate for a destructive change. As this may well be substantially greater than the amount those hurt by the change would be willing to pay to prevent it, a key question is, who has the initial property rights? The earlier inclination toward the nondestructive alternative could be based only on what some persons might regard as rather vague equity considerations.

In this chapter, although we do not make any assumptions about the priority of rights, results having much the same feel are obtained solely from considerations of efficiency. The major implication of our analyses of intertemporal conflict and uncertainty with respect to the use of a natural environment is that it will be efficient to proceed very cautiously with any irreversible modification. There is some benefit, for example, even from the point of view of one interested in maximizing the present value of the environment's resources, in refraining from irreversible development that appears warranted by relative benefits and costs when uncertainty is ignored.

If "irreversible" is identified with "destructive," the implication of the analysis of irreversibility under uncertainty is similar to that of the assignment of property rights to the nondestructive uses.

We readily concede that it is likely to be difficult, if not impossible, to apply some of these considerations in practice. Theory suggests that the existence of option value, and possible gains from trade between generations, may be relevant to a decision on whether to develop a natural environment. The difficulty for application in empirical work is that it does not spell out the precise quantitative adjustments to estimated benefits and costs that would be required. Does this mean that these concepts have no place in a volume on the economics of natural environments? We do not think so. Rather, the point of this chapter is that the traditional benefit–cost analysis of a resource development project in a natural environment may be incomplete as a basis for public decision on the project. The direction of the required adjustments, if not the magnitude, is apparent. As possible policy instruments for shifting valuation and allocation in the appropriate direction, we have suggested zoning of wilderness areas, and a subsidy to preservation.

REFERENCES

Arrow, K. J. 1966. "Discounting and Public Investment Criteria," in *Water Research*, Allen V. Kneese and S. C. Smith, eds. (Baltimore: Johns Hopkins Press).

———— and Fisher, A. C. 1974. "Environmental Preservation, Uncertainty, and Irreversibility," *Quarterly Journal of Economics*, vol. LXXXVIII, no. 2.

———— and Lind, R. C. 1970. "Uncertainty and the Evaluation of Public Investment Decisions," *American Economic Review*, vol. LX, no. 3.

Baumol, W. J. 1968. "On the Social Rate of Discount," *American Economic Review*, vol. LVIII, no. 4.

————. 1969. "On the Discount Rate for Public Projects," in *The Analysis and Evaluation of Public Expenditures: The PPB System*. A compendium of papers submitted to the Subcommittee on Economy of the Joint Economic Committee, 91 Cong. 1 sess. (Washington, D.C.: Government Printing Office).

Bohm, Peter. 1975. "Option Demand and Consumer Surplus: Comment," *American Economic Review*, vol. 65 (September).

Chase, S. B. 1963. *Asset Prices in Economic Analysis* (Berkeley: University of California Press).

Cicchetti, C. J., and Freeman, A. M. 1971. "Option Demand and Consumer Surplus: Further Comments," *Quarterly Journal of Economics*, vol. LXXXV, no. 3.

Conrad, Jon M. 1980. "Quasi-Option Value and the Expected Value of Information," *Quarterly Journal of Economics*, vol. 94.

Eckstein, Otto. 1958. *Water Resource Development: The Economics of Project Evaluation* (Cambridge, Mass.: Harvard University Press).

Fisher, A. C. 1973. "Environmental Externalities and the Arrow-Lind Public Investment Theorem," *American Economic Review*, vol. LXIII, no. 4.

―――― and Hanemann, W. Michael. 1984. "Option Value and the Extinction of
Species," University of California, Department of Agricultural and Resource
Economics, Working Paper No. 269 (Berkeley, Calif., October).

―――― and Krutilla, J. V. 1975. "Resource Conservation, Environmental Preservation, and the Rate of Discount," *Quarterly Journal of Economics*, vol.
LXXXIX, no. 3 (August).

Fisher, Irving. 1907. *The Rate of Interest* (New York: Macmillan).

Freixas, Xavier, and Laffont, Jean-Jacques. 1984. "On the Irreversibility Effect," in
M. Boyer and R. E. Kihlstrom, eds., *Bayesian Models in Economic Theory*
(New York: Elsevier Science Publishers).

Hanemann, W. Michael. 1983. "Information and the Concept of Option Value,"
University of California, Department of Agricultural and Resource Economics,
Working Paper No. 228 (Berkeley, Calif., November).

Henry, Claude. 1974. "Investment Decisions Under Uncertainty: The Irreversibility Effect," *American Economic Review*, vol. 64.

Hirshleifer, Jack. 1961. "Comments," in *Public Finances: Needs, Sources and Utilization* (Princeton: NBER-Princeton University Press).

――――. 1965. "Investment Decision Under Uncertainty: Choice-Theoretic Approaches," *Quarterly Journal of Economics*, vol. LXXIX, no. 4.

――――. 1966. "Investment Decision Under Uncertainty: Applications of the State-
Preference Approach," *Quarterly Journal of Economics*, vol. LXXX, no. 2.

Jones, Robert A., and Ostroy, Joseph M. 1984. "Flexibility and Uncertainty," *Review of Economic Studies*, vol. 51.

Krutilla, J. V., and Eckstein, Otto. 1958. *Multiple Purpose River Development*
(Baltimore: Johns Hopkins University Press for Resources for the Future).

Mäler, Karl-Goran. 1985. "Environmental Issues in Welfare Economics," in A. V.
Kneese and J. L. Sweeney, eds. *Handbook of Natural Resource and Energy
Economics* (New York: North Holland Publishing Company).

Marglin, Stephen. 1963. "The Social Rate of Discount and the Optimal Rate of
Investment," *Quarterly Journal of Economics*, vol. LXXVII, no. 1.

Miller, Jon, and Lad, Frank. 1984. "Flexibility, Learning, and Irreversibility in
Environmental Decisions: A Bayesian Approach," *Journal of Environmental
Economics and Management*, vol. II, no. 2 (June).

Mishan, E. J. 1971. *Cost-Benefit Analysis* (New York: Praeger).

Modigliani, Franco and Brumberg, R. 1954. "Utility Analysis and the Consumption Function: An Interpretation of Cross-Section Data" in *Post Keynesian Economics*, K. K. Kurihara, ed. (New Brunswick, N.J.: Rutgers University
Press).

Phelps, E. S. and Pollak, R. A. 1968. "On Second-Best National Savings and
Game-Equilibrium Growth," *Review of Economic Studies*, vol. XXXV, no. 2.

Pigou, A. C. 1932. *The Economics of Welfare* (London: Macmillan).

Ramsey, F. P. 1928. "A Mathematical Theory of Saving," *Economic Journal*, vol.
38, no. 152.

Samuelson, P. A. 1964. "Discussion," *American Economic Review*, vol. LIV,
no. 2.

Schmalensee, Richard. 1972. "Option Demand and Consumer's Surplus: Valuing Price Changes Under Uncertainty," *American Economic Review*, vol. 62 (December).

Scott, Anthony. 1955. *Natural Resources: The Economics of Conservation* (Toronto: University of Toronto Press).

Seagraves, J. H. 1970. "More on the Social Rate of Discount," *Quarterly Journal of Economics*, vol. LXXXIV, no. 3.

Strotz, Robert. 1955–56. "Myopia and Inconsistency in Dynamic Utility Maximization," *Review of Economic Studies*, vol. XXIII, no. 162.

Viscusi, W. Kip, and Zeckhauser, Richard. 1976. "Environmental Policy Choice Under Uncertainty," *Journal of Environmental Economics and Management*, vol. 3 (August).

Weisbrod, B. A. 1964. "Collective-Consumption Services of Individual-Consumption Goods," *Quarterly Journal of Economics*, vol. LXXVIII, no. 3.

Zeckhauser, Richard. 1969. "Resource Allocation with Probabilistic Individual Preferences, *American Economic Review*, proceedings volume (May).

PART II

APPLYING THE ANALYSIS: SELECTED CASE STUDIES

INTRODUCTION

In part I of this volume we have attempted to put in the framework of economic theory those aspects of environmental concerns that have their roots in the aesthetic dimensions of the environment. These concerns have found expression in a growing body of legislation applicable to public lands. This speaks to the importance of these lands in providing the amenity services for which an affluent society has exhibited an increasing demand. The implications of this legislation are extensive, since the natural environments under the administrative jurisdiction of public agencies represent vast areas of largely undisturbed land.

Except for specific land reservations designated for primary purposes (allowing only compatible related uses), most of the public land is still subject to allocation among alternative competing demands. On notable occasions one of the competing demands may be incompatible with another in perpetuity, i.e., it may destroy the substance of an amenity resource, eliminating access to its usufruct for all time. In chapter 2 we noted a problem in this connection in the assessment of the relative value of alternative uses of open access resources of the public lands. Where the beneficiaries of the flow of services from amenity resources are required to assume liability for the opportunity returns forgone from a prohibited destructive use, the benefits so measured are smaller than if they were measured as compensation for damages resulting from a destructive use of the environment. The reason for this turns on the difference between monetary income, on which the ability to pay depends, and real income, which depends as well on final consumption benefits derived from common property resources not necessarily matched by monetary income. Applied to nationally significant environmental modifications, these differences could be very large. Accordingly, any evaluation of benefits based on a willingness-to-pay criterion, under such circumstances, provides potentially only a lower bound estimate, depending on the assignment of property rights.

Results having somewhat the same implications are obtained from an analysis in chapters 3 and 4 of optimal investment planning (of a development project in a natural environment) under conditions including irreversibility of the investment and uncertainty as to its consequences. For example, we find under these conditions that there is likely to be a value, which we call option value, beyond the conventional (expected) consumers' surplus associated with preserving a natural environment. These theoretical considerations are worth exploring because they provide valuable guidance to the use and interpretation of data and results in applied studies. At the same time we recognize the hiatus between the relatively formal theory, on the one hand, and applied benefit–cost analysis, on the other.

One difficulty is that, strictly speaking, either an exact analytical solution to the problem of choosing projects of optimal scale or a computational algorithm for this purpose is required. But neither is likely to be within the capability of the analyst. The former is dependent on the specific forms of the benefit functions, which are not generally known, the latter on amassing and processing vast quantities of data, often at prohibitive cost. A "first approximation" approach that will be used in the case studies in part II, where applicable, will be to analyze in detail one or more development plans for which data on costs and alternative uses are at least to some extent available and then to make some inferences about the economics of other conceivable plans based on our knowledge of benefit functions in each case.*

> Let us also address another set of simplifications of the model in chapter 3, required for application to the data. Consider the evaluation of development alternatives as represented in expression (3-22a). This expression, along with (3-22b) can be simplified to aid in the exposition of our computational procedures in the following chapters. $\bar{S}(0)$, the scale of development prior to investment at a site, may be set equal to zero. The interpretation is either that there is in fact no prior development at the site, or that we are looking at the differential benefits from further development on a base of $\bar{S}(0)$. This results in dropping of the b_0^d term in expression (3-22b), the present value of the preserved environment. Further, since any preservation-related amenity service that can be enjoyed in the presence of development is generally also available with no development, we shall assume that the b_0^p term may be dropped from (3-22a), and then interpreted as representing only the differential benefits from the amenity resources in (3-22b). With these simplifications it is possible to represent the comparison between with-project and without-project benefits as one between expressions

> (1a) $\displaystyle\int_0^\infty e^{-\rho t}[b_0^d(\bar{S})e^{-rt} - C(I(t))]\, dt$

> and

> (1b) $\displaystyle\int_0^\infty e^{-\rho t}[b_0^p(\bar{S}(0))e^{\alpha t}]\, dt$

---

* The material set in indented type refers to the model of chapter 3, and may be skipped by those unfamiliar with that material.

A final simplification is to convert the continuous-time version of the present-value streams given above to a discrete-time version requiring a comparison of project net benefits expressed in terms of a stream of annual flows

(2a) $\sum_t b_0^d (1 + \rho)^{-t}(1 + r)^{-t}$

with, in the first instance, project investment costs

(2b) $\sum_t C(I_t)(1 + \rho)^{-t}$

where these costs are, however, incurred right at the outset, so that there are only one or two terms in (2b), and then if necessary, preservation benefits[1]

(2c) $\sum_t b_0^p (1 + \rho)^{-t}(1 + \alpha)^t$

It is possible that we shall have marginal cases under review, in which case carrying out the evaluation of the benefits and investment costs of development will suffice. That is, if the net present value of development is negative, it should not be undertaken regardless of environmental costs. Since a complete quantitative evaluation of environmental amenity services is likely to be difficult, if not impossible, in any event, our strategy is first to analyze each development plan critically, correcting for faulty elements in the evaluation to determine if development would be justified even if there were no environmental opportunity costs. Since some proposals are likely to be inefficient whether or not environmental costs are considered, such a strategy may avoid much unnecessary effort.

In chapter 5, then, we have a first look at the celebrated Hells Canyon case. Here for two out of the three proposals, a critical evaluation indicates that they should be rejected as inefficient without accounting for the environmental damages their construction entails. In one of the three, however, the most careful and critical review of the true social costs, exclusive of the environmental costs, indicates that the hydroelectric project shows net benefits. It is then necessary to consider whether the benefits thus estimated are greater or less than the benefits forgone from modifying a unique amenity resource in the interests of developing hydroelectricity. There are alternative energy supply options that will provide perfect substitutes for hydroelectricity as far as the ultimate consumers are concerned—the only difference is price. The canyon, on the other hand, represents an amenity resource with no close substitutes. Moreover, once

---

[1] Although we continue to use the terms ρ, r, and α defined for the continuous case, it should be recognized that a slight adjustment in their numerical values would be required for application to the discrete case.

its pristine character is destroyed, the action is irreversible in a nontrivial way, as discussed in chapter 3. The special considerations that must be brought into account in evaluating the worth of preserving the canyon in its present state are incorporated into the benefit–cost analysis in the complementary chapters 5 and 6.

In analyzing the preservation uses of Hells Canyon, we confront the problem of specifying a capacity constraint since the individual benefits associated with recreating in a primitive, undeveloped area are in part a function also of intensity of use. That is, low-density recreation seeks to provide for some freedom from intrusion upon solitude—an objective that is not realizable under congested conditions. In the Hells Canyon case, given the exigencies of public hearings, "expert opinion" on capacity was solicited. This is a time-honored practice in adversary proceedings, but is something less than adequate as a substitute for research. Testing the sensitivity of our quantitative estimates on the number of individuals the area could accommodate without erosion of the quality of the recreation experience, we discovered that while the ranking of alternatives in this case would not be changed, the quantitative significance could not be readily ignored.

In chapter 7 we address within a different context the approximation of the "optimal capacity" by exploring the relationship between the worth of an outing in a wilderness setting and the expected frequency of encountering others on the trip—and between the intensity of use and the expected frequency of encounters. This was done for the White Cloud Peaks area of Idaho, a scenic region capable of producing molybdenum (using openpit mining methods) as well as a wilderness type of outdoor recreation experience.

The conflict between incompatible uses in a natural area is not restricted to extractive or resource development projects on the one hand and preservation for the amenity and related services on the other. Indeed, the conflict over the Mineral King Valley of California relates rather to the question of which of two types of outdoor recreation—low-density undeveloped, or high-density developed—would represent the highest valued use. The problem for analysis is to develop a means for estimating the benefits of a developed facility introduced into an existing system of facilities, with expected attendant redistribution of the pattern as well as amount of use. This is a rather intricate problem in demand estimation, requiring the application of sophisticated econometric techniques.

The last two chapters relate to problems that are more regional than site-specific and which have more extensive ramifications partly for that reason. Chapter 9 discusses efficient allocation of prairie wetlands for nesting and breeding of migratory waterfowl in light of the overlapping common and private property resources involved. Chapter 10 addresses the issue of evaluating alternatives to the exploitation of Alaskan oil and routes for transporting it. It illustrates a different application of, and use for, economic analysis, in spite of its basic inadequacy for evaluating the environmental costs of raising and transporting Alaskan oil to market. Here the issue is to determine which of the suggested route and market combinations is preferable.

The cases investigated in part II represent different kinds of conflicts that have irreversible implications for natural environments, as well as problems requiring different levels of analysis, ranging from reconnaissance-grade investigations for planning purposes to very sophisticated theoretical and empirical studies. In sum, the cases are intended to provide a reasonable cross section of situations that will be encountered in the studies required for more efficient management of our natural environments.

CHAPTER 5

HELLS CANYON: ASYMMETRIC IMPLICATIONS OF TECHNICAL CHANGE FOR VALUE OF ALTERNATIVE USES

1. INTRODUCTION

A particular natural environment may represent a stock of resources, or a flow of resource services of both a production and a consumption variety. The extractive industries are typically involved in
converting resource stocks into the intermediate goods or services that
form the industrial raw materials from which final consumption goods are
produced. A given tract of land, or reach of river, may also at times provide an unusually aesthetic natural setting and related at-site amenity
services that enter directly into the utility function of ultimate consumers.
Through logging, mining, and developing complementary logistic support
facilities essential to their operations, extractive undertakings often alter
the original environment significantly, producing irreversible adverse consequences for the amenities otherwise available from the site. In this way
they tend to foreclose an option in perpetuity. The nondestructive alternative use of the amenity services, however, does not foreclose any future
options which are not reflected in the opportunity returns forgone by pre-
cluding extractive use. There are some asymmetric implications of alternative uses of such areas, of which the Hells Canyon is a prime example. We
shall analyze these in detail in this and the following chapter, but perhaps
this point should be elaborated before the Hells Canyon case is addressed
in specific detail.

Extractive activities typically result in outputs of goods and services
which are both producible and intermediate in nature. Because the activities are intermediate, there are more possibilities for substitution in the
production of final consumption goods and services. Advances in production
technology contribute to a broad spectrum of substitute intermediate inputs
for the production of final consumer goods. For example, printed circuits and

transistors are substitutes for copper wire circuits and vacuum tubes in communication equipment and do not alter quality or performance of the final
product.

More directly related to the problem to be discussed in this and the
next chapter is the inability of consumers to distinguish among kilowatt
hours of electricity produced from falling water, combustion of fossil fuel,
or nuclear reaction. Compared with consumer products, there is a high
degree of substitutability between hydroelectric and steam electric power
plants in the production of electricity and between fossil fuel and fission-
able material in the production of such energy in conventional steam cycle
power plants. Technical advances within either of the latter supply options
tend to reduce their real costs over time.

Consider now the use of a natural area for recreational and related
purposes. This will represent (1) use of nonproducible amenity services,
i.e., those provided through the chemistry of time, measured in eons, in
combination with geomorphologic and biologic evolutionary processes not
capable of replication by man, and (2) services entering directly into
the utility functions of individuals in final consumption. If the natural area
in question is characterized by some rare attributes that enhance recreation
and related amenity services, the range of substitutes may be both exceedingly narrow and grossly imperfect. In short, were the area to be devoted
to an incompatible (environmentally destructive) alternative purpose,
there would be very limited opportunity for substitutes to satisfy the preferences of those individuals who value such services highly (chapter 3,
section 2). Moreover, since such environmental resources are not reproducible, once destroyed, they are irretrievably lost. Anticipated growth in
the demand for such services cannot be matched by augmentation of supplies resulting from advances in technology of production.

We can see in this situation how the values of incompatible uses of an
area may be asymmetrically affected by technological progress. If the area
is dedicated to extractive or developmental purposes, it will produce an
intermediate good or service, e.g., hydroelectricity. Any increase in the
demand for electricity, say, can be met by increasing the supply from
various sources that substitute for each other perfectly insofar as producing
an indistinguishable final consumption service. And, if the advances in
technology that occur in the production of such intermediate goods or
services from alternative supply options are sufficient to permit increased
output over time at falling supply price (Barnett and Morse, 1963), the
value of the service flow of the extractive alternative will diminish as gains
occur in productive efficiency.

On the other hand, since a natural environment that provides amenity
services consumed on site cannot be produced by the efforts of man, general advances in productive technique have no positive implications for

increasing the stock of such nonproducible natural assets and their service flows. However, general advances in technology, representing as they do, increases in output and hence income per capita, result in increases in the demand for services of the irreproducible natural assets. The value of the annual service flow in the latter case appreciates with the passage of time as the relative scarcity increases. Accordingly, the effect of technical change on the value of the natural environment in alternative uses differs.

This chapter reviews the circumstances relevant to an analysis of the Hells Canyon case. Here we take into account the effects of technical change on the value of the benefits derived from hydroelectric development. We also address in more careful fashion the need for uniform treatment of discount rates for all actors on the proposed scene of development. This is necessary in order to eliminate the biases introduced in benefit–cost evaluation that stem from such practices as preferential tax treatment, subsidized investment through provision of capital at rates inconsistent with opportunity costs, and other similar aberrations that distort the results. Chapter 6 addresses the question of the value of retaining Hells Canyon in its present undisturbed state, and the expected appreciation of the benefits of preservation over time. The two chapters combined reflect the importance of taking into account in evaluating environmental alterations the expected changes over time in the relative value of the annual benefits from the alternative uses (see also Krutilla and Cicchetti, 1973; Smith, 1974).

2. THE PHYSICAL, INSTITUTIONAL, AND LEGAL SETTING OF THE PROBLEM

The lower Snake River, forming the boundary between the northeastern border of Oregon and the west central portion of the Idaho border, passes through about 200 miles of a geologic formation known as Hells Canyon. With the towering Seven Devils Peaks of Idaho rising on its east, and the beautiful Wallowa Mountains of Oregon rising on its west banks, the Snake River in this reach is one of the most scenic streams to be found anywhere and is in a most extraordinary natural environment (Leopold, 1969). At the same time, because of the volume of water flowing in the reach, its narrowness, the steepness of the canyon sides, and the excellent foundation conditions, there are a number of attractive sites for the development of hydroelectric and related water storage facilities. The incompatibility between the development of this reach of river for power and its preservation in an undisturbed state has sparked a controversy that has involved governmental agencies, courts, private electric utilities, and citizens' organizations.

The Hells Canyon reach of the Snake came under consideration for hydroelectric power development in some studies of the Columbia River and its tributaries conducted by the U.S. Corps of Engineers in the 1940s (House Document No. 531, 81st Cong., 2nd sess., 1950). During the 1950s, the Federal Power Commission (FPC) licensed three sites in the upper reaches of the canyon for development by the Idaho Power Company. Application for license by the Pacific Northwest Power Company (PNPC) to develop additionally the remaining lower 58 miles of the Hells Canyon reach by either of two alternative proposals, i.e., two low dams (one each at the Mountain Sheep and Pleasant Valley sites), or by a single high dam at Mountain Sheep, was made in a series of actions over a decade. License for development of the High Mountain Sheep facility was eventually issued by the commission in 1964.

The license issued to PNPC was challenged, however, by the Secretary of the Interior and appealed to the courts. In *Udall* v. *Federal Power Commission* (387 U.S. 428, 1967), the Supreme Court, noting that there was no evidence in the record of the hearings on certain issues of consequence, remanded the matter to the FPC for rehearing. Among the important considerations in the Supreme Court's opinion, for our purpose, was its concern that the Federal Power Commission had not considered adequately the issue of whether nondevelopment of the canyon might not be in the public interest. Citing section 10(a) of the Federal Power Act regarding the charge to select projects "best adapted to a comprehensive plan of improving or developing a waterway . . . and for other beneficial public uses, including recreational purposes," the Supreme Court said the following:

The objective of protecting 'recreational purposes' means more than that the reservoir created by the dam will be the best one possible or practical from a recreational viewpoint. There are already eight lower dams on this Columbia River system and a ninth one authorized; and if the Secretary is right in fearing that this additional dam would destroy the waterway as a spawning ground for anadromous fish [salmon and steelhead] or seriously impair that function, the project is put in an entirely different light. The importance of salmon and steelhead in our outdoor life as well as in commerce is so great that there certainly comes a time when their destruction might necessitate a halt in so-called 'improvement' or 'development' of waterways. The destruction of anadromous fish in our western waters is so notorious that we cannot believe that Congress through the present Act authorized their ultimate demise. (pp. 437–438)

and later in the opinion,

The issues of whether deferral of construction would be more in the public interest than immediate construction and whether preservation of the reaches of the river affected would be more desirable and in the public interest than the proposed development are largely unexplored in this record. (p. 449)

The question of giving consideration to preservation as well as development under the Federal Power Act was thus introduced explicitly in the Supreme Court's 1967 decision. Accordingly, in September of 1968, the FPC resumed hearings directed in part to addressing the question of the relative worth of the Hells Canyon site when devoted to the provision of amenity services compared with the production of hydroelectricity.[1]

From an analytical point of view, of course, the problem of resolving these issues is not inconsiderable. There are numerous difficulties associated with measuring the relative worths of the service flows from the two alternative ways of using the resources of the Hells Canyon. In the case of the "improvement" where a multiple-purpose storage reservoir is constructed for use in the production of power, reduction of flood damages, and improvement of navigation conditions on the river system, there has evolved a body of economic principles and analytical procedures that can be used to provide reasonably good estimates of benefits and costs if objectively applied in project evaluations (Eckstein, 1958). Even here, however, the peculiarities of the regional power system of which the Hells Canyon development is intended to be a part involve the need to develop some methodology in order to introduce the effects of technological progress into the evaluation of hydroelectric facilities.[2]

Aside from the problem of introducing appropriate technical change in computing power benefits, it is difficult to evaluate the alternative means of providing equivalent services because the regional power system is comprised of a mix of private, nonfederal public, and federal facilities. Whichever the assumed source of the increment to the power supply, whether Hells Canyon hydro or a thermal electric station, each alternative would be complemented in dissimilar amounts by federal transmission facilities. Moreover, the thermal alternative would rely on federal hydroelectric peaking facilities in part. Accordingly, with complementary facilities under different ownership participating to different extents, any nonuniformity in the treatment of any element of costs would tend to

---

[1] During the year previous to the reopening of the hearings, the Washington Public Power Supply System (WPPSS), which had competed with PNPC for license to develop this reach of the river, agreed with the latter to become a joint applicant for the projects. The rehearings dealt, then, with the joint application.

[2] The benefits from a hydroelectric development are taken to be the savings in costs as compared with the most economical alternative source of the same utility services (Steiner, 1965). In a mixed hydrothermal system the assumed thermal alternative to hydro for meeting capacity requirements will produce off-peak energy more economically than existing older, less efficient plants. Accordingly, advances in the efficiency of thermal generation can be credited to the thermal alternative if its off-peak energy displaces energy otherwise produced at higher cost, less efficient plants (see FPC, 1968, pp. 23–24). In an exclusively hydro system without existing thermal facilities such as the Columbia and tributaries system, but with thermal as the source of future growth, the introduction of the effects of technological change is more complicated, and will be treated on pp. 98 ff.

vitiate the evaluation. More specifically, since the land and water resource development programs have been a principal vehicle for disbursements from the congressional pork barrel, there are many subsidies in the accounting (as against real) costs of public facilities.[3] If federal transmission or peaking facilities participate in different degrees as complementary portions of the system in which the two alternatives being compared will operate, the evaluation will not be meaningful unless all costs are placed on the same economic footing regardless of the "accounting" costs permitted under various policies of the federal government. A particular problem in this phase of the analysis is to ensure that investment outlays, however made, bear a uniform imputed interest rate. Although this is perhaps an elementary point to economic theorists, we emphasize it here because the hearings data were not originally in this form, and accordingly had to be thoroughly reworked, and presented in separate exhibits and testimony in the rebuttal phase of the hearings.[4]

A second and more difficult problem relates to the value of the Hells Canyon resources when devoted to a nondevelopmental use. Responding to an invitation by the FPC to comment on the proposed development (which would flood portions of national forests), Secretary of Agriculture Orville Freeman in a letter dated November 8, 1968, characterized the recreation and aesthetic resources of the canyon region as follows:

The Snake River, in its present free-flowing state, is an awesome stream consisting of a series of swift white-water rapids flowing into deep pools in one of the deepest canyons in the United States. The immediate shoreline is principally a series of sheer rock faces dropping almost vertically into the river or stretches lined with great boulders interspersed by occasional sand bars in back eddies. There is no doubt that this stretch of the Snake River represents one of the last of this country's great rivers that has been little changed by man and still challenges his best efforts to tame. It represents a scene of ruggedness probably not equaled anywhere in the United States today. (FPC, 1970, p. 5 of exhibit)

and further in the letter:

This canyon of the Snake River is the locality in the United States having the greatest elevation difference between the canyon bottom and the tops of the immediately adjacent canyon rim crags in the Seven Devils Area. There is no way that the some 76 miles which encompass the swift water portions of this

---

[3] In addition to receiving concessions on interest and other features of capital costs, reliance on the "grandfather clause" introduces distortions in the evaluation procedure. For example, during a period in which the Water Resources Council required a 5 percent discount rate while throughout the remainder of the federal establishment a 10 percent rate was applied to public expenditures, the imputed interest rate on capital expended during the same time in the construction of the third powerhouse at Grand Coulee will be only 3⅛ percent.

[4] See Testimony of John V. Krutilla, Transcript R-5826 ff. and Exhibits R-669, 669-A, 671, and 671-A in Federal Power Commission (1970).

canyon can be mitigated or replaced. While there is archeological significance and recreational use significance in the canyon area for recreation associated with the free-flowing river, the outstanding natural resource is the canyon itself with the free-flowing river in it. This cannot be replaced nor is it duplicated elsewhere in the country. (p. 11)

While Secretary Freeman argued that the Snake River in this reach qualified for inclusion in the Wild and Scenic River System, no attempt was made to compare the relative value of the resources when used for alternative incompatible purposes. At any rate, as mentioned in chapter 1, methods of analysis were not readily available because of serious difficulties in evaluating the service flow of the resources retained in their undisturbed state.

The Snake River and the public lands that are adjacent to the canyon reach, primarily the national forests in that area, are for the most part open access resources. Since there is no annual receipt of user fees, the tendency has been to ignore the value of the service flow because the services do not generate revenues. Methods for estimating the demand for outdoor recreation under such circumstances, of course, have been known for a decade and a half now (Clawson, 1958), but their use in amenity resource allocation decisions has been largely ignored.[5]

In addition to the lack of studies which would make it possible to give recreation benefit estimates in the same terms as other hard-to-estimate benefits such as power and flood control, there are some other questions to which answers are not readily forthcoming. How does one measure the value of scientific research materials, particularly given some probability of serendipity? What is the value of an option in the face of an irreversible decision? Equally difficult is the question referred to in chapter 2 regarding the assignment of liability in the case of the "destructive" use of a common property resource. Depending on the assignment of liability, the value of the resources retained in an undisturbed state might be the sum that current and prospective users would be willing to pay for their use, on the one hand, or the amount they would require in compensation for the damages suffered from the destructive use, on the other. The latter, being unconstrained by the damaged parties' incomes, would typically be larger, and given the intensity of feeling on the part of some individuals regarding matters of this sort, probably a great deal larger.

Accordingly, we adopt the strategy of first examining the value of the developmental alternatives [expressions (2a) and (2b) in the introduction

---

[5] Although the method by which to estimate recreation benefits in the same metric as power, flood control, and similar water resource development benefits has been available for more than 15 years, the Water Resources Council, for example, still recommends that an arbitrary interim value be assigned (Water Resources Council, 1973).

to part II]. If it is possible to show that the net value of the most profitable development plan would be negative, even when no account is taken of environmental opportunity costs, then it will not be necessary to attempt the still more difficult evaluation of these costs. Conversely, if the present value of some development of the site is positive, attention must be given to the opportunity returns from preservation precluded by the proposed development. This latter question will be confronted in the next chapter.

3. ECONOMIC ANALYSIS OF THE
DEVELOPMENTAL ALTERNATIVES

Actual Proposals for Development
    There have been a number of proposals for the development of the lower Hells Canyon. Those most relevant to our analysis may be reduced basically to three. One involves a dam at the site of High Mountain Sheep located approximately a mile upstream from the confluence of the Snake and Salmon rivers at river mile 189.2 (see figure 5-1). It would develop the total head from that point to the tailwaters of the Hells Canyon dam of the Idaho Power Company. A second proposal, first advanced in the mid-1950s by PNPC, would be to develop this reach by two smaller dams, a low dam at the site of Mountain Sheep at river mile 192.5 and a second at Pleasant Valley, roughly 20 miles upstream (river mile 213.0). The two combined would develop virtually the same amount of head. A third proposal, the Appaloosa project, advanced by the Department of the Interior, envisions a relatively high dam, developing the total head of a reach of river from just above the confluence of the Imnaha and the Snake at the lower end (river mile 197.6) to the tailwaters of the Idaho Power Company's Hells Canyon Dam at the upper end. A reason for the location of the Appaloosa project upstream from the High Mountain Sheep site was to reduce the disturbance to salmon and steelhead spawning runs on the Salmon River, and to permit continued spawning on the Imnaha River.
    Initially upon resumption of the FPC hearings on remand from the court, the Appaloosa project was advanced for consideration by the Interior Department as an alternative to the nonfederal projects proposed for licensing. On August 12, 1969, however, the Department of the Interior took a position opposing any additional construction in the Hells Canyon. The issue before the commission then turned simply on the question of whether developing the remaining canyon reach of the river, by whichever of the PNPC alternative proposals, was justified in relation to environmental amenities destroyed by development. In short, whether, in the court's words, preservation of the reaches of the river was more in the public interest than the proposed development.

Partial Costs and Total
Benefits of Development

Although the projects proposed by PNPC were motivated by the applicants' interest in obtaining power for its system, a thorough analysis of the economic justification of the projects requires imputing relevant costs and benefits in addition to those associated with power. On the cost side, adverse environmental effects are to be included, but we exclude consideration of them in the first pass in analysis. On the benefit side, we would anticipate the possibility of some flood control and perhaps reservoir recreation benefits. Typically, when there are several functions performed by a multipurpose water resource development project, each separate function is analyzed to determine whether it qualifies for inclusion in the efficient project design. This is done by estimating the separable costs of that function, i.e., the costs that represent the difference between the costs of the project with the purpose included as compared with it excluded from the project design. If these separable costs exceed the benefits of the purpose, the purpose is dropped. If the estimated benefits from the purpose exceed the separable costs, the purpose is included. This matter is of some importance to the analysis of the Hells Canyon developmental alternatives.

Reservoir Recreation

Recreation plays a critical role in the evaluation of the alternative uses to which a natural environment, such as the Hells Canyon, can be devoted. Typically, the outdoor recreation benefits associated with undisturbed natural areas are an important part of the total benefits obtained from preservation of natural environments. But, it can be argued that the recreational benefits foreclosed by development may be offset to greater or lesser extent, or even exceeded, by the benefits from developed recreation associated with the reservoir. Indeed, since primitive or wilderness-type recreation in natural environments requires much land per recreation unit, the more intensively developed recreation facilities associated with reservoir recreation, it is claimed, can support many more recreationists and hence more recreation benefits than the area can if it is preserved for low-density recreational activities. Of course, the value per unit of the two different types of recreation may differ substantially and should always be investigated with great care. For the moment, however, we confine ourselves to an analysis of the comparison of benefits from reservoir recreation and its separable costs because this turns out to be significant for the selection of relevant costs of power facilities in the hydroelectric power benefit evaluation.

Analysis of the benefits to be associated with the introduction of a new recreation facility into an existing system of markets and facilities is a

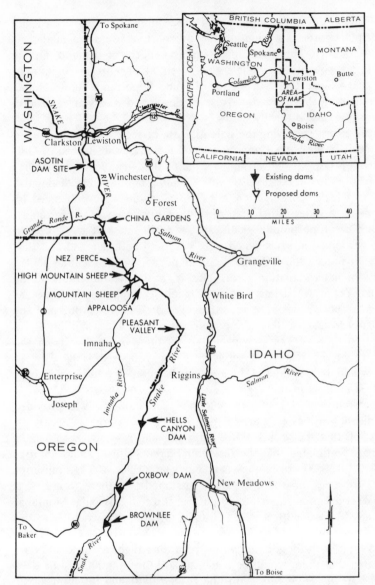

Figure 5-1. Sites for proposed development of Hells Canyon.

very complex problem, and has only recently been approached in a theoretically adequate manner (Burt and Brewer, 1971; Cicchetti, Fisher and Smith, 1972; also see chapter 8). The estimation of the benefits from reservoir recreation in connection with the proposed developments in the Hells Canyon did not rely on formal procedures of this sort. Basically three principal efforts at evaluating the prospective use were made, although none of them employed an economic concept of demand. Of the three, only one sought to evaluate the potential benefits in relation to separable costs. Since this is a matter of some importance, the attempts made at estimating the recreational use of developed reservoir recreation facilities are reviewed critically below.

One of the efforts surveying the potential use of recreational facilities of a new reservoir in the Hells Canyon was conducted by the Bureau of Outdoor Recreation (BOR). Unfortunately, the methods employed (and since discontinued) tended to confuse *use* with *demand,* and failed to distinguish the extent to which "participation rates" in a region were influenced by the existence of facilities rather than recreational preferences. Accordingly, an area with disproportionate facilities of a particular sort was likely to show high participation rates which were confused with demand and thus were likely to induce the BOR to recommend additional facilities in the light of the high participation rates. This is, basically, the result of the BOR study. Yet if we define "excess capacity" of existing facilities as the difference between heaviest recorded use for each reservoir, and the use in the survey year (1969), there were something like a million and a half recreation days of excess capacity in facilities on reservoirs in the region in which the recreation services of the proposed Hells Canyon reservoirs would be provided. The relevant tributary population is only about 50,000 persons in the aggregate.[6]

A second source of estimates of potential recreation use was provided by the applicant's witnesses, Larry Espey and F. D. Voorhees. Espey, on the assumption that the access to the dam site and reservoir would be a dead-end road, estimated that the reservoir recreation use would approximate 25,000 to 30,000 recreation days per year (FPC, 1970, Transcript R-467 ff). Voorhees, on the other hand, assumed that there would be a through road connecting Interstate 90 passing through Missoula, Montana, and Interstate 80 passing through La Grande, Oregon, that would cross the canyon in the vicinity of High Mountain Sheep Dam (FPC, 1970, Transcript R-4497).[7] With these assumptions regarding highway access, Voorhees estimated that there would be some 300,000 to 500,000 visitor days of recreation at the High Mountain Sheep Dam within a few years after the installation of facilities.

---

[6] This excess capacity was distributed as follows: McNary, 608,000; Chief Joseph, 55,000; Lower Monumental, 150,000; Little Goose, 200,000; Lower Granite, 200,000; Owyhee, 53,000; Brownlee (Farewell Bend), 95,000. Additionally, the Dworshak Dam and reservoir on the Clearwater was under construction and is currently available, adding a significant additional amount of flatwater recreation area.

[7] A check with the state highway departments of the two principal states indicates that there are no plans for an interconnecting highway such as the one postulated by witness Voorhees (FPC, 1970, Transcript R-4619–R-4623).

There appears to be some ambiguity in Voorhees' evaluation procedure. On cross-examination he conceded that there was excess reservoir recreation capacity in the Spokane and Lewiston, Washington, area that High Mountain Sheep might serve (FPC, 1970, Transcript R-4519–R-4520) and postulated that the bulk of the visitation would come from Northern California and the San Francisco Bay Area. Independent study of reservoir recreation in the Pacific Northwest, however, indicates that such facilities serve predominantly a local clientele. Analysis of seven Corps of Engineers recreational reservoirs in the Northwest reveals that approximately 80 percent of the visitation will come from within a 50-mile radius of the reservoir and over 90 percent will be drawn from within a 100-mile radius.[8] Records of attendance at even such nationally prominent reservoir recreation facilities as Flaming Gorge similarly suggest that 70 percent of all visitation will come from within 50 miles. These data do not support Voorhees' estimates that the bulk of the visitation to the proposed High Mountain Sheep facility would come from the bay area, some 650 miles distant.

Perhaps the most carefully conducted study of the recreational potential of the proposed reservoirs has been made by Dunlap (FPC, 1970, Transcript R-3879–R-3891), who exhibited intimate familiarity with the region, and with a recreation facility that, in his judgment, represented one most similar to the proposed High Mountain Sheep reservoir (FPC, 1970, Transcript R-4626–R-4634), namely the Owyhee Dam and Owyhee Lake State Park. This facility was built in the period 1928–1932 and was at that time the highest concrete arch-gravity structure built in the world (417 feet structural height). Located also near the Idaho–Oregon border, it occupies terrain, and has related characteristics very similar to the proposed High Mountain Sheep project. The Owyhee project has about 300 miles of shoreline, High Mountain Sheep about 200 miles, although the reservoir lengths are approximately equal, with the scenery outstanding at both locations (FPC, 1970, Dunlap Transcript R-4627). Dunlap finds

---

[8] These data will not hold for visitation at reservoir facilities located adjacent to interstate or U.S. highways. Such facilities often serve as comfort and convenience stops for persons en route to different, and not even recreational, destinations. An apparent confusion regarding data attaching to Farewell Bend State Park on U.S. 30 at the headwaters of the Brownlee Reservoir with the site of Brownlee Dam proper at the other end of the reservoir on a dead-end road, doubtless led witness Voorhees to the exaggerated estimates of visitation at the proposed High Mountain Sheep Reservoir.

Four separate surveys of the recreation facilities at the developed upper end of the canyon by the author revealed little use of these facilities. This came as something of a surprise in the light of the heavy use reported by the Idaho Power Company to the Federal Power Commission. A reported 10,000 camper nights at the campsite on Hells Canyon Reservoir, for example, could be accounted for only by utilization to full capacity over a 100-day season. During visits to the site on Labor Day, 1968; June 17, July 27, and August 15, 1969 we found that on only one occasion (July 27, a weekend) was there *any* use of the facility and even then it was not to capacity.

that over half of the visitors come from within a radius of 50 miles and roughly 90 percent from within a radius of 100 miles. This is similar to the experience elsewhere in the Pacific Northwest at Corps of Engineers reservoirs for which data were available. Dunlap then goes on to say:

With respect to population centers, the nearest population complex to Owyhee is the Ontario-Vale area about 30–35 miles to the north. Approximately 50–75 miles away in the State of Idaho we have Boise–Nampa and that area. Population centers at the Mountain Sheep are somewhat less as far as urban population. I was thinking in terms of Imnaha, White Bird, and Grangeville. I also anticipate some use would come from the Boise–Nampa area. (FPC, 1970, Transcript R-4630)

While the Dunlap analysis is the most thoughtful in terms of the comparisons of areas for similarity of attractions, location, and so forth, the tributary area of the Owyhee reservoir is substantially more populous than the area about Mountain Sheep. A check of the 1960 decennial census reveals no population for Imnaha (one building), or for Whitebird (some half-dozen buildings), and for Grangeville, 3,642 persons. The whole of Wallowa County in which Enterprise and Joseph as well as Imnaha are situated (the former on the shores of the popular Wallowa Lake and state park) is only some 7,000 persons. Within the 50–75 mile range of Lake Owyhee there are about 90,000 persons in the Boise–Nampa urban complex and 150,000 in the two counties (Ada and Canyon) in which the two cities are located. Within a comparable distance of Mountain Sheep there is the Lewiston–Clarkston urban place with only 18,700 persons and only 40,000 in the two counties (Asotin and Nez Perce). Aside from being much smaller in population, these towns have immediate access to the adjacent Lower Granite and Little Goose reservoirs on the lower Snake, along with the Dworshak dam and reservoir on the Clearwater. All of these are more accessible than Mountain Sheep. It seems likely also that the Mountain Sheep site would not attract many visitors from the Boise–Nampa area as it is over 200 miles distant, with almost a dozen intervening lakes and reservoirs.

With all the relevant information at hand, it is difficult to see how the Mountain Sheep site could attract visitation equal to that of Owyhee Lake, yet recreation specialists have projected a fivefold greater visitation. This conclusion hardly seems justified by experience with reservoirs in the region. Even so, because of the very high cost of access and recreation facilities, Dunlap found that the imputed recreation benefits did not equal their separable costs (FPC, 1970, Transcript R-3888 ff).[9]

[9] While the costs exceeded the benefits decisively for the High Mountain Sheep and Appaloosa projects, they favored the Low Mountain Sheep–Pleasant Valley project by a close margin, at imputed interest rates of 4.875 percent. With relevant opportunity costs of capital, however, the excess of separable costs of recreation facilities over estimated benefits was decisive for all of the reservoir recreation.

With the estimated benefits from the proposed recreation falling short of the estimated separable costs, construction and investment costs of the alternative plans of development were adjusted in our analysis to exclude costs of separable recreation and related access facilities. Basically the estimates of costs of the project, therefore, relate to the costs of power facilities because flood control is obtained as a by-product, i.e., without additional separable costs.

4. LOW MOUNTAIN SHEEP–PLEASANT VALLEY COMPLEX

The proposed Mountain Sheep–Pleasant Valley combination of two reservoirs permits the lower one to serve as a reregulating reservoir for discharges during peak load operations at the upper plant. With Mountain Sheep, the reregulating reservoir downstream from Pleasant Valley, the 1,570 megawatts of capacity installed initially can be increased to 2,735 megawatts ultimately as the hydroelectric plants become more extensively used for future peak load operations. Accordingly, the amount of capacity installed initially would be slightly greater (4 percent) than the amount in the high dam alternative in early years of operation, 30–35 percent greater during the intermediate years, and approximately 85 percent greater ultimately (FPC, 1970, Exhibit R-107-A).[10] The two-dam complex, representing a larger investment outlay and a larger amount of peaking capacity, will provide for greater gross benefits (i.e., the total cost of the most economic alternative source of power) compared with a single high dam at Mountain Sheep.[11]

Investment and annual cost of both the hydroelectric projects and the thermal alternative are given in appendix 5-B. Separate estimates of benefits and costs of Mountain Sheep–Pleasant Valley are made for each of three representative periods: the initial or predominantly hydroelectric period, 1976–1980; the intermediate period, while transition to a predominantly thermal system is taking place, 1981–1990; and the final period in

[10] For all practical purposes at the present time the regional power system in the Northwest, in which the Hells Canyon hydro would participate, is exclusively hydroelectric. But as the power demand grows large in relation to the supply of hydro energy, the demand will need to be met from thermal electric sources. By the time the thermal component of the system has grown large in relation to the hydro, it will become most economic to use thermal plants to generate energy for base load requirements, and to use hydro for peak load requirements. It is for this reason that provision is made for greater capacity to be used for evaluating benefits during the later years of the analysis.

[11] The two-project complex represents a lesser development in terms of storage capacity than would a single high dam at Mountain Sheep, resulting in a somewhat smaller annual flood control benefit ($87,000 compared with $245,000); but flood control benefits are in any event minor in relation to power benefits. There will be about 13 to 15 percent less energy (contrasted with capacity) produced by the two-dam complex, also as a result of the lesser storage.

which the regional power system has evolved into a predominantly thermal system, 1991–2025.

In addition to adjusting the cost of some components of the system to reflect application of uniform interest rates, the cost of the thermal alternative also had to be adjusted to allow for advances in the technology of thermal electric production. Some discussion of this matter is in order.

Typically, when a decision is made to invest, the technology embodied in the capital goods is frozen during the life of the investment. Now if we consider two production alternatives such as hydro and thermal electric facilities, the time over which the alternative is "locked in" by the state of technology existing at the time of investment is shorter, the shorter the life of the facility. That is, the shorter the life, the more frequently will the capacity be replaced by updated technology, and, other things remaining equal, the more efficient will the shorter lived alternative grow relative to the longer lived technologically fixed alternative.

Recalling that the benefit of a hydroelectric facility is given by the savings in cost over its least-cost alternative, we have noted that the savings (hence benefits) fall, other things remaining constant, with the technological updating of its shorter lived alternative. Accordingly, that portion of the benefits of a hydroelectric project which we call "capacity value" will be subject to reduction at the time the alternative against which it is compared is replaced by a technologically updated plant.

Technical change also affects the energy benefits of a hydroelectric project. The precise manner in which it affects the estimation of benefits, however, depends on the characteristics of the power system within which the hydroelectric plant will function. If the proposed hydro plant is considered for operation in a system with a substantial amount of existing thermal capacity, account must be taken of the difference between the efficiency of the older, more obsolete thermal plants and the technologically most advanced plant that is being considered. If the capacity is required because of growth in peak demands—hence is required for its capacity value—the capacity cost is attributable to the peak period operation. Any energy that the plant can provide during off-peak periods is available to displace energy that otherwise would be produced from the oldest, most obsolete, highest cost thermal facility (Brudenell and Gilbreath, 1958). The savings in fuel costs thus achieved are a credit to the thermal alternative, or alternatively, a debit against the savings (if any) in costs that a hydroelectric plant would otherwise show over its thermal alternative.[12] The economy achievable from using the newest plants at their highest

---

[12] Of course, if the hydro project would not exhibit any savings in cost over the thermal alternative without taking account of technical progress in the thermal sector, the "debit against the savings" would simply be an addition to the negative savings or excess costs. An example of this follows.

practicable plant factor is underscored by the experience that plant factors on fossil fuel plants have fallen to about 20 percent by the twentieth year (FPC, 1968, p. 24).

Conventional hydroelectric evaluation procedures will account for this gain in value of a thermal alternative due to technological advances in a mixed hydrothermal system (FPC, 1968). In the regional power system in which the Columbia River and its Snake tributary participate, however, the hydrolectric potential has been so large in relation to the power demands that until the present, for practical purposes, there has been no thermal component in the system. But, since the lower Snake River represents the last potentially economic hydroelectric energy (as distinguished from capacity),[13] project, additions to the regional power supply would need to be provided from thermal electric plants. This means that the thermal alternative to the Low Mountain Sheep–Pleasant Valley project initially would have no higher cost thermal energy to displace during off-peak periods. No savings in thermal energy costs are chargeable initially against the hydro plant's benefits. But, as the system expands in response to the growth in demand over time, additional thermal resources will enter the system. With advances in technology and lower energy costs, their off-peak energy will begin to displace some of the energy produced by the less advanced original thermal plant, thus reducing the energy benefits attributable to the hydro with advances in time and thermal electric production technology.

In appendix 5-A we present the computation model that is the more realistic version of the simple model introduced initially in chapter 3. The table giving the adjustments to energy costs that are necessary to bring the effects of technology into the evaluation process for the Hells Canyon hydro projects is also presented in this appendix. In these calculations a 30-year economic life was taken for the thermal plants. Initial plant factor was assumed to be 90 percent, with a decay of 3 percentage points per year. Accordingly, beginning with 90 percent, the plant factor is down to 30 percent by the twentieth year and zero, i.e., is replaced, in the thirtieth year. These figures, while broadly representative, were selected as well with an eye to computational convenience. Technological progress was assumed to fall within a range of 3 to 5 percent per year.[14] Results of the computa-

---

[13] Hydroelectric plants are sometimes developed simply for their capacity value, even with a net loss of energy, owing to the efficiency with which hydro plants can respond to surges in the load. This is the nature of pumped storage operations in which more *off-peak* thermal energy is used in pumping water into storage than can be obtained by releasing the water subsequently out of storage. The economy of the operation is explained by the fact that off-peak or "waste" energy is used in the pumping, whereas very valuable peaking power is obtained when the water is released at the appropriate time out of pumped storage.

[14] The rate of technological change was computed from data presented in the biennial reports of *Electrical World* over a period representing a consistent method

tions for different assumed rates of interest, rates of technological progress, and energy costs which were presented as relevant to the evaluation of thermal plant operations (FPC, 1970, Exhibit R-107-A) are given in table 5-3 in appendix 5-A.

The results of the analysis are shown in table 5-1. It is interesting to note that whatever the discount rate, within the range of 8 to 10 percent,[15] the costs exceed the benefits by a decisive margin. Annual costs exceed annual benefits by from $4 million to $6 million a year in the earlier years, falling a little in the later years as the power plants are assumed to begin operating with increased peaking capacity.[16] The present value of the excess of costs over benefits over the entire period runs on the order of $54 million to $57 million.

It is interesting to speculate why the applicants would manifest an interest in the undertaking when, in fact, its real costs would exceed the real benefits. There are, of course, several reasons why pecuniary benefits, or benefits to the applicants might exceed pecuniary private costs, in spite of the fact that social costs exceed social benefits for the case in point. One reason is that the Washington Public Power Supply System, being a quasi-public institution, benefits from a public policy granting tax exemptions for interest earnings on its debt instruments. This being the case, it is able to finance its facilities at private costs below the real costs to the economy, the public at large providing the subsidy. Secondly, a public policy that subsidizes the construction and operation of the federal transmission system in the regional power system similarly favors the use of

---

of reporting, 1950–68. It must be acknowledged that the model used for computation is applicable to the past, dominated by use of fossil fuels, and is not specifically relevant to the yet-unspecified changes in technology of the future which may be tied closely to nuclear reactors. The argument, however, is that while the relevant models would differ, the effects of technological change on costs of generation will be of the same or greater order of magnitude and should not be ignored. (See testimony of Krutilla, FPC, 1970, Transcript R-5838). Although, as noted earlier, at least some of the reduction in costs may be balanced by a rise in environmental pollution from the more efficient fossil fuel plants, estimated costs of dealing with the thermal pollution from a nuclear plant *are* included in our calculations (though not the possible but unknown costs of radioactive waste disposal).

[15] Discount rates of 8, 9, and 10 percent were used in the analysis because there appeared to be evidence that the opportunity costs of capital would fall within this range over the construction period of the projects. See, for example, testimony of Otto Eckstein (1968) and Arnold Harberger (1968); also see *Economic Analysis of Efficiency and Government,* Hearings before the Subcommittee on Economy in Government (Sept. 25, 30, Oct. 6, 1969).

[16] It should be noted that although the value of the hydro capacity *falls per unit* with the passage of time and advances in technology, the total value may increase because of the increase in the amount of capacity that is justified for a peak load operation. On balance, the latter influence countered the effects of technological changes as revealed by the lesser deficits of annual benefits compared with costs in the later years.

Table 5-1
Investment and Annual Costs–Benefits of Mountain Sheep–Pleasant Valley   ($000)

1976–1980	8%	9%	10%
1. Investment	$296,448	$300,919	$305,445
2. Annual costs	40,506	44,513	48,656
3. Gross annual benefits	35,704	38,985	42,412
4. Net benefits (3 − 2)	−4,714	−5,441	−6,157
1981–1990			
5. Investment	325,013	329,484	334,009
6. Annual costs	46,575	51,074	55,707
7. Gross annual benefits	42,035	46,133	50,105
8. Net annual benefits (7 − 8)	−4,540	−4,941	−5,603
1991–2025			
9. Investment	379,133	383,604	388,126
10. Annual costs	56,971	62,335	67,840
11. Gross annual benefits	53,106	57,758	62,604
12. Net annual benefits (13 − 12)	−3,865	−4,577	−5,236
13. Present value 1976–2025	−53,742	−55,042	−56,833

Sources: Appendix 5-B and Exhibit R-669.

facilities more remote from load centers than would be the case if the transmission charges over the longer distances represented their actual social costs. These conditions, which are not taken into account in conventional federal agency benefit–cost analyses, were necessary and of some importance to our analysis. Finally, a consideration to which some importance was apparently attached by the applicants (FPC, 1970, Transcript R-6534–R-6540) was the pecuniary advantage of a higher ratio of capital to operating costs in the face of anticipated continued inflation, as would be the case in having a hydro rather than a thermal electric plant.

While the analysis and adjustment of estimated costs in order to approximate the real cost of capital used in all of the facilities irrespective of ownership, public or private, makes a substantial difference in the perceived economic advantages of one alternative over the other, there is also the matter of the failure of the applicants to take into account the effects of technical advance in the alternative source of power. The question is, what is the quantitative significance of taking technical change into account? If we consult table 5-3 in appendix 5-A, we see that at a discount rate of 0.09 and an assumed rate of technical progress of 0.04/year, the failure to take technical change into account results in an overstatement of gross power benefits of approximately 7.5 percent. But since the overstatement is an absolute value expressed as a percent of *gross benefits,* it would be much greater expressed as a percent of *net benefits,* and hence as a percent of net present value. Under the conditions postulated, the failure to take technical progress into account will result in an understatement of the real costs of the hydro amounting to a present value of some $18,770,000, or an amount equal to roughly 50 percent of the unadjusted net loss. It is likely, therefore, that this item of nearly $19 million was simply overlooked in the calculations of the applicants.

While there may be some reasons (given the uneven distribution of capital subsidies and failure to consider long-run effects of technical change) why the applicants would prefer an economically unwarranted Mountain Sheep–Pleasant Valley hydro development over a thermal alternative, it is nonetheless true that there may have been real grounds for doing so at the time when the applications were first made. A great deal has occurred in the regional power system since the mid-1950s when the applications were first filed. All of the "first added" value of storage that would be attributable to the Hells Canyon projects in the 1950s has been eliminated by the acquisition of storage from domestic and Canadian sites on the Columbia and its tributaries (Krutilla, 1967a). The considerable value of incremental storage for production of firm energy and the substantial reduction of floodplain damages downstream that were originally attributable to the projects no longer exists due to the addition of the storage in the interim. But perhaps most significant will be the reduction in the alternative cost of power resulting from advances in the technology of thermal electric power production. In fact, calculation of the benefits and costs of the Mountain Sheep–Pleasant Valley project in terms of the circumstances relevant in the mid-1950s suggests that the projects at that time, compared with thermal alternatives, would have been quite economic (Krutilla Testimony, FPC, 1970, transcript page R-6566 ff).

The change in the relative economics of a project over time relates to the theoretical argument in chapter 3, section 4. With adverse changes in the relative value of two alternative means of meeting a power demand, the hydroelectricity would have had to be developed in some previous period or not at all. The problem, however, remains of discovering whether development in the present context is potentially economic at a different scale. We take up this issue below. Before proceeding, however, it is worth noting that, having analyzed the relative economics of the Mountain Sheep–Pleasant Valley project without attempting to evaluate the environmental opportunity costs of development, we learned the benefits did not equal the partial opportunity costs (i.e., excluding environmental opportunity costs). Thus the project should not be undertaken, quite independently of any environmental damage. In such cases we can avoid the difficult task of attempting an adequate evaluation of environmental opportunity costs.

5. ECONOMICS OF HIGH MOUNTAIN
SHEEP PROJECT

It is in some sense not entirely accurate to refer to the High Mountain Sheep alternative as a smaller scale development. With 2,250,000 acre feet of usable storage, its storage capacity would be over three and a half times as great as the Mountain Sheep–Pleasant Valley complex. Yet in spite of the greater storage, the amount of generating capacity that could be feasibly installed (1,400 megawatts) is rather limited. In order to install the amount of capacity that would permit the facility to serve ultimately as a peaking plant for the regional power system, a reregulating reservoir downstream would be required. A proposed dam and reservoir, the China Garden project potentially useful for this purpose, was not included in the application for license, but this is not ultimately of consequence because interdependent facilities ought to be evaluated jointly in any event. More significant is the fact that the China Garden project does not appear to be an economic project at any reasonable rate of discount (witness Chavez, FPC, 1970, Transcript R-5196). As a result, a substantially lesser amount of installed capacity, and correspondingly smaller total investment and gross benefit is associated with the High Mountain Sheep project than with the alternative Mountain Sheep–Pleasant Valley.

Table 5-2 shows the result of a benefit–cost analysis of the High

Table 5-2
Investment and Annual Costs–Benefits of High Mountain Sheep Project   ($000)

1976–1980	8%	9%	10%
1. Investment	$262,154	$266,786	$271,418
2. Annual costs	35,971	39,597	43,351
3. Gross annual benefits	37,741	40,901	44,394
4. Net benefits (3 − 2)	1,500	1,304	1,044
1981–1990			
5. Investment	262,154	266,786	271,418
6. Annual costs	35,971	39,597	43,351
7. Gross annual benefits	37,905	41,244	44,723
8. Net annual benefits (7 − 8)	1,934	1,647	1,372
1991–2025			
9. Investment	262,154	266,786	271,418
10. Annual costs	35,971	39,597	43,351
11. Gross annual benefits	36,985	40,241	43,635
12. Net annual benefits (13 − 12)	1,014	644	287
13. Present value 1976–2025	18,544	13,809	9,861

Sources: Appendix 5-B and Exhibit R-671.

Mountain Sheep project similar to that described in detail for Mountain Sheep–Pleasant Valley. Here we see that if the environmental costs are ignored, the project will show a positive net benefit at any of the discount rates used for analysis. This suggests then that even if we consider one of the divergent benefit trends, namely, the decline in the relative value of the hydro power from the Hells Canyon site due to the gains in technology over time in the alternative sources, *the value of the site for power production is positive*, when the environmental opportunity costs are not taken into account. It will be necessary then, in connection with High Mountain Sheep to attempt an evaluation of the opportunity returns precluded by its development.

Before the required analysis is carried out in chapter 6, it is necessary to address the question of the optimality of the selected scale, since only two scales of development were explicitly analyzed.

First, since all of the head between the sites and the upstream Hells Canyon project of the Idaho Power Company would be developed by either of the two proposals, building the dams to increased heights would only reduce the head at the existing upstream facility. There is the potential for a larger scale involving more developed head if a single large dam is located downstream. This, in fact, is similar to an old WPPSS proposal for development of the Nez Perce site. Being downstream, it could provide for more head, larger storage and greater streamflow because the contribution of the Salmon River flows would be added to the volume falling over the developed head at the Nez Perce site. While this represents an extraordinary hydroelectric site, WPPSS's application for license to develop this site was denied by the FPC Examiner's preliminary decision of October 1962. Denial was based largely on the feared destruction of the anadromous fisheries of both the Salmon and Snake rivers—a position to which the Supreme Court decision of 1967 gives support. Accordingly, enlarging the scale of development by relocating the site downstream does not appear to be a relevant alternative for possibly extra-economic reasons.

The possibility that a scale smaller than that defined by the High Mountain Sheep project might be even more profitable needs a word. The economics of hydropower production suggest that this is not likely. The reason is that, up to a point, there are economies of scale in dam building. The large fixed costs of foundation and spillway can be spread to an extent over a larger structure, so that increasing the scale of a single dam at Mountain Sheep should yield increasing returns—again, up to a point. Although we cannot *a priori* rule out the possibility of a project having some more desirable mix of characteristics, it would seem that the High Mountain Sheep project is the most promising, currently, and the one deserving study of its environmental effects.[17]

[17] It should be mentioned that the Appaloosa project represents in one sense a

Consideration of environmental effects suggests a possible problem with our conclusion. While it may be true that a smaller project would yield smaller net power benefits, it may also be true that the environmental benefits from a smaller project would be differentially greater (absolutely). This latter prospect is very unlikely, however, because even a fairly substantial reduction in project scale would not result in much of a reduction in its modification of the natural setting in that reach of the canyon. Put differently, the (declining) preservation benefit function is relatively flat over an interval including the various projects under consideration.

What this suggests is that the behavior of the benefit function in the case of the typical hydro project should be just a bit more complicated than the formal specification in chapter 3 would suggest. In fact, the possibility that incremental project benefits first increase was noted there. Here we are suggesting that the benefits associated with nonproject uses of the environment may fall rapidly with the introduction of even a relatively small project (breaking up the continuity of a long reach of free-flowing stream in canyon country). They may level off in a "middle region" and eventually fall more rapidly again with intensive development as, for example, in the movement from a High Mountain Sheep to a Nez Perce-type development. If this is true, the theoretical possibility exists that there may be more than a single point satisfying first-order optimality conditions, and a choice among such points could, in an empirical case, be made on the basis of calculations and comparisons of the opportunity returns and costs at each.

REFERENCES

Barnett, H. J. and Morse, Chandler. 1963. *Scarcity and Growth: The Economics of Natural Resource Availability* (Baltimore: Johns Hopkins Press).

Brudenell, R. N. and Gilbreath, J. H. 1958. "Economic Complementary Operations of Hydro Storage and Steam Power in the Integrated TVA System." Paper presented at the AIEE summer meetings, Buffalo, New York.

Burt, O. R. and Brewer, Durward. 1971. "Estimation of Net Social Benefits from Outdoor Recreation," *Econometrica*, vol. 39, no. 5.

Cicchetti, C. J., Fisher, A. C., and Smith, V. K. 1972. "An Economic and Econometric Model for the Valuation of Environmental Resources with

---

somewhat reduced High Mountain Sheep project. Being 70 feet lower, with a reservoir 8 miles shorter and storage of approximately 750,000 acre feet less than High Mountain Sheep, it represents a smaller project. But a combination of somewhat different mix of features, along with a lavish use of capital since it was designed on the presumption of the applicability of a 3⅛ percent interest rate, resulted in a substantially more costly structure. A preliminary examination of the project revealed that it was the least economic of the alternatives proposed (Krutilla, 1969a).

an Application to Outdoor Recreation at Mineral King." Paper presented at the annual meeting of the Econometric Society, Toronto.

————, Seneca, Joseph and Davidson, Paul. 1969. *The Demand and Supply of Outdoor Recreation* (Washington, D.C.: Bureau of Outdoor Recreation).

Clawson, Marion. 1958. "Methods of Measuring the Demand for and Value of Outdoor Recreation," Resources for the Future Reprint No. 10.

Eckstein, Otto. 1958. Water Resource Development: The Economics of Project Evaluation (Cambridge, Mass.: Harvard University Press).

————. 1968. *Economic Analysis of Public Investment Decisions: Interest Rate Policy and Discounting Analysis.* Hearings before the Subcommittee on Economy in Government of the Joint Economic Committee, 90 Cong., 2 sess., July 30, 31, and August 1, 1968 (Washington, D.C.: Government Printing Office).

Federal Power Commission. 1968. Hydroelectric Power Evaluation P-35 (handbook) (Washington, D.C.: Government Printing Office).

————. 1970. "In the Matter of: Pacific Northwest Power Company and Washington Public Power Supply System," Projects 2243 and 2273, hearings, Lewiston, Idaho, Portland, Oregon, and Washington, D.C., 1968–1970.

Harberger, Arnold. 1968. *Economics of Public Investment Decisions: Interest Rate Policy and Discounting Analysis.* Hearings before the Subcommittee on Economy in Government of the Joint Economic Committee, 90 Cong., 2 sess., July 30, 31, and August 1, 1968 (Washington, D.C.: Government Printing Office).

————. 1971. "Three Basic Postulates for Applied Welfare Economics: An Interpretive Essay," *Journal of Economic Literature,* vol. IX, no. 3.

Krutilla, J. V. 1967a. *The Columbia River Treaty: The Economics of an International River Basin Development* (Baltimore: Johns Hopkins Press).

————. 1967b. "Conservation Reconsidered," *American Economic Review,* vol. L, no. 4.

————. 1969a. *On the Economics of Preservation or Development of the Lower Portion of the Hells Canyon.* Draft Report to the Federal Power Commission.

————. 1969b. *The Differential Growth in Value of the Alternatives on the Lower Hells Canyon of the Snake River.* Draft Report to the Federal Power Commission.

————, and Cicchetti, C. J. 1973. "Benefit–Cost Analysis and Technologically Induced Relative Price Changes: The Case of Environmental Irreversibilities," in *Benefit–Cost Analyses of Federal Programs.* A compendium of papers submitted to the Subcommittee on Priorities and Economy in Government of the Joint Economic Committee, 92 Cong., 2 sess. (Washington, D.C.: Government Printing Office).

Leopold, L. B. 1969. "Quantitative Comparisons of Some Aesthetic Factors Among Rivers," Geological Survey Circular 620 (Washington, D.C.).

Potter, Neal and Christy, F. T., Jr. 1962. *Trends in Natural Resource Commodities: Statistics of Prices, Output, Consumption, Foreign Trade and*

Employment in the United States, 1870–1957 (Baltimore: Johns Hopkins Press).

"16th Steam Station Cost Survey." Reprinted from Nov. 3, 1969 issue of *Electrical World* (McGraw-Hill).

Smith, V. K. 1972. "The Effect of Technological Change on Different Uses of Environmental Resources" in *Natural Environments: Studies in Theoretical and Applied Analysis,* John V. Krutilla, ed. (Baltimore: Johns Hopkins Press).

————. 1974. *Technical Change, Relative Prices, and Environmental Evaluation* (Baltimore: Johns Hopkins Press).

Steiner, P. O. 1965. "The Role of Alternative Cost in Project Design and Selection," *Quarterly Journal of Economics,* vol. 79, no. 3.

Udall, Secretary of Interior *v.* Federal Power Commission, *et al.,* 387 U.S. 428 (1967).

U.S. Congress, House of Representatives, *Columbia River and Tributaries, Northwestern United States.* H. Doc. 531, 81 Cong., 2 sess. (1950).

Water Resources Council. 1973. *Establishment of Principles and Standards for Planning Water Related Land Resources, Federal Register,* Sept. 30, 1973.

TECHNICAL CHANGE ADJUSTMENT
COMPUTATIONAL MODEL (Exhibit R-670)

Over the first 30-year period, taken as the useful life of a thermal facility, let PVC_t represent the present value of annual costs per kilowatt of the thermal alternative in year t:

$$PVC_1 = C_1 + E(8760F)$$

$$PVC_2 = \left\{C_1 + [E8760(F - k)] + \frac{E}{(1 + r)}(8760k)\right\}\left(\frac{1}{(1 + i)}\right)$$

.
.
.

$$PVC_n = \left\{C_1 + E[8760(F - (n - 1)k)]\right.$$

$$\left. + \frac{E}{(1 + r)^{n-1}}[8760(n - 1)k]\right\}\left(\frac{1}{1 + i}\right)^{n-1}$$

for $1 < n < 30$

where

C_1 = capacity cost/kW/yr during first 30-year period
E = energy cost/kWh
F = the plant factor (0.90)
k = a constant representing the time decay of the plant factor (0.03)
i = the discount rate
r = the annual rate of technological progress

Writing out the nth term yields:

$$PVC_n = \frac{C_I}{(1 + i)^{n-1}} + \frac{8760EF}{(1 + i)^{n-1}} - \frac{8760Ek(n - 1)}{(1 + i)^{n-1}}$$

$$+ \frac{8760Ek(n - 1)}{[(1 + r)(1 + i)]^{n-1}}$$

These terms can be summed individually using standard formulas for geometric progressions[18] and then factored to form:

$$PVC_{1, \ldots, 30} = \sum_{n=1}^{30} PVC_n = (C_I + 8760EF)\left[\frac{1 - a^{30}}{1 - a}\right]$$

$$- \frac{8760Ek}{i}\left\{\frac{1 - a^{29}}{1 - a} - 29a^{29}\right\}$$

$$+ \frac{8760Ek}{(1 + r)(1 + i) - 1}\left\{\frac{1 - b^{29}}{1 - b} - 29b^{29}\right\}$$

where $\quad a = \left(\frac{1}{1 + i}\right)$

$$b = \frac{1}{(1 + r)(1 + i)}$$

Over years $31, \ldots, T$ the cost expressions are similar except that we are dealing with only a 20-year additional period and all terms thus get discounted by a factory of $(1/1 + i)^{30}$. Hence, using similar formulas for the sum of geometric series, the present value of annual costs per kilowatt from this latter period is determined to be:

$$PVC_{31, \ldots, T} = \sum_{n=31}^{T} PVC_n = \left(\frac{1}{1 + i}\right)^{30}\left\{(C_{II} + 8760E'F)\left[\frac{1 - a^{20}}{1 - a}\right]\right.$$

$$- \frac{8760E'k}{i}\left[\frac{1 - a^{19}}{1 - a} - 19a^{19}\right]$$

$$\left. + \frac{8760E'k}{(1 + r)(1 + i) - 1}\left[\frac{1 - b^{19}}{1 - b} - 19b^{19}\right]\right\}$$

where $\quad C_{II} = \frac{C_I}{(1 + r)^{30}}$

$$E' = \frac{E}{(1 + r)^{30}}$$

The overall present value is:

$$PVC_{1, \ldots, T} = PVC_1 + \ldots + PVC_{30} + PVC_{31} + \ldots + PVC_T$$

Traditional analyses are based essentially on the model given below.

$$K = \sum_{n=1}^{T} \frac{[C_I + E(8760F)]}{(1 + i)^{n-1}} \text{ or, which is equivalent,}$$

$$= [C_I + E(8760F)]\left[\frac{1 - a^T}{1 - a}\right] \begin{array}{l}\text{to be consistent with previous}\\\text{notation}\end{array}$$

[18] See p. 357 of the C.R.C. Standard Mathematical Tables, 12th ed., Cleveland: Chemical Rubber Publishing Co., 1961.

The adjustment factors in table 5-3 are obtained as follows:

$K/PVC_{1,\ldots,T}$

Appendix 5-B
ESTIMATING PROJECT COSTS AND BENEFITS

Estimated costs of the Low Mountain Sheep–Pleasant Valley project were obtained by taking from Exhibit R-100-A (FPC, 1970) the construction cost of project facilities, exclusive of indicated costs for recreation and related access facilities. To this was added interest during construction at 8, 9, and 10 percent, which, along with other items of expenditure preparatory to operations, led to investment in the project of $296,448,000, $300,919,000, and $305,444,000 respectively for initial level of development (1976–1980). With increased installation of supplementary peaking tory to operations, led to investment in the project of $296,448,000, $329,484,000, and $334,009,000 respectively for interest during construction at 8, 9, and 10 percent. For the period beyond 1990, the corresponding investment was estimated to be $379,133,000, $383,604,000, and $388,129,000. These investment outlays serve as the basis of the annual costs underlying Exhibit No. R-669, reproduced for convenience in this appendix.

Items 1 through 7 in table 5-4 from Exhibit R-669 display the costs of the proposed project. The table notes provide a detailed item-by-item explanation of the derivation of the various cost items. Since the remaining

Table 5-3

Overstatement of Hydroelectric Capacity and Energy Values by Neglecting Influence of Technological Advances

Discount rate/year $i =$	Technological advance rate/year $r_t =$	$/kW	Estimated hydro capacity values as a percentage of hydro generating values adjusted for influence of technological advance of various capacity and energy costs		
			Percent at 0.98 mill per kWh	Percent at 1.22 mills per kWh	Percent at 1.28 mills per kWh
0.08	0.03	$27.43	107.4	107.9	108.0
	0.04		109.0	109.6	109.7
	0.05		110.2	110.9	111.1
0.09	0.03	$30.08	105.9	106.4	106.5
	0.04		107.2	107.7	107.8
	0.05		108.2	108.8	108.9
0.10	0.03	$32.89	104.8	105.1	105.2
	0.04		105.8	106.2	106.3
	0.05		106.5	107.1	107.2

items given under "gross benefits (I)" and "gross benefits (II)" are dependent on the material developed in table 5-5, we skip them for a moment and consider the latter table before continuing down the list of items in table 5-4.

Items 1 through 4 in table 5-5 serve as the basis for estimating annual capacity cost per kilowatt of the nuclear alternative to the proposed hydroelectric development. A detailed explanation of the derivation of these figures is given in the table notes.

Under annual costs for generation and supplemental peaking are shown the annual capacity and energy values, and the total power generating costs as explained in notes e through g. Note for further use the estimated total annual power generating costs; namely, item 7.

The estimated supplemental peaking requirements and costs, as explained in note h, are developed, along with the related transmission costs for both the nuclear base load and the peaking supplement in items 9 and 10 as described in the notes. This provides an estimate of the total annual cost exclusive of generating costs, item 11.

Returning now to item 7, the total generating costs corresponding to each of the separate interest rates, we obtain the estimate of generating costs adjusted for technological advance, item 12, by dividing the appropriate factor taken from table 5-3 (the adjustment for technical change model) in appendix 5-A. For example, take from table 5-5 the total generating cost (item 7) for 1976–1980 corresponding to an interest rate of 9 percent. This will be $23,280,000. Now go to table 5-3 and select the block of technological advance adjustment factors corresponding to $i = 0.09$, and technological advance rate, $r_t = 0.03$, say, for a cost per kilowatt of capacity per year of $30.08 (corresponding to $i = 0.09$) and mills per kilowatt hour energy of 0.98 (corresponding to the cost of energy per kilowatt hour estimated to prevail in the period 1976–1980). Finding the technological advance adjustment factor to be 105.9, we divide it into the unadjusted generating cost of $23,280,000 (item 7 corresponding to $i = 9$ percent) which gives the adjusted generating cost $21,983,000 (item 12 in table 5-5) for $r_t = 0.03$ and discount rate of 9 percent. This adjusted generating cost is then added to item 11 (or total annual costs excluding generation, $17,269,000) to get item 13 or total annual costs of $39,252,000 for 1976–1980 at 9 percent.

For identical items for 1981–1990 and 1991–2025, the procedure would be the same except that we select from table 5-3 the adjustment factors corresponding to energy costs in mills per kilowatt hour of 1.22 and 1.28 respectively to correspond to costs of energy per kilowatt hour estimated to prevail in the two later periods of analysis.

If we were to go through the same set of steps for each of the other two estimates of total generating costs corresponding to interest rates of

8 and 10 percent, and the other eight adjustment factors corresponding to the three rates of technological advance and discount rates, we would get the other eight estimates of total annual generating costs given under item 13 for 1976–1980. The same is true for 1981–1990 and 1991–2025, using instead adjustment factors appropriate to the change in energy cost/kWh estimated to prevail in the periods corresponding to 1981–1990 and 1991–2025.

The nine estimates of total annual costs for each of the three time periods represent the estimated power benefit from the hydroelectric development following the rationale that the value of power can be no greater than the cost of the most economic alternative source (i.e., the benefit thus is the measure of the value of the resource savings, if any).

Having the estimated power benefits from hydroelectric development, we can return to table 5-4 to complete the analysis. Under the heading "gross benefits (I)" for 1976–1980 we are shown the imputed flood control benefit from the development, obtained as indicated in table note h. Next we can take the range of total annual costs given in table 5-5, corresponding to the range of technological advance of from 3 to 5 percent per year, and display them in the appropriate place in table 5-4. For example, consider the case of an interest rate of 9 percent for 1976–1980 in table 5-4. At $r_t = 0.03$, the estimated annual cost of the alternative is \$39,252,000; for $r_t = 0.05$, it is \$38,985,000. This is displayed as the power benefit (item 9) in the column corresponding to an interest rate of 9 percent. The power and flood control benefits (items 8 and 9) are summed to give us the total gross benefits (item 10) which range from \$38,872,000, based on an assumed rate of technological progress of 5 percent per year, to \$39,344,000, based on an assumed rate of technological progress of 3 percent per year.

We then subtract total annual costs from total gross benefits (I) (item 10) and get (at an interest rate of 9 percent) negative net benefits (item 11) ranging from \$5,169,000 to \$5,641,000. The same procedure would be followed to obtain the corresponding ranges of (negative) net benefits for assumed rates of interest of 8 percent and 10 percent.

Proceeding to the heading "gross benefits (II)," the method is the same as that for "gross benefits (I)" except that for the power benefits a rate of technological progress falling intermediate between 3 and 5 percent, namely $r_t = 0.04$, has been used, and as a result a single-valued estimate of the net benefits is provided as item 14. Assuming an interest rate of 9 percent and a rate of technological progress of 4 percent per year, we get estimated annual negative net benefits (losses) of \$5,441,000 for the period 1976–1980; \$4,941,000 for the period 1981–1990; and \$4,577,000 for the period 1991–2025. The first 5-year annual loss of \$5,441,000, discounted at 9 percent per year, gives a net present loss over the period

1976–1980 of $21,165,000 as shown in item 15 for 1976–1980. For the period 1981–1990 for the 9 percent discount with technological advance taken at 4 percent per year, the net annual loss of $4,941,000 obtained in the same way as described for the previous 5-year period gives a 1976 present worth (loss) of $20,604,000 and is shown as item 15 for 1981–1990. In the final period, the net annual loss of $4,577,000 over the remaining 35 years (1991–2025) when discounted at 9 percent gives a present worth of $13,273,000, again shown as item 15. The sum of these discounted annual losses, then, gives us a total net loss of $56,833,000 expressed in 1976 worth.

The estimated capital and annual costs and benefits for the High Mountain Sheep project follow the procedure described above. Exhibit R-671, giving the relevant estimated costs and notes, is reproduced in tables 5-6 and 5-7.

Table 5-4

Investment and Annual Costs–Benefits of Pleasant Valley–Low Mountain Sheep (Mountain Sheep Plan No. 2)

($000)

	1976–1980			1981–1990			1991–2025		
	8%	9%	10%	8%	9%	10%	8%	9%	10%
1. Investment (Excluding recreation and access)[a]	296,448	300,919	305,444	325,013	329,484	334,009	379,133	383,604	388,129
ANNUAL COSTS									
2. Fixed charges[b]	29,378	32,680	36,134	32,208	35,782	39,513	37,572	41,659	45,916
3. O & M[c]	1,966	1,966	1,966	2,388	2,388	2,388	2,941	2,941	2,941
4. A & G[d]	634	634	634	799	799	799	1,014	1,014	1,014
5. Total generation costs[e]	31,978	35,280	38,734	35,395	38,969	42,700	41,527	45,614	49,871
6. Transmission costs[f]	8,528	9,233	9,922	11,180	12,105	13,007	15,444	16,721	17,969
7. Total annual cost[g]	40,506	44,513	48,656	46,575	51,074	55,707	56,971	62,335	67,840
GROSS BENEFITS (1)									
8. Flood control[h]	87	87	87	87	87	87	87	87	87
9. Power[i]	36,002–35,488	39,252–38,785	42,637–42,257	41,098–41,634	45,823–46,316	49,814–50,267	52,772–53,327	57,455–57,930	62,324–62,758
10. Total gross benefits[j]	36,089–35,575	39,344–38,872	42,724–42,344	41,185–41,721	45,910–46,400	49,902–50,354	52,859–53,414	57,542–58,017	62,411–62,845
11. Net benefits[k]	-4,417– -5,018	-5,169– -5,641	-5,932– -6,312	-4,854– -5,390	-5,164– -6,014	-5,353– -5,805	-3,557– -4,112	-4,318– -4,793	-4,995– -5,429

114

GROSS BENEFITS (II)

(8) Flood control	87	87	87	87	87	87	87	87	87
12. Power[l]	35,705	38,985	42,412	41,948	46,046	50,017	53,019	57,671	62,517
13. Total gross benefits[m]	35,792	39,072	42,499	42,035	46,133	50,104	53,106	57,758	62,604
14. Net benefit[n]	−4,714	−5,441	−6,157	−4,540	−4,941	−5,603	−3,865	−4,577	−5,236
15. PV_d[o]	−18,809	−21,165	−23,335	−20,748	−20,604	−21,403	−14,185	−13,273	−12,095
Total PV_d (1976 worth)	−53,742				−55,042			−56,833	

[a]Investment data from Exhibit R 100-A (see FPC, 1970) sheets 2 and 4 obtained from construction costs, adding interest during construction at 8, 9, and 10% and excluding cost of recreational facilities and access roads for recreational purposes.

[b]Interest and amortization (50-year schedule), interim replacement (0.14%), insurance (0.10%), and state and local taxes (1.5%) witness Froggatt, (FPC, 1968, p. 9 and table 36, p. 87).

[c]Exhibit R 100-A, less operation and maintenance associated with recreation.

[d]Exhibit R 100-A.

[e]Sum of items 2, 3, and 4.

[f]Transmission investment outlays obtained from witness Bell with annual cost adjusted for varying interest rates, operation and maintenance and administrative and general from Exhibit R-118 (witness Bell) and state and local taxes 1.5% of investment. Costs/kW are $5.20, $5.63, and $6.05 respectively for 8, 9, and 10% (Exhibit 107-A, line 36, column 8, 1,640 MW; 9, 2,150 MW; and column 10, 2,970 MW).

[g]Sum of items 5 and 6.

[h]Exhibit R 107-A, line 41.

[i]Total annual costs for nuclear alternative (item 13 in table 5-5) for respective years. For 1976–80, use $r_i = 0.03$ and 0.05.

[j]Sum of items 8 and 9.

[k]Item 10 minus item 7.

[l]Total annual costs for nuclear alternative (item 13 in table 5-5) for 1976–80, 1981–90, and 1991–2025, respectively, with $r_i = 0.04$.

[m]Sum of items 8 and 12.

[n]Item 13 minus item 7.

[o]Item 14, net annual benefits, discounted by appropriate factor to give sum of annual benefits in terms of 1976 worths.

Table 5-5

Investment and Annual Cost of Pleasant Valley–Low Mountain Sheep (Mountain Sheep Plan No. 2) Alternate Nuclear Base plus Supplemental Peaking

	Units	1976–1980			1981–1990			1991–2025		
		8%	9%	10%	8%	9%	10%	8%	9%	10%
1. Investment/kW^a	($)	203.45	208.38	213.30	203.45	208.38	213.30	203.45	208.38	213.30
ANNUAL COSTS/kW										
2. Fixed charges, plant^b	($/kW)	22.34	24.71	27.24	22.34	24.71	27.24	22.34	24.71	27.24
3. Fixed charges, fuel inventory^c	($/kW)	2.59	2.87	3.15	2.59	2.87	3.15	2.59	2.87	3.15
3a. Fixed operating costs^e	($/kW)	2.50	2.50	2.50	2.50	2.50	2.50	2.50	2.50	2.50
4. Total annual cost/kW^d	($)	27.43	30.08	32.89	27.43	30.08	32.89	27.43	30.08	32.89
Annual costs										
Generation costs										
5. Nuclear capacity^e	($000)	16,129	17,687	19,339	15,498	16,995	18,583	14,812	16,243	17,761
6. Nuclear energy^f	($000)	5,597	5,593	5,593	6,805	6,805	6,805	6,689	6,689	6,689
7. Total generating costs^g	($000)	21,722	23,280	24,932	21,303	23,800	25,388	21,501	22,932	24,450
8. Supplemental peaking^h										
(a) 982 MW added (1976–80)	($000)	10,321	11,499	12,756	10,321	11,499	12,756	10,321	11,499	12,756
(b) 468 MW added (1981–90)	($000)	—	—	—	4,338	4,806	5,293	4,338	4,806	5,293
(c) 745 MW added (1991–2025)	($000)	—	—	—	—	—	—	8,985	9,715	10,475
Transmission										
9. Nuclear base^j	($000)	1,607	1,705	1,809	1,546	1,640	1,740	1,476	1,566	1,661
10. Peaking supplement^i										
(a) 982 MW (1976–80)	($000)	3,849	4,065	4,282	3,849	4,065	4,282	3,849	4,065	4,282
(b) 1,450 MW (1981–90)	($000)	—	—	—	5,684	6,003	6,322	5,684	6,003	6,322
(c) 2,195 MW (1991–2025)	($000)	—	—	—	—	—	—	2,615	2,809	3,010
11. Total excluding generating^k	($000)	15,777	17,269	18,847	21,889	23,948	26,111	33,419	36,398	39,517

116

12. Generating costs adjusted for technical advance[l]										
(1) $r_t = 0.03$	($000)	20,225	21,983	23,790	19,745	22,368	24,156	19,908	21,532	23,241
(2) $r_t = 0.04$	($000)	19,928	21,716	23,565	19,437	22,098	23,906	19,600	21,273	23,001
(3) $r_t = 0.05$	($000)	19,711	21,516	23,410	19,209	21,875	23,704	19,353	21,057	22,807
13. Total annual costs[m]										
(1) $r_t = 0.03$	($000)	36,002	39,252	42,637	41,634	46,316	50,267	53,327	57,930	62,758
(2) $r_t = 0.04$	($000)	35,705	38,985	42,412	41,326	46,046	50,017	53,019	57,671	62,518
(3) $r_t = 0.05$	($000)	35,488	38,785	42,257	41,098	45,823	49,815	52,772	57,455	62,324

[a]Investment based on data in Exhibit R 81-B (FPC, 1970); construction costs $169.00/kW with interest during construction computed at 8, 9, and 10%.

[b]Fixed charges include: interest and amortization (depreciation) 35-year schedule, interim replacement (0.35%), regular insurance (0.25%), special insurance (0.55%) and state and local taxes (1.25%) for total of 2.40% plus debt service charges (Exhibit R 54-B, FPC, 1970).

[c]Relevant interest rate plus state and local taxes times $28.0/kW (fuel inventory/kW) based on Exhibit R 54-B (FPC, 1970).

[c']Exhibit R 618-A (FPC, 1970), sheet 1, line 13.

[d]Sum of 2, 3, and 3a, i.e., $27.43, $30.08, $32.89 per kilowatt respectively for interest at 8, 9, and 10%.

[e]Exhibit R 107-A (FPC, 1970) line 6 (588, 565, and 540 MW, respectively) multiplied by cost/kW (item 4).

[f]For 1976, use Exhibit R 107-A, line 27 (5,707 GWh) multiplied by 0.98 mill/kWh; for 1981–90, use 5,578 GWh × 1.22 mills/kWh; 1991–2025, 5,226 GWh × 1.28 mills/kWh.

[g]Sum of items 5 and 6.

[h]For 1976–80, use Exhibit R 107-A, line 22 as corrected (982 MW) multiplied by $10.51, $11.71, and $12.99 per kilowatt respectively for 8, 9, and 10% interest. See note h in table 5-6. For 1981–90, use Exhibit R 107-A, line 22, as corrected (1,450 MW) multiplying first 982 MW by $10.51, $11.71, and $12.99 per kilowatt for 8, 9, and 10% interest respectively and 468 MW by $9.27, $10.27, and $11.31 per kilowatt respectively for 8, 9, and 10%. See note h in table 5-6 for further explanation. For 1991–2025, use Exhibit R 107-A, line 22 as corrected (2,195 MW). Costs for first 1,450 MW supplemental peaking as given in item 8(b) remaining 745 MW at $12.06, $13.04, and $14.06 per kilowatt respectively for 8, 9, and 10% interest. Basic construction cost for pumped storage, annual costs, and pumping power provided by witness Chavez.

[i]Exhibit R 107-A, line 4 (576, 554, and 529 MW respectively) multiplied by $2.79, $2.96, and $3.14 per kilowatt for 8, 9, and 10% respectively. Transmission basic data provided by witness Bell.

[j]For 1976–80 and 1981–90, use Exhibit R 107-A, line 22 as corrected (982 and 1,450 MW, respectively) multiplied as $3.92, $4.14, and $4.36 per kilowatt for 8, 9, and 10% respectively. For 1991–2025, use Exhibit R 107-A, line 22 (2,195 MW) 1,450 MW of which are multiplied by $3.92, $4.14, and $4.36 per kilowatt for 8, 9, and 10% respectively and the remainder (2,195 − 1,450 =) 745 MW multiplied by $3.51, $3.77, and $4.04 per kilowatt for 8, 9, and 10%. Basic transmission data provided by witness Bell.

[k]Sum of items 8, 9, and 10.

[l]Item 7 divided by appropriate factors given in table 5-3, Exhibit R-670 (FPC, 1970).

[m]Sum of items 11 and 12.

Table 5-6

Investment and Annual Costs–Benefits of High Mountain Sheep (Mountain Sheep Plan No. 1)

($000)

	1976–1980			1981–1990			1991–2025		
	8%	9%	10%	8%	9%	10%	8%	9%	10%
1. Investment (Excluding recreation and access)[a]	262,154	266,786	271,418	262,154	266,786	271,418	262,154	266,786	271,418
ANNUAL COSTS									
2. Fixed charges[b]	25,979	28,973	32,109	25,979	28,973	32,109	25,979	28,973	32,109
3. O & M[c]	1,820	1,820	1,820	1,820	1,820	1,820	1,820	1,820	1,820
4. A & G[d]	528	528	528	528	528	528	528	528	528
5. Total generation costs[e]	28,327	31,321	34,457	28,327	31,321	34,457	28,327	31,321	34,457
6. Transmission costs[f]	7,644	8,276	8,894	7,644	8,276	8,894	7,644	8,276	8,894
7. Total annual cost[g]	35,971	39,597	43,351	35,971	39,597	43,351	35,971	39,597	43,351
GROSS BENEFITS (I)									
8. Flood control[h]	245	245	245	245	245	245	245	245	245
9. Power[i]	37,579–36,968	40,972–40,417	44,417–43,966	38,033–37,382	41,314–40,739	44,769–44,244	37,099–36,451	40,299–39,745	43,671–43,165
10. Total gross benefits[j]	37,824–37,213	41,217–40,662	44,662–44,210	38,277–37,627	41,559–40,984	45,014–44,489	37,344–36,696	40,544–39,990	43,916–43,410
11. Net benefits[k]	1,242–1,853	1,065–1,620	860–1,311	1,656–2,306	1,387–1,962	1,137–1,663	725–1,373	393–947	58–565

Gross benefits (II)

(8) Flood control	245	245	245	245	245	245	245	245	245
12. Power[l]	37,226	40,656	44,150	37,660	40,999	44,478	36,740	39,996	43,390
13. Total gross benefits[m]	37,471	40,901	44,394	37,905	41,244	44,723	36,985	40,241	43,635
14. Net benefit[n]	1,500	1,304	1,044	1,934	1,647	1,372	1,014	644	287
15. PV_d[o]	5,985	5,073	3,957	8,838	6,868	5,241	3,721	1,868	663
Total PV_d (1976 worth)			18,544			13,809			9,861

[a] Investment developed from construction costs, Exhibit R 101-A, and Exhibit R 102-A (FPC, 1970), corresponding to costs of capital of 8, 9, and 10% (interest during construction) plus costs of additional units given in Exhibit R-99-A.

[b] Fixed charges consist of relevant interest and amortization (50-year schedule), interim replacement (0.14%), insurance (0.10%) and state and local taxes (1.50%). (Froggatt testimony, FPC, 1968, p. 9 and p. 87, table 36).

[c,d] Operation and maintenance and administrative and general costs from Exhibit R 102-A less recreation operation and maintenance.

[e] Sum of items 2 through 4.

[f] Capital investment of $71,544,000 (witness Bell) with annual costs adjusted to correspond to witness Krutilla's fixed charges for interest rates from 8-10%; operation and maintenance and administrative and general from Exhibit R-118 (witness Bell) and state and local taxes 1.5% of investment. Cost/kW are $5.20, $5.63, and $6.05 respectively for 8, 9, and 10%.

[g] Sum of items 5 and 6.

[h] Exhibit No. R 107-A, line 41.

[i] Item 13 (1) and (3), table 5-7.

[j] Sum of items 8 and 9.

[k] Item 10 minus item 7.

[l] Item 13 (2), table 5-7.

[m] Sum of items 8 and 12.

[n] Item 13 minus item 7.

[o] Item 14, net annual benefits, discounted by appropriate factor to give sum of benefits in terms of 1976 worths.

Table 5-7

Investment and Annual Cost of High Mountain Sheep (Mountain Sheep Plan No. 1) Alternate Nuclear Base plus Supplemental Peaking

	Units	1976–1980			1981–1990			1991–2025		
		8%	9%	10%	8%	9%	10%	8%	9%	10%
1. Investment/kW[a]	($)	203.45	208.38	213.30	203.45	208.38	213.30	203.45	208.38	213.30
ANNUAL COSTS/kW										
2. Fixed charges, plant[b]	($/kW)	22.34	24.71	27.24	22.34	24.71	27.24	22.34	24.71	27.24
3. Fixed charges, fuel inventory[c]	($/kW)	2.59	2.87	3.15	2.59	2.87	3.15	2.59	2.87	3.15
3a. Fixed operating costs[e]	($/kW)	2.50	2.50	2.50	2.50	2.50	2.50	2.50	2.50	2.50
4. Total annual cost/kW[d]	($)	27.43	30.08	32.89	27.43	30.08	32.89	27.43	30.08	32.89
ANNUAL COSTS										
Generation costs										
5. Nuclear capacity[e]	($000)	19,201	21,056	23,023	18,049	19,793	21,642	17,363	19,041	20,819
6. Nuclear energy[f]	($000)	6,596	6,596	6,596	7,941	7,941	7,941	7,715	7,715	7,715
7. Total generating costs[g]	($000)	25,797	27,652	29,619	25,990	27,735	29,583	25,078	26,756	28,534
8. Supplemental peaking[h]										
(a) 807 MW	($000)	8,482	9,450	10,483	8,482	9,450	10,483	8,482	9,450	10,483
(b) 38 MW	($000)	—	—	—	352	390	430	352	390	430
(c)	($000)	—	—	—	—	—	—	—	—	—
Transmission										
9. Nuclear base[i]	($000)	1,914	2,030	2,154	1,800	1,909	2,025	1,733	1,838	1,950
10. Peaking supplement[j]										
(a) 807 MW	($000)	3,163	3,381	3,518	3,312	3,498	3,684	3,312	3,498	3,684
(b) 845 MW	($000)	—	—	—	—	—	—	—	—	—
11. Total excluding generating[k]	($000)	13,559	14,861	16,155	13,946	15,247	16,622	13,879	15,176	16,547

12. Generating costs adjusted for technical advance[l]

(1) $r_t = 0.03$	($000)	28,262	26,111	24,020	24,087	26,067	28,147	23,220	25,123	27,124
(2) $r_t = 0.04$	($000)	27,995	25,795	23,667	23,714	25,752	27,856	22,861	24,820	26,843
(3) $r_t = 0.05$	($000)	27,811	25,556	23,409	23,436	25,492	27,622	22,572	24,569	26,618

13. Total annual costs[m]

(1) $r_t = 0.03$	($000)	44,417	40,972	37,579	38,033	41,314	44,769	37,099	40,299	43,671
(2) $r_t = 0.04$	($000)	44,150	40,656	37,226	37,660	40,999	44,478	36,740	39,996	43,390
(3) $r_t = 0.05$	($000)	43,966	40,417	36,968	37,382	40,739	44,244	36,451	39,745	43,165

a Investment: Exhibit R 81-B (FPC, 1970) for construction ($169/kW) with interest computed at 8, 9, and 10% over 6-year construction period.

b Fixed charges include interest and amortization (depreciation) 35-year schedule, interim replacement (0.35%), regular insurance (0.25%), special insurance (0.55%) and state and local taxes (1.25%) for total of 2.4% (plus debt service charge Exhibit R 54-B).

c Interest plus state and local taxes times $28.0/kW fuel inventory, Exhibit R 54-B.

c' Exhibit R 618-A, sheet 1, line 13.

d Sum of 2, 3, and 3a, i.e., $27.43, $30.08, and $32.89 respectively for interest at 8, 9, and 10%.

e Exhibit R 107-A, line 6 (700, 658, and 633 MW, respectively) multiplied by total cost/kW, item 4.

f For 1976-80, use Exhibit R 107-A, line 27 (6,731 GWh) multiplied by 0.98 mill/kWh; for 1981-90 multiply 6,509 MW by 1.22 mills/kWh; for 1991-2025, multiply 6,027 MW by 1.28 mills.

g Sum of items 5 and 6.

h Exhibit R 107-A, line 22 as corrected (807 MW) due to required changes in transmission routing and attendant increases in transmission losses from 4.6 to 5.8% (witness Bell). Cost per kilowatt of supplemental peaking obtained by weighted average cost of units installed in Chief Joseph (570 MW, 1976) and Grand Coulee 3rd powerhouse (600 MW 1979) (Interior Exhibits 251 and 253), adjusting investment to reflect interest during construction at 8, 9, and 10%; interim replacement at 0.4%, insurance 0.2%; operation and maintenance as given (Exhibit 253), administrative and general expenses at 39% of operation and maintenance, and state and local taxes at 1.5% for $10.51, $11.71, and $12.99 per kW respectively for interest at 8, 9, and 10%. For 1981-90, 38 MW installed at $9.27, $10.27 and $11.31 per kilowatt respectively for interest at 8, 9, and 10%. Cost per kilowatt is weighted arithmetic mean of Grand Coulee (600 MW—Sept. 1980); Lower Monumental (405 MW, 1982); Little Goose (405 MW, 1983); Lower Granite (405 MW, 1984). For 1991-2025, 845 MW installed at costs related to 1976-80 and 1981-90.

i Exhibit R 107-A, line 4 (686, 645, and 621 MW respectively) multiplied by $2.79, $2.96, and $3.14 per kilowatt corresponding to 8, 9, and 10% interest respectively; transmission investment obtained from witness Bell.

j Exhibit R 107-A, line 22 (845 MW) as corrected (see note h) multiplied by $3.92, $4.14, and $4.36 per kilowatt corresponding to 8, 9, and 10% interest respectively.

k Sum of items 8, 9, and 10.

l Item 7 divided by appropriate factors given in table 5-3 (FPC, 1970, Exhibit R-670).

m Sum of items 11 and 12.

121

CHAPTER 6

HELLS CANYON CONTINUED: EVALUATION OF ENVIRONMENTAL COSTS

1. INTRODUCTION

In chapter 5 we examined the economic justification for a hydro power development in the Hells Canyon by means of conventional benefit–cost analysis. That is, as a matter of analytic strategy we explicitly stipulated that there were no environmental costs associated with development, historically an implicit assumption in applied benefit–cost analysis. We argued that, in the light of other aspects that tended to bias results of conventional benefit–cost analysis in favor of developing water resource projects, perhaps a critical cost analysis intended to reveal the true opportunity costs would demonstrate that the projects would not show a positive net benefit, even ignoring environmental costs. This is what we did indeed discover in our analysis of the Low Mountain Sheep–Pleasant Valley project. Because it was found to be uneconomic whether or not there were any environmental costs associated with its construction, we could counsel against development on economic grounds without requiring analysis of the environmental costs.

This strategy may serve a useful purpose in many cases involving developmental activities that affect pristine natural areas. This is because construction agencies with pronounced developmental biases, using guidelines for their economic analyses that often stem from anachronistic policies, will advance projects for development with ostensible benefit–cost ratios exceeding unity that, on careful analysis, will be shown to be actually uneconomic. But, of course, there will be other projects, as illustrated by High Mountain Sheep, where the net present value of the development (excluding environmental amenity benefits forgone) will exceed developmental costs even when the analysis is carefully and objectively done. In these cases attention will need to be directed to the evaluation of the amenities associated with the preservation of the area in its pristine state. That is, the benefits of the two alternative uses of the site must be compared because the benefits associated with the precluded use become part of the opportunity costs of the preempting use.

In this chapter we shall review the approach adopted in our attempt to evaluate the preservation benefits associated with the High Mountain Sheep site of the Hells Canyon. Again, it might be mentioned that the analysis was done originally in response to the Supreme Court's remanding of the case for rehearing by the Federal Power Commission. As a consequence, time and related constraints had a significant influence on the nature of the analysis. However, since the Water Resource Council's (WRC) guidelines for project evaluation do not in any event require that serious professional attention be paid to the estimation of preservation benefits,[1] our analysis provides an approach that can be useful in many cases where neither adequate time nor resources have been provided for evaluating this objective of resource management.

Under ideal circumstances, there would be an evaluation of each of the separable attributes associated with this quite remarkable natural area. While the Hells Canyon reach of the Snake qualifies for consideration under the Wild and Scenic Rivers Act of 1968, it also represents an area that may be valued for its scientific research materials and opportunities. Owing to the great vertical distance between the canyon floor and tops of the adjacent rim crags, virtually all of the ecological life zones on the North American continent can be found at some locations within only a half mile. The peculiar geomorphologic formation, moreover, provides matters of research interest for the earth scientist. Given its quite remarkable geological and ecological attributes, the area retained in its natural state has some value for scientific research. In this analysis, however, the value of this objective of preservation remained unquantified as much for present lack of knowledge of how to measure it, as for the constraints imposed by time.

Similarly, we have observed that when an activity having an irreversible consequence is undertaken, given the uncertainty as to the future supply of, and demand for, the preservation benefits of the natural area, there is a value in retaining a viable option that otherwise would be lost. We discussed this somewhat in chapter 4 where the matter was considered within the context of option demand and option value (Weisbrod, 1964; Cicchetti and Freeman, 1971) and "quasi-option value" (Arrow and Fisher, 1974). This also remains an unevaluated benefit, again as much because of the lack of a method for its quantification as for the time constraints imposed on the analysis by the circumstances.

Perhaps closely associated with option value is the value some individuals derive from the knowledge of the existence of unspoiled wilderness, wild and scenic rivers, and related phenomena of peculiarly remarkable

[1] See discussion of this issue in chapter 5, p. 90 (fn. 5).

quality. These persons differ from those who may experience option value because it is uncertain whether or not they may in the future have an occasion to enjoy the amenity services of such environmental resources, and thus may wish to preserve their options. In the case of existence value, we conceived of individuals valuing an environment regardless of the fact that they feel certain they will never demand *in situ* the services it provides (Krutilla, 1967). Superficially, at least, this appears to be a case that can be distinguished from option value proper. However, if we acknowledge that a bequest motivation operates in individual utility-maximizing behavior (Modigliani and Brumberg, 1954; Chase, 1963), the existence value may be simply the value of preserving a peculiarly remarkable environment for benefit of heirs. In that case, the matter appears again in the form of preserving options (for heirs). It should be noted in any event that the motivation to leave one's heirs an estate of maximum value may require a mix of public as well as private assets, and this service or attribute of the area in question escapes quantitative evaluation, as is true of option value proper and the value of the area for scientific purposes.

The three attributes of value alluded to above were not taken into account in our computations because there are no currently known techniques or methodology whereby one might do so. But there were also some studies for which methods of analysis existed that were not undertaken because of constraints on time and other research resources. Thus economic and econometric methods for estimating the demands for outdoor recreation services provided by the Hells Canyon and the river in that reach might have been employed (see Clawson, 1959; Clawson and Knetsch, 1966; and for appropriate modifications and extensions, Cicchetti and Smith, 1973; and Cicchetti, Fisher and Smith, 1972), given sufficient data on origins and travel costs of visitors to the recreation site and on other characteristics, such as income and education levels, that could be expected to influence demands for different services (hunting, fishing, boating, backpacking, and so on) provided at the site.

To summarize then, in confronting the need to evaluate preservation benefits, we find that there are a number of aspects of such benefits that we do not know how to estimate quantitatively. These are the value of natural environments that have remarkable qualities for scientific research; the value that individuals place on retaining an option when faced with actions having irreversible consequences; and the value that some individuals place on the knowledge of the mere existence of gifts of nature, even when they feel certain they will never have or choose an opportunity to experience them *in situ*. In addition, although methods for estimating the demand for outdoor recreation are known, neither time nor available research resources (nor, it might be added, the WRC standards and procedures) encouraged a serious professional effort directed toward the application of such methods.[2] Given these circumstances, an alternative strategy had to be adopted that would be responsive to the exigencies of the decision before the Federal Power Commission reviewing the Hells Canyon case.

2. AN ALTERNATIVE APPROACH FOR EVALUATING BENEFITS FROM ENVIRONMENTAL PRESERVATION

We have acknowledged that we do not understand fully how to evaluate the benefits of preserving a natural environment. In chapter 5, however, we demonstrated that it was not necessary to know how to estimate the value of preserving a natural environment to recommend against its despoliation under some circumstances. That is, if the development alternative was not economic in any event, it was unnecessary to demonstrate that there was some positive value to preservation, it being sufficient to avoid the waste associated with an uneconomic undertaking. In this chapter we can extend this approach some additional distance. That is, while we concede that we do not know how to estimate the value of numerous aspects of natural environments, it may not be necessary, in many cases, that we understand how to evaluate *all* of the benefits of preservation. It is conceivable that if we can estimate only some portion of the benefits precluded by development, we shall have a value that exceeds the estimated benefits of development, without knowing how to measure the more intractable benefits of preservation. The strategy that one might adopt, then, is to determine how large the benefits from preservation must be in order to at least equal the benefits from development, and determine whether the preservation benefits that *can* be measured equal or exceed this amount. This, in fact, is the approach that was followed in our Hells Canyon–High Mountain Sheep analysis.

Basically, there are two minor variations one might follow. That is, one might undertake a study of the measurable benefits obtained in the base year if the canyon is preserved in an undisturbed state. Then, by using some model that would stimulate the appreciation in annual values [e.g., the rate of value appreciation specified in the simplified model of expressions (3-22) and (1) and (2) in the introduction to part II], one could determine whether the measurable benefits of preservation are equal to or exceed the positive net benefits of the development alternative in chapter 5. This is a perfectly straightforward method, and one that might well be preferred if there is an opportunity (research funds and time) to do a

---

[2] It should be noted also that the FPC rehearing of the Hells Canyon case preceded enactment of the National Environmental Policy Act, and hence was not influenced by that legislation.

competent job of analysis using the developed methodology on recreation benefit estimation. On the other hand, since the Water Resource Council does not require this kind of analysis and there is insufficient experience both under the National Environmental Policy Act and with the Environmental Quality Council and the Environmental Protection Agency, to know at this time what would be required,[3] it is altogether possible that the majority of the cases will come up for decision without a careful assessment or survey of the recreational value of the undisturbed natural environment. In that event the second variation may serve the useful purpose of asking what the initial year's preservation benefits would need to be in order that the present value of preservation at least equal that of development. The next question might be: Is the threshold value readily judged to be within the limit of reasonable expectation as to what the preservation benefits might be—or, on the other hand, readily seen to be quite outside the limit that the preservation benefit reasonably can be expected to be? If informed judgment is unable to settle on one answer or the other, then it appears that a survey of measurable benefits is in order, whether or not it is called for by the Water Resource Council or the National Environmental Policy Act. It is because it seemed unlikely that an adequate analysis of the initial year's preservation benefits would be provided that the second variant or approach was adopted.[4]

In determining how large the preservation benefits must be in order for the present value to equal the developmental benefit, it is not sufficient simply to observe the initial year's developmental benefit, for as we have seen in chapter 5, this may well change over time in the Hells Canyon case. There are two reasons for this. The first is that the role which the hydroelectric facility would play in the regional power system may change as the system evolves over time, thus changing somewhat the annual benefits of the facility over the years. The second is that technological advances in alternative sources of power, other things remaining constant, will tend to erode the benefits from hydroelectric development. For that reason we obtain a single-discounted, present-value sum of the total time stream of benefits from the development project. Similarly, the benefit from the preserved natural environment will be subject to changes over time. What

[3] Actually, it is probably as likely that the more specific requirements of NEPA section 102(d) involving environmental impact statements may be prescribed by the courts in a series of rulings in connection with cases precisely of the sort addressed in the Hells Canyon case. See *Sierra Club* v. *Froehlke,* U.S. District Court, Southern District of Texas, Houston Division, in *Environmental Law Reporter* (1973) for the court's opinion on the Wallisville Reservoir in such a case.

[4] As circumstances unfolded, it developed that the applicants commissioned a study conducted cooperatively by the Oregon State Game Commission, the Idaho State Fish and Game Department, and the Forest Service, with an observer designated by the applicants to survey the extent and type of recreation use of the canyon. This did not become available before the rebuttal phase of the hearings.

we need then is a discounted present-value sum for the preservation alternative as well. But, if we do not know what the initial year's benefit may be, despite the possibility that we may devise an adequate way in which to describe its rate of appreciation over time,[5] how can we get a suitable present-value figure? What we can do is to take a given value, say a dollar's worth of initial year's preservation benefits, and as indicated in equation (2c) of the introduction to part II, i.e., $\Sigma_t b'^p_0 (1 + \alpha)^t (1 + i)^{-t}$, where i is the discount rate and $b'^p_0 = \$1.00$, obtain an appropriately discounted sum of annual preservation benefits related to a dollar's worth of initial year's benefits. Then we can ask how many dollars of initial year's preservation benefits would be required in order that the present value of preservation equal the present value of the development benefits. Simply dividing the present value of a dollar's worth of initial year's preservation benefits (growing at the rate α, and discounting at the rate i) into the net present value of the High Mountain Sheep project would provide the requisite initial year's preservation benefits.

This can be restated more formally as:

$$(6\text{-}1) \qquad b^p_0 = \frac{\sum_{t=1}^{T} b^d_0 (1 + i)^{-t}(1 + r)^{-t} - \left[C + \sum_{t=1}^{T} O^d_t (1 + i)^{-t} \right]}{\sum_{t=1}^{T'} b'^p_0 (1 + \bar\alpha)^t (1 + i)^{-t}}$$

where

b^p_0 = the amount of initial year's preservation benefits growing at $\bar\alpha$ and discounted at i, required for present value of preservation to equal present value of developmental benefits

b^d_0 = the initial annual benefits from development

C = the investment cost (including interest during construction)

O^d_t = the annual operating and maintenance costs

b'^p_0 = one dollar's worth of initial year's preservation benefits

i = a constant discount rate

r = a simplified representation of the combined effect of benefit change due to change in role of the facility in the power system and the rate of benefit erosion due to technological progress, more realistically presented in the technological change model, appendix 5-A, and in benefit–cost estimates in appendix 5-B

$\bar\alpha$ = an average annual rate (equivalent to the actually varying rate) of preservation benefit appreciation

T = relevant terminal year for developmental benefits

T' = relevant terminal year for preservation benefits

[5] See introduction to chapter 5 for the rationale supporting the expected asymmetric changes in value of alternative service flows over time.

One attribute of this model may warrant comment. It will be noted that the time horizon is given by both T and T', and while they may be equal under special circumstances, it is more likely that they will not. So long as either $r > 0$, or $\bar{\alpha} > 0$, the result will be similar to having a lower effective discount rate applying to the stream of preservation benefits than to the developmental benefits (Fisher and Krutilla, 1975) and this will have the effect of introducing a differential time horizon (Fisher, Krutilla and Cicchetti, 1972).

How then do we find b_0^p, the required initial year's preservation benefits? We have already developed in chapter 5, table 5-2, and in the relevant appendices from which data for the table were drawn, estimates of the value of the numerator to equation (6-1). Evaluating the denominator requires a means by which values for $\bar{\alpha}$ can be obtained over the relevant time horizon. This we do by a simple simulation model that takes into account the growth in demand over time as a function of the increase in population, income, and changing tastes.

There is one complication, however, that relates to the previously mentioned fact that a capacity constraint is involved. Initially, the rate of growth in annual benefits will be the result of a combination of a larger number of recreationists as the demand grows, along with a higher willingness to pay as a function of increases in income. Under these circumstances, the annual rate of appreciation will be a function of the annual percentage increases in both price and quantity demanded. Eventually as the capacity of the area is reached, and assuming a policy of rationing access to preserve the quality of the recreation experience, appreciation in annual benefits can occur only as result of increases in the willingness to pay for a fixed quantity of recreation services. Thus the rate of appreciation will change over time, and this is why we have written $\bar{\alpha}$, an equivalent to the changing rate. An adaptation of the computational model required to reflect these dynamic changes, developed by Cicchetti (Cicchetti and Krutilla, 1970), is presented in appendix 6-A.

3. APPLICATION OF THE SIMULATION MODEL

Given the computational model, we still need to obtain values for the variables in the model that enter into the determination of the summary rate of annual appreciation, $\bar{\alpha}$, of equation (6-1). These are r_y, γ, k, d, and m, representing respectively the rate of growth in the price, or vertical, component of demand shift; the quantity, or horizontal component of demand shift at zero price (γ is constant up to capacity); the year the area reaches capacity; the rate of decay of γ after year k (eventually to the population growth rate); and the year in which the horizontal component equals the population growth rate. The discount rate, of course, will be the same as that used in the evaluation of developmental benefits in chapter 5, and was taken to fall within the range of 8 to 10 percent.

Doubtless the most difficult numerical value for which to provide an adequate empirical case relates to r_y, the vertical component in the shift of the computational demand schedule. We know that the demand for the amenity services of environmental resources has been growing rapidly in affluent societies. We understand that these are income elastic; indeed, they fall within the class of luxury goods, with demand increasing more than proportionally with income (Boyet and Tolley, 1966). We surmise that increases in demand for the services of nonproducible assets in short supply, if there are no adequate substitutes, would result in relative price increases as the growing demand competes for services of growing scarcity. This is simply the Ricardian rent phenomenon. Yet we have little, if anything, of an empirical nature to rely on in guiding the selection of an appropriate rate of annual price increase relative to the price of goods and services more generally.

Recent efforts by Smith (1974) give us a theoretical basis for making some judgments, however. Since the environmental assets such as the Hells Canyon are not producible in any event, we cannot anticipate improvements in productive efficiency to augment supplies of the services they yield. On the other hand, the demand for these services is influenced by technological progress in the producible goods sector, i.e., influenced by gains in real income. Examining the differential incidence of technical advance among different types of goods in a general equilibrium model, Smith establishes the conditions that determine the relationship between the rate of change in relative prices and the rate of technological change. Basically three conditions are significant: (1) an income elasticity of demand for amenity services that is large relative to goods in the producible goods sector, (2) the absence of satisfactory substitutes for the amenity services in question, and (3) the ease or difficulty with which the economy is able to transform its resources into alternative commodity mixes. The third condition, of course, involves the irreproducibility issue. Since these conditions coincide with the circumstances encountered in relation to the amenity services of the Hells Canyon environmental resources, we draw support from Smith's work in basing our estimates of r_y on the anticipated rate of technological advance in the economy generally.

Accordingly we use rates of technical gain within the range of 2 to 4 percent (subject to subsequent sensitivity analysis) directly as rates of relative price changes. Since we did not correct for likely inflation premiums in the opportunity cost-based discount rate that is reflected in the interest rates of fixed value assets, and our prices are in absolute terms, we need for consistency to include a historically suggested 2 percent per year rate of increase in the general price level. Accordingly, our r_y used in computing the present value of preservation benefits involves alternative calculations at 4, 5, and 6 percent.

With regard to the estimated growth rate, γ, in quantity of recreation services demanded, data over a sufficiently long period of time do not exist for the Hells Canyon. The rather active use of the Snake River in the lower Hells Canyon, especially for commercial recreational boating, seems to have begun around 1963. The rapidity of growth in use since that time indicates that the demand has been increasing at something like 20 to 30 percent per year. These rates are impressive but it does not seem likely that they are really representative of a longer run rate of increase in use.[6] For that reason, it seemed more conservative to use growth rates more typical of undeveloped wild and scenic areas generally. U.S. Forest Service estimates of recreational use of National Forests show the greatest growth in use of undeveloped areas. Estimates of such use in the Pacific Northwest indicate a growth rate of roughly 10 percent per year, dating back to 1941. For Oregon specifically, for 1946 to 1960, a period over which the data series appear comparable, the rate of growth in use was about 14 percent per year—for Idaho over the same period, about 12 percent per year.

It is a fact, however, that obtaining accurate data on long-run trends in recreational use of undeveloped areas of national forests and other public lands is a difficult matter. And despite the fact that the applicants' evidence corroborates a 15 to 20 percent increase in use over the recent past for the general area within which the Hells Canyon is located [Federal Power Commission (FPC), 1970 Exhibit 538, p. 16], a more conservative approach appears more persuasive. Accordingly, for the purpose of the analysis, we have taken γ to be 10 percent per year until the capacity constraint is met, with alternative calculations at 7.5 percent and 12.5 percent in order to provide some perspective on how the results might be affected by an error of 25 percent in either direction.

The rate of growth for primitive, remote areas, of course, must eventually moderate. That is, with rates of growth in this recreational activity exceeding the population growth rate, assuming the amount taken by each individual remains constant, it would be only a matter of time before we would find ourselves assuming that all of the population would be engaged in this type of activity. Accordingly, we assumed that the growth rates observed would continue for some time (for purposes of the computations, until the capacity constraint was met) and then would diminish until they

[6] The record of the past dozen years of growth in recreation use of the Colorado River in the Grand Canyon, however, shows an average rate of increase of about 45 percent per year until the recent moratorium on increases in intensity of use.

would equal only the rate of population growth. Equal annual percentage rates of decay (d) in the growth rate were chosen such that the growth rate in the quantity of recreation demanded would fall to the population growth rate by the fiftieth year.

How was the choice of the specific values rationalized? As in similar cases where there is little hard empirical evidence by which to be guided, this choice is difficult and must rely ultimately on the reasonableness of the arguments brought forth to support the estimates. The arguments advanced during the FPC hearings (FPC, 1970, Krutilla, Transcript R-5867 ff.) take into account two considerations. First, while there is some suggestion of leveling off in the proportion of the population that engages in car or "easy access" camping and related moderately exacting outdoor activities, the past rapid growth of this type of activity ensures continued growth in the demand for remote-area recreation activity for another generation or two.

Research on the characteristics of campers engaged in "easy access" camping, on the one hand, and "remote" or "difficult-access" camping on the other, indicates a progression of the former to the latter (Burch and Wenger, 1967). The burgeoning of past demand for easy access camping is likely to influence the demand for the more remote, primitive area outdoor activities in the future. The Burch and Wenger research reveals that families with children tend to be overrepresented in easy access camping and childless families underrepresented. The combination of the disproportionate representation of children that are being introduced to experiences with camping and with opportunities to acquire tastes and skills required for more exacting types of outdoor recreation experiences, on the one hand, and the observable tendency toward movement from the less to the more exacting outdoor camping experiences on the other, suggest a continuation in the demand for remote-area, or difficult-access, outdoor recreation opportunities.

The second consideration involves recognition of the fact that demand for this type of recreation activity cannot continue to increase indefinitely at a rate higher than the population growth rate—again, assuming constant per capita consumption (as may result, for example, from rationing use of wilderness areas). These differential rates of growth suggest a change in tastes, in part, but even so, not everyone will share an interest in such activities. At the present growth rates, all of those in the population (and new recruits) who are likely to be interested in difficult-access, remote-area camping will have been introduced to such camping within the next two or three decades. Additional gains in numbers would have to come largely through additions to the population. Given the paucity of really good data on the number of total days of remote or primitive area recreation, and the average number of days per individual per year, good estimates of the number of individuals who participate in wilderness activities are rather difficult to come by. On the basis of evidence available, with allowances for some error, it was felt sufficiently reasonable to assume growth rates of 10 percent per year over the next two decades, followed by an equal percentage rate of decline in the annual growth rate over the next three decades, until by the fiftieth year the growth rate would be equal only to the population growth rate. These assumptions about data values used in our model, when applied generally to participants in these kinds of recreational activities, suggest that roughly 2 to 6 percent of the population would participate in this kind of activity by the fiftieth year, depending on the specific assumptions or interpretations of the rather sketchy data.

The canyon proper, the river breaks, and the backcountry beyond the breaks will experience recreation capacity limitations if a policy of maintaining a low-density, high-quality, primitive recreation experience is pursued. With a growth rate of 10 percent per year for the composite of the recreation activities that the canyon area can support, the capacity is likely to be reached somewhere midway in the 1990s, or roughly 20 years from the date (1976) proposed at the time of the hearings for the initial High Mountain Sheep operations. The increase in some kinds of activities, say fishing, implicit in the growth rates to 1990–2000, appears to be consistent with harvesting the sports fisheries without adversely affecting the quality of the experience as measured by the effort–success ratio. For some species of game, such as deer or elk on the Oregon side of the canyon, on the other hand, the constraint on the number of hunters that would be required in order to preserve a low effort–success ratio in an uncrowded environment may be reached sooner than postulated in the 20-year interval, based on a 10 percent per year growth rate. Other recreation activities, such as smallmouth bass fishing, resident trout fishing, chukar hunting, backpacking, and related remote-area activities, are not likely to reach capacity limitations for some time after the date implied by the average for the composite of all activities.[7]

Taking all of these considerations into account, then, we concluded that the capacity constraint would become effective in 15 to 25 years, depending on the associated growth rate employed in the calculations.

Using the variables and constraints given above, what is the value of the initial year's preservation benefits that would be required in order to equal the value of developmental benefits? First we show in table 6-1 the

[7] Information regarding the fish and game characteristics of the region was supplied through discussions and correspondence with John McKean and Robert Stein of the Oregon State Game Commission and with Monte Richards of the Idaho State Fish and Game Department. Estimates of the recreational carrying capacity were influenced also by information provided by George Stankey of the Forest Service Wilderness Research Project, and by independent observations from field surveys in the area.

Table 6-1

Present Value of One Dollar's Worth of Initial Year's Benefits Growing at α_t and Discounted at i (m = 50 years)

r_v	$\gamma = 7.5\%,$ $k = 25$ years	$\gamma = 10\%,$ $k = 20$ years	$\gamma = 12.5\%,$ $k = 15$ years
	$i = 8\%$		
0.04	$134.08	$169.86	$173.90
0.05	211.72	263.49	262.12
0.06	385.10	467.30	449.00
	$i = 9\%$		
0.04	$ 93.67	$120.07	$125.89
0.05	136.12	172.35	176.25
0.06	214.76	267.10	264.49
	$i = 10\%$		
0.04	$ 69.28	$ 89.45	$ 95.71
0.05	95.15	121.91	127.68
0.06	138.17	174.85	178.66

various values for the denominator of equation (6-1); namely, the present value of a dollar's worth of initial year's benefits growing at the varying rate α_t and discounted at i. It should be noted that the terminal year, T', for the present-value calculations was taken to be the year in which the discounted benefits of a dollar's worth of initial year's benefits, growing at α_t and discounted at i, would be only one cent.[8]

Second, we display in table 6-2 the various values that are obtained by dividing the denominator values from table 6-1 into the comparable numerator values obtained from table 5-2. We can now see the value of the initial year's preservation benefits that is required in order to equal the value of benefits from the developmental alternative. These will range from a minimum of about \$40,000 to a maximum of about \$150,000. If we have no additional information regarding the probable value of the present recreational and related services yielded by the Hells Canyon, we have at least a set of values about which we can speculate. The question would be: "Does it appear reasonable that the measurable and nonmeasurable values of preserving the Hells Canyon in its present undeveloped state exceed, as a minimum, \$150,000 as an initial year's annual value?" Different individuals, of course, perhaps would come to different conclu-

[8] Theoretically the time horizon is fixed at the point at which the discounted value of a future benefit falls to zero (Fisher, Krutilla, and Cicchetti, 1972). For practical purposes, however, it is useful to have the computer cut off when the present values approach negligible values. Hence, using 1 cent as the cutoff value results in time horizons limited to from 120 to 350 years, depending on the combination of growth and discount rates. This permits capture of all of the significant benefits while limiting the machine running time.

Table 6-2

Initial Year's Preservation Benefits Needed to Equal Benefits from Development
($m = 50$ years, $r_t = 0.04$)

r_y	$\gamma = 7.5\%$ $k = 25$ years	$\gamma = 10\%$ $k = 20$ years	$\gamma = 12.5\%$ $k = 15$ years
	$i = 8\%, PV_d = \$18,540,000$ᵃ		
0.04	$138,276	$109,149	$106,613
0.05	85,568	70,363	70,731
0.06	48,143	39,674	41,292
	$i = 9\%, PV_d = \$13,809,000$		
0.04	$147,422	$115,008	$109,691
0.05	101,447	80,122	78,336
0.06	64,300	51,700	52,210
	$i = 10\%, PV_d = \$9,861,000$		
0.04	$142,335	$110,240	$103,030
0.05	103,626	80,888	77,232
0.06	71,369	56,397	55,194

ᵃSource: Table 5-2.

sions,[9] but considering the unmatchable quality of this geomorphologic–hydrologic phenomenon, it is likely that most people would argue that they do.

Fortunately we do not have to rely entirely on speculation as to what the recreational uses and values of the canyon might be if only they were known (see footnote 4). The results of a cooperative survey on recreational uses of the canyon are given in the portion of table 6-3 dealing with stream-based uses. Complementing this study were data provided by a U.S. Fish and Wildlife Service Study (1968) and testimony of the state wildlife biologists regarding recreational hunting in the canyon. These data are presented as 1969 data in the second and third columns of table 6-3. On the basis of this information, 1976 values were projected to obtain time comparability with the originally proposed year of initial hydroelectric plant operations, and values per recreation day were imputed in the manner illustrated in column four.[10]

[9] The Pacific Northwest Power Company, for example, is quoted as arguing that, "There is the misconception that grows from generalized descriptions of Hells Canyon—the 'deepest' on the North American Continent—'steep walls'—'wild and uncultivated'—'remote and lonely.' It is remote and wild, however, principally because it has little to offer. It is in no sense a spectacular gash like the Grand Canyon of the Colorado." Quoted in *Audubon*, January 1970, p. 19. For a comparison, see the letter from the Honorable Orville Freeman, Secretary of Agriculture, portions of which are quoted on pages 89–90, chapter 5.

[10] Note that two assumptions are made in order that the benefits given in table 6-3 represent net benefits consistent with the benefits estimated for the High Mountain Sheep project in table 5-2. One assumption is that there are no adequate substitutes of similar quality, i.e., other primitive scenic areas are either congested or being rationed, conditions which are being widely encountered in national parks and over

Assuming for the moment that the values attributed per recreation day are acceptable, we observe that the estimated value of preservation benefits of close to $900,000 is roughly an order of magnitude greater than necessary to establish a case, on economic grounds, for preserving Hells Canyon in its present state. It should be emphasized also that this was achieved without knowing how to evaluate all of the benefits from preserving the natural environment of the canyon area. That is, in this case and perhaps in numerous cases with which resource managers will be dealing, quantitative analysis can be very useful even in the absence of its capacity to capture all of the values potentially attributable to preserving rare natural environments. By the same token, the results of such analysis giving measurable benefits of preservation that exceed benefits from development may be sufficient for a decision, but are not essential for making a case for preserving some unique natural environment. That is, since only a part of the benefits from preservation currently can be evaluated quantitatively, it goes without saying that such results cannot be used persuasively, except in extreme cases, to establish that the environmental values precluded by development do not exceed the developmental gains.

We concede that the analyses in chapters 5 and 6 have been rather complicated, and the question may be put as to whether a resource manager facing a difficult decision would find them worth the effort. Would we not, for example, have come to the same conclusion by simply taking the initial year's annual benefit from development and compared it with the benefits from preservation? The answer can be obtained by referring to table 5-2 where we see, corresponding to item 4, annual benefits in the initial period of $1 million to $1.5 million. These values compared with our estimated value of roughly $900,000 would tip the balance—for the quantifiable benefits—in favor of development. Moreover, if the more conventional benefit–cost analysis which did not take the effects of technical change into account were used, comparing total generating costs with and without adjustment for technological advance (appendix 5-B, table 5-7), we see that an additional $1.5 million to $2 million of power benefits would be used in the comparison. *In short, in order to take account of the asymmetric effects of technological progress on the value of the alternative uses to which the Hells Canyon site can be devoted, we need to perform the kind of analysis undertaken above.* In many cases, just as in this, taking these additional factors into account will produce results that will counsel a different course of action than that which would follow from more conventional benefit–cost analysis.

---

much of the wilderness system. Secondly, it is assumed that the demand unsatisfied by virtue of the transformation of the Hells Canyon would impinge on the margin in other sectors of the economy characterized by free entry and feasibility of augmenting supplies, i.e., incremental costs will equal incremental benefits.

136

Table 6-3

Opportunity Costs of Altering Free-Flowing River and Related Canyon Environment by Development of High Mountain Sheep

(1) Quantified losses	(2) Recreation days 1969[a]	(3) Visitor days 1969[b]	(4) Visitor days 1976
Stream-based recreation[c]			
Total of boat counter survey	18,755	28,132	51,000
Upstream of Salmon–Snake confluence	9,622	14,439	26,000
Nonboat access			
Imnaha–Dug bar	9,678	14,517	26,000
Pittsburgh Landing	9,643	14,464	26,000
Hells Canyon downstream			
Boat anglers	2,472	1,000	1,800
Bank anglers	9,559	2,333	4,000
Total stream use above Salmon River	40,974 plus[d]	46,753 plus[d]	84,000 at $5/day = $420,000
Hunting Canyon area[e]			
Big game	7,050	7,050	7,000 at $25/day = $175,000
Upland birds	1,110	1,110	1,000 at 10/day = 10,000
Diminished value of hunting experience[f]	18,000	18,000	29,000 at 10/day = 290,000
Total quantified losses		$895,000±25%	

Unevaluated losses
A. Unmitigated anadromous fish losses outside impact area
B. Unmitigated resident fish losses:
   (1) Stream fishing downstream from High Mountain Sheep
C. Option value of rare geomorphological–biological–ecological phenomena
D. Others

a"Recreation days" corresponds to definition as per *Supplement No. 1, Senate Document No. 97*; namely, an individual engaging in recreation for any "reasonable portion of a day." In this particular study, time involved must be a minimum of 1 hour, as per letter from Monte Richards, coordinator, Basin Investigations, Idaho Fish and Game Department.

b"Visitor day" corresponds to the President's Recreational Advisory Council (now, Council on Environmental Quality) *Coordination Bulletin No. 6* definition of a visitor day as a 12-hour day. Operationally, the total number of hours, divided by twelve, will give the appropriate "visitor day" estimate.

cSource: "An Evaluation of Recreational Use on the Snake River in the High Mountain Sheep Impact Area," Survey by Oregon State Game Commission and Idaho State Fish and Game Department in cooperation with U.S. Forest Service, Report dated January 1970; and memorandum, W. B. Hall, liaison officer, Wallowa–Whitman National Forest, dated January 20, 1970.

dNot included in the survey were scenic flights, nor trail use via Saddle Creek and Battle Creek trails. Thus, estimates given represent an under-reporting of an unevaluated amount.

e"Middle Snake River Study, Idaho, Oregon and Washington" Joint Report of the Bureau of Commercial Fisheries and Bureau of Sports Fisheries and Wildlife in *Department of the Interior Resource Study of the Middle Snake*, tables 10 and 11.

fThe figure 18,000 hunter days is based on witness Pitney's estimate of 15,000 big game hunter days on the Oregon side, and estimated 10,000 hunter days on the Idaho side (provided in a letter from Monte Richards, coordinator, Idaho Basin Investigations, Idaho Fish and Game Department, dated February 13, 1970), for a total of 25,000 hunter days (excluding small game, i.e., principally upland birds) in the canyon area, less estimated losses of 7,000 hunter days. This provides the estimated 18,000 hunter days, 1969 total, which, growing at estimated 5 percent per year for deer hunting and 9 percent per year for elk hunting, would total 29,000 hunter days by 1976.

4. EVALUATION OF QUANTITATIVE RESULTS

The analyses in sections 2 and 3, taken in conjunction with the analyses of developmental benefits performed in chapter 5, provide some quantitative information on which to base an economic judgment as to whether to develop the Hells Canyon or to preserve it. We concede that there has been a paucity of empirical information on some of the variables used in computing the results required in analysis. Where information is inadequate or unavailable, our approach consists of making assumptions on what the data would show, if we had them. That is, consistent with adversary proceedings, a great deal of "expert opinion" had to be substituted for estimates derived from careful empirical investigation. Given that to have been the case, and given the fact that similar circumstances are likely to be unavoidable in many instances in which judgments are required when significant decisions are to be made, what can we say about the firmness, or the lack of firmness, of our quantitative results?

It may be best to investigate this issue by trying to determine the effect on our results of alternative assumptions with respect to what the data would show, were data of the relevant sort available. Perhaps the place to start is to note the range of values that can be obtained by use of alternative assumptions in our computational model as reflected in the values given in table 6-1.

Upon inspection, it appears that the results of the computations are most sensitive to the assumptions regarding the vertical component in the shift in demand for the services of the Hells Canyon preserved in its current state. The difference in the computed value of preservation benefits varies as a factor of slightly under 2.0 between an $r_y = 0.04$ and $r_y = 0.06$ for the higher discount rate (10 percent) to slightly over 2.5 at the lower (8 percent) discount rate. Where the outcome regarding analysis of the relative values of developing or preserving a site is close, obviously, the decision could turn on this value, and unfortunately this value is one for which we have the least empirical data.

When relying on a mechanism that results in long-term value appreciation, we recognize the hazards of generating unbounded estimates. To check the plausibility of the results, therefore, we sought to compare the relationship of some of the intermediate results (i.e., the implicit price of the recreational services in the terminal year and the projected per capita income in that year) with what is currently known about such relationships for high-quality recreation activities that are privately provided. Our computed ratio of implicit price to per capita income for the terminal years was well within the range of values found to exist for Atlantic salmon fishing in Norway, for example, or for even the better trout streams in the United Kingdom today. Except for the vertical shift of 6 percent per year, the implicit price-to-per capita-income ratio was very modest—enough so that there should be no reason to hesitate using an r_y of about 0.05.[11]

While there is also considerable range in the computed results associated with different discount rates shown in table 6-1, these differences are not equally significant in a comparison of the developmental and preservation benefits. The reason for this is that the identical discount rate, whether high or low, is used for discounting benefits from both of the alternatives, and we can see that when this is done (table 6-2) the variation in results as a function of the discount rate is a relatively minor matter.

The assumption regarding the rate of growth of recreational services demanded, γ, similarly is not critical to the outcome, given the prior selection of the capacity constraint. The more rapid the rate of growth, the sooner the capacity constraint is met, setting a severe limitation on the rate at which the annual benefits appreciate beyond this point. More critical, of course, is the selection of the capacity constraint, which in this instance was done on the basis of judgment among a group of informed professional resource managers, rather than in a more scientifically supported manner.[12] While such a procedure is characteristic of evidence submitted in adversary proceedings in the absence of more scientifically established research findings, the matter of determining optimal capacity for a low-density recreation resource is worth additional research.[13] In any event, it is clear that a wide range of error could be accommodated in this connection without altering the outcome of our analysis, in the sense of the ranking of alternatives, for the High Mountain Sheep case.

A question may be asked whether the decay in the rate of growth in quantity demanded should be a function of capacity limitations at the facility in question, or a result of a general stabilization of the participation rate within the population. In our model we chose to relate the beginning of the decline in the rate of growth to the reaching of the capacity constraint. On the other hand, if we took arbitrarily a two-decade uninterrupted growth rate followed by a gradual decline until the fiftieth year, the result would not be affected appreciably. Similarly, whether 40, 50, or 60 years were selected as the date by which γ would equal only the popu-

---

[11] The implicit price to projected per capita income for the Hells Canyon recreation services expressed in terms of today's per capita income would give a user fee or price of from $8 to $10 per day. This compares with the fee per rod per day of $200 to $500 for Atlantic salmon fishing in Norway, and upwards of $100 per day for trout fishing on the better chalk streams in the United Kingdom.

[12] Analysis of computer output suggests that an error in fixing capacity of ±25 percent affects the estimated value of the preservation benefits by ±15 percent.

[13] Recognizing that results of the computations are more or less sensitive to the setting of the capacity constraint, work has been undertaken on defining optimal recreation capacity for this type of primitive recreation facility. See Fisher and Krutilla (1972), also Cicchetti and Smith (1973), and Smith and Krutilla (1975). The matter receives further attention as well in the next chapter.

lation growth rate, the estimates of the value of preservation benefits were not affected to any significant extent.

One additional matter perhaps deserves attention. That is the sensitivity of the values generated by our model projecting the rate of growth in annual benefits over time, to the shape of the computational demand curve described in appendix 6-A. This has been investigated and the results reported elsewhere (Fisher, Krutilla and Cicchetti, 1974). It turns out that the growth rate is in general independent of the functional form, whether linear or curvilinear, of the computational demand curve.

Finally, a word should be said regarding our imputed values per day of recreation given in table 6-3. Where access to game is permitted without payment of any fee, it is difficult to obtain expressions of the value to hunters and fishermen of a day of quality recreational hunting or fishing. We know that in countries where rights to game are privately vested, exceedingly high fees are charged. Current rates per rod/day of fishing on the better artificial ponds in the United Kingdom are around $9,[14] while a fee of $150/rod/day for the finest chalk streams is not uncommon.[15] Atlantic salmon fishing, to which steelhead fishing in the Pacific Northwest may be likened, commonly costs $200 to $500/rod/day. Grouse shooting may reach $750 to $1,200 per week and the privilege of taking the red stag in central Europe would cost $5,000 at predevaluation prices. This is not to suggest that the average American hunter could participate in so aristocratic an activity, but it can be assumed that much more would be paid in fees than is now customary, were access to hunting and fishing rationed by price.

The figures given in table 6-3 for each of the categories of opportunity benefits are exceedingly modest, and are used only to retain consistency with testimony of record. The imputed values thus represent the most conservative estimates possible and are considerably lower than those being provided by current research results.[16]

Having addressed the sensitivity of our results to changes in the value of γ, k, m, d, and i, and commented on the firmness of the imputed value per recreation day found in table 6-3, we should comment on one additional datum evaluation. This concerns the relation between the annual preservation benefits in the terminal year of analysis and the projected GNP for the terminal year. Here we discover that in spite of the annual appreciation in preservation benefits, the ratio of the terminal year's bene-

---

[14] The Packington Fisheries is an example.

[15] Prime beats on the Test will go for $160/rod/day with secondary beats at $120 per day.

[16] See for example Brown, Singh, and Castle (1965); Matthews and Brown (1970), and Pearse (1968) for more systematic evaluation of the steelhead–salmon fisheries and other big game resource values, and estimated willingness to pay per day of recreation.

fits to the corresponding year's GNP will be an order of magnitude less than the ratio of the applicants' current revenues to current GNP. In short, while working with unbounded estimates, the values out to the limit of our time horizon are modest in relation to associated economic magnitudes of the corresponding period.

Accordingly, while we have had to work with rather poor empirical information in some instances, the insensitivity of the outcome to rather large potential errors in some of the variables provides some reassurance in the case at hand. There is nothing in the results of analysis, whether intermediate or final, that produces implausible results in any of the tests we were able to devise.

5. SUMMARY AND CONCLUSIONS

The Hells Canyon case represents one of the very early environmental cases, one that was brought under careful scrutiny by virtue of a Supreme Court ruling that predated the National Environmental Policy Act. The charge from the court was similar to the requirements implicit in NEPA; namely, that a federal agency involved in a resource allocation decision having a significant environmental impact take into consideration that impact as well as other considerations theretofore considered relevant. Because there was an important decision pending, with a limited time, given a fixed hearings schedule, the testimony presented for the record was a mix of careful research results and "expert opinion," albeit opinion nonetheless. Similar constraints affected the analyses underlying testimony presented on the relative economics of the Hells Canyon alternatives. Accordingly, the results presented in the chapters 5 and 6, which are drawn from the hearings record as well as background research performed in connection with the testimony, partake of the general characteristics of such adversary proceedings. One exception should be noted. The testimony presented on the relative economics of the alternative uses of the Hells Canyon site, reproduced in substance in chapters 5 and 6, was given in the role of "Friend of the Commission," rather than on behalf of one or another of the adversaries, i.e., applicants or intervenors in this case.

As the first case in which environmental opportunity costs were to be taken into account in benefit–cost analysis, it presented a number of difficult problems. There was need to consider the true costs of both the hydroelectric and the alternative power supply facilities, which was made difficult by the distribution of ownership of facilities in the regional power system. This involved adjusting for the subsidy elements in various facility costs as result of the class of ownership (whether private, nonfederal public, or federal) and the differential terms on which capital can be obtained by virtue of the features of public policy applicable to each.

Accordingly, an exhaustive analysis was undertaken to determine the real, or true opportunity, cost of all of the facilities that would participate in the alternative systems (one with, and the other without, the hydroelectric development).

It is important to note that when careful analyses of real costs are undertaken, some facilities destined for development that have significant environmental costs can be shown to be unjustified economically, even without a demonstration of their environmental costs. Thus, a substantial class of environmentally disruptive activities can be shown to be unjustified by the faithful application of economic analysis, within a benefit–cost framework used initially to "justify" such projects.

It is true that many public projects in the water resource development field are a reflection of the pork barrel in operation, but there are projects that can be justified on strictly economic grounds when the environmental costs are left unevaluated. This was true of the High Mountain Sheep proposal for the Hells Canyon. In this instance there was need to develop to the best of professional ability, an estimate of the value of amenity and related services of the environmental resources so they could be compared with the estimates of benefits from hydroelectric development presented in chapter 5. It is clear that the evaluation of some preservation benefits, e.g., value of retaining options in the face of uncertainty, at the moment escape the capability of the benefit–cost practitioner. There are others that must remain unevaluated as well. But the question that is posed is: Is analysis irrelevant in the face of the inability to evaluate *all* of the benefits from preserving a natural environment? Just as in the case of the Low Mountain Sheep–Pleasant Valley complex, in many other cases it is not necessary to have all of the information regarding consequences of a proposed action to reach a judgment on the desirability of taking that action. This of course was true in the High Mountain Sheep case.

In the evaluation of High Mountain Sheep, we needed to have information additional to that required for a judgment on the alternative two-dam project. Even so, the information required was short of all the information regarding the values associated with retaining an undeveloped reach of the canyon in its present state. The estimates of the benefits of preservation that we were able to measure, however, turned out to be sufficient to answer the question in the High Mountain Sheep case. To a significant extent, the reason for this was the importance, i.e., the quantitative significance for evaluative purposes, of changes in the relative value of the services from alternative uses of the Hells Canyon. In chapter 5 we indicated how under given conditions the initial annual benefit of the hydroelectric development would tend to diminish over time as a function of advances specifically in the technology of production from alternative sources of energy. In this chapter we addressed the opposing tine of our asymmetry argument. Since the services of the natural environment are gifts of nature not producible by man, we cannot look to specific gains in productive efficiency to augment the stock of amenity-related resources such as the Hells Canyon. However, since complementary goods and services are producible, and particularly since the amenity services are income elastic—then with general technological progress increasing productivity and, hence, income per capita, we can anticipate a growing demand for a fixed stock of amenity-supporting natural environments. This leads to expected increases in the value of the services of such natural assets as the Hells Canyon when retained in its natural condition.

There will be other environmental cases in which more of the unevaluatable benefits will have to be assessed in order to reach a decision, and as time and experience with such problems is gained, analysis may be relied on to play an important role in a larger number of cases. It is important to note, however, that careful analysis using relevant concepts can be useful in a variety of cases without pretending to be capable of valuing all attributes of natural phenomena.

Authors' Note

Since the analysis of the Hells Canyon alternatives was prepared in 1969, the more recent gyrations in the market for energy commodities might well raise a question as to the continuing validity of our analysis. Several points should be made to assist in evaluating the final results.

First, it should be borne in mind that the thermal alternative determined to be the most economic by methods employed by the Bureau of Power of the Federal Power Commission was nuclear rather than fossil fueled; the market for only the latter of these has been in an uncertain condition. Even so, it is not clear that a fossil fuel alternative was not in fact, and does not remain, a lesser cost thermal alternative. The Bureau of Power's evaluative procedures incorporate the taxes that utilities pay as part of the cost of the energy from any given source. A Montana-based operation utilizing the thick-seamed strippable coal in eastern Montana would be charged with a percentage of taxes on investment reflected in the taxes paid by the Montana Power Company. It develops that, owing to the favorable treatment the Montana Power Company receives from the state public utilities commission in figuring its rate base, it earns very large profits as determined by the Internal Revenue Service and thus pays in federal income taxes about 85 percent more per dollar of investment than the weighted average of all utilities. Accordingly, what the peculiarities of the FPC evaluation practice produce is a result that reckons a half of the excessive *profits* of the company *as a cost* of producing thermal electric power from Montana energy sources.

Were the evaluation to be conducted on a conceptually more adequate basis, it is likely that stripmined eastern Montana coal would represent the lowest cost thermal alternative. And, given the impressive economy of mining very thick seams by modern, technically advanced specialized methods, even taking into account the costs of rehabilitating the areas disturbed by surface mining, it is not certain that the real *costs of extraction* have not taken a course different in direction from that taken by *prices* for energy commodities in general. Of course, it would require a very careful analysis of the changes in relative costs among alternative energy sources to speak definitively on the matter. This note simply intends to suggest that there is no *prima facie* evidence that the results of our analysis are vitiated by the aberrant short-run price behavior in the markets for energy commodities.

REFERENCES

Arrow, K. J. and Fisher, A. C. 1974. "Environmental Preservation, Uncertainty and Irreversibility," *Quarterly Journal of Economics,* vol. 88, no. 2.

Boyet, W. E. and Tolley, G. S. 1966. "Recreation Projections Based on Demand Analysis," *Journal of Farm Economics,* vol. 48, no. 4.

Brown, W. G., Singh, A., and Castle, E. N., 1965. "Net Economic Value of the Oregon Salmon-Steelhead Sport Fishery," *Journal of Wildlife Management,* vol. 29, no. 2.

Burch, W. R. and Wenger, W. D. 1967. *The Social Characteristics of Participants in Three Styles of Family Camping.* U.S. Forest Service Research Paper PNW-48. Pacific Northwest Forest and Range Experiment Station, U.S. Dept. of Agriculture, Portland, Oregon.

Chase, S. B. 1963. *Asset Prices in Economic Analysis* (Berkeley: University of California Press).

Cicchetti, C. J. and Krutilla, J. V. 1970. "Technical Note on Estimating the Present Value of a Non-Depreciating, Non-Reproducible Asset with Increasing Annual Benefits Over Time." Exhibit R-667. Federal Power Commission, "In the Matter of: Pacific Northwest Power Company and Washington Public Power Supply System," Projects 2243 and 2273, hearings, Lewiston, Idaho; Portland, Oregon; and Washington, D.C., 1968–1970.

———— and Freeman, A. M., III. 1971. "Option Demand and Consumer Surplus: Further Comments," *Quarterly Journal of Economics,* vol. 85, no. 3.

————, Fisher, A. C. and Smith, V. K. 1972. "An Economic and Econometric Model for the Valuation of Environmental Resources with an Application to Outdoor Recreation at Mineral King." Presented at the annual meeting of the Econometric Society, Toronto.

———— and Smith, V. K. 1973. "Congestion, Quality Deterioration and Optimal Use," *Social Science Research,* vol. 2, no. 1.

———— and Smith, V. K. 1975. *An Econometric Analysis of Congestion Costs: The Case of Wilderness Recreation* (forthcoming).

Clawson, Marion. 1959. "Methods of Measuring the Demand for and Value of Outdoor Recreation," Resources for the Future Reprint No. 10.

———— and Knetsch, J. L. 1966. *The Economics of Outdoor Recreation* (Baltimore: Johns Hopkins Press).

Federal Power Commission. 1970. "In the Matter of: Pacific Northwest Power Company and Washington Public Power Supply System," Projects 2243 and 2273, hearings, Lewiston, Idaho; Portland, Oregon; and Washington, D.C., 1968–1970.

Federal Power Commission. 1970. *An Evaluation of Recreational Use on the Snake River in the High Mountain Sheep Impact Area.* Survey by Oregon State Game Commission and Idaho State Fish and Game Department in cooperation with U.S. Forest Service.

Fisher, A. C. and Krutilla, J. V. 1972. "Determination of Optimal Capacity of Resource-Based Recreation Facilities," *Natural Resources Journal,* vol. 12, no. 3.

———— and Krutilla, J. V. 1975. "Resource Conservation, Environmental Preservation and the Rate of Discount," *Quarterly Journal of Economics,* vol. 89.

————, Krutilla, J. V. and Cicchetti, C. J. 1972. "The Economics of Environmental Preservation: A Theoretical and Empirical Analysis," *American Economic Review,* vol. LXII, no. 4.

————, Krutilla, J. V. and Cicchetti, C. J. 1974. "The Economics of Environmental Preservation: Further Discussion," *American Economic Review,* vol. LXIV, no. 5.

Fox, I. K. and Herfindahl, O. C. 1964. "Attainment of Efficiency in Satisfying Demands for Water Resources," *American Economic Review,* vol. LIV, no. 2.

Krutilla, J. V. 1967. "Conservation Reconsidered," *American Economic Review,* vol. LVI, no. 4.

————, Cicchetti, C. J., Freeman, A. M., III, and Russell, C. S. 1972. "Observations on the Economics of Irreplaceable Assets," in *Environmental Quality Analysis: Theory and Methods in the Social Sciences,* Allen V. Kneese and Blair T. Bower, eds. (Baltimore: Johns Hopkins Press).

Leopold, L. B. *Quantitative Comparisons of Some Aesthetic Factors Among Rivers,* Geological Survey Circular 620 (Washington, D.C.).

Matthews, S. B. and Brown, G. M. 1970. *Economic Evaluation of the 1967 Sport Salmon Fisheries of Washington,* Dept. of Fisheries Technical Report No. 2 (Olympia, Washington).

Mishan, E. J. 1968. "What Is Producer's Surplus?" *American Economic Review,* vol. LVIII, no. 5.

Modigliani, Franco and Brumberg, R. 1954. "Utility Analysis and the Consumption Function: An Interpretation of Cross-Section Data," in *Post Keynesian Economics,* K. K. Kurihara, ed., (New Brunswick, N.J.: Rutgers University Press).

Pearse, P. H. 1968. "A New Approach to the Evaluation of Non-Priced Recreation Resources," *Land Economics,* vol. 44, no. 1.

Smith, V. K. 1972. "The Effects of Technological Change on Different Uses of Environmental Resources," in *Natural Environments: Studies in Theoretical and Applied Analysis,* John V. Krutilla, ed. (Baltimore: Johns Hopkins Press).

————, 1974. *Technical Change, Relative Prices and Environmental Resource Evaluation* (Baltimore: Johns Hopkins Press).

————, and Krutilla, J. V. 1975. *The Structure and Properties of a Wilderness Users' Travel Simulator* (forthcoming).

U.S. Department of the Interior, 1968. "Middle Snake River Study, Idaho, Oregon and Washington," Joint Report of the Bureau of Commercial Fisheries and Bureau of Sport Fisheries and Wildlife, in *Department of the Interior Resource Study of the Middle Snake.*

Weisbrod, B. A. 1964. "Collective Consumption Services of Individual Consumption Goods," *Quarterly Journal of Economics,* vol. 78, no. 3.

Appendix 6-A
PRESERVATION BENEFIT
COMPUTATIONAL MODEL

Let

b'^p_0 = $1.00 of initial year's benefits

P_0 = initial vertical axis intercept (of a linear demand curve)

Q_0 = initial horizontal axis intercept

$D_0D'_0$ = initial year's computational demand schedule giving b'^p_0 = $1.00

r_y = rate of growth in vertical component of shift

γ = the historical rate of growth in the quantity demanded for $P = 0$; i.e., horizontal component of demand shift at zero price. γ is constant up until capacity (year k)

k = the year the area reaches recreational carrying capacity

d = the rate of decay of γ after year k which brings the rate of change in horizontal component of demand shift to rate of growth of population

m = the year in which the rate of the horizontal component of demand shift equals the rate of growth of population

i = rate of discount

Equations

$$P_t = (1 + r_y)^t P_0$$

$$Q_t = (1 + \gamma)^t Q_0 \text{ for } t \leqslant k$$

$$Q_t = Q_{t-1}(1 + \gamma_t) \text{ for } t > k$$

where $\quad \gamma_t = \gamma(1 + d)^{t-k}$

and $\quad d = \left[\dfrac{\gamma \text{ population}}{\gamma}\right]^{1/(m-k)} - 1$

$$PV^p_0 = \sum_{t=1}^{\infty} \frac{b_t}{(1 + i)^t}$$

$$b_t = 1/2 P_t Q_t \text{ for } t \leqslant k$$

i.e., the area under the computational demand schedule $D_tD'_t$. However, note that in the present-value equation, the assumed life expectancy of the preservation alternative is unbounded. In actual application this assumption is abandoned, as explained in the text.

$$b_t = 1/2P_tQ_t - 1/2P_t^*Q_t^* \text{ for } t > k$$

where

$$\frac{P_t^*}{Q_t^*} = \tan \theta_t = \frac{P_t}{Q_t}$$

$$\therefore \quad P_t^* = Q_t^* \times \frac{P_t}{Q_t}$$

and $\quad Q_t^* = Q_t - Q_k$

and $\quad b_t = 1/2P_tQ_t - 1/2(Q_t - Q_k)^2 \frac{P_t}{Q_t} \text{ for } t > k$

$\therefore \quad PV_b^p = b_t(t \leqslant k) + b_t(t > k)$, appropriately discounted.

An important parameter of the system is the annual percent increase in benefits. This is derived as follows:

$$b_t = 1/2P_tQ_t \text{ for } t \leqslant k$$
$$= 1/2[P_0(1 + r_y)^t][Q_0(1 + \gamma)^t]$$
$$= 1/2P_0Q_0[(1 + r_y)(1 + \gamma)]^t$$

but $\quad 1 = 1/2P_0Q_0$

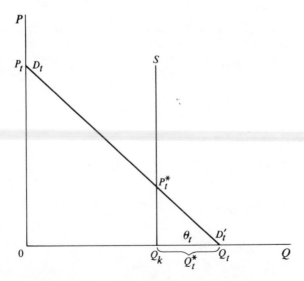

Figure 6-1. Demand curve in year t > k.

$$\therefore \quad b_t = (1 + r_y\gamma + r_y + \gamma)^t$$

$$\frac{db_t}{dt} = (1 + r_y\gamma + r_y + \gamma)^t \ln (1 + r_y\gamma + r_y + \gamma)$$

annual percent change in benefits $= \dfrac{db_t/dt}{b_t}$

$$\therefore \quad \frac{db_t/dt}{b_t} = \frac{(1 + r_y\gamma + r_y + \gamma)^t \ln (1 + r_y\gamma + r_y + \gamma)}{(1 + r_y\gamma + r_y + \gamma)^t}$$

$$= \ln (1 + r_y\gamma + r_y + \gamma) \text{ for } t \leqslant k$$

Note, that for r_y and γ close to zero, $\ln (1 + r_y\gamma + r_y + \gamma) \cong r_y + \gamma$, which is just the sum of the two shift rates. The rate of change in preservation benefits is identical to $(db_t/dt)/b_t$ when t is less than capacity, but since demand is expected to moderate when the canyon's capacity is reached, the rate of change in benefits begins to decline at capacity (k). Accordingly, $\dfrac{db_t/dt}{b_t}$ $(t \leqslant k)$ would exceed the $\bar{a}$ discussed previously.

Finally, the slope of the initial computational demand schedule (the area under which is equal to unity) may be varied and the effect measured, since:

$$P = a + sQ$$

$$\frac{P_0 \times Q_0}{2} = 1$$

and $\qquad P_0 = P$ when $Q = 0$

$$Q_0 = Q \text{ when } P = 0$$

$\therefore \qquad P = P_0 + sQ$

$$s = \frac{P_0}{Q_0}$$

$$sQ_0 = P_0$$

and $\qquad P_0 Q_0 = 2$

$$sQ_0^2 = 2$$

$\therefore \qquad Q_0 = \sqrt{2}/s$ and $P_0 = sQ_0$

This last result allows for the calculation of benefits for various initial slopes as well as varying demand shifts and supply constraints, thus completing the general derivation for the computation of benefits through time for linear demand schedules.

By using this model to calculate the present value of a dollar's worth of initial year's benefits, we obtain the denominator of equation (6-1). Having estimates of the numerator from analyses in chapter 5, we can perform the division to obtain b_0^p, or the aggregate initial year's benefits required to justify retaining the canyon area in its present state.

CHAPTER 7

THE WHITE CLOUD PEAKS: WILDERNESS RECREATION OR MINE–MILL OPERATIONS?

1. INTRODUCTION

In chapters 5 and 6 we reviewed the circumstances concerning one of the most outstanding wild and scenic rivers to be found anywhere on the North American continent. In addition to its remarkable setting, the Snake River in the Hells Canyon reach has some of the best hydroelectric power sites remaining in the coterminous United States. The stakes in the conflict between developmental and preservation uses, accordingly, are very large and have received intensive economic analysis by official parties. This chapter addresses a problem in wild and scenic land allocation that, while equally controversial, perhaps is not quite as well known, and for which no official benefit–cost analysis has been done. This case deals with the White Cloud Peaks Mountains in Idaho where prospective mining operations would be incompatible with retaining the area in its natural condition. The question then concerns the most efficient uses to which the area's resources may be allocated, taking explicit account of the mutual exclusiveness of some of the possible competing uses.

Since an official benefit–cost study has not been undertaken for the White Cloud Peaks, the analysis presented here does not have the kind of data typically available in federal, or federally regulated, water resource development benefit–cost studies. What we have done is use data which were made available through the broader Forest Service land-use planning basic studies, along with reconnaissance-grade estimates provided by the Forest Service in connection with recreation-related facilities, in order to permit results good to a first approximation. The objective was to organize what data were readily at hand or could be obtained in limited time to provide some guidance on the relative value of the commodity and amenity resources available from the area. The analysis is partial, as well as good only to a first approximation because the extractive activities incompatible with recreation were compared with only low-density recreation.

But, to get ahead of the analysis a bit, if it can be shown that an activity requiring an undisturbed environment can compete economically with an extractive activity, the grounds for massive landscape-degrading extractive activities can be questioned. Were that to be the case, there still would remain the question of the intensity of the recreational use. This is a matter that will receive attention under the recently passed Sawtooth National Recreation Area Act (1972), which directs the Park Service to evaluate the White Cloud Peaks for their potential suitability for inclusion in the National Park System.

2. THE CONFLICT IN LAND USE IN THE WHITE CLOUD PEAKS

The White Cloud Peaks, lying about 30 miles north of Sun Valley, Idaho, in the Challis National Forest (see figure 7-1), were little known nationally prior to the spring of 1969. In that year, having purchased some existing mineral claims (molybdenum) in the vicinity of Castle Peak and staked out additional claims, the American Smelting and Refining Company (ASARCO) applied to the Forest Service for a permit to build a mining access road across National Forest land in the expectation of more intensive activities in the area. Notice of the application attracted immediate and widespread attention among local conservation groups. And, as the road in question would be located along Little Boulder Creek to the base of Castle Peak—10 miles through presently roadless country—it soon attracted national attention through articles in such periodicals, among others, as the *Living Wilderness* and the *Smithsonian*.

Quite aside from the fact that the access road would have crossed an otherwise unroaded area,[1] the keen interest expressed by conservation groups was related to the characteristics of the area itself. The White Cloud Peaks, anchored at the southern end by Castle Peak, extend northward for about 10 miles of rugged peaks and razorback ridges. While the total area regarded as the White Cloud Peaks administrative unit by the Forest Service is put at 157,000 acres, the area actually occupied by the peaks and related high cirque basins is scarcely 20,000 acres in extent. In this belt there are well over a score of peaks rising to elevations in the range of 10,000 to nearly 12,000 feet. Viewed from the east, the White Cloud Peaks give the impression of a semicircular, self-contained "pocket mountain range." Individually the peaks are not more majestic than the peaks in the Pioneer Mountains to the southeast, for example, nor are they more numerous. What distinguishes them is their quality of self-

---

[1] Roadless areas are subject to consideration for inclusion into the Wilderness Preservation System.

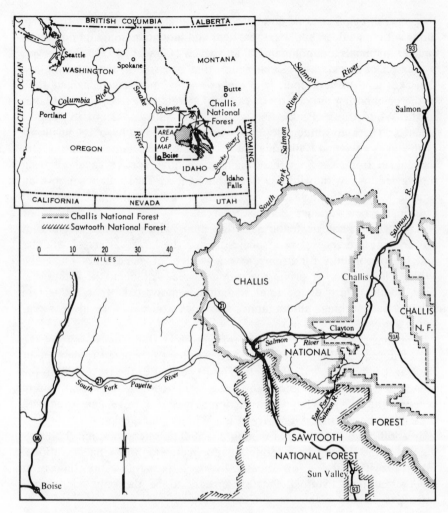

*Figure 7-1. Location of Sawtooth–Challis
National Forests.*

containment, clustered as they are in the circular arrangement. They appear physically isolated from other peaks and ranges, which along with their concentration and distinctive configuration, distinguishes them from the Boulder and Pioneer mountains, and collectively lends them a uniqueness which the peaks viewed individually probably would not merit.

Interestingly, not only are the White Cloud Peaks unusual in their concentration, but they and the adjoining lands also support a remarkable variety of the larger mammalian species of wildlife. Indeed, only within this general region can one find both the mountain goat and bighorn sheep, along with mule deer, elk, antelope, bear and mountain lion, and numerous smaller mammals and nonmammalian species (Gunnell, 1971). Moreover, by reason of the kind of glacial action that occurred in these mountains, the lakes tend to be deeper, with higher energy and oxygen budgets than in the neighboring mountain ranges (Schlatterer, 1972). Of the 120 lakes in the White Cloud Peaks, about half have sufficient depth to support fisheries. These are principally rainbow, cutthroat, and brook trout. Some of the lakes have had California golden trout and grayling introduced, and the golden trout has flourished when competitive species have not been introduced. As with wildlife, the White Cloud Peaks can support an unusual variety of game fishes, making the area interesting to anglers bent on bringing new varieties of fishes to creel.

The geomorphologic features of the area, which provide magnificent scenery; the presence of rare species among the large variety of wildlife; and the opportunity for fishing a wide variety of game fishes make the White Cloud Peaks a prime recreational area. Although the hunting is light, about a third of the total visitation is motivated by an interest in fishing. Backpacking, photography, and rock collecting are also recreational activities enjoyed in this area.

The construction of a high standard motorbike trail from the site of the old Livingston Mill into the Frog Lake area has contributed to damage of the fragile ecology.[2] And, while close to 40 percent of the travel within the area was by means of motorbike in the 1971 recreational season, future access to the area may require restriction to modes of travel consistent with preserving the ecological integrity of the White Cloud Peaks.

In addition to the potential mining and milling operations and the existing use of the White Cloud Mountains for recreation, the Challis National Forest provides grazing for domestic livestock, primarily cattle. Indeed, at the present time livestock grazing appears to be the only commercial extractive activity in the White Clouds area.

There are conflicts in resource uses, but with one notable exception, none are critical for each other. Grazing on the Big Boulder Creek Allotment inflicts some costs on recreationists, as the cattle graze in the Frog Lake and Quicksand Meadow areas, which are popular with recreationists, and up along Little Boulder Creek, also popular with fishermen. A range management plan is proposed for the allotment and will, with moderate adjustments at modest costs, eliminate the major sources of conflict. A somewhat more serious conflict involves the effects of possible mine–mill

[2] Prior to the construction of the motorbike trail, only 1 percent of the visitors listed bike riding as their principal interests. Following its construction, almost 20 percent listed biking. Report of White Clouds patrolman J. Palombi, Clayton Ranger District, Clayton, Idaho, September 26, 1971.

operations on utilization of range forage by wildlife as well as domestic livestock in the Germania Creek, Wickiup Creek, and Little Boulder Creek drainages. Even so, the better part of all four of the units making up the Big Boulder Creek Allotment, along with the Big Lake Creek Allotment, would be available for domestic livestock grazing.

The operation of an open-pit mine and ore beneficiation mill, however, would result in sufficient disturbance to the existing environment over a large enough area near the heart of the recreationally attractive portion of the White Clouds to be fatal to the amenities of a wilderness environment. Immense amounts of material would have to be removed and disposed of; tailings from the milling operations would also require disposal—and, for movement of all of this immense bulk, a transportation facility would need to be built that would be grossly out of character with the pristine conditions currently attracting the recreational activities.

Accordingly, the major conflicts in resource uses in the White Clouds involve the incompatibility of mining with wilderness recreation in an undisturbed natural setting. There may be some mutually exclusive activities involving mine operations and the Little Boulder Creek unit of the Big Boulder Grazing Allotment, but these instances appear to be relatively minor.

As explained in section 1, the data to inform judgments on the relative merits of the alternative uses of the White Cloud Peaks environment are rather informal. Accordingly, it might be thought that we face problems in adapting and applying some aspects of the theoretical format of chapter 3. In fact, the theoretical results will be helpful in organizing and interpreting the data we do have, as we shall suggest here and again in sections 5 and 6.

In the analysis of the Hells Canyon project in chapters 5 and 6 it was possible, on the basis of expectations that the value of the hydropower project would be declining over time relative to the value of wilderness recreation activity on the site, to achieve a considerable simplification in the investment criterion. Specifically, it was shown that any investment should be undertaken immediately, if at all. This in turn indicated a simple comparison of the present value of investing in the most profitable project there with the present value of the recreation activity that would be enjoyed only in the absence of the project. In the case of the White Clouds, the information we are able to develop concerning prospective trends in relative values suggests a similar, though not identical, simplification for evaluating investment in a mining project there.

Very briefly characterizing some of the empirical information reported in detail in section 3, we may say that benefits from recreation are expected to grow in much the same fashion, and for the same reasons, as the benefits from recreation in the Hells Canyon. (But see section 3 for discussion of a more sophisticated treatment of carrying capacity.) As indicated in section 5, the behavior of benefits from the incompatible extractive alternative is probably more complicated. It seems likely that extraction of molybdenum from this deposit at this time would yield negative benefits, even in the absence of environmental opportunity costs, and become profitable only some decades hence, if then.

Assume that wilderness recreation benefits are growing from the present, time t_0, at the rate α, and that returns to molybdenum extraction begin to grow from time t_1, $t_1 > t_0$, at the rate δ, where $\delta > \alpha$. Then, even if we also assume that the current flow of recreation benefits exceeds the current flow of extraction benefits, clearly the present value (at t_0) of extraction can exceed the present value of recreation. Equally clearly, however, development for mining beginning at t_0 would be wasteful, sacrificing recreation benefits from t_0 until such time t', $t' \geq t_1$, as some degree of mining operation becomes profitable. Instead, the present value of the natural environment, the maximand of chapter 3's optimality analysis, is maximized by preserving the environment for some time, until t', and only then starting operations. If the rate of appreciation of recreation benefits, α, in fact begins to decline after some time, as suggested for recreation at a single site in chapter 6, and all benefits are discounted to the present, it is likely that most of the (present) recreational value of the White Clouds, for example, will be realized roughly within the interim period before mining becomes profitable. Accordingly, it should suffice to assess the present value of recreation (and grazing) activity beginning immediately, on the one hand, and that of mining activity beginning some decades in the future, on the other. From the discussion above, however, it follows that a simple comparison of the two present values, as in the Hells Canyon case, will not be relevant.

We now look more closely at the several alternative uses and benefit flows, and begin by assessing the value of the White Clouds for recreational uses that are incompatible with the mine–mill operation based on the molybdenum in the Castle Peak location.

3. THE WHITE CLOUD PEAKS AS RECREATIONAL RESOURCES

The Setting of the Recreation Problem

The value of the White Clouds for recreational purposes depends on several factors. When a resource has a number of different uses, its value is not independent of the end to which it is put. There are various kinds of recreation activities, from those requiring highly developed facilities and resulting in relatively high density use to those with minimal development, or none, and low density use. Moreover, the resources take on different values as the demand for their services varies. In the latter connection, the White Clouds Peaks as recreational resources will have some kind of relationship with the Sawtooth Valley and the Sawtooth Mountains.[3]

Under recent legislation,[4] the Sawtooth Primitive Area has been reclassified as the Sawtooth Wilderness and made part of the statutory wilderness system. The Sawtooth Valley, along with the White Clouds, is designated as a National Recreation Area with the latter, under the act, to be examined by the National Park Service for its suitability for inclusion within the National Park System. Accordingly, while the Sawtooth Wilderness might be considered a competing recreational attraction for remote-area, low-density type recreation, the legislation creating the National Recreation Area will bring recognition to the White Cloud Peaks as recreational resources of national prominence. The additional publicity which the legislation involving both attractions brings is likely to stimulate increased demand for both areas' recreational resources. This prospect would be increased were the complex of resources, including the Sawtooth Valley portion of the National Recreation Area, to be regarded by the agency administering them as suited to provide complementary recreational services.

In the analysis of the White Clouds' recreational potentialities we make the following assumptions:

1. The Sawtooth Wilderness will be managed in a manner consistent with the retention of wilderness values and ecological integrity.
2. The Sawtooth Valley, being readily accessible by motor vehicles, will be used predominantly for recreational activities depending on developed facilities and consistent with higher use intensities.
3. The White Cloud Peaks, being relatively small, and ecologically fragile, will be carefully managed to provide recreation opportunities without activities or use intensities that would result in significant alteration of the ecological relationships.

Within the area covered by the legislation, therefore, a range of recreational opportunities could be provided to cater to various tastes. The more intensive development would be confined to the Sawtooth Valley and the bordering approaches to the west slopes of the White Clouds, while the more fragile areas on the upper eastern slopes would be protected against excessive use through appropriate management practices.

There was an estimated 4,500 to 5,000 recreation days' use in the upper cirque basin areas during the 1971 recreation season.[5] The use was

---

[3] The Sawtooth Mountains to the west of the White Clouds are separated from the latter by the Salmon River, which flows through the Sawtooth Valley.

[4] PL 92.400.

[5] Report of White Clouds patrolman J. Palombi, *op. cit.,* and correspondence with Don T. Nebeker, study coordinator, U.S. Forest Service, November 26, 1971.

not very evenly distributed, with a large concentration at Frog Lake. Part of this was accounted for by the reputation of the lake for yielding large fish, but a large part was also accounted for by day-use bike traffic, a very popular activity even before 1970 when the Forest Service built a 42-inch tread, high standard, motorbike road to the site of Frog Lake. Use of this area already exceeds the carrying capacity, if serious erosion of environmental quality is to be prevented. A second large concentration occurred at Walker Lake, with much of the remainder distributed among the Little Boulder Chain Lakes. Here also, the indicated present usage exceeds the sustainable capacity if sanitary conditions are to be maintained.

A number of related factors require attention if the ecology is to be preserved while the scenic and recreational attractions of the area are used. First, the area of prime recreational attraction is not particularly large. A fairly short, perhaps 2-day, overnight backpack trip per party might be regarded as typical.[6] With statutorily recognized national status and a clientele drawn from nonlocal sources, however, the average length of trip might tend to increase in the future. Secondly, to compound the problem related to size, the ecology is not very robust in these high, sparsely vegetated areas, and is readily damaged by concentrated use. Finally, the spatial distribution among recreationists has been very uneven; thus practices and facilities are required which will disperse the present concentrations at specific locations.

One of the more obvious actions that should be considered is the prohibition of trail bikes in the area. Damage from off-trail riding in the low meadows, and the short-cutting on trail switchbacks is the most urgent threat to the ecology.[7] Perhaps half of the concentration at Frog Lake, moreover, is accounted for by day-use bike riders.

If use beyond the present level of intensity is envisioned, some extension and relocation of segments of the present trail system is in order. The concentration at Frog Lake is partly accounted for by the convergence of several trails in the vicinity of the lake and the existence of a through-trail running adjacent to it. Perhaps relocation, or even elimination of a section of trail (No. 4179) between the lower of the Boulder Chain Lakes and its junction with the trail running along Red Ridge would be feasible. Frog Lake could then be serviced by a spur trail in a manner similar to the access to Little Redfish Lake (see figure 7-2).

Both because of the concentration on such a relatively small area, and the need to eliminate those uses which most tax the environment, horse

---

[6] It should be noted that a two-day, one-night, wilderness trip is currently the most numerous, irrespective of the wilderness area in question. See *Research Progress 1971*, Pacific Southwest Forest and Range Experiment Station, Berkeley, California.

[7] Regulations have been introduced prohibiting off-trail use of motorbikes. How effectively these can be enforced is not at the moment known.

traffic should be restricted from access to areas above Frog Lake and Little Redfish Lakes, with dispersed corrals built to accommodate tethered stock while the upper cirque areas are enjoyed by travel afoot.

In addition to these possible actions necessary to preserve the environment in a largely unmodified condition, carefully designed and located toilets will be required to deal with a sanitation problem that would become acute in some localities. They should be designed for aesthetically pleasing conformity with the alpine surroundings[8] as much as for the functional objectives of eliminating threats of pollution.

Finally, in order to reach maximum ecologically sustainable recreation, additions to the present trail system are required, both to assist in dispersal of presently occurring concentrations of visitors as well as to increase the number of more readily accessible areas.[9] Several specific loop routes have been suggested and are as follows:

Trail I. Beginning at the top of Railroad Ridge (see figure 7-2) and proceeding down the mountain to the site of Tin Cup Lake, the trail would then go on to Quicksand Meadow and down Big Boulder Creek.[10] This trail would terminate at the Livingston Mill site.

Trail II. Beginning at the Livingston Mill site, the trail would proceed to Walker Lake and Big Boulder Lakes, then over the divide to Boulder Chain Lakes and down to Frog Lake and back to the point of origin. If the trail from the lower Boulder Chain Lakes were relocated to avoid contributing to the traffic through the vicinity of Frog Lake, the trail between the lower of the Boulder Chain Lakes and the old Livingston Mill site would bypass Frog Lake.

Trail III. This trail would enter the White Clouds area via the Little Boulder Creek trail and proceed to its intersection with Forest Service Trail No. 4179. At that point, several options exist that would use segments of other trails to complete loop routes. Essentially the same sets of options exist for trail loops entering the area up Wickiup Creek and Germania Creek drainage trails.

Trail IV. Given the working assumptions adopted above, access from Warm Springs Creek or the Sawtooth side leading to the vicinity of Born Lakes would not be completed over the divide to the Boulder Chain Lakes. Establishment of the Sawtooth National Recreation Area will very likely

[8] For discussion of means to blend structures to conform with the environment see Burton Litton, "Aesthetic Dimensions of the Landscape," unpublished manuscript, p. 200 ff.

[9] Whether the benefits from such investments justify the cost, of course, would need to be evaluated.

[10] There is a possibility that this trail would adversely affect a band of mountain goats, perhaps causing them to abandon this section of the range. This information was supplied by Dan Pence, district ranger, in correspondence dated January 22, 1973.

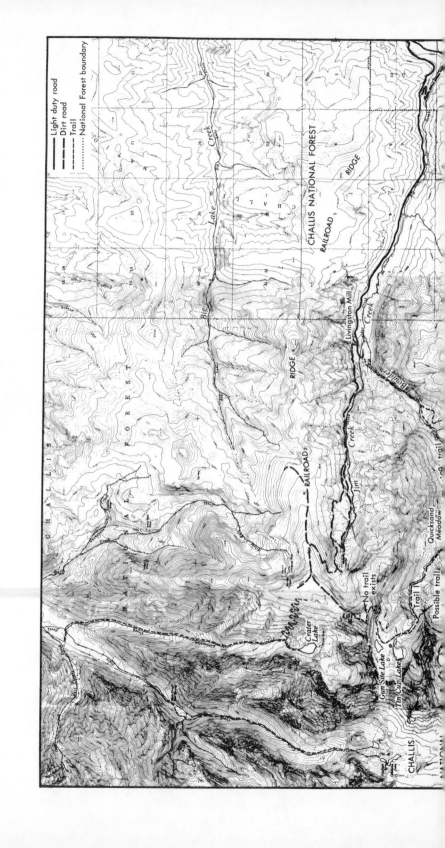

Figure 7-2. Trail system in White Cloud Peaks.

encourage too large a visitation for the Sawtooth Valley to be compatible with preserving the environment as a resource for wilderness experience.

With these trail additions and relocations, it is variously estimated that the carrying capacity for recreational purposes could be increased from two to three times the present level without causing damage to the natural environment. In order to maintain the present water quality in the currently more heavily used lakes (Frog and Walker), as well as to accommodate an expansion of use, expenditures would be necessary for sanitary facilities.[11] A rough estimate of the requirement suggests a need for approximately nine toilets for the area. Accordingly in table 7-1 we present the required capital outlays for the trail system, which current expenditure experience suggests is necessary to maintain some of the more difficult trail segments, and the investment and operating expenditures associated with the sanitary facilities. These are in turn summarized as present values of the combined investment, replacement, and operating costs.

Valuation of Recreation Benefits

Do the benefits to be obtained from recreation justify the expenditures that make it possible? To answer this question we will need an estimate of the value of the recreation in the White Clouds with the added trails and sanitary facilities, along with an estimate of the value of the recreation in the absence of additional facilities. This will be needed to determine whether the increment in benefits exceeds the increment in costs. But this will tell us only whether the *additional* expenditures necessary to secure the *additional* benefits from recreation are justified. There will remain the question of whether or not the recreational benefits, at whatever appears to be the optimal level, are sufficient to secure the use of the area for recreation as against alternative incompatible uses. We defer this matter until after our analyses in sections 4 and 5.

Ideally, in order to evaluate the recreation and related benefits of an undisturbed natural environment, we would need to undertake the kind of analyses described in chapter 6, pages 123–124, along with an adequate economic or econometric analysis of the recreation demand. And, as in the case of Hells Canyon where a low-density, primitive setting recreational experience is sought, the analysis would have to take into account the potential change in per unit value to recreationists as increasing numbers demand the services of the area, thus potentially crowding it. Once such a functional relation between willingness to pay and congestion is established for current users, the demand function would need to be made to reflect, by simulated demand function shifting, the growth in demand over time and its effect on the per unit and total value of the recreation benefits

---

[11] In the opinion of the district forest ranger, limitation of use to an appropriate level for these lakes will have to be solved by regulation. *Ibid.*

Table 7-1A
Trail Extensions for White Clouds Threshold Wilderness Recreation

		Present value of costs		
Trail extensions		7% discount	10% discount	13% discount
Capital outlays				
Trail I	$11,000	$ 11,000	$ 11,000	$ 11,000
Trail II	12,000	12,000	12,000	12,000
Trail III	—ᵃ	—	—	—
Trail IV	—ᵃ	—	—	—
Maintenance outlays/yr.				
Trail I	$ 5,500	$ 77,770	$ 54,505	$ 41,855
Trail II	6,000	84,840	59,463	45,660
Trail III	90	1,273	892	685
Trail IV	322	4,553	3,191	2,450
USFS 4179	180	2,545	1,784	1,370
Total trail present value of costs		$193,981	$142,835	$115,020

ᵃTrails III and IV are existing trails which will link up with segments of trails I and II to provide loop routes.

Table 7-1B
Sanitary Facilities for White Clouds Threshold Wilderness Recreation

		Present value of costs		
Sanitary facilities		7% discount	10% discount	13% discount
Year/capital outlays				
1	Nine toilets @ $750/toilet equals $6,750	$ 6,750	$ 6,750	$ 6,750
30	Nine toilets, $6,750	887	387	173
60	Nine toilets, $6,750	114	20	4
Present value of capital outlays		$ 7,751	$ 7,157	$ 6,927
Maintenance and operation outlays, $100/year		$ 1,414	$ 990	$ 759
Present value of total sanitation cost		$ 9,165	$ 8,147	$ 7,686
Present value of all recreation capital and annual costs		$203,145	$150,982	$122,706

Sources: Information transmitted by letter dated 11/26/71 and 1/21/72 (Nebeker) and discussions with recreation specialists and study coordinator 4/24–26/72.

of the White Clouds. This would be required to fix capacity constraint at the point at which wilderness-type recreation benefits are maximized.

Neither time nor resources permitted the kind of sophisticated survey research and econometric analysis that would provide a demand function for recreational services specific to the White Clouds. A companion study

of the Spanish Peaks Primitive Area (Cicchetti and Smith, 1973) however, provides some surrogate data that might be used.[12] Conditions in the
White Clouds are not precisely the same as those in the Spanish Peaks,
but the nature of the experience, in part, and the characteristics of the
users may be sufficiently close to warrant using for the White Clouds some
of the relationships found to exist in the Spanish Peaks data.[13] Cicchetti
and Smith (1973) found the relation between the users' expressed willingness to pay for the wilderness trip and the number of encounters to be of
the following sort:

(7-1) $\log(WP) = a_0 + a_1Ln + a_2Tn + a_3Cn + a_4SE + U$

where

WP = willingness to pay

Ln = length of trip in days

Tn = average number of trail encounters per day

Cn = number of nights of camp encounters

SE = socioeconomic characteristics

U = error term

If we restrict the analysis to trips of an average of two, or at most three
days, and if we set all variables at their mean values except for the dependent variable (WP) and the two independent encounter variables, we
can observe the numerical relation between user willingness to pay and
the expected congestion. We illustrate this in the table.

*Relation Between Willingness to Pay and the Expected Number of Encounters
in Spanish Peaks Primitive Area (no encounter = 1)*

Number of Encounters—Camp	0	1	2	3
Trail				
0	1.00	0.81	0.66	0.53
1	0.89	0.72	0.59	0.47
2	0.79	0.64	0.52	0.42
3	0.70	0.57	0.46	0.37
4	0.62	0.51	0.41	0.34
.	.	.	.	.
.	.	.	.	.
.	.	.	.	.

---

[12] See also Cicchetti and Smith, "An Econometric Analysis of Congestion Effects
in Wilderness Recreation" (forthcoming).

[13] Indeed, it was precisely because George Stankey had found an inverse relation
between satisfaction obtained from the trip and the number of other parties encountered on four widely separated wilderness areas, that prompted the econometric study
of the Spanish Peaks. See Stankey (1972).

Two observations might be made on the Cicchetti–Smith results. First, the relationship satisfies the hypothesis which is intuitively suggested; namely, that individuals who seek experiences in the wilderness for the solitude and privacy such experiences afford find the satisfaction from the outing diminished as encounters with other parties increase. Secondly, it provides confirmation of the Stankey findings that campsite encounters entail greater disutility—are more unsatisfactory encounters. Both of these points in the Stankey work are reconfirmed by the multivariate analysis of the Spanish Peaks data. The Cicchetti–Smith results, therefore, not only conform with those of Stankey (unpublished) on the Spanish Peaks but also with findings on four other separate wilderness areas studied by Stankey (1972) previously. Since the general nature of the relationships is consistent across several different kinds of wilderness areas, we feel justified in using results as surrogates, pending a specific study addressed to these issues on the White Clouds.

Given the relation between the intensity of use and users' valuation of the recreation experience, there can arise a socio-psychological consideration in addition to the ecological that may counsel restriction of entry to control density. That is, since there is a tradeoff between the number of individuals using the area and the value of the experience to each individual, there is a point at which use must be rationed in order not to reduce the total value of the recreation services by an excessive number of users.[14] Having an expression for the relationship between willingness to pay and the number of encounters, what is needed next is a relationship between the intensity of use (or number of users per unit time) and expected number of encounters. This is a relation that could be obtained from a wilderness traffic simulator, which would mimic the traffic flows and patterns through the area. With a simulator that related the increasing expected number of encounters as the number of users increased per unit time, the tradeoffs could be computed and the point at which the incremental cost to others from an additional user just equaled the incremental benefit would give the maximum aggregate benefit, or optimal capacity.[15]

While such a wilderness traffic simulator was being developed,[16] it was not available for application, nor did the detail of analysis justify its use. Rather, we had to rely on a very rough, intuitive judgment on the relation between expected number of encounters and increases in the number of users. Since the area is dotted with numerous lakes, thus providing many

[14] For a more complete discussion of this issue, and the relation between ecological and socio-psychological capacity constraints, see Fisher and Krutilla (1972).

[15] See Fisher and Krutilla (1972) for discussion of the use of travel behavior simulation as a means of estimating the expected number of encounters.

[16] Work on the development of a simulation model has since been completed at Resources for the Future under a cooperative research agreement with the U.S. Forest Service and IBM. See Smith and Krutilla (1975).

attractive campsites, campsite capacity is not likely to be a limiting factor. In the judgment of four knowledgeable individuals, approached independently, a figure of 60 parties was proposed as daily capacity potential, without any problem of congestion.[17]

An effort was made then to use what knowledge of the area and trail use was available to approximate crudely a relationship between expected number of parties and encounters by place of encounter (camp or trail), and to relate this to the tradeoff between encounters and willingness to pay. Given the Cicchetti–Smith model for measuring the effects of congestion on willingness to pay in the Spanish Peaks Primitive Area, it is possible to derive some approximate adjustments to the vertical shifter (r_y) in the demand function, to account for such reduction in service quality.

Assume, for the moment, that only trail encounters will be considered. The estimated coefficients from the Cicchetti–Smith model measure the percentage change in willingness to pay as trail encounters change. We know from the nature of wilderness recreation that as the intensity of use of a given wilderness area increases, the expected intrusions upon solitude any user can anticipate will also increase. Accordingly, if one can link encounters to use intensity, and the intensity to time (through growth in demand over time), then it is possible to provide a dampening adjustment to r_y to account for the effects of quality reduction.

$$\beta = [dWP/dt]_c/WP = a_2(dTn/dx)(dx/dt)$$

where

$a_2 =$ coefficient for trail encounters (Tn) in equation (7-1)

$\beta =$ congestion adjustment to growth in willingness to pay

$x =$ use intensity

$t =$ time

$[dWP/dt]_c =$ change in willingness to pay due to congestion

Moreover, since we need to project the shift in the demand function for recreational services over time, it is convenient to partition the sources of growth into their two constituent elements. First, the quantity demanded is likely to grow over time as a direct result of the growth in population.[18] Secondly, the price, or willingness to pay for such services is likely to increase over time as well. If one assumes that the quality of the service will be protected by management practices, then the price will increase with income growth and technical change.[19] Consequently, we might postulate that the rate at which the price intercept is shifting upward is a func-

[17] The individuals approached included the district ranger and the White Clouds patrolman, among other knowledgeable outdoorsmen.

[18] See chapter 6, p. 130 ff.

[19] *Ibid.* and Smith (1972).

tion of the rate of technological change, and the characteristics of the community's demand structure given below:

$$r_y = \frac{dWP/dt}{WP} = f(T, D_1, \ldots, D_n)$$

T = rate of technological advance

$D_1, \ldots, D_n$ = parameters describing the nature of community demand

Since we do not have precise knowledge of the relation between encounters and intensity of use that would be given by a traffic simulator, we have relied on informed judgments on the White Cloud Peaks area to approximate the term $(dTn/dx)(dx/dt)$ with the first two terms of a Taylor expansion, testing for the sensitivity of results to the parametrization of the approximation. This approach produces crude approximations only, depending as it does on educated guesses, but does permit introducing the effects of reduced willingness to pay as the intensity of use is increased to an optimal point.

With this refinement over the Hells Canyon model to determine the variable rate of appreciation (α_t) of the recreational services, we can represent the present-value computational model compactly as below:

$$PV = \sum_{t=1}^{T'} b_0 (1 + \bar{\alpha})^t (1 + i)^{-t}$$

where

b_0 = the benefit in the first year

$\bar{\alpha}$ = an average rate of appreciation equivalent to the actually varying rate of appreciation, α_t

i = the discount rate

t = the index of time measured in years

T' = the terminal year of the computation or the year in which the present value of an initial dollar growing at the rate α_t, discounted by the relevant rate i, falls below 1 cent

Computing the present value requires an estimate of the value of recreation in the beginning year, the rate of annual value appreciation, and the rate of discount. Here we have relied on a frequently used discount rate of 10 percent, with sensitivity checks made using alternatively 7 and 13 percent. Just prior to the time of this analysis, 10 percent was being recommended for federal projects by the Office of Management and Budget (OMB) as well as numerous economists (U.S. Congress, 1968). A rate of 13 percent represents an average of views regarding the interest rate given by economists at hearings held by the Joint Economic Committee of the Congress (Seagraves, 1970) but has been chosen by us more specifically to provide symmetry to the range for sensitivity tests since a rate of 7 percent is also used. The latter is not economically derived, but rather is a rate politically negotiated between the Office of Management and Budget and the Water Resources Council. It represents a political compromise midway between current rates used by the Council and the 10 percent recommended by OMB.[20]

We used, as in the Hells Canyon case, a projected growth in use (γ) of 10 percent per year (with sensitivity tests assuming growth at alternatively 7.5 percent and 12.5 percent) until the capacity constraint was reached, with a gradual decline in the horizontal shifter of the demand curve to a rate equal only to the population growth rate by the fiftieth year. The vertical demand shifter (r_y) was rationalized as described in chapter 6, pp. 129–132.[21] The vertical shift of the demand function was taken to be 4 percent per year initially, dampened by the effects of increased encounters over time on the willingness to pay. The annual rate of appreciation, $\bar{\alpha}_t$ will be a function of the two growth rates (r_y and γ_t) until the capacity constraint is met. Since no further increase in number of users can be accommodated after the constraint becomes effective, α_t increases thereafter only as a function of the increase in value of services over time as their scarcity relative to demand increases.

The model was formulated in a perfectly general form, i.e., in terms of $1 of initial year's benefit, just as in its application to the Hells Canyon study. It can therefore be applied to the White Clouds by simply multiplying the present value of the $1 (growing at α_t and discounted by i) by the number of dollars estimated for the value of recreation services in the White Clouds for the initial year of analysis.

As already mentioned, no survey research effort designed to develop willingness-to-pay estimates could be undertaken in connection with the White Cloud Peaks recreation. However, considering the results of the Spanish Peaks survey and related information, an average imputed value of $10 per day is not unreasonable. Taking the recreation days at roughly 4,600, we would estimate an initial year's benefit from White Clouds recreation at about $46,000. It is this initial year's figure that we use as the basis for the following analysis.

Table 7-2 shows the range of estimated recreation benefits under varying assumptions with respect to interest rate, growth rate, and the nature of the functional relation between encounters and time. In sections A through E the high and low estimates reflect the difference in assumption

---

[20] It should be noted that since the time of this analysis the Congress, by attaching a rider to the 1974 omnibus Rivers and Harbors Bill, legislated a 5 percent discount rate.

[21] For a formal proof see Smith (1972).

Table 7-2
Present Value of Wilderness Recreation Benefits of White Clouds

A.	$i = 10\%, \gamma = 10\%, r_y = 4\%$		D.	$i = 10\%, \gamma = 7.5\%, r_y = 4\%$
	Low	\$1,577,340		Low	\$1,426,000
	Medium	1,680,320		High	1,560,320
	High	1,793,080			
B.	$i = 7\%, \gamma = 10\%, r_y = 4\%$		E.	$i = 10\%, \gamma = 12.5\%, r_y = 4\%$
	Low	\$3,448,160		Low	\$1,861,620
	High	4,919,940		High	2,192,940
C.	$i = 13\%, \gamma = 10\%, r_y = 4\%$			
	Low	\$ 994,520			
	High	1,108,140			

as to the way encounters are related to the intensity of use. That is, the low estimate in each pair assumes a relatively higher encounter rate for any level of use than does the high estimate of recreation benefits. The range is given in the light of our imperfect knowledge as to precisely how encounters relate to the intensity of use. Moreover, the encounters are assumed to obtain under conditions in which the current uneven distribution over time and space is modified by appropriate management practices.

In section A of table 7-2, with a discount rate of 10 percent, growth rate of 10 percent per year, and an annual rate of appreciation of 4 percent (dampened to take into account the effect of increased encounters on willingness to pay as use increases), the benefit estimates will range from a low of \$1,577,340 to a high of \$1,793,080. If the discount rate is varied as in sections B and C, we see that the present value of the estimated benefits will vary as a factor of about three and a half. It should be noted, however, that while the discount rate makes a great difference in the present-value computation, the same discount rates would be applied to the estimated benefits of any alternative incompatible use and therefore the change in values shown does not convey anything in an absolute sense. Finally, sections D and E show the differences in present value of estimated recreational benefits when differences in the rate of growth in demand are postulated. The difference in present values between the 7.5 percent and the 12.5 percent growth rates favors the more rapid growth rate by 30 to 40 percent.

It must be stressed that these present-value computations represent rather crude approximations. While conceptually the analysis takes into account the most significant relevant factors, the empirical relationships have not all been established specifically with respect to the White Clouds. There is particular need for application of the sophisticated survey research and econometric analysis undertaken in connection with the Spanish Peaks in order to get better initial-year benefit estimates. Moreover, the relationship between expected number of encounters and level of use that could be obtained by application of a wilderness traffic simulator was not available at the time of this effort. Nevertheless, this analysis has provided at least a first approximation to the present value of the recreational services of the White Cloud Peaks when managed for wilderness type recreation.

While we have a first approximation of the total present value of the wilderness recreation, assuming that the necessary investment in trails and related facilities is made, we need also to consider whether an increase in recreational value from the investment is warranted by the investment cost. If we assume that the present use is as intense as could be permitted without additional expenditures for management and facilities, we can note the increment in benefits between the present and the expanded levels of use and compare it with the increment in costs of the inputs required for the more intensive, more carefully managed option. Table 7-3 shows the estimate of the present value of use restricted to current levels and management practice.

The differences between the values in table 7-3 and those for the implicit midpoint calculations of Table 7-2 are given in table 7-4, along with the relevant differences in costs obtained from table 7-1.

Based on the analysis above, the range of potential values for wilderness recreation of the White Clouds is indicated, subject to all qualifications noted, in table 7-2. Moreover, the present value of the additional expenditures considered to be necessary to achieve the potential benefits appears warranted by the incremental value associated with the costs (table 7-4).

4. THE WHITE CLOUDS WATERSHEDS AS RANGE RESOURCES

Second in economic importance to recreation in the White Clouds is the grazing of domestic livestock on portions of the National Forest and on adjacent lands belonging to the Bureau of Land Management (BLM) and the state of Idaho. There are two grazing allotments on the National Forest either bordering on, or within, the scenic and recreationally attractive area of the White Cloud Mountains' eastern slopes. One

Table 7-3

Present Value of Current Level of Recreation without Additional Investment in White Cloud Peaks Trail and Sanitary Facilities with $r_y = 0.04$

γ	$i = 7\%$	$i = 10\%$	$i = 13\%$
7.5%	—	$1,236,480	—
10.0%	$2,732,860	1,289,984	$833,980
12.5%	—	1,332,160	—

Table 7-4

Incremental Benefits and Costs of Increased Expenditures on White Clouds Trail
and Related Recreational Facilities with $r_y = 0.04$ ($000)

γ		$i = 7\%$	$i = 10\%$	$i = 13\%$
7.5%	Incremental B	—	$257	—
	Incremental C	—	151	—
10.0%	Incremental B	$991	$390	$218
	Incremental C	203	151	122
12.5%	Incremental B	—	$694	—
	Incremental C	—	151	—

is comprised of three units situated in the Big Lake Creek drainage, and appears to be free of any appreciable conflicts with recreation activities. The second, the Big Boulder Creek Allotment, is comprised of four units. The first unit is a combination of Forest Service, BLM, and state of Idaho land located along the bottomlands of the East Fork of the Salmon River. The second unit of the allotment occupies the Bluett Creek drainage, while the remaining two occupy respectively the major portions of the Little Boulder and Big Boulder Creek drainages. Since only the Big Boulder Creek Allotment overlaps portions of the choice recreation areas, and in turn would be affected by the prospective mining operation, we can confine our analysis to this allotment.

Years of sheep and cattle grazing, sometimes to excess, have been responsible for range conditions which are in places quite poor. Some of the most overgrazed range occurs on public land adjacent to private lands along the East Fork of the Salmon River. This area is vital winter range for deer and bighorn sheep (Pence, 1971, p. 3). One of the priority objectives of the management plan will be to improve conditions of this critical winter range. This is feasible in part because the Bluett Creek drainage which abuts the land along the East Fork of the Salmon River currently is getting little use. Because there are no fences, cattle left on this unit tend to stray into the adjacent allotment used by a neighboring permittee. Fencing these units and scheduled rotation, along with related improved management practices, should improve the winter forage in this area.

Elsewhere range conditions are variable, tending to reflect overgrazing on favored areas and inefficient utilization of the forage on less choice areas. Achievement of a more uniform forage harvest will require confining grazing stock to restricted areas, thus encouraging uniform foraging within a given fenced unit before rotation to the next unit. It is believed that in the absence of an explicit management program of this sort to upgrade the range conditions, the number of grazing animals will have to be reduced by approximately 40 percent (Pence, 1975, p. 5).

Conflicts between grazing and recreation occur at Frog Lake, Quicksand Meadows, and Big Meadow in the Little Boulder Creek drainage. Heavy grazing of meadows around the lakes that are used for recreation tends to trample the areas and adversely affect the aesthetic conditions. The conflict between recreation and grazing takes on another aspect as well, i.e., competition for forage, when pack animals are used in recreational travel. If the rest–rotation involving a permittee's livestock is to have the desired effect, recreational livestock must not be allowed to graze on the favored areas of the unit being rested. A coordinated effort, manipulating access to differentiate between recreationists moving on foot without pack animals and those travelling on horseback, would permit restriction of access to allotment units being grazed, with foot access directed to resting units. This would tend also to separate horse and foot traffic along trails, a desirable objective from the standpoint of limiting conflict among recreation participants using different travel modes.

In summary, the objectives of the range management program would be improvement of plant vigor, plant density, and species composition to increase the grazing capacity of the range; melioration of the conflicts between grazing and recreational uses of the White Clouds in areas on the allotment; and provision of forage for wildlife, particularly in the critical winter range along the East Fork of the Salmon. The program also would have the effect of improving ground cover essential to watershed conservation. Table 7-5 summarizes the basic information regarding the Big Boulder Creek C & H Allotment (see also figure 7-3).

Investments in various improvements must be made in order to achieve the management objectives. For the desired control over the movement of grazing cattle on the allotment, 9 miles of fence must be built. By itself, this would provide the necessary separation of basic units to ensure a feasible rest–rotation program. But in the absence of further investment in water development, a section of secondary range in unit III would remain unproductive. The incremental gain to forage production, and its value, must be considered in relation to the increment in costs to determine whether the water development projects merit the cost. Finally, range improvement programs consider the merit of removing undesirable or inferior species of plants for reseeding of superior forage species. In this case herbicides are used to remove unwanted species. They are incidentally capable of removing important cover for wildlife, particularly antelope young and sage grouse. Accordingly, use of herbicides is being proposed only after adequate consultation with wildlife biologists and examination of candidate areas to ensure that the spraying would not impinge on key habitats of the area's wildlife. In any event, the cost of spraying the recommended areas will need to be considered with this project.

Table 7-6 identifies the separate projects in the proposed program,

Table 7-5
Big Boulder Creek C & H Allotment—Allotment Acres

Unit	Primary range	Secondary range	Unsuitable, not used	Unsuitable, used	Timber	Barren	Lake area	Total allotment area
I	35.0	-0-	-0-	12.5	-0-	-0-	-0-	47.5
II	1,414.5	(10.0)[a]	3,387.5	892.0	1,635.0	3,370.0	250.5	10,949.5
III	1,080.0	720.0	1,427.5	-0-	44.5	150.0	-0-	3,422.0
IV	2,175.0	(15.0)[a]	3,248.5	267.5	5,020.0	4,245.0	187.5	15,143.5
Totals	4,704.5	720.0	8,063.5	1,172.0	6,699.5	7,765.0	438.0	29,562.5

Source: Big Boulder C & H Allotment Development Plan, Clayton District, Challis National Forest.
[a]Suitable acres located outside allotment grazing area. Forage is often used by recreation livestock, but is not included in grazing capacity calculations for the allotment. Acres are carried in Unsuitable-Not Used totals.

173

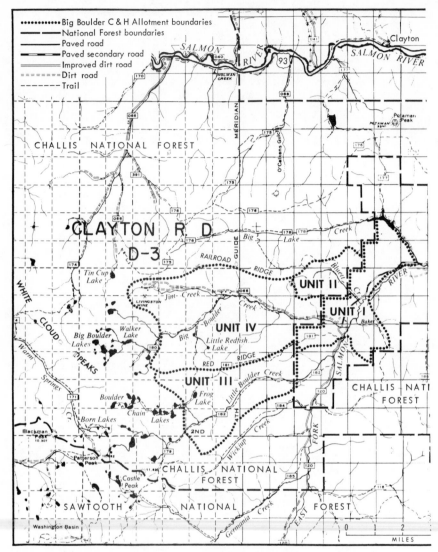

Figure 7-3. Big Boulder C&H grazing allotment.

along with the estimated project costs. An item of $1,150 for fencing that would be incurred in the event of mining operations by ASARCO appears in the table, but is excluded in the initial computations undertaken below.

We can reassemble the program costs by project type, i.e., fencing, water development, and spraying, to compare the estimated costs and gains for each program increment individually. First, however, it is desirable to

Table 7-6
Planned Projects

Year	Construction by	Description	Material furnished by	Fund	Estimated cost				
					FS	Per-mittee	Per-mittee	BLM	Total
First	FS	Spray 899 acres	FS	052	$ 5,394	$	$	$	$ 5,394
	Permittee	1 mile fence in Little Boulder	FS	053	675	500			1,175
	Permittee and other	3 miles fence between allotments	FS	052	2,025	750	750		3,525
	FS	7 water troughs	FS	053	420				420
	BLM	2 water troughs	BLM	—				120	120
	BLM and FS	material & installation of water troughs	BLM & FS	053	1,500			400	1,900
Subtotal for first year					$10,014	$1,250	$750	$520	$12,534
Second	Permittee	1 mile fence on lower herdground	FS	052	$ 675	$ 500	$	$	$ 1,175
	FS	0.5 mile fence and 16-ft heavy-duty cattleguard across Little Boulder Creek Road	FS	053	1,150				1,150
Subtotal for second year					$ 1,825	$ 500	$-0-	$-0-	$ 2,325
Third	FS	3.5 miles fence (suspension), 0.5 mile log fence, trail cattleguard and metal gate on Red Ridge	FS	053	$ 7,000	$	$	$	$ 7,000
Subtotal for third year					$ 7,000	$-0-	$-0-	$-0-	$ 7,000
Total of all projects					$18,839	$1,750	$750	$520	$21,859

Source: Big Boulder C & H Allotment Development Plan, Clayton District, Challis National Forest.

ᵃFS = Forest Service; BLM = Bureau of Land Management.

175

indicate the nature of the computations that need to be carried out to evaluate the economic merit of the management plan. It should be noted that the plan intends to restore the range to an improved condition and, in effect, maintain it on a sustained yield basis. It is therefore necessary to cumulate the discounted benefits and costs in perpetuity. Of course with relatively high rates of discount, whether 7, 10, or 13 percent, annual increments in time will produce present worths of greatly diminished amounts, tending toward zero in the limit. It is useful, under these circumstances, to calculate both benefits and costs only to the point where their discounted value is non-negligible as described in chapter 6, pp. 132–134. As a practical matter, for convenience and economy, the cutoff point taken in the computations below is the point at which the present value of a dollar's annual benefit or cost falls below 1 cent. Accordingly, the present-value formula for a program of N projects with economic lives of T years can be given as:

$$PV = \sum_{n=1}^{N} \left[\sum_{t=y_n}^{T_n+y_n} \frac{B_t^{(n)} - O_t^{(n)}}{(1 + i)^t} - \frac{C_n}{(1 + i)^{y_n}} \right]$$

where

$n =$ number of discrete capital outlays (projects)

$T_n =$ project life in years

$y_n =$ year in which nth project goes into operation

$B_t^{(n)} =$ gross benefit of project n in year t; $[B_t = B_0(1 + \alpha)^t]$

$O_t^{(n)} =$ operation and maintenance costs of project n in year t

$C_n =$ the investment cost in project n

$i =$ rate of discount

To summarize the cost of the range management plan by program then, we show the results in table 7-7.

What now are the indicated results of each program of the range management plan? It must be clear that for the plan to accomplish any of the range restoration established as a management goal, it is necessary to erect and maintain fences in order to control grazing. We can consider this basic to the plan. Incrementally, we can consider water development on unit III for harvesting of the forage on the secondary range. Finally, undesired species would be removed to allow reseeding of more desirable plants. Table 7-8 shows the estimated results of each program.

The value per animal unit month (AUM) will differ with different qualities of range. For the Challis National Forest, independent study has established the value to be $6.11 (Williams, 1968), a figure used by the Forest Service in its analyses, and the one adopted for this study.

There is, however, another matter that requires attention. The income elasticity of beef as well as the population growth rate indicate strongly

Table 7-7
Estimated Costs of Management Programs for Big Boulder Creek Allotment

Costs		PV of costs @ 7%	PV of costs @ 10%	PV of costs @ 13%
Fencing costs				
Y	C			
1	$4,700	$ 4,700	$ 4,700	$ 4,700
2	1,175	1,098	1,068	1,040
3	7,000	6,114	5,785	5,482
31	4,700	577	245	106
32	1,175	135	56	24
33	7,000	751	301	124
61	4,700	81	14	3
62	1,175	20	3	1
63	7,000	121	17	5
Fence maintenance $100/year		1,414	997	769
Total PV of fencing		$14,260	$13,386	$12,245
Water development				
Y	C			
1	$1,900	$ 1,900	$ 1,900	$ 1,900
31	1,900	233	99	43
60	1,900	33	6	1
Water development maintenance		707	495	385
Total PV of water development		$ 2,873	$ 2,500	$ 2,329
Herbicidal spray				
Y	C			
1	$5,394	$ 5,394	$ 5,395	$ 5,394
17	5,394	1,708	1,067	675
34	5,394	541	211	85
51	5,394	171	42	11
68	5,394	70	8	3
Total PV of spraying		$ 7,864	$ 6,722	$ 6,168

that the demand for grazing will increase into the indefinite future, but public range is in fixed supply. Private land often associated in use with the public range frequently lies in the bottomlands and is suitable for the production of hay and other higher valued crops. Accordingly, the opportunity cost of this land for grazing is very high. Because the public range in the intermountain region is suitable largely only for wildlife and livestock grazing, it is likely to remain in grazing, but at increasingly higher values as demand grows over time.[22] Just as in the case of certain types of recreation activity, there are grounds for assuming that the value per unit of forage will increase relative to the level of prices generally and in particular, to the level of natural resource commodity prices. The relationship we postulate is:

[22] These points we owe to Delworth Gardner and Darwin Nielson.

$$B_t = B_0(1 + \alpha)^t$$

where

B_t = the gross benefit or value of the forage in year t

B_0 = the gross benefit or value of forage in the initial year

α = the annual rate of increase in forage value per unit

t = time measured in units of a year

the present value will be

$$PV = \sum_{t=1}^{T'} B_0(1 + \alpha)^t(1 + i)^{-t}$$

with T' again given by the year in which the present value of $1 of initial-year benefits falls to $0.01.

In our present-value computations we take α variously as 0.03, 0.04, and 0.05. Table 7-9 presents the results of the benefit estimation, along with the costs presented in table 7-7. The benefits and costs are calculated separately for each program. We can see that the program as a whole produces benefits exceeding costs at any rate of discount. At the highest discount rate, however, i.e., 13 percent, the value of the forage produced falls short of the cost of the separable spraying project.

It should be noted in any event that the value of the grazing services of the White Cloud Peaks range is relatively modest. This is true of the value of the range without any improvements (carrying capacity of 510 AUMs), as well as of the net value of the increment in AUMs (618) accomplished by the range management program. The combined total will sum to a present value within the range of $100,000 to $200,000, depending on assumptions with respect to rate of annual value appreciation and the discount rate.

Table 7-8

Estimated Potential Increase of Range Management Allotment
(Adjusted for one unit remaining fallow each year)

Unit	From fencing AUMs[a]	From water development AUMs	From spraying AUMs	Total increase[b] AUMs
I	3.0	–0–	–0–	3.0
II	130.2	–0–	–0–	130.2
III	25.9	141.3	88.5	255.7
IV	229.5	–0–	–0–	229.5
Totals	388.6	141.3	88.5	618.4

[a]AUM represents an animal unit month, or an average daily dry weight forage of 33 pounds for a 1,000-pound cow with 300-pound calf.

[b]These data apply only to U.S. Forest Service lands and do not include BLM or state lands.

Table 7-9

Benefits of Big Boulder Creek C & H Allotment Management Plan

($)

	7% discount			10% discount			13% discount		
	$r = 0.03$	$r = 0.04$	$r = 0.05$	$r = 0.03$	$r = 0.04$	$r = 0.05$	$r = 0.03$	$r = 0.04$	$r = 0.05$
Fencing									
Benefits	58,733	78,342	117,513	33,568	39,171	47,005	23,503	26,114	29,366
Costs	14,260	14,260	14,260	13,186	13,186	13,186	12,245	12,245	12,245
Net benefits	44,473	64,082	103,253	20,382	25,985	33,819	11,258	13,869	17,121
Water development									
Benefits	21,359	28,490	42,735	12,208	14,245	17,094	8,547	9,497	10,679
Costs	2,873	2,873	2,873	2,500	2,500	2,500	2,329	2,329	2,329
Net benefits	18,486	25,617	39,862	9,708	11,745	14,594	6,218	7,168	8,350
Spraying									
Benefits	13,378	17,844	26,767	7,646	8,922	10,707	5,353	5,948	6,689
Costs	7,864	7,864	7,864	6,722	6,722	6,722	6,188	6,188	6,188
Net benefits	5,514	9,980	18,903	924	2,200	3,985	−835	−240	501
Total net benefits	68,473	99,679	162,018	31,014	39,930	52,398	17,476	21,037	25,972

Source: "Allotment Management Plan: Big Boulder Creek C & H Allotment," Challis National Forest, Clayton Ranger District, Clayton, Idaho (1971).

Note: The benefits included above cover only the value of the incre-mental forage for domestic livestock resulting from the management program. Potential benefits which cannot be reckoned adequately in AUMs are related to the potential improvement of the winter range in unit I for deer and especially for the dwindling band of bighorn sheep.

5. THE WHITE CLOUDS AS A SOURCE OF MINERAL SUPPLIES

The geology of portions of the White Clouds is propitious for mineral deposits. The interfaces between granitic and sedimentary rocks are places where silver, lead, zinc, and molybdenum are frequently found. The area on the east slopes of the White Cloud Peaks abounds in such zones. There are other known deposits of silver, lead, zinc, copper, gold and antimony within or near the White Cloud Peaks area (U.S. Dept. of Interior, 1972). The old Livingston Mill, in fact, worked an area on the upper Jim Creek drainage, a tributary of Big Boulder Creek, producing lead, zinc, and silver. The East Fork of the Salmon, including the Germania Creek drainage; and Boulder Creek, including both streams; along with Lake Creek represent the two main districts within the White Clouds that are generally mineralized. Unfortunately, these are the areas that have the most attractive recreation opportunities as well.

The molybdenum occurrence in this area is of low grade, and would be open-pit mined. Molybdenum is a comparatively rare mineral, occurring in the earth's crust in a ratio of about 5 parts per million. The concentration in commercial ores is from 1 to 3 parts per thousand, or 2 to 6 pounds of molybdenum per ton of ore. With low grade deposits, then, one could expect the removal and disposal of a half ton of ore and tailings for every pound of molybdenum concentrate (Sheridan, 1970, p. 335) exclusive of the associated overburden. Mining a large deposit of low-grade ore such as the one found in the vicinity of Castle Peak would have an enormous impact on the landscape. Initially the stripped overburden would be used to create, it has been suggested, a 700-foot high earth-fill dam in the Wickiup Creek drainage, which is planned as a site for solid waste disposal. The reservoir behind the dam would serve as a settling pond and general tailings disposal area. Figure 7-4 outlines the sites of the major activities against a photographic background of the heads of Little Boulder, Wickiup, and Germania Creek drainages.

Until recently there were only two primary producers of molybdenum; Molybdenum Corporation of America (MOLYCORP), and the Climax Molybdenum Division of American Metals Climax (AMAX). Approximately a quarter of total production, however, is the result of by-product or co-product production through the processing of molybdenum-bearing copper, tungsten, and uranium ores. Kennecott Copper Corporation is the largest producer of by-product molybdenum, although the Duval Corporation and the Magma Copper Company are significant by-product producers. The by-product production is significant because it represents a source of supply which is over half of the total U.S. industry demand. It thus offers additional sources of supply in what otherwise would be a very noncompetitive market.

The United States has been the principal producer of molybdenum outside the Socialist bloc countries and has been producing about double its domestic requirements. In recent years there has developed a condition of excess supply and growing inventories (Kuklis, 1970, p. 727). Despite the present excess supply, past decisions have committed the industry to record expenditures for new mines. The most significant of these developments is Climax Molybdenum's Henderson Mine (Colorado) where, upon completion, there will have been invested about a quarter of a billion dollars for a production facility that will enable AMAX alone to produce as much as the domestic industry's current supply, which is roughly double the country's domestic consumption (Kuklis, 1970, p. 727). A co-product copper–molybdenum mine with reported developmental costs of $165 million was placed into operation just recently by Duval Sierrita Corporation near Tucson, Arizona, adding to the prospect of excess supplies for some time into the future.

Perhaps equally important have been exploratory and developmental activities in Canada, the second largest molybdenum producer outside the Socialist bloc. Several large developments in British Columbia are underway in response to the Japanese market. Chile and Peru are also developing as sources of competition for the American producers of molybdenum destined for foreign markets (Kuklis, 1970, pp. 734–735).

Given the present excess productive capacity in the domestic industry, and the development of additional capacity that is well advanced, the prospects for reasonable returns on further expanding capacity that uses low grade ore appear remote. The competition is expected to be so vigorous, from both by-product as well as primary producers, along with the growing foreign sources, that commodity analysts are projecting constant prices for the remainder of this century despite the need to resort to lower grade ores (Sheridan, 1970, p. 340). With ASARCO's return on equity, averaging over 14 percent for the past decade, it is difficult to believe that it could be seriously interested in what would be at best a marginal undertaking.

Mineral exploration in the Castle Peak area has not been sufficient to determine either the extent of the ore body or the exact molybdenum content of the ore. The ore appears as an outcropping to which limited access could be obtained without removing overburden, but stripping to any depth would result in increased overburden as a function of ore removed.[23] The estimated molybdenum content, based on inadequate sampling to date,

[23] Obtained from Keith Whiting, ASARCO field representative, Spokane, Washington, in telephone conversation June 23, 1972.

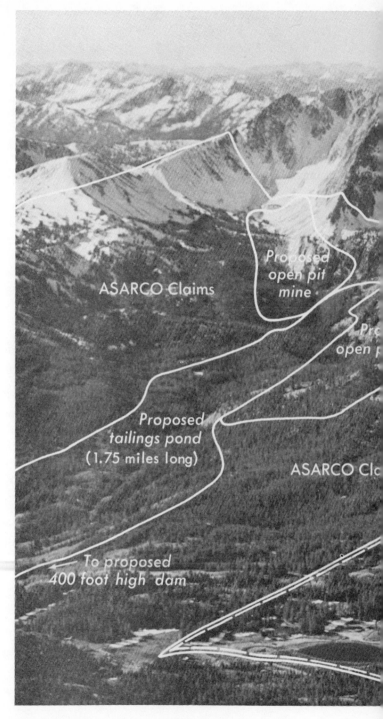

Figure 7-4. Sites of proposed molybdenum mining and milling operations in White Clouds area.

eak

Taylor Mining Company Claims

ke

(Photo courtesy of Ernest E. Day and *Smithsonian* magazine.)

runs within the range of 0.17 to 0.20 percent.[24] This suggests a marginal deposit with a high waste-to-metal ratio, if early samples are indicative of the larger ore body.

Because of the limited data available for evaluating the worth of the proposed molybdenum mine–mill operation, it is most difficult to develop a precise estimate that could be compared with the values that would be precluded by development of the mineral resource. But, considering the indicated marginal character of the undertaking, and the indicated excess capacity in the industry for the forseeable future, it is difficult to visualize any early development. The present value of the deposit if extraction is deferred for any considerable length of time would not be very great, however, at any reasonable rate of discount. For example, assume that the operation of the proposed mine could not begin until after, say, 30 years. Assume that the developmental costs would be $100 million and would yield a rate of return of 14 percent (ASARCO's rate of return), or $14 million annually from the thirty-first through the sixtieth year. The net present value of this stream of deferred income, discounted at 10 percent would be only $2.3 million. For any yield lower than that assumed above, of course, the net present value would be smaller; in particular for a yield of $10 million annually, the net present value would go to zero. If development outlays were begun earlier, cumulating to $100 million by the thirtieth year, the calculations, of course, would be less favorable to molybdenum extraction.

Assume for the moment that the present value today of the workings, even when deferred, would be greater than the net present value of the alternative incompatible recreation services. Would this greater present value counsel the early initiation of the mining operation as a socially optimal decision? The answer, as given by the optimality analysis of chapter 3 and suggested in section 2 of this chapter, of course is negative. The reason, it is clear, is because some part of the recreation benefits that are realizable between the present and the moment the mining operation would become commercially feasible would be lost to society. If the decision involved a choice between development of the White Cloud molybdenum deposits now or never, then under a simple present-value criterion the project ought to be undertaken now. However, this is really not the choice, for deferral of the mining activity would permit the realization of (growing) recreational benefits from the area during an interim period before the mining became economic. Furthermore, when a potentially irreversible modification is contemplated, the uncertainty of the supply and demand for the extractive commodity requires that there be an additional positive net benefit from the development to justify the action.[25] With the ultimate commercial feasibility of the mining operation open to substantial ques-

[24] *Ibid.*
[25] See chapter 4, p. 69 ff.

tion, the decisive net positive gain that would have to be indicated to warrant a deleterious modification of the White Clouds' landscape at this time is wholly lacking. Under the circumstances, it appears that the decision to establish the White Cloud Peaks as part of the protected Sawtooth National Recreation Area reflects sound economic judgment.

6. CONCLUSIONS

The analysis of the conflict in resource use in the White Cloud Peaks area is the second study addressing wild and scenic land (and river) allocation problems. Here even more so than in the Hells Canyon case, the data and analysis have been more in the nature of a reconnaissance investigation of the comparative resource values. In the case of the recreation benefit evaluation, we obtained estimates by using surrogate data adapted from the Spanish Peaks Primitive Area on which a more intensive recreational analysis had been conducted. A more adequate analysis of the White Cloud Peaks would have required the same kind of survey research and econometric analysis as was performed for the Spanish Peaks. Secondly, the recreational value was based on the assumption that the White Clouds would be devoted to wilderness-type recreation services. Of course, it was necessary to identify what type of recreational services were being postulated in order to relate the density of use appropriately to the activity and hence the value of the resources when used for that particular type of recreation. It would have been equally appropriate to have postulated that the area would be used for higher density recreation experiences, such as those depending on the kind of intensively developed facilities and use levels found in national parks. Indeed, under the Sawtooth National Recreation Area Act, the Park Service has been directed to evaluate the White Cloud Peaks area to ascertain whether it might not qualify for National Park status. It is conceivable that the recreational value from this kind of use would be greater than the area's use as a wilderness recreation facility. Thus, our analysis is partial in the sense that while it has compared the relative value of recreation versus extractive activities, it has not compared the value of two mutually exclusive (high versus low density) recreational activities. An intensive analysis of this kind of problem will be taken up in the next chapter where we address the question of choosing between mutually exclusive recreational uses of the Mineral King Valley environmental resources.

Granting the limitations of the level of detail in analysis and coverage, we have reason to believe that the use of the White Cloud Peaks for recreation will exceed the value of the incompatible molybdenum mining alternative. Should it develop that the kind of more intensive recreational activity that would be considered in connection with national park status would exceed the value of the recreational services from the wilderness-type use of the area, the immediately significant decision would not be affected. That is, what was at issue in the White Cloud Peaks was the potential massive degradation of a very scenic and ecologically attractive area. Whichever of the recreational activities might be selected as the most valued, the widespread physical degradation of the environment caused by mining molybdenum would be compatible with neither. Accordingly, for the decision at issue, the inevitable disturbance of the environment that would attend more intensive and extensive exploration and/or mining in the area does not at this time appear warranted on economic grounds. This is true, moreover, even if the annual benefits from mining at some future date would exceed the recreational benefits sufficiently that the discounted stream of deferred income from mining would exceed the present value of the stream of recreation benefits. It seems clear that the option that will maximize the benefit from the environmental resources of the White Cloud Peaks area is preservation for recreation and related compatible uses at this time.

We have come to these conclusions essentially on the economic basis of the willingness of users of the present recreational amenities of the White Cloud Peaks to pay for such services. This basis, as discussed in chapter 2 under the general issue of assigning liability in connection with mutually exclusive uses of open access environmental resources, is established as the most conservative position (Mohring and Boyd, 1971) that can be advanced in favor of preserving the natural environment.

Were we to have adopted the Rothenberg (1970) argument that the party responsible for initiating a use that is destructive of the environment is liable for the costs associated with restoring the welfare status of those who suffer as result of the destructive action, the argument in favor of retaining the White Cloud Peaks in an undisturbed natural state would be even stronger. The liability assignment problem, however, has not been ultimately resolved in the courts, although they appear to be attentive to this problem and perhaps are even leaning toward the Rothenberg position. However, it is still too early to be certain. Whatever the ultimate disposition of the liability assignment problem, it is clear that the burden of proving the ultimate wisdom of massive landscape degradation in the White Cloud Mountains has not yet been shouldered.

REFERENCES

Arrow, K. J. and Fisher, A. C. 1974. "Environmental Preservation, Uncertainty, and Irreversibility," *Quarterly Journal of Economics,* vol. 88, no. 2.
Bieniewski, C. L. *Demand and Supply of Molybdenum in the United States.* (Washington) Department of the Interior, Bureau of Mines (U.S. Bureau of Mines Information Circular 8446).

Cicchetti, C. J. and Smith, V. K. 1973. "Congestion, Quality Deterioration and Optimal Use: Wilderness Recreation in the Spanish Peaks Primitive Area," *Social Science Research,* vol. 2, no. 1.

Fisher, A. C., Krutilla, J. V., and Cicchetti, C. J. 1972. "The Economics of Environmental Preservation: A Theoretical and Empirical Analysis," *American Economic Review,* vol. LXII, no. 4.

————, Krutilla, J. V. "Determination of Optimal Capacity of Resource-Based Recreation Facilities," *Natural Resources Journal,* vol. 12, no. 3.

Gunnell, Frank. 1972. *Wildlife Analysis of the Proposed Sawtooth National Recreation and Wildnerness Areas,* U.S. Department of Agriculture, Forest Service, Intermountain Region.

Federal Power Commission. 1970. "In the Matter of: Pacific Northwest Power Company and Washington Public Power System," Projects 2243 and 2273, hearings, Lewiston, Idaho; Portland, Oregon; and Washington, D.C. 1968–1970.

Hope, Jack. 1971. "In Idaho's White Clouds: Mines or a Park—or Both," *Smithsonian* (January).

Krutilla, J. V., ed. 1972. *Natural Environments: Studies in Theoretical and Applied Analysis* (Baltimore: Johns Hopkins Press).

Kuklis, Andrew. 1970. "Molybdenum," in Bureau of Mines *Minerals Yearbook,* vol. 1, pp. 727–736.

Merriam, J. H. 1970. "Idaho White Clouds: Wilderness in Trouble," *The Living Wilderness,* vol. 34, no. 109.

Mohring, Herbert and Boyd, J. H. 1971. "Analyzing Externalities: Direct Intersection vs. Asset Utilization Frameworks," *Economica,* vol. 38, no. 152.

Pence, Dan. 1971. *Environmental Analysis Report Big Boulder Creek C & H Allotment Development Plan,* Clayton Ranger District, Challis National Forest.

————. 1971. *Allotment Management Plan Big Boulder Creek C & H Allotment,* Challis National Forest, Clayton Ranger District.

Platt, W. S. 1972. *Aquatic Environment and Fisheries Study Proposed Sawtooth National Recreation and Wilderness Areas,* U.S. Department of Agriculture, Forest Service, Intermountain Region.

Roberts, N. K. 1963. "Economic Foundations for Grazing Use Fees on Public Lands," *Journal of Farm Economics,* vol. 45, no. 4.

Rothenberg, Jerome. 1970. "The Economics of Congestion and Pollution: An Integrated View," *American Economic Review,* vol. LX, no. 2.

Seagraves, James. 1970. "More on the Social Rate of Discount," *Quarterly Journal of Economics,* vol. 84, no. 3.

Sheridan, E. T. "Molybdenum" in *Mineral Facts and Problems,* 1970 edition. U.S. Bureau of Mines.

Schlatterer, Edward, *White Cloud–Boulder–Pioneer Mountains Comprehensive Land Management Planning Study, Interim Ecological Evaluation,* U.S. Department of Agriculture, U.S. Forest Service, February 1971.

Smith, V. K. 1972. "The Effects of Technological Change on Different Uses of Environmental Resources," in *Natural Environments: Studies in Theoreti-*

cal and Applied Analysis, John V. Krutilla, ed. (Baltimore: Johns Hopkins Press).

————, 1974. *Technical Change, Relative Prices, and Environmental Resource Evaluation* (Baltimore: Johns Hopkins Press).

————, and Krutilla, J. V. 1975. *The Structure and Properties of A Wilderness Users' Travel Behavior Simulator* (forthcoming).

Stankey, G. H. 1972. "A Strategy for the Definition and Management of Wilderness Quality" in *Natural Environments: Studies in Theoretical and Applied Analysis,* John V. Krutilla, ed. (Baltimore: Johns Hopkins Press).

U.S. Congress. 1968. *Hearings on Economic Analysis of Public Investment Decisions: Interest Rate Policy and Discounting Analysis,* before a Subcommittee on Economy of Government of the Joint Economic Committee, 90 Cong. 2 sess. (1968).

U.S. Department of Interior Task Force. 1972. White Cloud Mountains Idaho Status Report.

————, "Wilderness Use Study Completed," *Research Progress 1971,* Pacific Southwest Forest and Range Experiment Station, Berkeley, California.

Williams, R. G. 1968. "Determining Market Areas for Livestock Grazing," unpublished Master's thesis, Utah State University.

CHAPTER 8

MINERAL KING VALLEY: DEMAND THEORY AND RESOURCE VALUATION

1. INTRODUCTION

In the theoretical discussions of chapters 3 and 4 we generally assumed that decisions about the use of a natural environment would be made on the basis of expected values. In chapter 5 problems of measurement in an empirical case were addressed in an effort to assess the value of the Hells Canyon site for hydroelectric power production. Although this and subsequent efforts in chapters 6 and 7 yielded results which we believe are of some interest and value to researchers and policymakers, it must be acknowledged that the methods, constrained by limits on research resources, were relatively crude. Moreover, the strong implications for policy in both the Hells Canyon and White Clouds cases derive at least in part from assumptions about the dynamic behavior of the alternative benefit streams, based on trends in the demand for wilderness recreation and the technology of extractive resource use.

A question might then be raised concerning our ability to assess a project to develop an area for recreational purposes, as proposed for Mineral King, where there is no dramatic difference in the dynamic behavior of benefits from extractive and nonextractive uses. In such a case, a more sophisticated approach to the measurement of the net gains at each moment or short period in time from each of the alternative uses of the environment is indicated. In particular, closer attention must be given to the link between value and demand, and to the specification and measurement of demand.

Recall that in the Hells Canyon case, net benefits from power production were measured as the difference in costs between the least-cost alternative source and a project of given size, neglecting the potential welfare gain from increased consumption of electricity as a function of a lower price. Although the neglect was justified there, clearly it is not when we consider the effect on consumption of ski recreation following the development of a high-density facility at Mineral King. In addition to the reduction in costs that will be experienced by skiers located nearer to Mineral King than existing sites, it may be expected that they (and others) will be induced by the reduction to take more recreation, as measured by trips over a season, than formerly. On the other hand, facilities that to some extent substitute for Mineral King could experience a reduction in demand as a result of competition. What is required to capture these effects, then, is a careful specification and estimation of the demand for trips to ski recreation sites in the Mineral King market area.

Such an estimate will be useful also in dealing with the link between demand and value. Recall that in the Hells Canyon study the benefits imputed to recreational users of the area in its natural state were based on fragmentary evidence concerning prices paid for similar kinds of activities (fishing, hunting) on private streams or preserves. Although we believe the imputed values are realistic, and the ranking of alternatives is not sensitive to substantial changes, it seems preferable in this case to infer value from explicitly estimated demand. As demonstrated in the analysis of the Mineral King project, this is done by integrating the system of estimated demand equations between the new and old price vectors (with and without the project) to obtain the change in a willingness-to-pay measure of consumers' surplus associated with the introduction of a new facility. Essentially the same methods may be used to estimate the demand for and value of outdoor recreation at the Mineral King site in its present state.

In section 3 of this chapter we present an econometric model of the demand for developed ski recreation sites in California. In section 4 the demand coefficients are used, in the manner suggested above, to infer the change in benefits associated with the development and introduction of a new site in this area, namely, Mineral King. Primary attention is given to the derivation and discussion of these estimates because the theoretical and statistical techniques developed and adapted for the purpose are in our judgment innovative in certain respects. In this connection it should be noted that much of the material of sections 3 and 4 is based on a study by Cicchetti, Fisher, and Smith (1972). Although our main concern here is to develop and apply a methodology for estimating project benefits, section 5 covers estimates of costs, including the environmental opportunity costs, and the benefits forgone if the Mineral King project is implemented. Less attention is given to the estimation of preservation benefits, partly because the method of estimation represents an application of existing technique, and partly because we are reporting results of an unpublished doctoral dissertation by Stanley (1973).

Before going any further, the reader may find it helpful to have a better idea of just what and where Mineral King is, its physical characteristics, and the nature of the development plan.

2. THE NATURAL ENVIRONMENT
AND PROPOSED MODIFICATIONS

The Physical Setting

Mineral King is a small valley surrounded by eight alpine bowls and a number of peaks rising about 4,000 feet above the valley floor, to heights of 12,000 feet above sea level, in the Sierra Nevada Mountains of south-central California (see figure 8-1). By way of comparison, it is about twice as high, and maybe a sixth as large, as the much better known Yosemite Valley a hundred miles to the north and west across the rugged Sierras. Mineral King lies 228 miles northeast of Los Angeles and 271 miles southeast of San Francisco.

Part of the "problem" with Mineral King, i.e., the reason for its being a source of contention between developers and preservationists, is that, although not part of Sequoia National Park, it is almost completely surrounded by it. This has led some persons to contend that it is in fact ecologically a part of the park. A number of small streams flowing into the valley join there to form the headwaters of the East Fork of the Kaweah River, which in turn flows westward out of the valley and through the park. Similarly, access to Mineral King is via a very narrow, and largely unpaved road that winds its way for several miles through the park west of the valley, and which is blocked (by snow) for all but a few summer months. A major part of the development project for Mineral King would in fact consist in construction of a larger, straighter, all-weather access road, more or less along the existing right of way which follows the stream through the park. Moreover, Mineral King is a part of the migratory cycle of several species of park animals, and was presumably for this reason designated in 1926 as the Sequoia National Game Refuge, a part of the Sequoia National Forest, then as now, administered by the U.S. Forest Service.

The area serves today as a base for exploring the surrounding wilderness, as well as the site of several types of outdoor recreation, most prominently hiking, fishing, and camping, which together account for nearly two-thirds of visitor days, as shown in table 8-1. From the table it is apparent that there is also a certain amount of use, nearly 23 percent, associated with recreation residences on the site. This raises the question of whether Mineral King can legitimately be considered an unmodified natural environment, even in the absence of the high density ski facility planned for the site. Proponents of the project argue precisely this point; namely, that existing development would in any case preclude classification as wilderness under established standards. To shed some light on this question, we turn to a brief historical sketch of development at Mineral King, followed by a discussion of the much larger project currently under consideration.

Table 8-1
Current (1970) Uses of Mineral King

Activity	Visitor-days use (thousands)	Percent of total
Auto (drive-motor)	1.3	1.1
Ice-snow craft (drive-motor)	0.1	0.0
Foot (hiking-walking)	18.4	16.6
Horse (horseback riding)	0.2	0.1
Fishing, cold water	13.0	11.7
Camping, general	19.4	17.6
Camping, auto	8.6	7.8
Camping, tent	21.9	19.8
Resort-comm. pub. service, general	0.1	0.0
Recreation residence	25.2	22.8
Skiing	0.1	0.0
Hunting, big game	1.9	1.7
Composite total	110.2	99.2

Source: RIM Center, U.S. Forest Service.

A History of Development and Development Plans

Mineral King takes its name from the mining activity of the late nineteenth century there. At the time it was expected that the search for various metals, including gold and silver, would be more fruitful than it turned out to be in fact. Though the prospectors and miners have long since abandoned the site, remnants of their activity remain. Some of the old mining shacks have even been converted into summer cabins, some of the "recreation residences" cited in table 8-1. Currently there are perhaps 60 of these structures, along with a couple of other buildings, some campsites, and signs of the early mining activity. In the 1920s the present access road was put in, though it should be noted that this is little more than a dirt trail in the section that approaches the valley through the park. One's overall impression of the approach and existing on-site development is that, though it may preclude the area from qualifying as "wilderness" in the sense of being roadless and otherwise unmodified by man, it is unobtrusive and not inconsistent with park status and hence is suitable for inclusion within the surrounding Sequoia National Park.

According to a Forest Service report, the area has from the beginning of skiing interest in the U.S. been considered potentially ideal for this purpose because of the challenging slopes of the eight alpine bowls and the high elevation of the valley itself.[1] In response to the growth in skiing activity after World War II, the Forest Service in 1949 issued a prospectus for

[1] See U.S. Forest Service (1969). This report is the source also for other details, unless noted, of development planning for Mineral King.

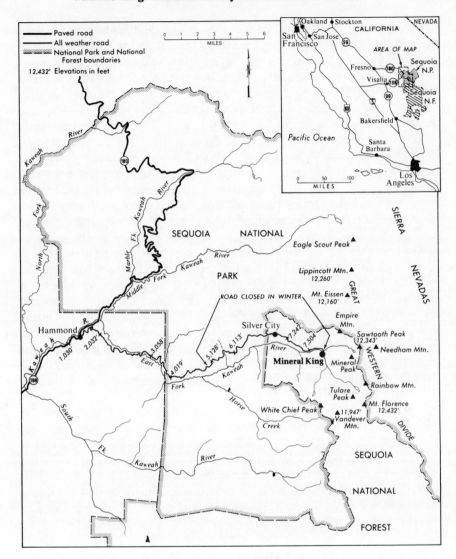

Figure 8-1. Location of Mineral King Valley.

development of a ski facility at Mineral King, but apparently the cost of access, of building a 25-mile all-weather road to the site, was too great to induce bids from private developers. In 1953 a Congressional hearing on the subject of Mineral King ski development was held, eliciting support from various quarters, including the Sierra Club, now a leading opponent of development. The Sierra Club, however, argues that its early support for development was based on the original prospectus, which envisioned a relatively minor modification of the environment, and further, that a large part of the basin has since reverted to *de facto* wilderness, the scarcity of which has greatly increased in the region.[2] In any event, access remained the major problem, and nothing further happened until 1965, at which time the Forest Service issued a second prospectus, much more ambitious than the first, and the California State Highway Commission, along with other relevant legal entities, approved funding (via California gas tax payments) of an all-weather access road. Late in the year the Forest Service selected, from the six submitted, a proposal by Walt Disney Productions to develop a ski (and other) recreation facility at Mineral King. At this point the Sierra Club and others raised substantive objections to the Forest Service prospectus and the Disney proposal, citing a variety of legal grounds for their position. The legal questions are interesting, and we shall return to them with a brief survey of the unfolding court proceedings. First, let us see just how Disney and the Forest Service plan to develop the area.

A point to bear in mind is that the details given here are based on the plan as of about 1969, when the court proceedings began. It calls for a smaller scale of development than originally envisioned by Disney, and quite conceivably could be further revised, in one direction or the other. But the figures cited were double-checked in an interview in April 1972 with a Disney representative.[3] Moreover, as we shall see, plan revisions resulting in greater or lesser capacity, hence greater or lesser costs and benefits, are readily accommodated by the econometric model in sections 3–5.

The plan calls for, in addition to the all-weather access road through the Sequoia National Park, construction of an "Alpine Village" (hotel complex, restaurants, etc.) mostly within the valley, with at least one restaurant atop a peak; a multilevel parking structure occupying 4½ acres just below the valley; and of course the lift facilities on the major slopes, affecting in some degree much of the remaining 13,000 acres. In addition, there would be a great variety of service facilities including employee housing, shops, a theater, and modifications for waste treatment and flood control, these latter apparently involving the construction of dams and some stream diversion and channelization. It is envisioned that average weekend day use of the facilities might be about 10,000 (visitors), with a peak of perhaps 12,000 or a little more.

Beyond these details, there is a great deal of controversy between the development planners, as represented in the Forest Service report (see footnote 1) on the one hand, and those opposing the current project, as

[2] *Sierra Club Bulletin,* November 1967, p. 7.
[3] In another (written) communication from Disney just prior to the interview it was noted that the project is "inactive" until such time as the legal issues are resolved by the courts, and might at that time be "re-evaluated."

represented in the *Sierra Club Bulletin* (see footnote 2) on the other, regarding the effects of this construction and activity, not only on the site of the present game refuge, but perhaps more importantly on the surrounding park, through which would run the access road and power lines, as well as the drainage from Mineral King. As one example, the Sierra Club cites a report to the state highway commission indicating that erosion due to construction of the new highway would endanger half of the giant sequoias below the road, whereas the project brochure claims that none of these trees will be jeopardized. Certainly there are unresolved questions here of interest to ecologists and others, but further discussion is beyond the scope of this study.

Although detailed discussion of the legal issues and court proceedings is also beyond the scope of the study, we can indicate for those interested the status of the matter in the courts. Following public hearings held late in 1966 by the National Park Service on whether certain parts of Sequoia National Park should be included in the National Wilderness System, and other hearings held by the California Division of Highways in connection with its planning of the access road, at both of which the related question of development of Mineral King was considered, the Forest Service in early 1969 approved the Disney plan described above. This action was in turn followed in June 1969 by the filing of a suit in U.S. District Court in San Francisco by the Sierra Club against the Secretary of Agriculture (the Forest Service is part of the Department of Agriculture), the Secretary of the Interior, and members of their departments. In July 1969 the court granted a preliminary injunction against both on-site and road construction, which is still in effect. In December 1969, however, attorneys representing a number of different parties, including the U.S. Department of Justice, filed an appeal in the Ninth Circuit Court of Appeals, which resulted in September 1970 in a judgment against the Sierra Club, on the grounds that it had no standing to sue. The Sierra Club, in turn, appealed to the U.S. Supreme Court, which in April 1972 ruled 4 to 3 that a person has standing only if he can show that he himself has suffered or will suffer injury. Since the Sierra Club did not assert this "individualized" loss, this might have been the end of the matter, except that the majority opinion, sympathetic in tone to the substance of the Sierra Club's position, invited a resubmission of the suit in the lower courts, on amended grounds that would fall within the majority guidelines on standing. As of this writing (spring 1973) the amended suit is back before the District Court.[4]

We shall not attempt to set out in any detail the complicated legal issues

---

[4] For more discussion of the economic implications of the Supreme Court decision, see Cicchetti and Fisher, "Economic Values of Environmental Resources: Some Comments by Economists on the Supreme Court Decision in the Mineral King Case," unpublished manuscript.

raised by the original suit, but note only that they involve (1) charges of illegal activities on the part of the Forest Service in connection with the management and leasing of the Mineral King area, and (2) charges of illegal activities on the part of the National Park Service in connection with the planning and construction of the road and power line through the Sequoia National Park. Also, the Sierra Club charges that no public hearings were held as required on the development or the road through the park— although, as noted above, the Forest Service claims that these issues were addressed in hearings held for other purposes.

Where does all of this leave us? Briefly, it is our impression that the question of what use to make of the site is still open, and that there is therefore a role for analysis of the sort provided in the following sections.

3. THE DEMAND FOR SKI RECREATION SITES IN CALIFORNIA

Elements of the Theoretical Approach

Estimation of demand for recreation sites is not a straightforward application of well-known methods for estimating the demand for goods and services exchanged in organized markets. The reason is that the services of the sites are ordinarily provided in extra-market fashion, at a zero or very low price that does not reflect imputed site rent. Although this pricing policy may be efficient, in the absence of congestion, it does make estimation of a market demand relationship difficult. It should be clear that the price we are speaking of is for access to the resources—the slopes—not for use of lift facilities. In what follows we shall assume that lift charges do not vary appreciably from one group of sites, as defined for purposes of the empirical analysis, to another. The charges are roughly the same, on average, for the use of lifts in the Tahoe area, say, as they are in the June Mountain–Mammoth Mountain area. We have some confidence in this assumption because these charges are for the most part closely regulated by the Forest Service. Even where there are small differences in day rates, it may be that these reflect differences in the quantity or quality of facilities, so that the unit price of constant quality services is roughly the same everywhere. The only component of the "price" for ski services that does vary to the consumer is his travel cost to different areas, as discussed below.

An ingenious method for measuring demand and value for the recreation site was first proposed, rather sketchily, in a letter from Harold Hotelling to the director of the National Park Service in 1947. Hotelling's suggestion was developed in detail by Marion Clawson (1959), and the resulting approach discussed at greater length in a more general work on the economics of outdoor recreation by Clawson and Jack Knetsch (1966). In what follows we first describe the Hotelling–Clawson–Knetsch (HCK) procedure, and then show how it can be extended to take account of substitution effects in a system of sites, such as the California ski sites.

The key to HCK lies in the recognition that, though there may be little explicit charge or none for his use of a site, the recreationist does pay a price, measured by the substantial travel costs to the ordinarily remote, resource-based recreation area. The first part of the procedure is then to infer demand for the site using travel cost as the measure of price. This is done by relating the rate of use, as measured, say, in visitor days divided by population, for each of a number of suitably defined visitor origin zones, to the costs of visiting from the zone. In principle these costs include not only all direct, or out-of-pocket expenditures, such as those on automobile maintenance and operation, but also the indirect elements such as the value of the traveler's time and the disutility of travel. The use–cost, or quantity–price, relationship is represented in linear form for simplicity, in figure 8-2.

In this construction, there is associated with a travel cost of $10 a visit rate of 4, with a travel cost of $20 a visit rate of 3, and so on. The visit rate from each zone can also be interpreted as the expected use by a representative individual from that zone.

In order to achieve this simple two-dimensional representation, a number of considerations that may influence use of a recreation site have been ignored. First, as hinted above, the presence of alternative facilities

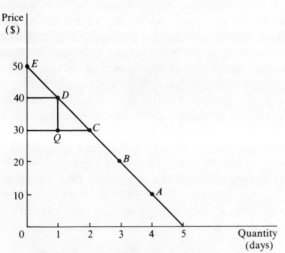

Figure 8-2. Travel costs, demand, and consumer's surplus from a recreational site.

which are at least partially substitutable for the site in question can affect demand for the site. For example, if travel costs to the site from one origin zone (A) are $10, and from another (B) $20, and these are the only influences on use of the site, then we can explain the higher visit rate from A, as represented in figure 8-2, by the difference in costs. But if there is another recreation site, on the "other side" of B, to which travel costs (from B) are just $15, then some part of the observed difference in visit rates to the first site may be explained by the presence of the lower cost substitute. Accordingly, to avoid bias in the estimation of a site's own price coefficient, we shall want to specify a model of a demand system that includes, in each equation, the prices (travel costs) of relevant alternatives.

Also omitted in the simple price–quantity relationship of figure 8-2 are the socioeconomic characteristics that are generally thought to influence demand, such as income, level of education, age, and so on, for the recreationists from each zone. Demand for a site may then be hypothesized to depend on these variables, in addition to its own price and the prices of substitutes. In our empirical work a sequential estimation technique will be used to discriminate between variables that ought to remain in a particular demand equation and those that ought to be omitted.[5]

A number of other potential difficulties in the extended HCK approach to demand estimation also deserve mention. Suppose (winter) visitors to a ski site are going for other purposes as well, simply to play in the snow, say, or to enjoy the social environment. Is this a problem? We don't think so. If the mix of activities varies across sites (and we don't know that it does), presumably this is due to differences in site characteristics. Nothing in the demand model says the sites must be perfect substitutes in consumption (except in the special case of introduction of a new site, and then only in a limited portion of the system, as discussed below). In any case, though we shall speak of demand for ski sites, it should be understood that the demand we observe may be for the sites as inputs to other activities as well.

A related but perhaps more serious difficulty is that in estimating demand for ski and related winter use of the California sites, we fail to provide a framework for assessing the benefits claimed for summer use of the proposed new development at Mineral King. This issue is addressed later on in the chapter, in the discussion of current summer use of the site.

A final point here is that the approach as outlined thus far works only if visits are approximately the same length.[6] That is, each visit or trip must be regarded as a member of a class of homogeneous goods (trips to a particular site), one characteristic of which is its length. The problem is solved

[5] For a discussion of sequential estimation, see Wallace and Ashar (1972).
[6] For a more general model of demand for recreation sites and other environmental resources which in principle considers the determination of time on site, or length of visit, see Cicchetti, Fisher, and Smith (1972).

in our case by considering only weekend trips to the California ski sites. This is also justified on the grounds that most use of these sites is of this sort. One explanation for the lack of variation in length of visit may lie in an institutional constraint on leisure time, restricting skiers for the most part to weekend excursions. Later on in our benefit calculations, weekday use is added back in. Perhaps 25–30 percent of California skiing is non-weekend, so total benefits may be approximately a third greater than weekend benefits. This is further discussed in the section on benefit estimation.

The second part of the HCK procedure infers the value of a site by integrating to obtain a consumers' surplus measure of the area under the demand curve.[7] With reference to figure 8-2, for example, the surplus accruing to the representative individual in the $10 travel cost zone is the area under the demand curve and above his (constant) marginal cost line, or triangle 10EA. This area is multiplied by the number of individuals in the zone to obtain the aggregate consumers' surplus in the zone. Proceeding similarly for each of the zones, the sum of the surpluses over all zones provides the measure of value associated with the site.

In case the foregoing discussion is not clear, an analytical formulation may help. Let the HCK demand be represented by $q = f(p)$, where q is the visit rate and p is price or travel cost; p_i = the price for zone i; p_0 = the price for the zone from which the visit rate falls to zero; and n_i = the population in zone i. Then the aggregate consumers' surplus associated with the use of the recreation site is given by

$$(8\text{-}1) \qquad \sum_i n_i \int_{p_i}^{p_0} f(p)\, dp$$

The introduction of a new site is easily represented within this framework. Suppose a site, say for ski recreation, is developed to perfectly substitute for the existing site considered in figure 8-1 and equation (8-1). The only difference between the sites is that the new one is closer than the old to at least some zones of visitor origin. In particular, again consulting figure 8-2, suppose an individual is in a $40 zone with respect to the original site and a new site is developed that reduces his travel costs to $30. A measure of the benefits (to him) from the new site is then the associated *change* in consumer's surplus, or the trapezoid 30 40 DC in figure 8-2. Two components of the gain are conveniently distinguished, namely the saving in cost to the original level of use, represented by the rectangle 30 40 DQ, and the surplus associated with the new use, represented by the triangle QDC. Note that the former, the saving in real resource costs made possible by a project (in this case to build a ski

---

[7] For a detailed discussion of the concept of consumers' surplus, and especially its relation to the area under the demand curve, see Mishan (1971), and also chapter 9.

facility), is exactly equivalent to the benefit measure employed in chapter 5 in the study of the Hells Canyon power project. The new element here is the benefit from additional use induced by the project, represented by triangle QDC. Analytically, the measure of benefits from the new facility, the change in aggregate consumers' surplus, is given by

$$(8\text{-}2) \quad \sum_i n_i \int_{p_i'}^{p_i} f(p) \, dp$$

where $p_i' = $ the price of site-based services after the introduction of the new site; other symbols are as before.

We earlier suggested that it would be desirable to capture the effects of the development of a new site on demand for existing sites that it may partially substitute for, and that to do this, an extension of the HCK method to take account of the substitution effects—as well as to obtain unbiased own price coefficient estimates—is required. In the remainder of this section we discuss the specification and estimation of a system of interrelated demands for ski recreation sites in California. Following this, in section 4, problems of benefit estimation are considered.

An Econometric Model of Demand

There is a developing literature on the specification and estimation of demand or expenditure systems, which we shall review briefly.[8] One approach, as originally developed by Stone (1954), consists in basing the estimation of linear expenditure functions on a particular utility specification. Stone's objective was to derive a linear expenditure system that was globally compatible with classical demand theory. In contrast, Leser (1961) and Powell (1966) have regarded such systems as convenient linearizations of an underlying nonlinear system. Accordingly, these approximations satisfy classical demand restrictions for a given set of initial conditions rather than for all possible sets. It is not possible in either case to derive the demand equations from the estimated expenditure functions. Since it is our objective to evaluate the benefits from the development of a new skiing facility in terms of a consumers' surplus measure, some estimates of the relevant structural demand functions for each site are necessary.

The structural demand approach has been taken by Parks (1969) and Byron (1970), who report methods for estimating systems of demand equations integrating the restrictions implied by classical demand theory. It is not, however, possible to adopt their suggested specifications. These are based on analyses of the complete market basket, to which restrictions of budget exhaustion and homogeneity of degree zero in income and all prices apply. In the case of demand for ski recreation, we are dealing with a subset of the consumer's expenditures and consequently may not appeal

[8] For a more thorough review, see Brown and Deaton (1972).

to these restrictions. On the other hand, for purposes of benefit estimation, a particularly important restriction is that of *symmetry*, which requires that the cross price coefficients in the site demand equations be equal. Since this restriction can be imposed only in linear demand equations, our system is specified to be linear in prices. An additional reason for the linear specification has to do with the complications nonlinear demand equations can cause for benefit estimation.[9]

Our task, then, is to estimate a system of linear demand equations whose errors may be contemporaneously correlated and whose coefficients are related via exact restrictions.[*] A restricted Aitken estimator may be derived by minimizing a quadratic objective function subject to the exact linear restrictions. The Lagrangian expression is given in (8-4), if the system of demand equations is as given in (8-3).

(8-3) $Q = P\beta + V$

(8-4) $S = (Q - P\beta)^T \Sigma^{-1}(Q - P\beta) - 2\lambda(T\beta - t)$

where

$$Q = \begin{bmatrix} \bar{q}_1 \\ \bar{q}_2 \\ \cdot \\ \cdot \\ \cdot \\ \bar{q}_K \end{bmatrix}$$ a $KT \times 1$ vector of T observations of the visit rates for each of K sites

$$\beta = \begin{bmatrix} \beta_1 \\ \beta_2 \\ \cdot \\ \cdot \\ \cdot \\ \beta_K \end{bmatrix}$$ a $KR \times 1$ vector of coefficients for the R independent variables in each of K demand equations

$$P = \begin{bmatrix} \bar{P}_1 & 0 & 0 & \cdot & \cdot & \cdot \\ 0 & \bar{P}_2 & 0 & \cdot & \cdot & \cdot \\ 0 & 0 & \bar{P}_3 & \cdot & \cdot & \cdot \\ \cdot & & \cdot & & & \\ \cdot & & & \cdot & & \\ \cdot & & & & \cdot & \\ & & & & & \bar{P}_K \end{bmatrix}$$ a $KT \times KR$ matrix of T observations for each set of R regressors for each of the K equations. P may include more or less information than the set of all site prices

[9] For a discussion of these problems, see Cicchetti *et al.* (1971).

[*] The material set in indented type, developed by Kerry Smith, deals with the derivation of an estimator. It may be skimmed by those not familiar with or especially interested in theoretical econometrics.

T = a $N \times KR$ matrix of coefficients which specify the linear restrictions on the coefficients β

t = a $N \times 1$ vector of additive components to the linear restrictions (i.e., $T\beta = t$)

V = a $KT \times 1$ vector of disturbances, K in total each with T observations

$\Sigma = \Omega \otimes I_T$, where Ω is a $K \times K$ covariance structure for the errors associated with each demand equation's structural errors.

Solution of the first-order conditions yields, following rearrangement, an expression for the estimator

$$(8\text{-}5) \quad \hat{\beta} = (P^T\Sigma^{-1}P)^{-1}P^T\Sigma^{-1}Q + (P^T\Sigma^{-1}P)^{-1}T^T[T(P^T\Sigma^{-1}P)^{-1}T^T]^{-1}$$
$$[t - T(P^T\Sigma^{-1}P)^{-1}P^T\Sigma^{-1}Q]$$

The first term on the right-hand side of (8-5) is the seemingly unrelated regressions estimator (SUR) of β. The second term adjusts these estimates by the extent to which they fail to satisfy the *a priori* restrictions.[10]

The Data

The market area, or region we hypothesize is likely to contain significant alternatives to the proposed new facility, is the state of California. Accordingly, demand will be estimated from visit rates to most of the ski sites in the state, including all of the major ones.

The first consideration, however, is which of these ought to be selected as the existing site for which the Mineral King facility will perfectly substitute. Of course, the more natural approach to the measurement of demand for and benefits from Mineral King would be estimation and integration of the demand for its services directly, especially as it may be difficult to identify another site that provides services which are perfect substitutes. Since the demand for Mineral King cannot be estimated in advance, however, and we wish to know something about the value of the project there before it is undertaken, it is first necessary to select, from the existing sites for which demand can be estimated, one that provides services which most closely substitute. Once we have an estimate of this demand, it is then possible to calculate one component of the change in surplus resulting from the introduction of Mineral King, as discussed above and represented in figure 8-2 and equation (8-2). The site selected as most similar to Mineral King is actually a composite of two sites, June Mountain and Mammoth Mountain. They were chosen because they are close

---

[10] In general the regressors will differ across equations and it is these differences which differentiate the first term in (8-9) from ordinary least squares (OLS). It should also be noted that we are necessarily assuming that Ω is not diagonal.

together, closer than others to Mineral King, have good (dry) snow conditions for skiing similar to those at Mineral King, and currently account for a large fraction of the Los Angeles area use that project planners envision for Mineral King.[11]

In addition to the June–Mammoth composite site, five others have been defined for estimation purposes and are designated as follows: Tahoe, Dodge Ridge–Mt. Reba, Mt. Shasta–Lassen Park, Badger Pass, and China Peak. As the names indicate, some of these are also composites, and Tahoe includes the following seven sites: Alpine Meadows, Boreal Ridge, Echo Summit, Heavenly Valley, Sierra Ski Ranch, Squaw Valley, and Sugar Bowl. As with June–Mammoth, the composites are defined for reasons of proximity and similarity in other characteristics. Our hypothesis with respect to these sites is that the cross price terms will be positive, with the fall in price of June–Mammoth services resulting from the introduction of Mineral King leading to a reduction in demand for the alternative sites.

The reader familiar with skiing in California may note that a number of sites have not been mentioned. In particular, sites in the Angeles National Forest and San Bernardino National Forest in southern California are not considered substitutes for other sites in the California system because of the poor quality of skiing conditions there (often more mud than snow) as well as the very limited capacity. It might be said, in the framework of Lancaster (1966), that the characteristics of these sites are not sufficiently similar to those of the included sites to permit them to function as substitutes. Also omitted from the demand analysis are a small number of sites scattered throughout the state. This was because data on visitor use were not available for the 1969–70 season over which use at the other sites was observed. The omission is probably not significant, however, as figures for 1967–68 suggest that the sites not in our present sample are not only few in number but also used very little.

The data on visit rates are derived from a 1969 U.S. Forest Service survey of the ski sites in which the county origins of arriving automobiles were recorded. By assigning on the basis of independent observation an average number of visitors to each automobile for the weekend visits, it is possible to derive the visitation rates (visitors per thousand population) for each of the fifty-eight counties in California for each site. The travel cost was determined by measuring the shortest road distance from the site configuration to the center of population mass in the county and multiplying the distance by a cost per mile. The measure of cost per mile is further discussed in the section on benefit estimation.

---

[11] Information about snow conditions at June–Mammoth, as well as some of the other information about the characteristics of sites and users in California has been furnished by Craig Stanley, whose work has been cited earlier, and Pete Wyckoff, Mineral King staff specialist, Sequoia National Forest.

Estimates of Demand Parameters

Ordinary least squares (OLS) regressions of visit rates on the price (travel cost) variables for each of the six sites indicated that not all sites can be considered substitutes for each other.[12] Geographic considerations evidently preclude some sites from functioning as effective substitutes for others. It is clear that the specification of the demand equation system will influence the estimated benefits to be derived from the development of ski facilities at Mineral King. Tables 8-2 through 8-5 present two alternative sets of specifications. Table 8-2 is based on the restricted and table 8-3 on the unrestricted estimates of the system for the first specification, which takes account of the geographic barriers to substitution. Again, by restricted we mean that the cross price coefficients are constrained to be equal. With respect to barriers to substitution, we see that the Shasta–Lassen site of extreme northern California, for example, does not substitute for sites south of Tahoe such as June–Mammoth. Accordingly, p_4, the price for Shasta–Lassen, does not appear in the second row of tables 8-2 or 8-3, the restricted and unrestricted equations respectively for June–Mammoth. Although in some of the equations the estimated cross price effects for selected sites are less than zero, it is not possible in any of these cases to reject the null hypothesis of no positive association.

The second specification eliminates the price variables whose estimated coefficients are negative but not significant. This is done on the grounds (in addition to statistical insignificance) that complementarity between the sites' services, as negative cross price effects would imply, is unlikely. Although it is conceivable that certain recreational facilities, such as Disney World in Florida, may have served to increase the demand for other facilities in the area, the proposed development at Mineral King is intended to provide facilities for skiing that will substitute for those elsewhere in California. Thus tables 8-4 and 8-5 present the restricted and unrestricted estimates of this specification of the demand system (i.e., the cross price effects in the restricted set are all positive).

It should perhaps be emphasized that inclusion of a price variable in the *restricted* specification is based on a loss function somewhat different from the one traditionally employed in the literature.[13] Although the included coefficients are not, in all cases, significantly different from zero,

---

[12] This specification was derived after examining the effects of income and demographic measures for the counties of origin as determinants of the demand. These variables were not significant and did not appear to be reflecting the effects economic theory would suggest. Ideally, we would like to know the income and characteristics of the actual users, but these were unavailable. Consequently the county data were used as proxies, and we are unable to assess whether it is true that income, for example, is not an important influence on participation, or that county income is not a good proxy for visitors' income.

[13] For an interesting discussion of related aspects of statistical inference, see Wallace and Ashar (1972).

Table 8-2

Restricted Estimates—Specification No. 1[a]

Site	Inter-cept	p_1	p_2	p_3	p_4	p_5	p_6
1. Tahoe	15.49[b] (7.46)	−2.27[b] (1.07)	0.52 (0.97)	1.21 (1.40)	0.34 (0.48)	−0.60 (1.05)	— —
2. June–Mammoth	60.11[b] (25.42)	0.52 (4.10)	−7.09[c] (4.25)	0.90 (6.38)	—	0.38 (6.10)	1.32 (5.05)
3. Dodge Ridge–Mt. Reba	5.56 (9.77)	1.21 (1.55)	0.90 (1.64)	−3.41 (2.42)	—	1.44 (2.30)	−0.34 (1.90)
4. Shasta–Lassen	1.34 (1.09)	0.34[b] (0.14)	— —	— —	−0.29[b] (0.10)	— —	— —
5. Badger Pass	5.06[c] (2.87)	−0.60 (0.45)	0.38 (0.45)	1.44[c] (0.79)	—	−1.52[b] (0.58)	— —
6. China Peak	−1.74 (3.77)	— —	1.32[c] (0.76)	−0.34 (0.41)	—	—	−0.83[c] (0.49)

[a]The numbers in parentheses are standard errors.
[b]Significantly different from zero at the 0.05 level.
[c]Significantly different from zero at the 0.075 level.

Table 8-3

Unrestricted Estimates—Specification No. 1[a]

Site	Inter-cept	p_1	p_2	p_3	p_4	p_5	p_6
1. Tahoe	0.33 (6.79)	−4.69[b] (1.00)	0.96 (0.88)	0.47 (1.30)	2.02 (0.44)	1.08 (0.97)	— —
2. June–Mammoth	44.20[c] (24.75)	4.76 (4.02)	−19.19[b] (4.12)	3.00 (6.24)	−6.40 (5.97)	—	14.93[b] (4.89)
3. Dodge Ridge–Mt. Reba	10.37 (9.35)	2.44[c] (1.52)	−1.99 (1.56)	−6.42[b] (2.35)	—	6.67[b] (2.26)	−1.19 (1.86)
4. Shasta–Lassen	1.77[b] (0.59)	0.17[b] (0.07)	— —	— —	−0.19[b] (0.05)	— —	— —
5. Badger Pass	5.29[b] (2.35)	−0.42 (0.37)	0.17 (0.37)	1.05[c] (0.65)	—	−1.11[b] (0.48)	— —
6. China Peak	1.11[b] (0.33)	— —	0.09 (0.07)	0.04 (0.04)	—	—	−0.17[b] (0.04)

[a]The numbers in parentheses are standard errors.
[b]Significantly different from zero at the 0.05 level.
[c]Significantly different from zero at the 0.075 level.

it is not clear that the ordinary test of significance is applicable to jointly constrained estimates, as in the restricted specification. The coefficients have been included on the basis of significant estimates with the *unrestricted* format, to which the test does apply. Then, since (as discussed below) economic theory requires the symmetry restrictions for benefit estimation with a system of demand equations, and since we fail to reject the null

Table 8-4
Restricted Estimates—Specification No. 2[a]

Site	Inter-cept	p_1	p_2	p_3	p_4	p_5	p_6
1. Tahoe	14.39[b]	−2.36[b]	0.25	0.93	0.45	—	—
	(6.72)	(0.93)	(0.83)	(0.86)	(0.45)	—	—
2. June–Mammoth	60.59[b]	0.25	−6.23[c]	1.12	—	—	0.96
	(25.18)	(3.98)	(4.19)	(5.22)	—	—	(3.87)
3. Dodge Ridge–Mt. Reba	4.59	0.93	1.12	−2.65	—	0.48	—
	(9.33)	(1.46)	(1.46)	(2.54)	—	(1.87)	—
4. Shasta–Lassen	1.05	0.45[b]	—	—	−0.35[b]	—	—
	(1.30)	(0.16)	—	—	(0.12)	—	—
5. Badger Pass	4.29[b]	—	—	0.48[b]	—	−0.72[b]	—
	(1.63)	—	—	(0.24)	—	(0.27)	—
6. China Peak	−1.57	—	0.96[c]	—	—	—	−0.77[c]
	(3.98)	—	(0.60)	—	—	—	(0.52)

[a]The numbers in parentheses are standard errors.
[b]Significantly different from zero at the 0.05 level.
[c]Significantly different from zero at the 0.075 level.

Table 8-5
Unrestricted Estimates—Specification No. 2[a]

Site	Inter-cept	p_1	p_2	p_3	p_4	p_5	p_6
1. Tahoe	2.99	−5.11[b]	1.29[c]	1.62[b]	1.91[b]	—	—
	(6.53)	(0.91)	(0.81)	(0.83)	(0.44)	—	—
2. June–Mammoth	48.65[b]	4.96	−18.93[b]	−0.10	—	—	11.00[b]
	(24.58)	(3.93)	(4.10)	(5.16)	—	—	(3.78)
3. Dodge Ridge–Mt. Reba	7.96	2.77[b]	−2.31[c]	−6.31[b]	—	5.49[b]	—
	(8.41)	(1.34)	(1.32)	(2.32)	—	(1.72)	—
4. Shasta–Lassen	1.75[b]	0.16[b]	—	—	−0.19[b]	—	—
	(0.59)	(0.07)	—	—	(0.05)	—	—
5. Badger Pass	4.37[b]	—	—	0.41[c]	—	−0.67[b]	—
	(1.60)	—	—	(0.24)	—	(0.26)	—
6. China Peak	1.02[b]	—	0.14[b]	—	—	—	−0.18[b]
	(0.32)	—	(0.05)	—	—	—	(0.04)

[a]The numbers in parentheses are standard errors.
[b]Significantly different from zero at the 0.05 level.
[c]Significantly different from zero at the 0.075 level.

hypothesis of symmetry (for each pair of equations tested separately) on the basis of the unrestricted estimates, the restricted estimates in table 8-4 are considered appropriate. The restrictions derived from economic theory are accepted with certainty and imposed on the data so that the resulting estimates conform. These estimates, from table 8-4, are then the basis for the benefit estimation of the next section. An alternative, Bayesian approach might call for the use of sample information to update our prior information concerning symmetry (see Zellner, 1971). That is, the restrictions could be stochastic, and the resulting posterior distribution would depend both on the nature of the prior probability distribution and the sample information. Although this approach has some appeal, traditional benefit estimation would not be possible.

4. BENEFITS FROM INTRODUCTION
OF A NEW SITE: MINERAL KING

Before the benefit figures are presented, a couple of theoretical issues should be addressed. The more important of these is the relationship of the symmetry restriction on the estimates to benefit evaluation. In particular, the issue arises with respect to the consumers' surplus measure of benefit derived by integrating the demand equation, or as in the present case, the system of demand equations. It has been known at least from the definitive analysis by Hotelling (1938) that this measure may be affected by the path of integration, the sequence of price changes. In other words, the measure is not well defined if different sequences yield different values. On the other hand, it is known (see any advanced calculus text) that the value of the line integral is independent of the path of integration if the symmetry condition is satisfied. In symbols,

$$\int_c Q \, dp$$

(where Q is the system of demand equations) is independent of the path C, if $\partial q_j / \partial p_i = \partial q_i / \partial p_j$, for all i, j pairs, $i \neq j$, where q_j is the quantity demanded of site j and p_i is the price of site i, and so on.

The question then is, what determines whether the symmetry condition is satisfied, and in particular, is it likely in our case, so that we may proceed with confidence to the evaluation of benefits? It turns out that if expenditures on an item, such as visits to ski recreation sites, account for a "small" fraction of the consumer's budget, then the symmetry condition is approximately satisfied.[14] This follows from a property of the well-known Slutsky equation of comparative static consumer demand theory. Writing this equation for any two sites, i and j, as

$$(8\text{-}6) \quad \frac{\partial q_j}{\partial p_i} = \left(\frac{\partial q_j}{\partial p_i}\right)_{\text{utility constant}} - q_i \left(\frac{\partial q_j}{\partial Y}\right)_{\text{prices constant}}$$

and

$$\frac{\partial q_i}{\partial p_j} = \left(\frac{\partial q_i}{\partial p_j}\right)_{\text{utility constant}} - q_j \left(\frac{\partial q_i}{\partial Y}\right)_{\text{prices constant}}$$

[14] However, this is not the only means of satisfying the condition. For a discussion of this problem see Mohring (1971) and Silberberg (1972).

where Y = income, recall that the first terms on the right-hand side of each equation, the pure substitution terms, must be equal. The question then turns on the second terms, which represent the income effects of price changes. Writing the income change induced by the price change for the first equation, say, as $dY = q_i dp_i$, so that $q_i = dY/dp_i$, it is clear that the less the importance of the good q_i in the budget, the less the effect on income of a change in its price p_i. It seems plausible, and we shall assume, that expenditures on visits to the several ski recreation sites in our sample account for a sufficiently small fraction of the representative consumer's budget that the second, or income, terms of the Slutsky equations can be neglected, leaving us with the symmetry condition at least approximately satisfied.

The other issue with which we might deal with at this point is just what is and is not being measured here. What is being measured, as has been noted, is a change in consumers' surplus associated with the introduction of a new ski facility at Mineral King. It must be admitted, however, that we propose to capture only that portion of the surplus associated with changing patterns of site use. Not accounted for is the change in surplus associated with the change in purchases of related goods and services, as for example, ski equipment. Also not accounted for is any change in producers' surplus associated with the change in the pattern of consumer expenditures.

Ideally, in a complete, or general equilibrium, analysis these effects would be accounted for. One reason why they are not in the present analysis is simply that we are unable to track all of the repercussions, in all markets, of a particular price change. Another, and perhaps better reason, is that they are likely to be, as suggested by Eckstein (1958), of the "second order of smalls." Moreover, it should be emphasized that previous empirical studies of the effect on economic surplus of a price change generally have not moved beyond the most partial equilibrium analysis, neglecting all changes in markets for related goods. This is noted also by Harberger (1971), in his critique of applied welfare analysis, where consideration of the more general equilibrium is urged. This study is an attempt to move at least part of the way in this direction, in that it does take account of changes in demand, and consumers' surplus, for what should be the most important substitutes for the good experiencing the price change.

Now let us indicate the results of our benefit calculations, presented in compact form in table 8-6. Three alternative travel mileage costs have been specified, partly because each may be plausible, depending on the circumstances, and partly for sensitivity analysis. The first is based on a recent U.S. Department of Transportation (1970) study, which reports variable costs of 5.5 cents per mile for operating an automobile. Since independent observation indicates an average of 3.2 persons per vehicle in trips to the California ski sites, the per visitor cost is 1.7 cents per mile. The second is based on a statistical study by Burt and Brewer (1971) which suggests a variable cost of 14.2 cents per vehicle mile for trips to recreation sites, or about 4.4 cents per visitor, assuming 3.2 visitors per vehicle. The difference presumably arises from the presence of other out-of-pocket costs in addition to those counted in the automobile operating costs. For the third figure, note that if all travel time in our sample were valued at some average wage rate, say $3 per hour, another 6 cents per mile (assuming an average speed of 50 miles per hour) would have to be added to travel costs, producing a figure of 10.4 cents per mile per visitor. Finally, it is intuitively plausible, and can be shown, that increasing travel costs by a given proportion with linear demand schedules has the effect of increasing benefits by the same proportion. Alternative benefit estimates corresponding to alternative travel cost assumptions are then readily derived.

The capacity constraint referred to in the table, with the associated reduction in benefits from the project, arises in the following way. The econometric results indicate that about 194,000 visitors will come to the area over the weekend, whereas capacity has been pegged at not more than 25,000, or a little over 12,000 per day, as noted in section 2. With annual benefits from weekend use of $5.8 million, assuming a 20-week season and the middle travel cost, and use by 194,000 visitors per weekend, the average increase in consumer's surplus per visit is approximately $1.50. If access to the area were rationed in such a way that each prospective visitor had an equal chance of admission, then annual benefits would be reduced to less than $0.8 million.

Earlier we noted that total (weekend plus weekday) use of California ski sites is about a third greater than weekend use alone. Assuming the population of weekend users, annual benefits from both uses together can be calculated simply by augmenting annual benefits from weekend use by a third. For example, annual benefits under the capacity constraint with the middle travel cost would be $1.0 million, as indicated in the table. But it is also possible to interpret the use predictions as suggesting that (in the absence of constraint) some 258,000 visitors (194,000 × 4/3) would come to Mineral King over the course of a week. If it is further assumed that the predicted weekday use of 64,000 would be evenly spread over the five days, then virtually all could be accommodated (5 × 12.5 thousand = 62.5 thousand). This is admittedly an unusual pattern of use, but let us just work out the implications for project benefits. Use over the 20-week season would be 1.75 million (12.5 thousand × 7 × 20), and still assuming the middle travel cost and an average surplus of $1.50, benefits would be $2.6 million, as indicated in the table.

Since assessment of the Mineral King project requires a comparison of benefits with investment items, the costs of facilities, and access, some attention must be given to the time pattern of benefits. We suggested earlier that project benefits might be expected to behave in this case like the benefits from preserving the area. Both are likely to be increasing over time. Still, there is reason to believe that demand for the amenities of Mineral King in its present, largely undeveloped state is likely to grow somewhat relative to demand for the project services. Figures on use of a larger area that includes the valley as a key feature indicate an increase of nearly 100 percent from 1967 to 1970.[15] This growth, about 25 percent (compounded) per year, is, as we have observed in the discussion of Hells Canyon, not unusual for wilderness recreation areas in recent years, and seems likely to continue.

The demand for outdoor recreation generally, on the other hand, is increasing much less rapidly. Although the use of ski facilities appears to be increasing at a rate closer to the demand for wilderness, this increase includes supply shifts as well. Growth in demand is probably more moderate. In this connection it should be remembered that, as discussed in footnote 12, measures of the mean and dispersion of origin zone income distributions, along with other demographic variables, were not significant in ordinary least squares estimation of the separate site demand equations. These results would suggest *no* growth in demand, hence a constant flow of benefits, for a given project capacity. In the terminology of chapter 3, the adjustment parameter r, the rate of growth in project benefits, is just equal to zero. The adjustment parameter α, the rate of growth in preservation benefits, on the other hand, is presumably positive for the same reasons as in the Hells Canyon and other cases. Besides, as long as r is expected to be less than α, as proposed just above, we may appeal immediately to the proof in chapter 3 that determination of the optimal use of the environment requires only a comparison of the present value of development now with the present value of preservation.

The first item considered in the comparative evaluation is the present value of benefits from the project. This is slightly more complicated than has thus far been indicated because only 55–60 percent of projected capacity could be accommodated during the first year of the project, so that benefits would be correspondingly reduced. Use would grow, presumably steadily, to the previously noted level of 12.5 thousand per day by the fifth year of operations. The present value of benefits, then, given this modified capacity constraint, assuming the middle travel cost, no growth in demand, and discounting annual flows at 9 percent, would be $8.2 million for weekend use, $10.9 million in total (augmented by a third), or $26.7

[15] This information comes from a report prepared by the RIM Center, U.S. Forest Service.

million (allowing for weekday per day use equal to weekend). After introducing investment costs, we return to the benefits to consider the effects
of assuming some growth in demand for project services over time.

First, a source of possible bias in the benefit estimates should be noted.
The problem arises because, although it is not possible to have a negative
visit rate, the estimated demand equations can, and in some cases do, result
in negative predictions for particular county-site pairs. One way of
proceeding in these circumstances would be to drop just the county demand
equation(s) for the particular site(s) for which negative visits are predicted, while at the same time retaining, for the system benefit estimate,
the county demand equations for the other sites. Even in this case, the
possibility of bias exists. Thus, suppose the predicted June–Mammoth visit
rate for a county is negative at the initial (without project) price, but
positive at the new (with project) price. Dropping this county-site demand
equation then results in the omission of a gain in surplus. On the other
hand, for one of the substitute sites, if the predicted visit rate is first
positive and then negative, a loss in surplus is ignored.

But the problem is more serious. If we proceed as suggested above,
dropping one or more (but not all) site equations (for a county), then the
path of integration is no longer consistent across the system of equations,
and the quadratic system benefit function

(8-7) $$\sum_i (1/2 P_i^T \beta P_i + P_i^T \alpha)$$

where

$P_i = 6 \times 1$ vector of prices for county i
$\beta = 6 \times 6$ matrix of estimated coefficients
$\alpha = 6 \times 1$ vector of estimated intercepts

derived by integrating the system of estimated demand equations is not
defined. Accordingly, to achieve a consistent path we are constrained to
adopt a second adjustment, dropping the county's demand (and contribution to benefits) for all of the six sites in the system, and not just those
for which predicted visit rates are negative. It should be observed, however,
that although this is in principle a serious omission, the relative magnitudes
in the present case are such that results are not much affected, because only
a small minority of the fifty-eight counties are involved, all having small
populations.

5. INVESTMENT AND OPPORTUNITY COSTS
OF THE MINERAL KING PROJECT

Investment Costs

The figures presented in this section are simply the planned
private and public expenditures on project facilities, including, importantly,

the access road. Planned on-site investment expenditures are about $36 million, distributed over a 10-year period in installments of (roughly) $6 million spread evenly over the first 3 years, $16 million over the next 2, and $14 million over the next 5.[16] The present value of these costs, again discounting at 9 percent, comes to just over $25 million. As for the access road, planned expenditures are $25 million, presumably all within the first year of operations. It might be noted, however, that expected costs of the road have risen since it was proposed in 1966, and many persons now feel that actual costs would be much higher than $25 million, perhaps double. Indeed, the *Sierra Club Bulletin* argued this point as far back as 1967. Accepting for the moment the $25 million figure, and combining it with the on-site costs, we obtain a present value of direct investment costs of $50 million.

Comparing this amount with the benefits in table 8-6, it seems that the project would be inefficient in the Kaldor–Hicks sense. But what of the possibility, suggested earlier, that demand for the project's services could grow over time? Of course it was also pointed out that observed rates of increase in ski recreation activity generally in the United States are due at least in part to increases in the supply of ski facilities. And we did not find a significant correlation between income and demand in the cross-section of California counties. Accordingly, it is not clear what rate of growth in benefits, other than zero, would be appropriate. We can, however, ask the question: What would the rate have to be for the present value of benefits to just equal investment costs? Suppose annual benefits from completed capacity use were $1.0 million, based on the assumptions noted earlier. Then, even assuming this level of use from the first year of operations, and a 9 percent discount rate, benefits would have to grow at the equivalent of 7 percent in perpetuity to have a present value of $50 million. Since the capacity constraint would be binding from the start, this seems unlikely. Alternatively, suppose annual benefits were $2.6 million, the difference due to the assumed heavier weekday use. In this case benefits would have to grow at the equivalent of 4 percent in perpetuity—again, even if the full $2.6 million could be realized in the first year.

If this too is considered unlikely, then following the empirical strategy outlined in the introduction to part II, the project could indeed be judged inefficient, even without counting environmental costs. Since we do not feel it is possible to speak definitively on the basis of the evidence presented above, some knowledge of the environmental costs could be helpful. Actually, proponents of the project argue that benefits from current

[16] This represents the most recent planning for which figures are available, as communicated in a private interview with Robert Hicks of Walt Disney Productions in the spring of 1972.

Table 8-6
Benefit Estimates for Mineral King Development[a] (millions of $)

	Benefits		
Travel cost	(Weekends only)	(Weekends + weekdays)[b]	(Weekends + weekdays)[b]
	Annual		
1.7¢	2.3	3.0	
4.4¢	5.8	7.7	
10.4¢	13.6	18.1	
	Annual, with capacity constraint[c]		
1.7¢	0.3	0.4	1.1
4.4¢	0.8	1.0	2.6
10.4¢	1.8	2.3	6.1
	Present value,[d] with capacity constraint		
1.7¢	3.1	4.1	11.3
4.4¢	8.2	10.9	26.7
10.4¢	18.5	24.6	62.6

[a]These estimates are based on restricted specification No. 2 given in table 8-4. For cases in which negative predicted quantities were encountered for the single site for either initial or terminal price, the particular county's contribution to system benefits was excluded.

[b]The assumptions behind each of the two weekend plus weekday use benefit computations are given in the text.

[c]The capacity constraint is explained in the text.

[d]Present values are obtained by discounting annual flows at 9 percent in perpetuity. No growth in demand is assumed for these figures. See the discussion in the text for justification of the no-growth assumption, and also for the effect on present values if it is relaxed.

summer uses of the site would not be sacrificed. First, some uses at least would not be displaced, and second, summer use of project facilities could compensate for those that are displaced. These issues are addressed in the discussion of the value of the site for current recreation uses.

Preservation Benefits: Opportunity
Costs of the Project?

Adopting the HCK method of demand and value analysis essentially as presented in section 3 of this chapter, Stanley (1973) has observed visit rates, estimated demand, and calculated (annual) consumers' surplus for current recreation use of Mineral King.[17] His origin zones, instead of the California counties, are rings defined in terms of distance from the site, with the most distant an open-ended "out-of-state." This latter poses a problem, in that it is not clear which of the many observed travel costs from this zone should be used as the benchmark (corresponding to $50 in

---

[17] A number of other approaches to the measurement of consumers' surplus, along with a wealth of detail concerning the site and visitor use are presented in Stanley's work.

the illustrative example of section 3). Stanley settles, perhaps conservatively, on the average. On the basis of this figure, and the observed costs and visit rates for the closer zones, the consumer's surplus for the representative individual in each zone is calculated. Summing over all individuals and all zones, as in equation (8-1) of section 3, aggregate consumers' surplus for current recreation use of Mineral King comes to just under $0.7 million for 1971.

A number of qualifications are in order with respect to this estimate. In the first place, it assumes, for the same reasons as does the estimate of recreation benefits reported in chapter 6, that there are no (good) substitutes for the particular preserved environment, in this case Mineral King (at least for the great majority of users, from southern California), so that virtually all of the triangular surplus of figure 8-2 is lost in the event the area is removed from their consumption opportunity set.

Secondly, the figure of $0.7 million excludes the surplus accruing to an important class of users, the on-site cabin owners, who accounted for 26.8 percent of total visitor days in 1971. We might assume, as Stanley suggests, that per capita surplus to this group is just equal to that of the included groups. This seems reasonable, if again a little conservative, and accordingly benefits may be adjusted by a factor of 1.366, yielding a more comprehensive estimate of just under $1 million.

To put the preservation benefits, say $1 million in 1971, on the same footing with development benefits and costs, it is necessary to convert the annual flow to a present value. Use of the Mineral King area has been increasing in recent years, and if unconstrained seems likely to continue to do so for much the same reasons as discussed in chapters 6 and 7. On the other hand, no attempt has been made to determine the capacity of the area for recreation of the low-density type, and it may be that use is already at or near that level. Of course, from what has been said earlier, it follows that even if use does not increase, per capita surplus is likely to, and hence also the flow of benefits. In the earlier terminology, the appreciation parameter α is likely to be greater than zero. Let us be very conservative in imputing a present value to preservation, and for the purpose of our numerical calculations assume that there is no appreciation, due either to increasing use or increasing per capita surplus, in the benefit flow. Then, discounting at 9 percent in perpetuity, the present value of preservation-related recreation benefits from Mineral King comes to approximately $11 million. Clearly, in the framework of this simplified application, an alternative and probably more realistic assumption of a small positive α is easily substituted, in effect by reducing the 9 percent discount rate by the particular α assumed. This would result in increasing project opportunity costs to a level greater than the $11 million in the table corresponding to an α equal to zero.

It was noted above that some or all of current summer use of the site might not be displaced by the project. In view of the substantial modification of the environment the project would involve, and the likely reaction to this by current users (recall chapter 3's discussion of the preferences of wilderness users), we are frankly skeptical of the claim that current values would not be sacrificed by development. In any event, we have presented an estimate of these values. The reader is free to judge for himself whether, as we tend to believe, they are appropriately counted as opportunity costs of the project.

It has also been suggested that summer use of project facilities, even if by different people, would more than make up for any losses sustained by users of the preserved environment. This is possible, but here too we have some doubts. It is difficult to see why people would travel 200 miles and more from the Los Angeles area to eat in restaurants, swim in pools, or even play tennis or golf, when facilities for these and other similar activities are available so much closer to home. In other words, it is difficult to see a gain in consumers' surplus here corresponding to that for the skiers who would benefit from reduced travel time. Of course, if the summer facilities were to be unique, or even to have no good substitutes, then conceivably surplus would be generated, but it would be necessary to await development and operation of the facilities in order to estimate directly demand and value. In the meantime, assuming the middle present value of winter use of $10.9 million (see table 8-6), value would have to exceed $50 million, or five times that estimated for winter use, in order to reverse the ranking of the alternatives. Assuming a present value of $26.7 million, value would have to exceed $34 million, still well above the winter use figure. This calculation assumes no growth in demand for either alternative, probably favoring the project for reasons given above, and also ignores road-related losses.

No value has been attached to the damage that would result from construction and use of the access road through Sequoia National Park. This represents in a sense an external cost, but the reasons it is not included in our estimates are, first, there are considerable differences in just the predictions of physical damages (see section 2), making valuation difficult, and second, it would only add to the preponderance of project costs over benefits, and thus not affect the qualitative results. It may, however, be important if we are to consider alternative project sizes, as in the Hells Canyon analysis of chapters 5 and 6. Indeed, choice of the optimum use of Mineral King requires such consideration (see chapter 3). Our empirical results indicate that the particular project envisioned by Disney and the Forest Service is not likely to exhibit a positive net present value, but nothing in the results, or the analysis, indicates that a project of substantially different scale would be similarly inefficient.

Relating this to the question of damage to the surrounding environment by the access road, a larger project would presumably call for a more elaborate and therefore more disruptive access, as well as increased on-site and congestion costs. On the other hand, the greater capacity would mean greater benefits, following the admission of some or all of the additional users our econometric results indicate would be forthcoming. But an even better prospect would probably be the much smaller project, a few lifts and a ski hut, for example, originally envisioned by the Forest Service and the Sierra Club. The losses, if any, from such a project to users of the present environment possibly would be less than the gains (net of the minimal investment costs) to skiers, and the project therefore would be efficient.

6. CONCLUSIONS

We have sought in this chapter to present a rigorous quantitative analysis of the benefits of a proposed high-density ski recreation project in the Mineral King area of California. Results of an econometric analysis of a generalized Hotelling–Clawson–Knetsch model of demand for recreation suggest that these benefits are likely to be substantially less than costs, even under some rather conservative assumptions about costs.

The analysis is relatively formal because it is important to measure as accurately as possible static demand and value for each of the alternative uses of the environmental resource, since behavior over time may not be that different. This contrasts with the anticipated asymmetry, for example, in the Hells Canyon case of chapters 5 and 6, where the static analysis was correspondingly less formal. Now, as it turns out, much of the benefit predicted from the ski site demand estimation in this chapter is dropped owing to a capacity restriction. This does not mean, however, that the exercise was not worth doing. In the first place, of course, the result that predicted that use of the new site would exceed planned capacity was not known until the empirical work was completed. Secondly, and more importantly, the total benefit estimates *with* the capacity restriction are derived from average benefit estimates *without* the restriction. Finally, development of the model and estimating procedure for use in this case should make possible improved measurement in many formally similar cases to which they can now be applied.

REFERENCES

Brown, A. and Deaton, A. 1972. "Surveys in Applied Economics: Models of Consumer Behavior," *Economic Journal,* vol. 82, no. 328.

Burt, O. R. and Brewer, Durward. 1971. "Estimation of Net Social Benefits from Outdoor Recreation," *Econometrica,* vol. 39, no. 5.

Byron, R. P. 1970. "The Restricted Aitken Estimation of Sets of Demand Relations," *Econometrica*, vol. 38, no. 6.

Cicchetti, C. J., Fisher, A. C. and Smith, V. K. 1972. "An Economic and Econometric Model for the Valuation of Environmental Resources." Paper presented at Econometric Society Meetings, Toronto.

————, Freeman, A. M., III, Haveman, R. H., and Knetsch, J. L. 1971. "On the Economics of Mass Demonstrations: A Case Study of the November 1969 March on Washington," *American Economic Review*, vol. LXI, no. 4.

————, Seneca, Joseph, and Davidson, Paul. 1969. *The Demand and Supply of Outdoor Recreation* (Washington, D.C.: Bureau of Outdoor Recreation).

Clawson, Marion. 1959. "Methods of Measuring the Demand for and Value of Outdoor Recreation," Resources for the Future Reprint No. 10.

———— and Knetsch, J. L. 1966. *Economics of Outdoor Recreation* (Baltimore: Johns Hopkins Press).

Eckstein, Otto. 1958. *Water Resource Development: The Economics of Project Evaluation* (Cambridge, Mass.: Harvard University Press).

Harberger, A. C. 1971. "Three Basic Postulates for Applied Welfare Economics," *Journal of Economic Literature*, vol. 9, no. 3.

Hotelling, Harold. 1938. "The General Welfare in Relation to Problems of Taxation and of Railway and Utility Rates," *Econometrica*, vol. 6, no. 3.

Lancaster, K. J. 1966. "A New Approach to Consumer Theory," *Journal of Political Economy*, vol. 75, no. 2.

Leser, C. E. V. 1961. "Commodity Group Expenditure Functions for the United Kingdom, 1948–1957," *Econometrica*, vol. 29, no. 1.

Mishan, E. J. 1971. *Cost–Benefit Analysis* (New York: Praeger).

Mohring, Herbert. 1971. "Alternative Welfare Gain and Loss Measures," *Western Economic Journal*, vol. 9, no. 4.

Parks, R. W. 1969. "Systems of Demand Equations: An Empirical Comparison of Alternative Functional Forms," *Econometrica*, vol. 37, no. 4.

Powell, Alan. 1966. "A Complete System of Consumer Demand Equations for the Australian Economy Fitted by a Model of Additive Preferences," *Econometrica*, vol. 34, no. 3.

Sierra Club Bulletin, November 1967.

Silberberg, Eugene. 1972. "Duality and the Many Consumer's Surpluses," *American Economic Review*, vol. LXII, no. 5.

Stanley, Craig. 1973. "The Estimation of Activity Demand for a Non-Priced Recreational Resource: Mineral King, California," unpublished Ph.D. dissertation, Claremont Graduate School, California.

Stone, R. D. and Rowe, D. A. 1954. *The Measurement of Consumer's Expenditure and Behavior in the United Kingdom, 1920–1938*, vol. 1 (Cambridge: Cambridge University Press).

Wallace, T. D. and Ashar, V. G. 1972. "Sequential Methods in Model Construction," *Review of Economics and Statistics*, vol. 54, no. 2.

Zellner, Arnold. 1971. *An Introduction to Bayesian Inference in Econometrics* (New York: Wiley).

U.S. Dept. of Transportation. 1970. *Cost of Operating an Automobile* (Washington, D.C.).

U.S. Forest Service. 1969. *Mineral King: A Planned Recreation Development* (Washington, D.C.).

U.S. Forest Service. 1971. *Recreation Use Information—California Region.*

CHAPTER 9

ALLOCATION OF PRAIRIE
WETLANDS

1. INTRODUCTION

The study reported in this chapter is different from those of earlier chapters in several respects. In the first place, although an effort is made to blend it in with earlier theoretical and empirical materials, with some differences of emphasis from the original, it represents work done primarily under a grant by the Natural Environments program at RFF to Gardner Brown and Judd Hammack. References are made throughout to the published work of Brown and Hammack; the reader interested in a great variety of detail and qualification beyond that presented here might refer to *Waterfowl and Wetlands*. This chapter is essentially a summary version of their work, modified in a way appropriate to this volume.

Secondly, the resource at issue is not, like the Hells Canyon, the White Cloud Peaks, or Mineral King, a single publicly held (unique) environment; rather it is composed of many private holdings scattered over a relatively large area. The issue is the allocation of the prairie wetlands of the north central United States (Minnesota and the Dakotas) and neighboring provinces in Canada. The disadvantages of having marshes and ponds on his land encourage the individual farmer to drain and convert them to cropland. Drainage increases the supply of arable land and eliminates the costs of tilling around potholes (Brown and Hammack, 1972). If left in their natural state, on the other hand, these wetlands play a vital part in the life cycle of migratory waterfowl, which are valued objects of hunting, viewing, and so on. Brown and Hammack, citing Crissey (1969), observe that the quantity and quality of the birds' wintering grounds are believed to be adequate, with their summer nesting and breeding grounds the critical factor in determining population. More than 55 percent of all ducks produced in North America in an average year are produced in the prairie wetlands, on just 10 percent of the continental breeding area. Compounding the conflict in resource use is the fact that, although resting and feeding areas along the migration routes are in large part on public

219

lands of the Wildlife Refuge System, most of the nesting areas are privately owned. Since the private owners bear the costs of producing the recreational resource but do not share in the benefits, there is at least a presumption that a socially optimal number of ponds would be greater than that determined by market forces alone.

A third difference between the case of prairie wetlands allocation and the other problems addressed in earlier chapters is that conversion of the wetlands may not be irreversible. The Brown–Hammack model for the determination of an optimal number of ponds, similar in other respects to that in chapter 3, is formulated as if reconversion is possible; evidence on methods for producing new wetlands is reported from a publication by Ducks Unlimited (Brown and Hammack, 1972, p. 194). This seems to be a matter of some controversy, however, since Russell Train, the administrator of the Environmental Protection Agency, has suggested that the conversion is in fact irreversible. The distinction may be that, although the draining of a natural pond is in fact irreversible, Ducks Unlimited and Brown and Hammack are talking about the production of biologically acceptable substitutes. Assuming that they are correct in the sense that it is technically possible to create new duck-producing ponds, might it not still be true, as we have argued earlier, in chapter 3, that preferences of the affected recreationists rule out the substitution in consumption of a man-made for a natural environment? Although we believe this is true for unique environments of the sort discussed in preceding chapters, it seems less likely for individual ponds in this area. In the first place, there are already many such ponds, and more importantly, they are not experienced directly, but rather serve as factors of production for a commodity (migratory waterfowl) that is "consumed" hundreds and even thousands of miles away. In what follows, then, we describe the approach and results of Brown and Hammack. The next section describes an optimal control model similar to that in chapter 3.

2. A MODEL FOR THE OPTIMAL ALLOCATION OF WETLANDS

The objective, as in chapter 3, is to maximize the present value of the net benefits (here from use of the wetlands), where benefits are represented by an aggregate consumers' surplus (the willingness to pay of waterfowl hunters), and costs by the opportunity costs of the ponds, presumably in agricultural output forgone. In the Brown–Hammack symbols, the objective is to maximize

(9-1) $$\int_0^\infty [NV(K, Y, S, E) - C(P)]e^{-\rho t}\,dt$$

where
> N = the number of hunters
>
> V = the individual hunter valuation function
>
> K = the bagged waterfowl kill
>
> Y, S, and E = socioeconomic characteristics of the hunter population
>
> C = the pond cost function
>
> P = the number of ponds
>
> ρ = an appropriately chosen discount rate

The problem is to choose the sequence of P and K that maximizes (9-1), subject to a constraint on the waterfowl population, written in the form of a differential equation (again adopting the Brown–Hammack terminology) as

$$(9\text{-}2) \qquad \frac{dW}{dt} = -W + s_2[I + s_1 W - c_3 N K]$$

where
> W = the number of mature birds
>
> I = the number of immatures
>
> s_1 = an instantaneous rate corresponding to the survival fraction of adults from May to September (the summer nesting and breeding season on the northern wetlands)
>
> s_2 = an instantaneous rate corresponding to the survival fraction of the fall flight not killed by hunters from September to May
>
> c_3 = an adjustment for unbagged kill

It is assumed, and indeed empirically demonstrated, as we shall see in the next section, that the valuation function V is concave in K, so that, further assuming a linear or convex cost function C, and given an initial value $W(0)$ for the state variable W, there is a solution to the problem.

As in chapter 3, this is an optimal control problem, which may be solved by applying the maximum principle of Pontryagin et al. (1962). However, it should be pointed out that there is a difference between the two problems that also affects the issue of irreversibility. Recall that the main analytical result of chapter 3 was that, in the presence of time-varying benefit functions, if there exists an interval of time over which it is anticipated that preservation-related benefits will be growing relative to development-related benefits, so that the instantaneous optimum size of a development project will be decreasing, then the net present value of the environmental resource (the project site) will be maximized by stopping investment at some point before the start of the interval. The interpretation of this result is that, given the irreversibility of development, it may be profitable to take some near-term losses as forgone returns from expanding development in exchange for a reduction in future losses resulting from too much development at a time when less is preferred. Now, since the value and cost functions in equation (9-1) are not functions of time, i.e., are stationary, a result of the sort obtained in chapter 3 is precluded. Put another way, the lack of a restriction on reversibility has less analytic significance. With a stationary value function (and only one type of "capital"), the Brown–Hammack system will evolve toward a stationary, or steady-state solution for values of P, K, and W.

Let us briefly indicate the solution. The Hamiltonian

$$(9\text{-}3) \quad H = [NV(K, Y, S, E) - C(P) - \lambda(W - s_2(I + s_1W - c_3NK))]e^{-\rho t}$$

where λ is an auxiliary variable is maximized with respect to the control variables K and P, yielding the necessary conditions

$$(9\text{-}4) \quad \frac{\partial H}{\partial K} = \frac{\partial V}{\partial K} - \lambda s_2 c_3 = 0$$

and

$$(9\text{-}5) \quad \frac{\partial H}{\partial P} = -\frac{\partial C}{\partial P} + \lambda s_2 \frac{\partial I}{\partial P} = 0$$

I is a function of P since, as noted earlier, P is a factor in the production of I. The remaining condition is given by

$$(9\text{-}6) \quad -\frac{d\lambda}{dt} + \rho\lambda = \frac{\partial H}{\partial W} = -\lambda\left(1 - s_2\frac{\partial I}{\partial W} - s_1 s_2\right)$$

I is a function of W since W, along with P, is a factor in the production of I.[1]

Economic interpretations of equations (9-4), (9-5), and (9-6) are provided by Brown and Hammack, and the reader would do well to consult them. Here we essentially reproduce part of their interpretations, using in some cases slightly different language and simplifying where possible. First of all, note that from the Pontryagin conditions $dW/dt = \partial H/\partial\lambda$, so that the auxiliary variable λ may be interpreted as the shadow price of the waterfowl capital, W. Then equation (9-4) says that the bagged kill level K at any time should be set such that the marginal value of the kill to hunters, $\partial V/\partial K$, is just equal to the value of the marginal bird, λ (since the adjustments s_2 and c_3 are close to unity).

Equation (9-5) says that the factor P should be employed up to the point where its price, $\partial C/\partial P$, equals the value of its marginal product, $\lambda \partial I/\partial P$ (since the adjustment s_2 is close to unity).

---

[1] For details, see Arrow and Kurz (1970).

Again letting the adjustments s_1 and s_2 equal unity, purely for expositional purposes, the negative of the expression in parentheses on the right-hand side of equation (9-6), $-1 + s_2\, \partial I/\partial W + s_1 s_2$, becomes $\partial I/\partial W$, or the marginal productivity of waterfowl capital. Then equation (9-6) may be rewritten as $-d\lambda/dt + \rho\lambda = \lambda\, \partial I/\partial W$, and in the stationary state in which $d\lambda/dt = 0$, as $\rho = \partial I/\partial W$. In words, the steady-state optimal stock of waterfowl capital is that for which the marginal productivity, or rate of return, is just equal to the discount rate.

The dynamics of this result are also subject to straightforward interpretation. Suppose the system is not in equilibrium, so that $(d\lambda/dt)/\lambda = \rho - \partial I/\partial W$. If, for example, the productivity of waterfowl capital is greater than the discount rate, this will be reflected in a falling price of capital $[(d\lambda/dt)/\lambda < 0]$ as the stock expands along the optimal path to the steady-state level. This assumes, of course, that the production function $I = h(W,P)$ is concave, i.e., that the marginal productivity of W is diminishing, and indeed this hypothesis is verified in a statistical estimation by Brown and Hammack. It is also consistent with biological experience, in that the waterfowl exhibit "compensatory mortality," fewer young per breeder surviving as the number of breeders increases.

It will obviously be interesting to substitute values for the discount rate, pond cost, number of hunters, and also—and more precisely than the approximations in the preceding discussion—for the adjustment parameters, in order to compare optimal solution values for the number of ponds, the breeding stock, and annual kill, with recently observed magnitudes. Such an exercise is undertaken, subject to serious qualification, by Brown and Hammack, and the results (and qualifications) are reported below. First, however, further explanation of the crucial valuation and cost functions, V and C respectively, in the functional expression (9-1) is provided.

3. VALUE AND COST OF WETLANDS

The Valuation Function

In chapter 8, consumer's surplus was calculated as the area under an estimated (travel cost) demand curve for trips to a recreation site. On the assumption that the income effect was negligible, this area coincided with both the compensating variation and the equivalent variation measures of consumer's surplus.[2] The consumer's surplus measure of value, the dependent variable V in the present case, however, is not arrived at in this fashion. Instead, Brown and Hammack adopt a version of the Davis (1963) interview technique, in which a sample of users of the recreational

---

[2] For a discussion of the relationships of the two measures to each other and to the area under the demand curve, see Mishan (1971).

resource is queried directly concerning the value each attaches to use of the resource. Although it is true that economists (at least these economists) generally prefer the method of indirectly estimating demand and value, as developed and applied in chapter 8, because of its reliance on observed behavior rather than responses to hypothetical questions, there are good grounds for choosing the Davis technique in this case. One additional problem it does raise, however, is the necessity for choosing among the alternative consumer's surplus measures. That is, should users be queried concerning their willingness to pay for waterfowl hunting (the compensating variation), or their willingness to sell—the amount they would have to receive in order to forgo the right to hunt waterfowl (the equivalent variation)?

Before considering the pros and cons of travel cost versus interview methods for eliciting consumer's surplus in this case, we address the question of appropriate measure. In chapter 2 we reviewed essentially this same problem, namely, the effect of the assignment of property rights on the determination of value. Since the prairie wetlands are already privately owned for all practical purposes, it seems reasonable not to implicitly assign property rights to waterfowl hunters, as would the equivalent variation approach. Instead, Brown and Hammack rely on the compensating variation measure of willingness to pay. More specifically, the Davis technique which they employ seeks to avoid the purely hypothetical character of a direct question concerning willingness to pay by asking instead about the amount the hunter's costs would have had to have risen to keep him from hunting that season.

Now, from the wetlands owners' viewpoint, since the wetlands are in fact privately owned, it seems the appropriate measure is in effect the equivalent variation, i.e., the amount the owners would have to be paid to leave a pond in its natural state. Some alternative estimates developed by Brown and Hammack are in fact consistent with this approach, as indicated in the discussion of pond cost functions below.

Returning to the problem of choice of method—travel cost or interview —one very good reason for not using the travel cost method in this particular case is that it is site-specific. That is, demand can be inferred only for a single site, or perhaps simultaneously for a relatively small number of specific sites, on the basis of information concerning visitor origins and alternative recreation opportunities. Yet there are millions of ponds in the prairie region, and probably thousands of hunting sites along the migratory routes. Application of the travel cost method to yield results on the value of waterfowl and wetlands would then require information about the travel patterns of hunters to all these sites. Moreover, since the hunting sites are not the waterfowl production sites, it is not clear that the value of hunting derived from the demand for a particular configuration of hunting sites would be equivalent to the value of the wetlands in the production of waterfowl.

Other reasons for the choice of the Davis interview method are discussed by Brown and Hammack in the lengthier monograph version of their study (Hammack and Brown, 1974). Although we are not in agreement with all of the remarks there concerning the properties of the two methods generally, the interested reader might want to consult the discussion in their chapter 2.

One other point that might be explored before turning to the empirical results is the exclusive reliance on hunter valuation since, as indicated at the beginning of the chapter, migratory waterfowl are valued also as objects of viewing or photographing. In defense of the Brown–Hammack approach, expert opinion in this area holds that even a substantial reduction in the amount of wetlands would leave "sufficient birds of all species . . . capable of meeting a greatly increased demand for outdoor recreation in the form of bird-watching, photography, etc." (Crissey, 1969, p. 171). Or, as paraphrased by Hammack and Brown, "The value of nonconsumptive use is presumed to be insensitive to changes in the total size of the population and is therefore unaltered by relevant changes in the supply of nesting habitat" (1974, p. 3). The value of the consumptive use (hunting) would, however, be affected by a substantial reduction in ponds, and is therefore the appropriate focus of this study.

As noted in expression (9-1), the hunter valuation (V) just discussed is hypothesized to be a function, in addition to seasonal bagged kill (K), of a number of socioeconomic variables: hunter (annual) income (Y), the number of seasons of waterfowl hunting (S), and hunter costs for the season (E). Using data obtained from a questionnaire sent to a sample of waterfowl hunters in the seven states—Arizona, California, Idaho, Nevada, Oregon, Utah, and Washington—that lie within the Pacific flyway, Brown and Hammack (1972, pp. 182–183) estimate the following equation:

(9-7) $\ln V = 1.54 + 0.443 \ln Y + 0.163 \ln S + 0.149 \ln E + 0.409 \ln K$
    (t values)   (8.4)   (4.4)   (5.6)   (12.9)
    [\$256]   [\$12.1](000)   [16.2]   [\$322]   [23.9]

$$R^2 = 0.217, \quad n = 1511$$

The numbers in brackets are the means of the untransformed variables.

The logarithmic transformation apparently gave the best fit of those tested. The authors note that an untransformed linear regression is ruled out by the restriction that the second partial derivatives of V with respect to the independent variables be negative. This property is easily verified for the double log form in the case in which the coefficients are between 0 and 1, as in equation (9-7). In response to an objection by Scott (1965) that responses to hypothetical valuation questions may confuse actually incurred costs with valuation, another regression was run, omitting the variable E. This yielded very slight differences in the estimates of the coefficients of the remaining variables, differences which are not significant even with the relatively small standard errors of estimate.[3]

Pond Cost Function

The function $C(P)$ in expression (9-1) represents the cost of holding (or creating) undrained wetlands in terms of the net returns to agricultural production forgone. If a pond is left in its natural state to serve as a factor of production for waterfowl, then clearly the value of agricultural output that would be obtained following drainage and conversion to cropland is lost. Presumably there are costs incurred in the conversion process, but evidence on the rate of conversion, especially of U.S. wetlands, suggests that these costs are less than the benefits obtained by farmers, at least so far.[4] Of course, this evidence suggests nothing about the desirability from the social point of view of further, or even existing, conversion of wetland to cropland, since the private decision-makers have little incentive to take into account in their profit calculations the value of wetlands in waterfowl production. They may even believe, perhaps mistakenly according to existing statistical evidence, that crop damage varies with the size of the waterfowl population (Hammack and Brown, 1974, p. 84).

The cost function is not estimated, and although the theoretical formulation of section 2 allows for the possibility of convexity, the empirical specification is in all cases linear, i.e., the cost of a marginal pond, $\partial C/\partial P$, is constant. The assumption is that wetlands are homogeneous factors of production in the agricultural as well as the waterfowl alternative (Hammack and Brown, 1974, p. 69). This seems questionable, at least where a substantial increase in the number of ponds is indicated, but the very fragmentary nature of the data on the costs of obtaining this land evidently did not permit parametric estimation, as for the valuation function.

Even assuming a constant pond cost, it is not clear from the available data just what that cost is. A Canadian government program for the annual purchase of easements suggests a figure of $5.60 per acre for recently acquired land in Alberta, or $4.76 per pond, since the average pond and supporting wetland is about 0.85 acre (Hammack and Brown, 1974, pp. 69–70). Of course, it is not clear that a large number of additional ponds, in Alberta or elsewhere, would be forthcoming at this rental price.

Another estimate of wetland costs is provided by the value of only marginally productive land, which would presumably be most readily

---

[3] Again, much additional detail, along with alternative specifications and estimation, is provided in Hammack and Brown.

[4] See Brown and Hammack (1972), p. 172.

available for a wetlands preservation program. Hammack and Brown cite a recent study indicating a value of $17 per acre for marginally productive land, again for Alberta (1974, p. 70). In addition to these estimates of opportunity costs, Ducks Unlimited calculates that recent projects to create new wetlands cost slightly more than $1 per acre (Hammack and Brown, 1974, p. 70). Where creation of new wetlands is involved, then, this amount should be added to the opportunity cost of the land, if any, to obtain the correct cost figures. In the application of the model of the preceding section, alternative cost specifications of $4.76, $17, and $12 per pond are tried, the latter representing an arbitrarily selected intermediate value. It is to this application that we now turn. We are interested particularly in the optimal solution value for the number of ponds in the steady state, and in how this compares with recent observation.

4. SOLUTION OF THE OPTIMAL CONTROL
MODEL AND COMPARISON WITH RECENT OBSERVATION
AND A BIOLOGICAL "OPTIMUM"

There are problems in attempting to solve the model for numerical results, problems with the data that are forthrightly acknowledged: "On the economic side, only hunters in the Pacific flyway were studied (figure 9-1). The physical relations are continental. Joining the two parts requires either that the economic relations be broadened or that the physical functions be reduced from the continent to the Pacific flyway" (Brown and Hammack, 1972, p. 195). In fact, the data are further fragmented in that the estimated valuation function refers to all waterfowl, whereas the estimated physical production function refers only to mallards, and only to Canadian prairie ponds. A further assumption that the valuation function can be legitimately applied separately to mallards, a single component of total waterfowl (about 30 percent of bagged birds along the Pacific flyway), would then seem to be required for use of the model with continental mallard data in addition to the assumption that it can be legitimately applied to all hunters in Canada and the United States.

Alternatively, optimal kill values are set for all waterfowl as 3.33 times optimal mallard kill, since as just noted, mallards constitute about 30 percent of the waterfowl bagged along the Pacific flyway. This procedure, in turn, would seem to require the assumption that the estimated production relationship between ponds and mallards is representative of that between ponds and all waterfowl. To further complicate the story, this latter exercise is carried out only for Pacific flyway kill. Although a rigorous decomposition of the production function is ruled out because the estimated relationship does not exhibit constant returns to scale (see below), mallard

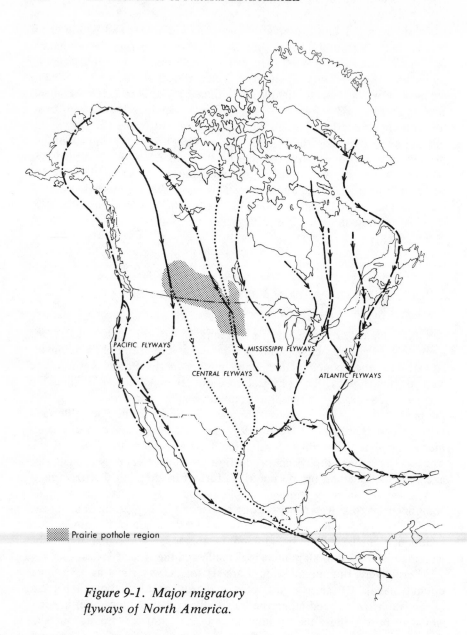

Figure 9-1. Major migratory flyways of North America.

and other waterfowl kill is broken out for the Pacific flyway on the basis of its proportion of the continental hunter population.

Results of the solution for optimal steady-state numerical values of breeders, ponds, and kill on the basis of the assumptions described here, and other assumptions about parameter values noted below and explained in Brown and Hammack (1972, pp. 189–196), are presented in table 9-1, a modified version of table 6.3 in Brown and Hammack (1972).

Probably the most striking aspect of these results is the substantial increase in the number of ponds, and also of breeders and kill, called for by the optimal solution, even for the high pond cost of $17, as compared to the historically observed values reported in the last column of table 9-1. Thus the historical value of 1.3 million ponds is expanded by over 200 percent, to 4.0 million, in the $17 pond cost solution, and by nearly another 200 percent, to 6.3 million, in the intermediate $12 pond cost solution. These results, though admittedly not definitive, owing to the weak data base, do tend to confirm the presumption stated in the introduction: namely, that a socially optimal number of ponds will be greater than the number determined by market forces.

Another interesting comparison that can be made on the basis of models and results developed in the longer study (Hammack and Brown, 1974) is between the optimal values for the level of breeding stock, W and total kill, X, where $X = c_3NK$, and the values consistent with a biological "optimum," maximum sustained physical yield for a given pond count.

Maximum sustained yield can be calculated from a two-equation waterfowl population dynamics model consisting of the production function $I = f(W,P)$ and the physical balance equation, in discrete form

$$(9\text{-}8) \qquad W_{t+1} = s_2(I_t + s_1W_t - X_t)$$

Table 9-1
Illustrative Stationary Economic Optimal Values[a]

	Pond cost			Historical values
	$4.76	$12.00	$17.00	
Breeders (W) (millions)	33	15.2	11.4	7.8[b]
Ponds (P) (millions)	22	6.3	4.0	1.3[b]
Marginal value of waterfowl (λ) (dollars)	1.90	3.10	3.70	—
Continental mallard kill (millions)	27.4	12.2	9.1	3.7[b]
Mallard kill, Pacific flyway (millions)	4.5	2.0	1.5	0.9[b]
Total kill, Pacific flyway (millions)	14.8	6.6	4.9	3.5[c]

[a]Assumptions about parameter values: $s_1 = 0.95$, $s_2 = 0.84$, $c_3 = 1.25$, discount rate = 8 percent. The number of hunters in the Pacific flyway is 0.279 million, and in total, 1.715 million.
[b]1961–1968.
[c]1965–1969.

A specific form must be chosen for the production function, and a plausible one is the ordinary multiplicative

(9-9) $I_t = AW_t^\alpha P_t^\beta,$ $0 < \alpha < 1,$ $0 < \beta < 1$

where A, α, and β are constants.[5]

Following Hammack and Brown (1974, p. 45) we write $W_t = W_{t+1} = W^*$, using the asterisk to denote a steady-state value. Then equation (9-8) may be rewritten as

(9-10) $W^* = s_2(I^* + s_1 W^* - X^*)$

and solving for the sustained yield, as

(9-11) $X^* = I^* - cW^*$

where $c = (1 - s_1 s_2 / s_2)$. Note that since $0 < s_1 < 1$ and $0 < s_2 < 1$, $c > 0$. The interpretation of equation (9-11) is that the sustained yield, the number of waterfowl that may be killed by hunters in each hunting season, X^*, is equal to the annual output of new birds, I^*, less the number required to compensate for adult mortality due to natural causes over the year (cW^*).

The next step is to determine the maximum sustained yield, the value of X that is the largest that can be sustained. Substituting equation (9-9) into equation (9-11) we obtain

(9-12) $X^* = AW^{*\alpha}P^{*\beta} - cW^*$

The necessary condition for a maximum is found by differentiating with respect to W^* and setting the result equal to zero:

(9-13) $\dfrac{\partial X^*}{\partial W^*} = \alpha A P^{*\beta} W^{*\alpha-1} - c = 0$

Solving for W^*, we have

(9-14) $W^{**} = (c/\alpha A P^{*\beta})^{1/\alpha-1}$

where a double asterisk denotes a maximum steady-state value. Substituting the expression for W^{**} in terms of estimated parameters (see below) and a given pond count into equation (9-9) then determines I^{**}, and substituting I^{**} into equation (9-11) in turn determines X^{**}.

To obtain numerical values for W^{**}, I^{**}, and X^{**}, it is necessary to first obtain estimates of the production parameters A, α, and β, to be used along with the survival parameters s_1 and s_2, and a specified pond level. Although the model of this section, including the production function, equation (9-9), has been developed for all waterfowl, as noted earlier the

[5] An alternative form is also discussed in Hammack and Brown (1974).

production parameters are estimated with data on mallards. Apparently the data on mallards are much superior to any available data on other species, and there are reasons for believing mallards to be representative of the migratory waterfowl considered in the study (Hammack and Brown, 1974, p. 41). The estimated relationship is

$$(9\text{-}15) \qquad \ln I \quad = 1.36 + 0.269 \ln W + 0.460 \ln J$$
$$\text{(t values)} \qquad\quad (1.6) \qquad\quad (6.7)$$
$$R^2 = 0.83, \quad n = 13$$

where the empirical counterparts of the variables specified in equation (9-9) are as follows.

All variables are represented in a time series of annual observations running from 1955 through 1968. The dependent variable, I, is the number of immature birds in September. W is the continental breeding population in the preceding May, and P is the number of Canadian prairie ponds in July of the same year. Equation (9-15) is taken from Brown and Hammack (1972, p. 189). Estimates on the basis of a different measure of ponds, and other modifications, including alternative functional forms, are also presented in the 1974 study (pp. 48–50).

For values of s_1 and s_2 equal to 0.95 and 0.85 respectively, and a mean 1958–1968 July pond value of 1.4 million, the maximum steady-state, or sustained-yield values for breeders, immatures, and kill are $W^{**} = 10.11$, $I^{**} = 8.49$, and $X^{**} = 6.21$ respectively (Hammack and Brown, 1974, p. 51, table 7). Although the calculations are made for a constant annual wetland figure, the results are apparently little affected by the introduction of random influences via a simulation model of fluctuations in the pond count (Hammack and Brown, 1974, pp. 53–55). Comparing these results now to the economic optima reported in table 9-1, we observe that the economic solution calls for a larger breeding stock at all pond cost levels, and allows a considerably larger mallard kill. Of course, the differences are due to the much larger number of ponds in the economic solution.

The disparity in the results of these two approaches to determining an "optimal" stock of waterfowl is worth some discussion, as it illustrates in our judgment the superiority of the bioeconomic approach of Brown and Hammack over what might be regarded as the conventional, purely bio-logical approach. There are essentially two problems with the biological, or maximum sustained yield solution. One, indicated in the comparison of the two solutions, is that the amount of wetlands must be constant and not subject to policy control. Put another way, there is a (different, in general) maximum sustained yield solution corresponding to each and every possible pond count. For example, for a pond value of 3.0 million (and a survival fraction $s_2 = 0.80$), $W^{**} = 11$, $I^{**} = 12.3$, and $X^{**} = 9.04$ (Hammack and Brown, 1974, p. 87). How is the biologist, or the resource manager, or anyone else for that matter, to choose between this set of values and that corresponding to a pond count of 1.4 million? It seems obvious that some measure of the gains and costs associated with each must be brought to bear on the decision, just as the optimizing model has done.

The other problem with maximum sustained yield as a guide to policy is that it implicitly assumes that even for a given amount of wetland environment, hunters and others in society would prefer that the same amount of waterfowl be harvested each year, in perpetuity, rather than (say) increasing the harvest for a few years by drawing down the breeding stock and thereby reducing future harvests. Given a high enough discount rate, the latter option is by no means irrational from the point of view of present-value maximization.[6]

5. CONCLUDING REMARKS

We noted in the introduction and in section 1 that a major difference between the Brown–Hammack optimal control problem and that formulated in chapter 3 is that the Brown–Hammack problem has a steady-state solution, due in part to the specification of stationary value and cost functions. Accordingly, a "conservative" policy of the sort obtained in chapters 3 and 4—of holding back on development investment in anticipation of greater returns flowing from an unmodified environment at some future date—is ruled out.

It seems to us, however, that further work on the wetlands issue may well suggest the same sort of relative benefit behavior over time as that anticipated in the Hells Canyon, White Clouds, and Mineral King cases, for example. In each of these cases we anticipate that benefits from the preservation-related alternative are likely to grow relative to benefits from the development project, at least over some interval of time. If our remarks in earlier chapters concerning the dynamic behavior of relative values of extractive versus nonextractive uses of the environment are not too wide of the mark, then the same effect may be expected to take hold in this case as well.

At this point irreversibility again enters the picture. So long as conversion of wetlands is reversible, as assumed by Brown and Hammack, the presence of shifting benefit functions, although complicating the analysis, does not pose an intractable problem for the land use planner. As we also noted earlier, however, the reversibility of conversion is a matter of some disagreement. If those who suggest that the drainage and development of wetlands are in fact irreversible are correct, then, even without working through the formal analysis, it seems clear that a still more conservative policy with respect to wetlands drainage than that derived by Brown and

---

[6] For an excellent short discussion of this and related points, see Plourde (1970).

Hammack would be indicated. Of course, the degree of reversibility here is an empirical question, and as such ought ultimately to be answered on the basis of reliable data.

There is another aspect of the study which we should like to comment on in closing. As discussed in some detail in the preceding section, the empirical base is relatively weak, requiring substitution of assumptions for data in places. What the work of Brown and Hammack indicates is *not* that the attempt to apply sophisticated economic models to problems of environmental resource management is ill-advised, however. We have seen, just above, for example, the clear advantages of this sort of approach over the traditional maximum sustained yield, rooted in a rather ambiguous "biological optimum." On the contrary, the work of Brown and Hammack indicates the desirability of a more focused program of data collection to fill the gaps noted in the text and to provide a stronger empirical base for application of a well-defined and potentially fruitful optimizing model.

REFERENCES

Arrow, K. J. and Kurz, Mordecai. 1970. *Public Investment, the Rate of Return, and Optimal Fiscal Policy* (Baltimore: Johns Hopkins Press).

Brown, G. M., Jr. and Hammack, Judd. 1972. "A Preliminary Investigation of the Economics of Migratory Waterfowl," in *Natural Environments: Studies in Theoretical and Applied Analysis,* John V. Krutilla, ed. (Baltimore: Johns Hopkins Press).

Crissey, Walter. 1969. "Prairie Potholes from a Continental Viewpoint," *Saskatoon Wetlands Seminar,* Canadian Wildlife Service Report, Series No. 6 (Ottawa: The Queen's Printer).

Davis, R. K. 1963. "The Value of Outdoor Recreation: An Economic Study of the Maine Woods," unpublished Ph.D. dissertation, Harvard University.

Hammack, Judd and Brown, G. M., Jr. 1974. *Waterfowl and Wetlands: Toward Bioeconomic Analysis* (Baltimore: Johns Hopkins Press).

Mishan, E. J. 1971. *Cost–Benefit Analysis* (New York: Praeger).

Mohring, Herbert and Boyd, J. H. 1971. "Analyzing Externalities: Direct Interaction vs. Asset Utilization Frameworks," *Economica,* vol. 38, no. 152.

Plourde, C. G. 1970. "A Simple Model of Replenishable Natural Resource Exploitation," *American Economic Review,* vol. LX, no. 3.

Pontryagin, L. S., *et al.* 1962. *The Mathematical Theory of Optimal Processes* (New York: Interscience).

Scott, Anthony. 1965. "The Valuation of Game Resources: Some Theoretical Aspects," *Canadian Fisheries Reports,* No. 4 (Ottawa: The Department of Fisheries of Canada).

CHAPTER 10

THE TRANS-ALASKA PIPELINE: ENVIRONMENTAL CONSEQUENCES AND ALTERNATIVES

1. INTRODUCTION

In November of 1973 Congress amended the Mineral Leasing Act of 1920 and provided authorization for the Trans-Alaska pipeline (TAP) to short circuit some difficult legal issues pending before the courts. This marked the end of a long period of deferred action due to the controversy over the environmental impact from exploiting and transporting oil that had been discovered on the North Slope of Alaska's Brooks Range.

The planned transport facility, a hot oil pipeline destined to cross arctic tundra and some very active seismic zones in its near-800 mile length, has many and varied environmental hazards that are discussed in section 2. In the light of these problems, environment and conservation-conscious citizen groups had intervened to ensure that an adequate environmental evaluation be undertaken before a permit was issued for rights of access across federal lands. The process of undertaking the necessary studies and sorting out the legal tangles that ensued took nearly 3½ years. One of the important studies that played a significant role in identifying and evaluating the alternatives, and in illuminating related public policy issues, was Charles Cicchetti's *Alaskan Oil: Alternative Routes and Markets,* from which the materials and analyses of this chapter are largely drawn.

Since completion of Cicchetti's study early in 1972, when the decision on the pipeline was still pending, several important developments have occurred. The decision for which the Cicchetti analysis was relevant[1] has since been made in favor of the Trans-Alaskan route. The price of imported crude—an element in the analysis—has roughly quadrupled in the wake of the Arab oil embargo and the OPEC pricing policy. Nevertheless, to the extent that the inflation in construction costs has not offset the rise

---

[1] The Cicchetti proposed alternative, a Trans-Canada pipeline, was reflected in the Bayh–Mondale amendment which failed passage in the Senate by a tie-breaking vote cast by then Vice-President Spiro Agnew.

in imported crude prices, the change in the price structure between the time of analysis and the present reinforces Cicchetti's conclusions. And despite the fact that the decision to proceed with TAP has been made, the analysis as an illustrative case is both valid and valuable. Accordingly, while most of the issues to which this chapter is addressed are now moot from the decision standpoint, the study is presented as part of a series of cases illustrating the kind of analyses that can and should be undertaken in environmentally relevant areas that involve public decisions.

In the case studies in chapters 5 through 9 we have addressed problems in which it was possible to develop meaningful estimates of the costs of environmental modification or estimates of at least significant portions of the benefits that attach to retaining a natural environment in an undisturbed state. We discovered that in many instances it is possible to counsel in favor of preserving an environment even in the absence of all the information that would be potentially relevant in very close decisions. In some cases studied here, the nonenvironmental costs alone were sufficient to justify rejection of an extractive or developmental project. In other cases, while nonenvironmental opportunity costs alone were not sufficient to reject a developmental project, estimates of readily evaluated opportunity returns from environmental amenities precluded by development were sufficient to tip the balance without an exhaustive analysis of all environmental costs.

In this chapter, the problem addressed was basically of a different order of evaluative difficulty. Quantitative evaluation of environmental impact, or the probability of environmental damage from the pipeline expressed in monetary terms, defied the analyst's best efforts. The problem of deciding whether the undertaking was warranted in the face of environmental hazards ultimately was an ethical and political one. In this instance the analyst found it difficult to argue on the basis of the objective scientific evidence that the costs of this resource extractive activity, including the expected costs of the environmental damage, outweighed the economic benefits. But in any event, there remained the question of the relative economic and environmental costs of alternative routes and markets. The study of the Trans-Alaska pipeline, then, was an exercise in carrying out the requirements of the National Environmental Policy Act [sections 102 (c) and (d)] to evaluate the alternative transportation possibilities in the face of the need to raise and bring to market the North Slope oil. Because of our utter inability to assess environmental costs of the pipeline in monetary terms, as well as prospective changes in the value of North Slope oil over time, no attempt was made to fit the Cicchetti analysis into the formal dynamic framework of chapters 3–8. Instead, as in chapter 9, we mainly report the results of analysis carried out independently, with some simplifying assumptions.

2. NORTH SLOPE OIL DISCOVERY AND ENVIRONMENTAL IMPLICATIONS

Between 1968 and 1970, exploration for petroleum on the North Slope of the Brooks Range in Alaska led to the discovery of a major oil field. Proven reserves of the Prudhoe Bay field approximate 10 billion barrels as estimated by the American Petroleum Institute. Because the field is on the arctic side of Alaska, the problem of bringing oil from Prudhoe Bay to market is a serious one. Several transportation routes and modes, such as an all-water route involving ice-breaking tankers, an overland oil pipeline crossing Canada in large part, and a combination overland route across Alaska, completed by tanker transshipment from the south of Alaska to West Coast ports in the United States, were considered. Ultimately, the oil companies involved, operating through the Alyeska Pipeline Service Company, favored transportation by a pipeline from Prudhoe Bay across Alaska to the southern port city of Valdez for transport to the "lower 48." The planned Trans-Alaska pipeline will be 789 miles in length and will require 373 miles of new service road along the portion between the north bank of the Yukon River and Prudhoe Bay.

While a great deal of the general region south of the Yukon River is essentially undeveloped, the presence of the highway between Valdez and the proposed Yukon crossing reflects some strip development of the area through which the pipeline will pass. The region to the north of the Yukon River, however, is completely roadless. Here is to be found the largest expanse of authentic wilderness remaining within the continental United States. It is over this region that the large (quarter of a million head) arctic caribou herd migrates and where we find the large (9 million acre) Arctic National Wildlife Range.

The objection of environmentalists to the intrusion of additional development and extractive activities into the last really vast, authentic, wilderness remaining in the United States can be readily understood. In addition to the disruption of an area that has escaped, to date, evidence of the activity of a highly industrial society, the nature of the potential disturbances occasioned by the pipeline and its construction is of some significance. The pipeline will pass through something like 750 miles of territory characterized by permafrost. Permafrost is a condition in which the soil and related materials at or near the surface of the ground remain permanently at or below the freezing temperature of water. In an undisturbed state, permafrost protected by tundra vegetation will remain in a relatively stable condition. Modification of the environment by construction activities disturbing the tundra, however, can cause thawing of the permafrost by changing the thermal balance at the surface. This can be caused by gravel pads, damage to the organic surface layer, or disturbed surface drainage.

Another hazard to the stability of the permafrost will come from burying the hot oil pipeline itself. Such instability in the soils and related materials could cause pipeline displacement, resulting in serious damage to it (U.S. Dept. of Interior, 1972, vol. 2, pp. 7–10, 97), although those who favor the construction of a hot oil pipeline argue that design specifications could be stipulated to withstand the stresses that are likely to be imposed.

The difficulty, of course, is that design and construction costs mount disproportionately as the safety factor is increased. Doubtless the pipeline will be built with specifications short of those that will guarantee a zero probability of pipeline damage and oil spill in the arctic tundra. It is worth noting that each mile of pipeline is reported to contain double the amount of oil involved in the Santa Barbara spill of 1969 (Aspin, 1971). Moreover, the pipeline will cross several major navigable rivers and as many as 350 additional smaller streams. Potential problems with spring ice breakup and ice jams raise difficult questions which may never be answered adequately for the assured protection of the arctic environment.

While minimum-risk construction of the pipeline facility across permafrost may be the most challenging engineering problem, the hazard of earthquake damage is another serious problem. Approximately 70 percent of the southern portion of the route lies within 25 miles of a recorded epicenter (Lewis, 1971). There have been 23 large earthquakes with Richter ratings of 6 or higher during the past 70 years in the vicinity of the TAP route. Moreover, the most frequently mentioned tanker route from Valdez to the U.S. West Coast will pass through areas with a notable concentration of previously recorded epicenters (Cicchetti, 1972, p. 39). To sum up, the Department of the Interior's findings on exhaustive investigation were as follows:

Seismic shaking or surface faulting accompanying a large shock could rupture the pipeline directly or cause failure in the foundation material that could lead to rupture. Furthermore, large earthquakes could trigger landslides and sea waves that could jeopardize the integrity of the pipeline. (U.S. Dept. of Interior, 1972, vol. 2, p. 11)

Accordingly, the problem appears to be, quoting Cicchetti (1972):

The as-yet unresolved controversy is whether it is possible to construct a pipeline that can withstand major earthquakes in this range along the proposed route and—short of such an accomplishment—whether a system of shutoff valves, retaining dikes, or walls can be constructed to contain or minimize the damage to the wilderness and the many streams and rivers the proposed pipeline will cross. (pp. 39–40)

The hazards to the environment of transporting North Slope oil through the Trans-Alaska pipeline are not confined to the area along the pipeline route. Upon delivery at Valdez, the oil will be transferred to ocean-going oil tankers for delivery to West Coast ports. Roughly two million barrels of oil per day will be moved across Prince William Sound, with about half that amount moving through Puget Sound. The Department of the Interior's assessment of the treacherous weather and navigation conditions attending this tanker route is sobering. A translation of the hazardous conditions into annual equivalent spills suggests an amount up to 140,000 barrels per year (U.S. Dept. of Interior, 1972, vol. 4, p. 474).

Quite aside from oil spills that occur as a result of tankers running aground or colliding, and similar large-scale adverse events, there will be a continuous low-level contamination of the terminal port waters. There are two sources of this low-level contamination, (1) normal spillage associated with loading and unloading operations involving the prospective 2 million barrels a day, and (2) the discharging of ballast water from tankers on return to Prince William Sound. There is great variation in the estimates of the likely amount and effect of this contamination, but the higher range estimates provide grounds for grave concern about the Prince William Sound fisheries among a group of Cordova fishermen economically dependent on them. The concern is of sufficient gravity to have resulted in a legal action seeking to prevent the use of Prince William Sound for these operations.

To sum up, it is doubtless true that the problem of transporting oil from Prudhoe Bay across Alaska and thence from the port of Valdez on Prince William Sound to the Puget Sound and California ports is attended by enormous risks of environmental damage. There is no question that the risks can be reduced by increasing expenditures for engineering design and construction features directed toward fail-safe characteristics in the transport system. It must be acknowledged, however, that engineering and construction costs become prohibitive in any economic sense before fail-safe features are incorporated which would guarantee that there was no possibility of breaching the integrity of the pipeline under the difficult permafrost and seismic conditions, or that there was a zero probability of offshore marine mishaps, given the treacherous weather and navigation conditions. What this suggests is that it is certain that there will be somewhere, sometime during the period of oil exploitation from the Prudhoe Bay field, an accidental spill of some kind involving the transport system. But, of course, the severity of the environmental impact could not really be assessed with sufficient precision, given information on engineering and construction safety stipulations existing at the time the analysis was undertaken. It has not been meaningful to attempt any serious quantitative (monetary) estimates of the environmental impact from accidental breaches of the transport system's physical integrity.

Aside from the environmental impacts from breaks in the pipeline or offshore oil spills, of course, there are other environmental impacts such as

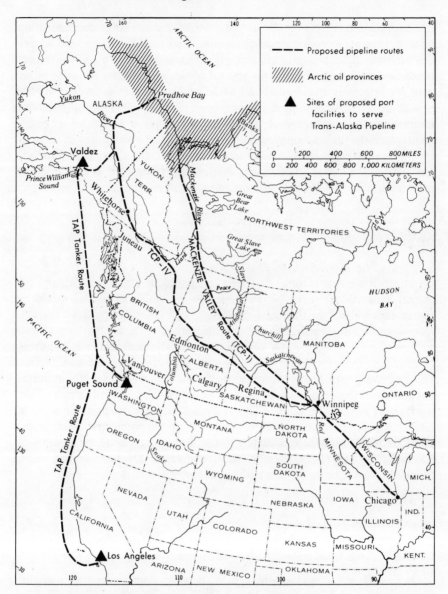

Figure 10-1. Alternate routes and markets for Alaskan oil.

the unevaluated effects on the caribou herds, the low-level contamination of offshore waters from normal operations, and the like. Even here we are dealing with risks and probabilities rather than certainty as to the impact on the environment. There is no general consensus whether we are dealing with an extremely low probability of an environmental disaster; a higher probability of relatively more frequent lower level environmental contaminations; or near certainty of numerous individual instances of environmental damage that in sum would not be expected to exceed the net value of raising, transporting, and utilizing in the most efficient manner the Prudhoe Bay petroleum. How great, then, is the net value of the North Slope petroleum reserves? We address this question in section 3.

3. ESTIMATING THE ECONOMIC VALUE OF NORTH SLOPE OIL[2]

The Nature of the Evaluation

If we can assume, as we in fact can, that there is a demand for the oil available from the North Slope, the net value of the oil would be the market value less the costs of raising and transporting it to market, ignoring for the time being the environmental costs we have not been successful in quantifying. Of course if oil of identical grade is available from alternative sources, since both would serve the same demand, the net value of the North Slope oil would be no more than the favorable difference in costs (resource savings) if any, using North Slope oil in lieu of the lowest cost alternative source. This is consistent with the basic analysis of alternatives in estimating the net value of the hydroelectric sites in the Hells Canyon discussed in chapter 5[3] and also in part with the analysis of Mineral King and alternative ski sites in chapter 8. The net value of North Slope oil, then, can be represented in summary as below:

(10-1) $b = C_A - C_{NS}$

subject to: $B_{NS} = B_A \geqslant C_{NS}$

---

[2] This section is based entirely on the analysis presented in chapter 1 of Cicchetti's study, *Alaskan Oil*.

[3] In comparing the relative advantage of different prime movers of dissimilar characteristics in a power system, care is taken to design alternative system components such that both will provide precisely the same service. With the service provided by both identical (and the value of the service exceeding its cost), the benefit of the preferred alternative can be no greater than the difference in costs, if any, between the two. In the case of comparing North Slope oil with the most economical alternative source, the comparison, of course, must be made with reference to the same markets, and with crude of the same grade. In his analyses, Cicchetti adjusted the prices for the specific gravity of North Slope crude ($26°$–$26.9°$ API) and related adjustments for sulfur content, in order to achieve comparability. See Cicchetti (1972), appendix A.

where

b = net benefits

B_{NS} = gross benefit of North Slope crude oil

B_A = gross benefit of alternative oil

C_{NS} = delivered cost of North Slope crude

C_A = delivered cost of oil from lowest cost alternative source

In short, the net benefit of North Slope oil is the favorable difference in cost (if any) between the delivered real costs[4] of crude from the two sources, subject to the conditions that the crudes are of comparable value per barrel, and that their unit value exceeds their unit delivered costs.

The objective here, of course, is to obtain relevant data to provide an estimate of the size of b, the net benefits or value of the Prudhoe Bay oil, to weigh the tradeoff that would be involved if we were to opt for the alternative, namely, avoidance of environmental risk by a decision not to raise and transport North Slope oil to market. We begin by estimating the delivered cost of oil from an alternative source to the market (West Coast) identified by the TAP promoters. Secondly we consider the delivered cost of North Slope crude to the market and obtain the difference which provides our estimate of the net value of the oil as transported by TAP and tanker to West Coast markets.

Delivered Cost of Crude from Alternative Sources

The most likely alternative source of low-cost crudes to serve the intended Alaskan Oil–TAP market at the time of analysis was the Persian Gulf petroleum fields. To calculate the delivered cost of the most economic foreign alternative to Alaskan oil via TAP and tanker to the West Coast, Iranian Light 34° API (1.4 percent sulfur) was selected as the specific reference crude. Table 10-1 is a summary of values prepared in connection with Cicchetti's analysis of delivered costs of imported crudes.[5]

Although the 1971 estimated delivered price, as indicated in the table, was $2.36 per barrel, the U.S. tariff of 10.5 cents per barrel is an internal (U.S.) monetary transfer and hence should not be included in the real cost

---

[4] The term *real*, associated with the delivered costs, is used to distinguish between real costs of production and transportation, and "pecuniary" costs associated with taxes and similar transfer of funds among individuals, rather than net resource costs to society. In the case of North Slope oil, severance and other taxes would be excluded from the *real* delivered costs. Since severance taxes or royalties paid foreign governments on imported crudes represent deferred claims against resources within the U.S. economy, such taxes would represent real costs in the delivered price of foreign, or imported, crudes.

[5] These data appear as table 9, p. 20, of Cicchetti (1972).

Table 10-1
Average Costs for Persian Gulf Oil Delivered to U.S. Coastal Ports   (dollars per barrel)

	Iranian light 34° API (1.4% sulfur)	
	1971	1975
Production[a]	0.10	0.11
Payments to foreign governments[b]	1.11	1.27
Other costs[c]	0.30	0.30
FOB price at destination	$1.51	$1.68
Transportation costs[d]	0.74	0.45
Total cost to U.S. (delivered)	$2.25	$2.13
U.S. tariff	0.105	0.105
Delivered price	$2.36	$2.24
Average	$2.30	

[a]See M. A. Adelman, *The World Petroleum Market* (Johns Hopkins Press, 1972). Adelman's calculation is best viewed as an overall average for the Persian Gulf and not necessarily for the Iranian Light 34° API that is used in this analysis.

[b]See *Platt's Oilgram Price Service*, August 25, 1971; and *Oil and Gas Journal*, June 21, 1971, for crude price postings in 1971 and 1975. Payments to foreign governments are based on a calculation of 49 percent of the posted price that has been approximately determined by Mikesell for Iran. See Raymond F. Mikesell, *Foreign Investment in the Petroleum and Mineral Industries: Case Studies of Investor–Host Country Relations* (Johns Hopkins Press, 1971), especially p. 247.

[c]These costs include all other transportation and gathering costs and payments made to determine the FOB price at point of destination. This FOB price was estimated to be $1.30 in New England Council and others, "Rebuttal Statement of the New England Parties on Oil Import Controls to the Cabinet Task Force on Oil Import Control," submitted to the Cabinet Task Force, August 15, 1969. At the old posting of $1.80 and Adelman's production costs of 10¢, this would mean a difference of 30¢, which is denoted as "other costs."

[d]A high and low cost for transportation are shown to be consistent with the Cabinet Task Force calculations.

of imported oil delivered to U.S. coastal ports. An additional adjustment of 12 cents per barrel was based on the 8° API difference in specific gravity (at 1.5 cents/1° API), thus leaving an adjusted delivered real cost of crude comparable to the North Slope crude of $2.13 per barrel (Cicchetti, 1972, p. 21, and footnotes 18 and 19).

Transportation Cost of Alaskan
Oil Moved via TAP and Tanker

Since all of TAP capacity must be built in advance of any movement of petroleum from Prudhoe Bay to Valdez, it represents a fixed capital outlay irrespective of the level of throughput or rate of utilization. The original Alyeska throughput schedule assumed a 5-year buildup beginning with a 350,000 barrel per day throughput in the first year, ultimately reaching capacity throughput (2 million barrels per day) in the fifth year. Alternatively, an accelerated throughput, assuming capacity operation beginning in the first year, represented a utilization rate that would effect a per-unit transport cost reduction because the fixed costs could be allocated at capacity utilization rates from the outset. A second consideration in estimating the transport cost per barrel was the difference in the time distribution of capital outlays, and oil deliveries. To deal with the latter problem, Cicchetti reduced both the costs and the barrels of oil delivered to time-equivalent, or present-value, terms. Below are given both the present-value computation model for obtaining the present equivalent of oil throughput and the results of the computations.

$$(10\text{-}2) \quad PV_{1971} = \sum_{t=1}^{T} DTP_t(365)(1 + i)^{-t}$$

where

PV_{1971} = the present equivalent of the throughput

DTP_t = the average daily throughput in year t

i = the rate of discount

T = the shorter of either the useful life of the transportation system or the expected production period

Table 10-2 presents the results of the computations employing this present equivalent conversion model. It gives the relevant equivalent throughput estimates for the two alternative schedules at each of three discount rates; 10 percent is used as the rate for the basic computations, with alternatively 8 and 12 percent used for testing the sensitivity of the conclusions to the estimates of appropriate discount rate.

To obtain the estimated capital cost per barrel, the data displayed in table 10-2 must be divided into the estimates of capital outlays for TAP. The latter range from $1.75 billion to $2.5 billion and are displayed in the upper portion of table 10-3.[6] In the lower portion of the table are displayed the results of the division, giving the capital costs in cents per barrel.

In addition to the per barrel fixed capital charges, there is an estimated operating cost of about 13 cents that must be added to the figures given in table 10-3 (Cicchetti, 1972, pp. 11–12). Finally, while these costs

[6] These data, of course, are much out of date, owing both to the delays encountered before final clearance to begin construction, the required improvements stipulated for safety reasons in the design of the system, and, of course, the course of inflation in construction (and other) costs. These costs have been more than matched by the price behavior of foreign oil following the Arab–Israeli conflict of October 1973, the Arab oil embargo, and the OPEC pricing policy adopted in the wake of the embargo. The analysis is presented using the original data since the changes in costs and prices tend to reinforce rather than reverse the results of Cicchetti's analysis.

cover delivery of the oil from Prudhoe Bay to Valdez, there is an additional charge required to cover the tanker leg of the trip from Valdez to the ports in the "lower 48." Transported in U.S. bottoms, as required by the Jones Act, an estimated 35 cents per barrel appeared appropriate for this leg of the trip (see Cicchetti, table 7). The sum of these costs, representing the total real transport cost of North Slope oil to a West Coast port, is shown in table 10-4.

A final cost element was necessary in order to determine the net savings in the delivered cost of crude from the North Slope compared with the most economical alternative (Persian Gulf) source. This related to the cost of raising and collecting the oil in the field in preparation for transporting it to tidewater at Valdez. Various estimates were presented within a reasonable range and we shall employ the average, 24.5 cents, as used by Cicchetti (p. 22). Table 10-5 displays the total real cost of raising, collecting, and transporting North Slope crude to the Los Angeles market.

Table 10-2
Present Equivalent Barrels of Oil Throughput

Total undiscounted throughput	Alyeska throughput	Accelerated throughput
	(billions of barrels)	
	16.74	18.25
1971 equivalent at 8%	5.16	6.19
1971 equivalent at 10%	4.04	4.98
1971 equivalent at 12%	3.22	4.08

Source: Cicchetti (1972), p. 11.

Table 10-3
Capital Costs per Barrel for TAP and Terminal Facility

	Investment ($ billion, 1971)			
Discount rate	1.75	2.00	2.25	2.50
	Alyeska throughput schedule (cents per barrel)			
8%	33.9	38.8	43.6	48.5
10%	43.3	49.4	55.7	61.9
12%	54.4	62.2	69.9	77.7
	Accelerated throughput schedule (cents per barrel)			
8%	28.3	32.3	36.4	40.4
10%	35.2	40.2	45.2	50.2
12%	42.9	49.1	55.2	61.3

Source: Cicchetti (1972), p. 13.

Table 10-4
Transport Cost of North Slope Oil to Los Angeles via Trans-Alaska Pipeline and Tanker of U.S. Registry

	Investment ($ billion, 1971)			
Discount rate	1.75	2.00	2.25	2.50
	Alyeska throughput schedule (dollars per barrel)			
8%	0.82	0.87	0.92	0.97
10%	0.91	0.98	1.04	1.10
12%	1.02	1.10	1.18	1.26
	Accelerated throughput schedule (dollars per barrel)			
8%	0.76	0.80	0.84	0.88
10%	0.83	0.88	0.93	0.98
12%	0.91	0.97	1.03	1.09

Note: The estimates in this table are based on tanker costs of 35 cents per barrel and terminal operating cost of 13 cents per barrel.

Estimated Net 1971 Value
of North Slope Oil

If we substitute in equation (10-1) $2.13 as the cost ($C_A$) of equivalent grade Persian Gulf crude delivered to Los Angeles, using selected values from table 10-5 as the values of C_{NS}, we can obtain the per barrel savings in costs of North Slope oil over equivalent grade crude from the most economical alternative source.[7] Next, if we wish to get an aggregate net 1971 value of North Slope oil, we can multiply this difference per barrel by the corresponding 1971 equivalent barrels of oil obtained by equation (10-2), displayed in table 10-2. These computations are performed and the results shown in table 10-6. Of course, all of the computations assume that the measure of value per barrel, the price differential, remains the same over the life of the project. Admittedly this was a strong assumption, but as we noted earlier, the myriad uncertainties surrounding the future course of delivered oil prices, especially from the Middle East, did not permit the substitution of an alternative trend with any degree of confidence. Accordingly, the assumption of a steady flow of benefits was made in the interest of simplicity, and for lack of more defensible assumptions.

[7] Although the real resource costs of raising and transporting Persian Gulf oil to U.S. markets were not affected by the October war, the price to importers and hence real costs to them was increased. What the ultimate long-run cost to importing countries may turn out to be if OPEC cartel agreements do not hold fast is not predictable. The price, however, is not likely to result in a delivered cost of less than $2.13; hence this figure represents a lower bound estimate. Any departures in the upward direction not offset by equivalent increases in costs simply reinforce the conclusion of Cicchetti's analysis.

Table 10-5

Total Real Cost of Delivering North Slope Oil to Los Angeles via Trans-Alaska Pipeline and Tanker of U.S. Registry

	Investment ($ billion, 1971)			
Discount rate	1.75	2.00	2.25	2.50
	Alyeska throughput schedule (dollars per barrel)			
8%	1.06	1.11	1.16	1.21
10%	1.16	1.22	1.28	1.34
12%	1.27	1.35	1.42	1.50
	Accelerated throughput schedule (dollars per barrel)			
8%	1.01	1.05	1.09	1.13
10%	1.08	1.13	1.18	1.23
12%	1.15	1.22	1.28	1.34

If we take the discount rate of 10 percent for our comparative estimates, we see that the savings in costs using North Slope oil will range from a low of around $3.19 billion as a 1971 worth (capital cost of $2.5 billion and Alyeska throughput schedule) to a high of around $5.2 billion (capital costs of $1.75 billion and accelerated throughput schedule). Corresponding variations for discount rate changes between 8 and 12 percent are presented for inspection. The values given in table 10-6 will vary from $3.2 billion to $6.9 billion, depending on assumed investment in the pipeline, rate of discount, and throughput schedule. Observing the case of variation in all variables except for the discount rate held at 10 percent will give the $3 billion to $5 billion range noted above. This represents a net resource cost savings apart from other potential desirable characteristics (national security advantage?). It was this magnitude of net present value that would have been forgone if a decision had been made to forgo exploitation of North Slope oil in the interest of environmental protection.

The question turns essentially on whether the public interest in avoiding the expected deleterious effects of TAP and tanker transport—which involves both an assault upon the northern Alaskan wilderness as well as other environmental insults associated with oil spills—was sufficient to trade off $3 billion to $5 billion of benefits through resorting to other, higher cost sources of petroleum. There are doubtless some persons who would have unhesitatingly subscribed to the belief that it was. There are others who thought otherwise, noting additional considerations such as national security achieved from reduced reliance on imported foreign sources and the associated adverse environmental impacts from expected oil spills associated with transportation of Persian Gulf oil to the United

Table 10-6
Aggregate Net Present (1971) Value of Savings in Costs, North Slope Oil
Compared with Lowest Cost Alternative

Discount rate	Pipeline investment ($ billion, 1971)			
	1.75	2.00	2.25	2.50
	Alyeska throughput schedule ($ billion, 1971)			
8%	5.52	5.26	5.01	4.75
10%	3.92	3.68	3.43	3.19
12%	2.77	2.51	2.29	2.03
	Accelerated throughput schedule ($ billion, 1971)			
8%	6.93	6.69	6.44	6.19
10%	5.23	4.98	4.73	4.48
12%	4.00	3.71	3.47	3.22

States. The merits of one position over the other cannot be effectively demonstrated, of course, since they depend as much on values and ethical predispositions as on the objective probabilities attaching to the risks involved.

In the absence of scientific and related objective information that would yield more demonstrable conclusions, there was a need for a consensus to be reached by public debate, which in fact was conducted through various media. In this debate, at least two potentially important issues, among others, were sorted out. One was the question of whether the Prudhoe Bay oil field should be exploited or not. The second was, assuming that a decision was to be made to do so, whether the choice of transport mode and market was appropriate. It was on the assumption that the first issue would be resolved in the affirmative that the second question was addressed. The analysis that resulted is presented in the next section.

4. EVALUATING ALTERNATIVE ROUTES AND MARKETS

The Nature of the Evaluation

Section 3 discussed the economic advantage of raising and transporting oil from the North Slope to the West Coast market by means of TAP and tanker, as proposed by the promoters of TAP. We looked to the most economical alternative source, the Persian Gulf petroleum fields, to determine whether or not the market could be supplied as economically without disturbing the arctic environment. Since both sources would serve the same market, the price of the Iranian reference crude could be adjusted for comparability with North Slope oil to represent benefits which were then equivalent per barrel of crude. To determine the relative economics of the two as sources of oil for the Los Angeles market, we needed only to compare the costs. Since there was a savings in cost favoring the North Slope source, we were able to develop estimates of the net value of the North Slope oil to compare with the anticipated environmental impact. In this case the expected environmental damages would need to be on the order of $3 billion to $5 billion before the damages could be considered in excess of benefits.

Such an analysis is useful for comparing the expected benefits of a given proposal with its expected costs. But it is not inconceivable that an equal, or even greater, benefit might be achieved at a lesser economic and environmental cost by considering an alternative route and market. This issue will be addressed below, but first it is important to consider the difference in the nature of the evaluation when the same source of oil is destined to supply, alternatively, different markets by different transport routes and modes, in contrast with the case in which different sources of oil and transport modes are used to provide oil for the same market. In the previous case the gross benefits at market were the same for both sources of oil; production and transport costs differed. In the case we consider below, production costs are going to be the same for oil destined for different markets, but the market value of the petroleum per barrel may differ, apart from the difference induced by transportation cost differentials. Understanding why the clearing prices in different markets might differ by an amount that is more or less than the transportation cost differentials requires some background on the institutional features of the domestic petroleum industry, along with other related factors. First, however, we shall indicate how the rationale for the analysis will differ in this case from the evaluation in the previous section. Here we shall seek, not an estimate of the net value of the North Slope oil field, but rather an evaluation of the relative economics of alternative routes and markets. That is, for the net benefit of TAP to be positive,

$$(10\text{-}3) \quad (B_{NS}^i - C_{NS}^i) > (B_{NS}^j - C_{NS}^j)$$

where

B^i = the gross value or benefit of a barrel of oil at market i served by TAP and tanker

C^i = the total cost of a barrel of North Slope oil delivered at market i

B^j = the gross value or benefit of a barrel of oil at the alternative market, j, served by the alternative transport mode and route

C^j = the total cost of a barrel of North Slope oil delivered at market j

In short, if TAP is to emerge as the most economical route and transport mode serving the most economical market, the net benefits of TAP, the left-hand expression, must be greater than the net benefit of the alternative route, mode and market, or the value of the expression to the right of the inequality.

Gross Benefits or Market Value
of Oil in Alternative Markets

To understand why the gross benefit of a barrel of oil might differ in different markets, one must understand the administered nature of the price structure in the domestic petroleum products market. The United States has not been self-sufficient in oil for some time, relying in part on imported Canadian, Indonesian, Persian Gulf, and Venezuelan oil.[8] However, on the presumption that more intensive exploration for oil would occur if the domestic producers would have greater profit incentives, the institution of the oil import quota was adopted to artificially restrict the amount of imported oil and thus provide for a generally higher level of prices for petroleum products in the United States. A feature of the Mandatory Oil Import Quota Program is the division of the United States into five Petroleum Administration for Defense (PAD) Districts. PAD District I and especially PAD Districts II and V are the most relevant for our purpose. Included in PAD District V are Alaska, Hawaii, and the Pacific coastal states, along with Arizona and Nevada. All of the Midwestern states east of the Rockies and west of the Appalachians (excluding, of course, the Gulf Coast states) are included in PAD District II. We shall refer to District II as the Chicago market. In District I are all of the Atlantic coastal states; we shall use New York as the reference market. The policies adopted with respect to the amount of petroleum to be imported under the quota program in the different districts gave rise to price differentials, in addition to the differences in prices attributed to transportation cost differentials among different markets.

In PAD District V, domestic production was completely protected against foreign competition at a predetermined historical price ($3.17 per barrel of 26°–26.9° API crude for reference purposes). If the quantity of oil demanded at that price exceeded the amount supplied from domestic sources and Canada (the latter of which is limited by the throughput capacity of the Trans-Mountain pipeline from the Alberta fields to the Puget Sound), the difference was permitted to be supplied from foreign imports. Given the domestic production in District V and the capacity limitation on Canadian petroleum entering District V, the foreign imports have been representing about 12.2 percent of the total up to at least mid-

[8] Oil imports were about 30 percent of domestic production in 1970.

1973, at which time the restrictions on imports were relaxed in light of the "energy crisis."

Administration of the import quotas in the districts east of the Rocky Mountains was quite different and resulted in a different clearing price in eastern markets. Petroleum products (excluding residual fuel oil) permitted under the import quota were set at 12.2 percent of domestic production, a percentage that happens to be quite coincidentally equal to that in District V. Canadian crude oil in this case, however, is figured as part of the foreign imports governed by the quota. Finally, the domestic production was influenced by state demand prorationing restrictions. Prorationing results in higher cost domestic production than otherwise possible for any given quantity supplied. Producers with both high and low marginal costs, within limits, were assigned a given allowable monthly production level. This resulted in a higher rate of output from high-cost wells than would have been required if there were no output restrictions on low-cost wells. Accordingly, petroleum supplied from domestic sources east of the Rockies was marketed generally at a higher price than if it had been market determined in the absence of prorationing restrictions.

The result of the prorationing and the effects of the operation of the Mandatory Oil Import Quota Program, produced a substantial price differential between the Pacific Coast District V ($3.17/barrel) and the Districts (I and II) east of the Rockies ($3.81 and $4.06) respectively.[9] The significance of these price differentials is that the value of the North Slope oil is not independent of the market in which it is sold. An examination of transportation costs to different markets must be undertaken for comparison of cost differentials with corresponding price differentials before a judgment can be made regarding the economics of alternative routes and markets. But, first there was need for some adjustments to the reference price due to the different values placed on crude oil of the same specific gravity and sulfur content, other things being equal, in different markets.

Consumers value products made from crude oil differently in different markets. Gasoline bulks dominantly in the product mix of refineries on the West Coast. Because it represents a product from the lighter end, the lighter the crude oil used, the more economical is the production of gasoline from it. A higher proportion of fuel oil for home heating is demanded in the Midwest and as this represents a refinery product toward the heavier end, the heavier North Slope crudes are relatively more valued by midwest refineries and consumers than is true on the West Coast. A rough indication of this is the difference in penalty per degree API specific gravity on the West Coast (6–7 cents) compared with the Midwest (2 cents). On

---

[9] See Cicchetti (1972), appendix A, table A-5, p. 131.

the other hand, the North Slope crude may be lighter than the 26.9° API used for reference purposes, and thus, for example, the Alyeska Service Company suggested a 5 to 10 cent per barrel downward adjustment for Alaskan oil in Midwest markets (Cicchetti, 1972, pp. 78–79).

Another matter of potential significance was that domestic crudes supplying the Midwest market are typically of lower sulfur content than anticipated for North Slope crudes. A difference of 11 cents per barrel existed between a barrel of West Texas Sour and West Texas Intermediate Sweet, other things remaining equal. Accordingly, there could be a total downward adjustment of up to 18 cents per barrel from the reference price for North Slope oil in the Midwest market, as suggested by Alyeska representatives. This would have reduced the reference price to $3.63. On the other hand, early analysis of North Slope crude indicated that it scored particularly high with hydrocracking refining techniques then being introduced in the Midwest and thus the adjustment for the sulfur difference could be in the opposite direction. Taking into account factors that were not considered by Alyeska, the upper bound reference price as estimated by Cicchetti was placed at $3.93 per barrel.

Delivered Cost of Crude
to Alternative Markets

Having bracketed a range for the market value, or gross benefit, of North Slope oil in the Pacific Coast and Midwest markets, it remained to determine whether the difference in transport costs from the North Slope to Chicago was greater than the difference in the value of petroleum in the two markets.[10] The estimated cost of delivering North Slope crude to the Los Angeles market was presented in section 3, and is used below in our comparison of cost and value differentials. But first estimates of costs involved in delivering North Slope crude oil to Midwest markets are required.

Obtaining a valid estimate of the construction and operating costs of a Trans-Canadian pipeline (TCP) was difficult and perhaps unduly complicated. The reason is that the estimates which were available in published sources vary a great deal because vastly different assumptions were made in what were regarded as preliminary estimates. Some involved assumptions that both gas and oil pipelines would be built, with costs of such facilities giving estimates highest in the range. Others were prepared with an eye to combining current facilities, i.e., looping existing pipelines, using

---

[10] Since the difference in market price (25 cents per barrel) between Chicago and New York is equivalent to the difference in transport cost per barrel from Chicago to New York, the two will cancel out and it is necessary only to compare one of the districts, i.e., the Midwest, with the Pacific Coast in evaluating alternative routes and markets.

rights-of-way supporting existing facilities, or combining gas and oil transport facilities with joint costs allocated in some reasonable proportions.
The Cicchetti estimates were developed with an eye to maintaining comparability in assumptions with TAP, and thus the same investment per
mile (excluding port transshipment facilities) was used as in the estimates
developed for TAP (1972, table 14, p. 62). Investment costs in the
Prudhoe Bay to Edmonton leg of the route run from $2 billion to $2.75
billion and are displayed in table 10-7.

Investment in transport facilities for the Edmonton to Chicago leg of
the route also varied widely, depending on the nature of the assumptions
with respect to possibly looping or using existing facilities or excess capacity on the Interprovincial pipeline. An investment of only $0.1 billion
represented the lower end of the range while an estimated $3.5 billion
represented the highest estimate. The estimates used here, following Cicchetti, are the ones that were advanced in various early oil company
reports (Atlantic-Richfield, 1971) adjusted to 1971 price levels, with a
spread ranging from $0.6 billion to $1.0 billion. Capital costs per barrel
based on this range of estimated investment outlays are displayed in
table 10-8.

With capital charges for the two legs of the North Slope to Chicago
TCP as given above, operating costs need to be included for total transportation costs per barrel. The three major oil companies involved in

Table 10-7
Capital Costs for Trans-Canada Pipeline from North Slope to Edmonton

	Investment ($ billion 1971)			
Discount rate	2.00	2.25	2.50	2.75
	Alyeska throughput schedule			
	(dollars/barrel)			
8%	0.39	0.44	0.49	0.53
10%	0.50	0.56	0.62	0.68
12%	0.62	0.70	0.78	0.86
	Accelerated throughput schedule			
	(dollars/barrel)			
8%	0.32	0.36	0.40	0.45
10%	0.40	0.45	0.50	0.55
12%	0.49	0.55	0.61	0.68
	Accelerated throughput schedule following 2-year delay			
	(dollars/barrel)			
8%	0.38	0.42	0.47	0.52
10%	0.49	0.55	0.61	0.67
12%	0.62	0.69	0.77	0.85

Source: Cicchetti (1972), p. 63.

Table 10-8

Capital Costs for Trans-Canada Pipeline when Full Throughput Is Sent
from Edmonton to Chicago

Discount rate	Investment ($ billion 1971)		
	0.60	0.80	1.00
	Alyeska throughput schedule (dollars/barrel)		
8%	0.12	0.16	0.19
10%	0.15	0.20	0.25
12%	0.19	0.25	0.31
	Accelerated throughput schedule (dollars/barrel)		
8%	0.10	0.13	0.16
10%	0.12	0.16	0.20
12%	0.15	0.20	0.25
	Accelerated throughput schedule following 2-year delay (dollars/barrel)		
8%	0.11	0.15	0.19
10%	0.15	0.19	0.24
12%	0.19	0.25	0.31

Source: Cicchetti (1972), p. 66.

North Slope oil exploitation estimated operating costs for the North
Slope–Edmonton–Chicago line, operating at full capacity, or 2 million
barrels per day, to be approximately $0.30 per barrel. Components of
their cost estimation are displayed in table 10-9.

Given the two sets of capital outlays—one of four estimates for the
North Slope to Edmonton leg of the Trans-Canada pipeline, and one of
three estimates for the Edmonton to Chicago leg, we have a combination
of twelve estimates of capital costs per barrel which, combined with the
30-cent estimated operating costs per barrel gives a set of estimates of total
transportation costs from the North Slope to Chicago by the Trans-Canada
pipeline as displayed in table 10-10. These costs now can be compared
with the estimated costs of transporting North Slope crude from Prudhoe
Bay through Valdez to Los Angeles by means of the Trans-Alaska pipeline
and tanker combination. The latter estimates are given in table 10-4 of
section 3.

With the transport cost estimates provided, along with the estimated
range of values for the North Slope crude in each of the two markets, we
can carry out the evaluation implicit in equation (10-3). This can be performed for any of the twelve combinations of investment costs; however,
in the interest of minimizing detail, the display is reduced to a comparison
of only four estimates for each of the markets—for any given discount

Table 10-9

Operating Costs per Barrel for Full Capacity Throughputs

	North Slope to Edmonton	Edmonton to Chicago
Expenses for personnel, materials, maintenance, service, administration, oil measurement losses, and fuel (Can. $)	35,300	41,220
Depreciation (Can. $)	42,400	14,830
Total annual operating costs (Can. $)	77,700	56,050
Maximum annual throughput (mil. bbl.)	547.5	547.5
Operating costs/bbl. at maximum throughput (Can. ¢)	14.2	10.2
Linear increase in costs/bbl. to a throughput level of 2 MMb./day (Can. ¢)[a]	18.9	13.6
	32.5	
Conversion to U.S. dollars, Can. $1 = U.S. 1971 $0.93 (U.S. ¢)	17.4	12.6
	30	

Source: Canadian Bechtel, Ltd., *Mackenzie Valley Pipeline Research Limited, Preliminary Report* (June 1970).

Note: n.a. = not applicable. Monetary costs of property taxes and interest have not been included above.

[a]If costs are expected to increase linearly when throughput is increased from 1.5 MMb./day, the assumption is that savings from economies of scale are offset by additional pumping costs. This assumption has been utilized generally in the estimates found in the various Arctic pipeline costs reports prepared for or by the oil industry

rate. This is done by selecting the middle estimate of investment outlays ($0.8 billion) for the Edmonton to Chicago leg to combine with each of the four investment outlay estimates of the North Slope to Edmonton leg for the Trans-Canada pipeline, as the difference per barrel among transport costs estimates for the Edmonton–Chicago leg is quite small and thus permits the reduction of detail with minimum reduction of information (see table 10-8). In table 10-11 are shown the differences between the value per barrel of North Slope oil in each market and the corresponding transportation cost.[11]

If it is understood that the difference in value per barrel of North Slope oil between the West Coast ($3.17) and the minimum estimated value for the Midwest ($3.63) was $0.46, it is clear that the difference in the transport costs per barrel to the two markets was substantially less. When both differences are taken into account, it is seen that the net difference favored the Trans-Canadian pipeline route and the Midwest market by a large margin. Indeed, were we to compare the differences between the market value on the Pacific Coast, and the lowest estimated transport cost to that

[11] The estimated production cost was not included in the data shown in these tables because this would be equal for each market, since it depends on the same source of petroleum. Accordingly, the *differences* between corresponding estimates in the two sets presented in tables 10-11 and 10-12 are not affected.

Table 10-10

Transport Cost for Trans-Canada Pipeline from North Slope to Chicago via Edmonton

Discount rate	Investment ($ billion, 1971)											
	2.6	2.8	3.0	2.85	3.05	3.25	3.10	3.30	3.50	3.35	3.55	3.75
	Alyeska throughput schedule (dollars/barrel)											
8%	0.81	0.85	0.88	0.86	0.90	0.93	0.91	0.95	0.98	0.95	0.99	1.02
10%	0.95	1.00	1.05	1.01	1.06	1.11	1.07	1.12	1.17	1.13	1.18	1.23
12%	1.11	1.17	1.23	1.19	1.25	1.31	1.27	1.33	1.39	1.35	1.41	1.47
	Accelerated throughput schedule (dollars/barrel)											
8%	0.72	0.75	0.78	0.76	0.79	0.82	0.80	0.83	0.86	0.85	0.88	0.91
10%	0.82	0.86	0.90	0.87	0.91	0.95	0.92	0.96	1.00	0.97	1.01	1.05
12%	0.94	0.99	1.04	1.00	1.05	1.10	1.06	1.11	1.16	1.13	1.18	1.23
	Alyeska throughput schedule following 2-year delay (dollars/barrel)											
8%	0.79	0.83	0.87	0.83	0.87	0.91	0.88	0.92	0.96	0.93	0.97	1.01
10%	0.94	0.98	1.03	1.00	1.04	1.09	1.06	1.10	1.15	1.12	1.16	1.21
12%	1.11	1.17	1.23	1.18	1.24	1.30	1.26	1.32	1.38	1.34	1.40	1.46

Table 10-11

Estimated Differences Between Market Value and Transport Cost per Barrel of North Slope Oil for Pacific Coast Compared with Midwest Markets

Discount rate	Investment ($ billion, 1971)							
	1.75	2.00	2.25	2.50	2.08	3.05	3.30	3.55

Alyeska throughput schedule
(dollars/barrel)

	Pacific Coast market $(B_{NS}^i - C_{NS}^i)$				Midwest market $(B_{NS}^i - C_{NS}^i)$[a]			
8%	2.35	2.30	2.25	2.20	2.78	2.73	2.68	2.56
10%	2.26	2.19	2.13	2.07	2.63	2.57	2.51	2.45
12%	2.15	2.07	1.99	1.91	2.46	2.38	2.30	2.22

Accelerated throughput schedule
(dollars/barrel)

8%	2.41	2.37	2.33	2.29	2.88	2.84	2.80	2.75
10%	2.34	2.29	2.24	2.19	2.77	2.72	2.67	2.62
12%	2.26	2.20	2.14	2.08	2.64	2.58	2.52	2.45

[a] B_{NS}^i or the benefit of North Slope oil in the Midwest market, was taken to be the minimum ($3.63) estimate in the range for these calculations.

market, with the highest estimated transport costs associated with the Trans-Canada pipeline and the lowest estimated market value in the Midwest (for comparable discount rates), we would see that there still remained a substantial margin of advantage in the selection of the Midwest market and the Trans-Canada pipeline route, factors other than those considered in the analysis remaining equal.

One of the factors not considered in the analysis to this point, however, does not remain equal. This factor concerns the differential environmental impact of the alternative routes to the different markets. To quote the U.S. Department of Interior (1972) environmental impact study:

One factor involved in viewing potential Trans-Alaska-Canada Alternative routes from an environmental impact standpoint is the potential oil and gas resource situation of the entire Arctic and prospective future pipeline development. This is important because the fewer the corridors, pipelines, or other transport systems which might ultimately be used, the lesser would be the injury to nature.

and, again:

The mountain chains are major obstacles to movement and construction. Less severe, but nevertheless important are the topographic hindrances imposed by the intervening hills, plateaus and uplands. If only topography were considered, the most favorable corridor from Prudhoe Bay to Edmonton would follow the coastal plain lowlands and interior plains around the outer margins of the mountains. . . .

On the basis of recorded earthquakes . . . it appears that each of the (TCP) corridors traverses areas of much lower seismic activity and risk than the proposed Trans-Alaska pipeline. In particular, all the new corridors avoid the very high seismic zone in the Prince William Sound area. . . . (vol. 2, p. 115ff.)

One of the two possible Trans-Canada routes would move across the mountains to the Fairbanks area and then follow the right-of-way of the Alcan highway, thus making use of an already disturbed area. Offsetting considerations here are that the route would traverse some of the active seismic zones in the Fairbanks area, and would not exploit the possibility of consolidating both Prudhoe Bay oil and gas transport systems and corridors with those most likely to be introduced by the discovery and exploitation of Canadian arctic petroleum resources. A disadvantage of the consolidation of the Alaskan and Canadian transport facilities through Northern Canada is the hazard that one variant poses to the 9-million-acre Arctic National Wildlife Range, which borders Canada and adjoins the Beaufort Sea. On balance, however, it was the conclusion of the Department of Interior study that the routes through Northern Canada would be superior to the Trans-Alaska pipeline on environmental grounds (U.S. Dept. of Interior, 1972, vol. 2, p. 320ff.).

To summarize then, it appeared that given the decision to exploit the Alaskan oil, the use of the Trans-Alaska pipeline for transporting it to market was the least desirable method on two counts. First, it was not economic compared with alternative transport routes and markets, and second, it was inferior on environmental grounds as well.

This conclusion has implications for the net value of the Alaskan oil. That is, if the Trans-Canada pipeline and the Midwest market provide for a net gain in their favor, the additional net benefits per barrel of oil will be reflected in a larger net value of the Prudhoe Bay field than initially estimated ($3 billion to $5 billion) in section 3. There are some qualifications in reaching this judgment, however, to which we give attention in section 5.

5. CONSIDERATION OF SOME FACTORS
NOT REMAINING EQUAL

Given the indicated advantages of the Trans-Canada pipeline, other factors remaining equal, the question can be advanced as to why these advantages could not have been perceived as readily by the Alyeska Service Company as by an economic analyst.

Assuming the analysis itself is correct, there may be many reasons for a divergence between private and social benefits and costs or between pecuniary and real benefits and costs that could lead private parties to opt for actions quite advantageous to themselves that would be less than socially optimal. There are in this instance a whole set of institutional restrictions on free market operation that leave numerous opportunities for private parties, working within the policies and laws affecting their activities, to take advantage of actions that would not be feasible within an unconstrained socially optimal course of action. As an example, it is known that members of the Alyeska Service Company were alert to the possibility of diverting some (or all) of Alaskan oil to Japanese markets rather than to the West Coast under an import-for-export plan. That is, the Alaskan oil sent to Japan was expected to be marketed at roughly the world price of $2 per barrel, thus reducing the oil companies' per barrel tax liability on North Slope oil to the state of Alaska. Compensating for the lower price of oil sold in Japan was the higher price of oil sold in New York ($4.06 per barrel), imported from Venezuelan fields under the import-for-export arrangement, and the opportunity of avoiding provisions of the Jones Act requiring shipment in higher cost U.S. bottoms. There is no need to detail the numerous possibilities under which the returns to the Alyeska Pipeline Service Company, given existing laws, policies, and institutional arrangements, would exceed returns from pursuing the alternative environmentally (and economically) most desirable course of action. These have been examined in rich detail in Cicchetti's study;[12] thus we note them only in passing. There was one factor, however, relating to another real element in the problem, which does not fit neatly into the distinction between private and social nonconformities in objectives.

One implicit assumption, or factor taken to be remaining equal, in our evaluation of the alternative transport modes and markets, was that access to a Canadian right-of-way would not be delayed compared with the time that would be required for a similar right-of-way across lands in Alaska. Given the fact that access across public lands was required in Alaska, and that this required compliance with the National Environmental Policy Act and a provision on rights-of-way of the Mineral Leasing Act of 1920,[13] it was not clear that seeking a permit through Canada would necessarily involve a longer period of negotiation and preparation than the attempt to obtain a permit from the Department of the Interior for a right-of-way to build a service road and line across public lands in Alaska.[14] Assuming,

[12] See Cicchetti (1972), especially chapters 4 and 5.

[13] Provisions of the Mineral Leasing Act restricted the width of rights-of-way to 24 feet, a limitation that was inconsistent with the proposed methods of construction contemplated for TAP until the action taken by Congress November 16, 1973, amending the original provisions of the Act.

[14] In 1970 the Environmental Defense Fund, the Friends of the Earth, and the Wilderness Society joined in a legal action seeking injunction against issuance of a permit pending the filing of an environmental impact statement under provisions of PL 91-190, 91st Congress. Following the filing of a final environmental impact statement, the courts, without ruling on the environmental issue, ruled on the inconsistency of the plans involving a right-of-way exceeding limits imposed by the Mineral Leasing Act of 1920. Subsequently Congress liberalized the provisions for width of rights-of-way across public lands to enable the project to meet rights-of-way provisions, following which all formal opposition to the TAP ceased.

Table 10-12

Estimated Difference Between Market Value and Transport Cost per Barrel of
North Slope Oil for Trans-Alaska Pipeline and Trans-Canada Pipeline with
2-Year Delay

Discount rate	Investment ($ billion, 1971)							
	1.75	2.00	2.25	2.50	2.08	3.05	3.30	3.55
	Accelerated throughput schedule Pacific Coast market (dollars/barrel) $(B^i_{NS} - C^i_{NS})$				Accelerated schedule with 2-year delay Midwest market (dollars/barrel) $(B^i_{NS} - C^i_{NS})$; $B^i_{NS} = \$3.63$			
8%	2.41	2.37	2.33	2.29	2.80	2.76	2.71	2.66
10%	2.34	2.29	2.24	2.19	2.65	2.59	2.53	2.47
12%	2.26	2.20	2.14	2.08	2.46	2.39	2.31	2.23
					$(B^i_{NS} - C^i_{NS})$; $B^i_{NS} = \$3.93$			
8%					3.10	3.06	3.01	2.96
10%					2.95	2.89	2.83	2.77
12%					2.76	2.69	2.61	2.53

however, that the problem of obtaining access across lands in Canada, involving as it does a foreign power, would incur additional delays, the economics of the alternative routes and markets would be changed, and with sufficient delay in the Canadian over the Alaskan route, actually reversed.

Simply in order to gain perspective on this problem, let us assume that the time required to obtain access rights-of-way, build, and put into operation a transport facility across Canada would involve 2 years in excess of the time the TAP facility could otherwise be put into operation. We can observe the effects of this in table 10-12, which is drawn from the appropriate section of table 10-10, section 4.

At first sight, the change in the difference between market value and transport cost, assuming an accelerated throughput schedule but with a 2-year delay for the Trans-Canada pipeline, appears to have an effect that only approximates the difference between the Alyeska throughput and the accelerated throughput schedules examined before. Comparing the differences, we see that even at the lowest estimated market value in the Midwest, i.e., $3.63, the accelerated schedule with a 2-year delay in operation of the Canadian facility still has a large favorable net advantage over TAP with the assumed accelerated throughput schedule when viewed in the net difference per barrel perspective. However, a 2-year delay implies that the benefits will not be received as soon, and this will have an effect equivalent to a reduction in number of 1971 barrels for the delayed throughput.[15] To

[15] Compare equation (10-2) and table 10-2.

give an indication of the magnitude of the effect, we compare the two in table 10-13.

The effect of a 2-year delay at discount rates in the range of 8 to 12 percent can be seen to be rather substantial. If the favorable difference in the per barrel net benefit for the Trans-Canada pipeline and Midwest market is weighted by the unfavorable difference in the time equivalent barrels that a two-year delay would occasion, the comparison of the Trans-Alaska and Trans-Canada pipelines becomes much more difficult. The combined effects of the difference in time-equivalent barrels and the net benefits per barrel for the two alternative routes and markets are illustrated in table 10-14. Here it is readily seen that at a discount rate of 10 percent, there is no unambiguous way in which to distinguish the economic superiority of one over the other, when the Trans-Canada pipeline is assumed to be delayed 2 years longer than TAP. At the lowest estimated market value of North Slope oil in the Midwest market ($3.63), the 1971 net value of TAP and tanker in the Los Angeles market exceeds the Canadian alternative route and Midwest market by approximately three-

Table 10-13
Time-Equivalent Barrels of Oil Throughput

	Accelerated throughput	Accelerated throughput with 2-year delay
	(billions of barrels)	
Total undiscounted throughput	18.25	18.25
1971 Equivalent at 8% discount	6.19	5.31
1971 Equivalent at 10% discount	4.98	4.12
1971 Equivalent at 12% discount	4.08	3.25

Table 10-14
Comparative 1971 Equivalent Values of Trans-Alaska Pipeline and Trans-Canada Pipeline Delayed a Differential 2-Year Period

Discount rate	Investment ($ billion, 1971)							
	1.75	2.00	2.25	2.50	2.08	3.05	3.30	3.55
	Accelerated throughput schedule Trans-Alaska pipeline and tanker ($ billion, 1971)				Accelerated schedule with 2-year delay Trans-Canada pipeline; Midwest market ($ billion, 1971) $B_{NS}^i = \$3.63$			
8%	14.92	14.67	14.42	14.18	14.87	14.66	14.39	14.12
10%	11.65	11.40	11.16	10.91	10.92	10.67	10.42	10.18
12%	9.22	8.98	8.79	8.49	8.00	7.77	7.51	7.25
					$B_{NS}^i = \$3.93$			
8%					16.46	16.25	15.98	15.72
10%					12.15	11.91	11.66	11.41
12%					8.97	8.74	8.48	8.22

quarters of a billion dollars. Alternatively, at the higher estimated market value of North Slope oil in the Midwest market ($3.93), the 1971 net value of TCP-transported North Slope crude in the Chicago market exceeds the Trans-Alaskan alternative route and Los Angeles market by approximately half a billion dollars. At lower discount rates, the Trans-Canada alternative will naturally appear to improve slightly, whereas at higher discount rates the nondelayed alternative will benefit differentially.

Accordingly, it is conceivable that expectation of a differential delay, along with the need to consider compensation to Canada for rights-of-way may have figured significantly, along with other incentives to consider a non-Canadian route and West Coast markets.[16] It may well have seemed reasonable at the time of the proposed Trans-Alaska pipeline that a longer time would be required for the Canadian than for the Alaskan route, and that would have made a significant difference in the relative economics. Whether the same rationale will hold in retrospect is uncertain, but even if as little as a 2-year delay were anticipated, assuming accelerated throughput schedules for the two routes, the relative economics would leave little to choose between them. Even so, the lesser environmental impact of the Trans-Canadian pipeline would remain at issue, and here we would encounter the inconsistency between private and public objectives and values.

6. CONCLUSIONS

The decision to raise and transport North Slope oil across arctic tundra and seismically active zones represented an option having environmental impact of such potentially large magnitude that it may appear questionable whether conventional economic analysis can be applied without severe qualifications. The smaller scale the decision, the more applicable is benefit–cost analysis. On the one hand, from the standpoint of the total energy supply situation, perhaps, North Slope oil might be considered a relatively modest increment to total petroleum resources. On the other hand, from the standpoint of new investment in energy supplies, or of environmental impact, we cannot be too comfortable relying ultimately on techniques of marginal or incremental analysis.

[16] Cicchetti does not emphasize this point by virtue of his conclusions derived from analysis of the relative size of the Pacific Coast and the Midwest and East Coast markets. A two million barrel per day throughput would approximately double the supply of crude oil on the West Coast, but would increase the supply east of the Rockies by only approximately 17 percent. Accordingly, he assumes the Alyeska throughput schedule for delivery of crude from Prudhoe Bay to be applicable to the Pacific Coast market, and recognizes on the other hand, that the total supply of Alaskan oil could be readily absorbed in the Midwest and Eastern markets with an accelerated throughput schedule following a 2-year delay. Cicchetti concludes that the payments to Canada could increase costs as much as 20 percent and the delay compared with the Trans-Alaskan pipeline could go up to 3 years without tipping the balance away from the Trans-Canada pipeline and Midwest and Eastern markets (Cicchetti, 1972, p. 121).

In addition to the limitations of the analysis for the reasons cited above, we are dealing with a problem having monumental imponderables. These appear not only with respect to the more conventional variables in benefit–cost analysis, e.g., the trend in future relative price of imported foreign crudes, hence the relative benefits of North Slope oil (for simplicity assumed to remain constant in the analysis) but also in connection with the uncertainty attending potentially massive damage in a particularly fragile environment. These considerations counsel viewing the economic analysis with perhaps greater circumspection than in the more typical problems represented by the previous cases analyzed.

Since it is ultimately not clear whether we are talking about a fairly high probability of numerous relatively low-level contaminations on the one hand, or a low probability of an ecological catastrophe, it may be that neither expected values of benefits and costs nor the present-value criterion are as defensible, as welfare-analytic concepts, as they were in the more customary problems we have addressed. A very low probability of an ecological catastrophe can be expected to yield a relatively modest "expected value" in terms of environmental costs; yet should it occur, and the effects continue in perpetuity, the costs to future generations may well be so extreme that we would elect to reject economic comparisons based on expected present values. We have discussed the deficiencies of the present-value criterion involving intergenerational resource allocations in section 2 of chapter 4. It was there illustrated that changes in the vantage point from which present values are to be calculated, i.e., from one generation to the next, make the present-value criterion a possibly ambiguous policy guide. This may not be all that serious in cases where the variance about the expected values is not great and the magnitude of the decision impacts is also relatively modest. But these conditions are not so likely to obtain in the case of raising and transporting North Slope oil to markets. For this reason the economic analysis of the costs and gains, under the severe qualifications cited above, must be considered as only a part of the input in reaching a public decision in this case in particular. The outcome of the political process, if resulting from free and open public debate of the issues, with the economic considerations entering as part of the relevant information for public choice, is doubtless a more reliable guide to decision in this matter than exclusive reliance on economic information on relative costs and gains, when undertaken under the rather severe conditions of this case.

Yet while the issue whether to raise and transport North Slope oil may be debatable, once given the decision, the selection of market and route seems clearly to favor the Trans-Canadian alternative. Here the TCP alternative dominates TAP; i.e., it appears to have been preferable not only environmentally but economically as well. Accordingly, while economic analysis may not be definitive on the first issue, it does provide useful evidence on the second.

REFERENCES

Adelman, M. A. 1972. *The World Petroleum Market* (Baltimore: Johns Hopkins Press).

Aspin, Les. 1971. "It's Not Too Late to Stop the Alaska Pipeline—Maybe," *Not Man Apart*, vol. 1, no. 8.

Atlantic-Richfield Co. 1971. "The Trans-Canadian Alternative Route," memorandum submitted to the Department of the Interior, September 10, 1971.

Canadian Bechtel, Ltd. 1971. *Mackenzie Valley Pipeline Research Limited, Preliminary Report.*

Cicchetti, C. J. 1972. *Alaskan Oil: Alternative Routes and Markets* (Baltimore: Johns Hopkins Press).

Lewis, C. R. 1971. "Comments on the Draft Environmental Impact Statement for the Trans-Alaska Pipeline," (submitted to Department of the Interior).

Mikesell, R. F. 1971. *Foreign Investment in the Petroleum and Mineral Industries: Case Studies of Investor–Host Country Relations* (Baltimore: Johns Hopkins Press).

U.S. Department of the Interior. 1972. *Final Impact Statement Proposed Trans-Alaska Pipeline*, vols. 2 and 4.

CHAPTER 11

SUMMARY, CONCLUSIONS, AND POLICY RECOMMENDATIONS

REVIEW OF PART I

As result of the rise of environmental awareness in the United States, particularly in connection with the more widespread sensitivity to the aesthetic dimensions of the environment, land management agencies have been encouraged to broaden their responsibilities for resources occurring on the public lands. The Wilderness Act of 1964, the Wild and Scenic Rivers Act of 1968, and the National Trails System Act of 1968 were only the elaboration and explicit extensions of the spirit motivating the earlier multiple-use acts that sought to extend the concept of resource management beyond commodity resources to amenity resources as well. The Environmental Policy Act of 1969 not only added emphasis to this concept but also provided the means by which concerned citizens might challenge the responsiveness of the resource management agencies to the new directives contained in the legislation.

As new public interests evolve to challenge traditional interests in the use of a given tract of land or reach of river for a purpose that is incompatible with amenity uses, it is to be expected that controversies over the allocation of resources should arise. This is because resources in the public sector are allocated by specific administrative decision rather than more impersonally by the market. Thus we have seen the land and water resource management agencies brought to court under the National Environmental Policy Act by various conservation and environmental organizations. Moreover, because of the elevation of the status of common property resource claimants before the courts, quite independently of NEPA, actions are being taken by citizens' groups who feel deprived of rights without due process.

Some of this activity may be due to the difficulties of managing well an interrelated complex of resources, with their mix of overlapping private and common property claims. But in addition, there is the possibility that the management of public resources that has been characteristic from the earliest days of the conservation movement has not contributed to the development of a corpus of management principles, or to a cadre of management personnel that are immediately available or competent to handle the range of new and complex responsibilties mandated by recent legislation and the changing public climate regarding resource use.

It is perhaps for this reason that the Public Land Law Review Commission encountered difficulties in finding information within the land management agencies' files that would assist it in determining the value of commodity as compared with amenity resources. This kind of evaluation is essential if the land management agencies are to administer the public's resources to maximize their net benefits.

The extent of the public lands administered by the resource management agencies is enormous. While the distribution of the commodity resources may be more sparse than on an equivalent expanse of private lands in the United States, the distribution of the natural areas of any great size, with their attendant amenity resources, is doubtless much greater. Accordingly, with approximately a third of the United States' lands under public management, increases in the efficiency of such management represent potential welfare gains, or public benefits, of many billions of dollars. It is important then, considering the extent and value of the resources under the management of public agencies, to develop principles and practices that will conform to the new policies and the broader objectives in resource management.

Since the amenity services of natural environments enter directly into consumption, unlike the predominantly intermediate goods character of commodity resources, perfect or reasonably close substitutes are often difficult to find for a significant body of consumers. Because these are gifts of nature, not reproducible by man, the destruction of the natural environment on which such services depend represents an irreversible event carrying a cost for present and future generations that normally does not attend the use of commodity resources. Accordingly, the improvement of management principles and practices would not only represent many billions of dollars of benefit to the public, but by incorporating the special considerations associated with decisions having significant irreversible consequences, environmental costs otherwise incurred in perpetuity could be avoided. It is therefore of great urgency that the theory and practice of managing irreplaceable assets be advanced as rapidly and comprehensively as possible.

In this volume we have attempted to provide theoretical and applied analytical techniques for addressing some of the difficult problems that come up for decision in the management of public lands. First we have indicated the extent of the overlapping of private and common property attributes of resources found on the public lands. Some of these common property, or open access, characteristics are a matter of law and policy and could be modified by public choice. Others, however, have their origin in technical conditions that are not subject to "correction" by legislation or changes in policy. Accordingly, while a virtue of the market is its impersonality in the allocation of resources (with perhaps an attendant vice in its impersonality in the distribution of welfare), the inefficiencies or transaction costs of market allocations involving resources on the public lands are thought to be excessive. It is for this reason, for example, that the Bureau of Land Management, which is responsible for the administration of what remains of the public domain, is increasingly being directed to take on more of the responsibilities of a land management rather than a land disposal agency. It is on the verge of obtaining an organic act that will specify, as in the case of other resource management agencies, its changed and larger management responsibilities. However, having public agencies administer the privately unappropriated lands of the public domain does not by itself resolve some of the difficult problems associated with an attempt to allocate efficiently the resources found in association with these lands.

One problem that remains relates to the assignment of liability for the damages suffered by one group of users of common property resources from preemptive, incompatible uses by another group. For example, the benefit that an incompatible (destructive) extractive use of an area would need to show if it were to exceed the benefits derived from the amenity services thus foreclosed would differ depending on whether the aggregate amount that recreationists would be willing to pay for continued enjoyment of the amenities were used as a measure of the damages (benefits), or whether the aggregate amount that would be required to leave the recreationists indifferent between the proffered compensation and the recreation opportunity threatened with foreclosure were used. The reason for the difference is that in the first instance the aggregate willingness (ability) to pay is constrained by the recreationists' money incomes. In the second instance, the benefits would represent real income of beneficiaries resulting from access to the common property resources, quite independent of the ability to match the amount out of their money incomes.

This outcome represents a conceptual dilemma for public land resource managers in estimating benefits from alternative courses of action until either by legislation or through court decision the priority of rights, i.e., the sanction for "unequal access," to the common property resources is established. In this case, perhaps the stipulation in the 1960 Multiple Use and Sustained Yield Act that the productivity of the land be maintained, may be interpreted to assign liability for damage to the party engaged in the destructive use of the environment. This appears to be consistent with features of the common law which provide for taking the usufruct of a resource without affecting its substance. It is also reflected in the economics literature in the partially defined distinction between a destructive and a constructive use of the environment. Some possibility exists of establishing a hierarchy of rights or priorities (essentially unequal access) that would satisfy the essential conditions for determining which measure of benefits is appropriate in cases involving incompatible uses of common property resources. To our knowledge, however, there has been no court action directed specifically to this question, and the law remains at best ambiguous.

Since natural environments are the product of biological evolution, geomorphology, and related natural processes involving time spans greatly exceeding that of human civilization, significant modification represents irreversible alterations. We recognize that a decision, once taken, cannot be "untaken" subsequently, and in this trivial sense all decisions are irreversible. But in a more significant sense, decisions that have consequences which endure virtually undiminished over a very long time span can be distinguished from decisions that have ephemeral results. That is, there are some decisions the consequences of which can be regarded as virtually permanent, notwithstanding any attempted offsetting compensatory actions. These can be distinguished meaningfully from those that, while still irreversible, can be offset by subsequent action. While not every environmental modification is irreversible in a nontrivial sense, there are those that affect very unusual, if not unique, natural phenomena that are significant. The irretrievable loss of genetic information with the extinction of a species, or the modification of a uniquely scenic landscape fall into the category of nontrivial irreversibilities.

One interesting distinction here is between the conversion of a natural environment, the problem we focus on, and the use of an exhaustible extractive resource from the environment. A common feature of studies of the latter problem is that the resource has value only when extracted, or regarded as a store of future extractions. A general theme of this volume is that the resource may have another value, realized only if it is *not* extracted. Moreover, it is the loss of this value which may be more importantly irreversible than use of an exhaustible resource such as a source of energy. Technical progress has more than compensated for the use of particular sources of supply. Although the use is irreversible, this may not matter very much if substitute fuel materials are available at progressively lower cost, as historically they have been for the United States. The same option does not exist for the nonproducible amenity resources, which remain available only if they are protected from mining and other disruptive activities. Just as economic theory would predict in these circumstances, the value of these resources appears to be rising relative to the value of the commodity resources.

The implications of this behavior are explored in a model of irreversible investment in the development of a natural environment. It is shown that for an interval of time over which development benefits are (expected to be) decreasing relative to preservation-related benefits, (1) the optimal scale of development is decreasing, and (2) the net present value of the environment will be maximized by stopping investment at some point before the start of the interval—i.e., while it is still (currently) profitable to expand development. The sacrifice of some near-term gain is a consequence of the restriction on reversibility, which is required to avoid greater future loss from too much development. As a special case of this general proposition, if development benefits are *always* decreasing relatively, as we have some reason to expect, it will be optimal to invest immediately, if at all. A useful implication is that the planner need consider only the present value (net of environmental costs, of course) of a single investment, as in the standard benefit–cost computation not derived from a more general model of the scheduling of investment.

The analysis is carried further to show that environmental modifications having irreversible consequences may require a premium, over and above all costs, in order to be efficient. The premium is the value of retaining an option to consume the amenity services of an unspoiled environment under conditions of uncertainty as to future demand for the services. Put another way, the irreversible development carries a cost—the loss of option value. A rather similar result emerges from consideration of the effect of shifting vantage points on the evaluation of alternative uses of an environment. This point may best be understood through an example. Hetch Hetchy Valley in Yosemite National Park was flooded to provide a water supply reservoir for the city of San Francisco in 1914. Although a few people such as John Muir objected at the time, a benefit–cost analysis of the project might have shown it efficient, given the alternatives for water supply and the then-extensive wilderness environment of the region. With changes in technology, the supply of wilderness, and consumer preferences over the past 60 years, construction of a dam across the lower Yosemite Valley for water or power now seems unthinkable. And many could wish, for the same reasons, that it were possible to have an unflooded Hetch Hetchy as well.

This intertemporal "inconsistency," along with the existence of option value (and perhaps also considerations of liability for destruction of common property amenity resources on the public lands), suggests the addition, for planning purposes, of a charge or something akin to a "severance" tax, to the conventionally calculated costs of a development project. Legislative zoning of wilderness areas, with provisions to make rezoning more difficult, might similarly compensate for the asymmetric consequences of irreversibility.

REVIEW OF PART II

Having reviewed the complex interrelation of uses that have over-lapping claims against both common and private property resources on the public lands, along with the additional complications for choice that non-trivial irreversible decisions entail, we then analyzed a number of controversial cases involving modifications of the natural environment where some of the above problems are reflected. In the Hells Canyon case the hydroelectric potential is proposed for development. An opportunity cost of the development, of course, is the value of the amenity resources that would be destroyed if the canyon were modified in the manner contemplated by the developers. Moreover, since many of the proposed developments involving public lands, or streams over which the federal government has jurisdiction, are themselves public projects or represent projects that require complementary facilities built by the public construction agencies, an additional complication arises. The cost of facilities built at public expense are traditionally understated because only part of the opportunity cost of public capital is reflected in the computed costs of such facilities. This will result in an inflated estimate of net benefits from development.

Facilities over which the power would be transmitted to load centers as well as the peaking facilities in some federal dams that could serve as alternatives to the Hells Canyon project are built with subsidized public capital. Moreover, one of the two entities presenting themselves as the combined applicant for license before the Federal Power Commission was a local quasi-public utility enjoying access to subsidized capital via preferential tax treatment. An element of spurious savings or understated costs was introduced into the official analysis of comparative costs of hydropower and its less capital-intensive thermal alternative for this reason as well. Accordingly, the cost of all facilities in the system that would participate in developing and delivering Hells Canyon power to market, along with the postulated thermal alternative, had to be reestimated in order to obtain a valid comparison.

A second feature of the benefit estimation also required attention. Typically, the off-peak energy from the postulated thermal alternative to the hydro project is credited with the savings available from displacing energy otherwise required from older, less efficient plants in the system. But since the regional power system in which the Hells Canyon project would operate is currently a hydroelectric system, for all practical purposes, no value for off-peak displacement energy was credited against the thermal alternative's cost. This is understandable in the present, but during the period in which the project would function, the regional power system would begin immediately evolving from an exclusively hydro, to a mixed hydro-thermal, and eventually to a predominantly thermal system. Advances in technology and gains in efficiency associated with new thermal energy entering the system would erode benefits initially attributed to the hydro plant.

Making the necessary adjustments to all the costs, hence benefits of the hydro projects, it was found that two of the three proposals advanced for the development of the Hells Canyon would not be economic in any event —even without the opportunity costs associated with the preemption of the amenity services otherwise available from the Hells Canyon preserved in its natural state.

This is an important conclusion. Given the various subsidies—whether the understatement of capital costs for public projects, preferential tax treatment for extractive industries, or deficit sales of timber from the national forests—many extractive or developmental activities having adverse implications for environmental values appear to be economic (disassociated from their environmental impacts) only because their costs are understated. Under such circumstances the public will incur both the subsidized portion of the uneconomic developmental or extractive activities as well as the burden of the associated environmental degradation. A first step, then, in any procedure to weigh the value of extractive uses and environmental values is a careful auditing of the ostensible cost—and hence genuine economic benefit—of many of the public or public-related commodity resource activities. In a significant number of cases a professionally competent analysis of the true costs will make unnecessary the more difficult task of estimating the environmental values precluded by the extraction of commodity resources.

While a careful screening will reveal many proposed projects and programs with ostensible benefits exceeding costs that would not pass muster on careful professional analysis, there will, of course, be many that would. This appears to be the case for the proposed High Mountain Sheep project, which survived a rigorous cost analysis to which its two companion alternative proposals for development of the Hells Canyon succumbed. In such cases, it is necessary to make as careful and comprehensive an analysis of the value of the environmental amenities as possible, even though it must be acknowledged that it is not possible to fix the value of every attribute of the amenity resources enjoyed by the public. However, in a significant class of cases it will not be necessary to measure the benefit of every environmental attribute. Here an accurate professional evaluation of true resource costs, coupled with estimates of only those environmental values that can be measured, will be sufficient to establish that such a *lower bound* estimate of the measurable environmental values exceeds the benefits of development. It was not possible to encompass the value of all of the attributes of preserving the Hells Canyon intact, yet owing to the relatively thin margin of advantage of the hydro over its most economic alternative source of energy when correctly analyzed, those environmental values that could be estimated were shown to exceed the value of the site if used for power production. Accordingly, while a complete and comprehensive evaluation of all environmental values may not be possible, there will be a class of cases for which it will not be necessary. An assessment of only those values susceptible of measurement may provide lower bound estimates that suffice for the resource allocation decision.

An important element of our analysis was to incorporate expected changes in the relative value of the two alternative uses of the Hells Canyon over time. Here we introduced the asymmetric implications technological progress will have for the value of the site in alternative uses. Expected continued advances in the efficiency of energy conversion and the logistic support industries for the electric utility industry suggest that the initial nonpeaking power benefits of the hydro plant, as explained above, would diminish over time. On the other hand, the advances in technology occurring throughout the economy result in increases in output, hence income, per capita. Given that the demand for the amenity services provided by natural environments is income elastic—and such amenity services are irreproducible gifts of nature not capable of augmentation by man—the annual benefits of the canyon retained in its natural state would appreciate over time, reflecting the growing scarcity of supply relative to demand.

This is an important general result. Historically, the cost and price of resource commodities relative to the price of goods and services generally has been constant or declining, with the exception of softwood saw timber. Conversely, the demand for environmental amenity resources has been increasing, and as some of these are nonproducible gifts of nature in fixed supply, the effect will be an expected rise in relative value. This anticipated change in the relative value of alternative uses of the environment has not been reflected in traditional benefit–cost analysis, but requires serious attention in the future if the relative commodity and amenity resource values of particular outstanding, if not unique, natural areas are to be properly weighed.

Next, applying our methods of analysis to the White Cloud Peaks area of Idaho, we address a conflict that arises between recreation (with compatible grazing uses) and the potential open-pit mining of molybdenum at a location that would effectively destroy the pristine character and the sense of remoteness and solitude of a major part of the most scenic area in the White Clouds. Basically the problem presents a choice between environmental preservation for recreational purposes and an environmentally destructive extractive activity. The recreation use, of course, could be either a type of higher density use associated with developed facilities such as those found within the older, longer established, national parks, or a lower density, essentially wilderness or primitive-type recreation use.

Since the area is presently geared to a low density use, and the higher cirque basins of interest to backpackers support a very fragile ecology, the analysis was conducted assuming a low density use. Here an attempt was made also to incorporate a conceptually more sophisticated treatment of the relation between individual benefits received from a wilderness experience and the expected frequency of encountering others in camp or on trail. This was done to fix in a less arbitrary manner the optimal density of recreational use, i.e., to define a capacity that would maximize the benefits from low density recreation use, a matter that was handled more crudely in the Hells Canyon case.

Analysis of the potential benefits of molybdenum mining reveal a condition in which deferred net benefits, at best, would be anticipated. Production capacity in the industry currently exceeds both domestic and foreign demand, and past decisions to expand capacity promise a doubling of current domestic capacity in a single facility of one of the producers. Since molybdenum is also a by-product of other mine–mill operations, it is felt by industry analysts that there will be downward pressure on molybdenum prices to the end of the century. Given the expected low grade of the molybdenum ore in the White Clouds area, the commercial feasibility of this deposit appears remote at best and then not until there is a change in the present relation between demand and supply—a condition that is not expected to change sufficiently to be of significance for the White Clouds area deposits until beyond the turn of the century, if ever.

Should the relative costs and prices of molybdenum change in the future sufficiently to indicate a higher expected present value from working the deposits than from recreation (which is not suggested by our analysis), the optimal strategy would not be, as suggested by a simplistic application of the present-value criterion, to undertake now activities that would preclude realizing recreation benefits during the interim. Maximizing benefits from management of the area would require deferment of environmentally destructive activities detrimental to the realization of recreation benefits until conditions had changed sufficiently to promise early commercially feasible mine–mill operations.

It should be noted that, having found the benefits from a preservation use that promises to exceed the present value of the benefits from an extractive use, it is not immediately important to establish that the preservation use selected is the optimal recreation use. If the area is in any event secured against irreversibly destructive uses, the question of which use—a wilderness area or a national park—is ultimately of higher value can be determined subsequently. Indeed, the matter is currently under review by the National Park Service under terms of the Sawtooth National Recreation Area Act (passed subsequent to this analysis) which protects the White Cloud Peaks area and establishes the Sawtooth Wilderness. In some instances the conflict in potential uses may revolve around the nature of the recreation use itself. Indeed, this is the source of conflict in the legal proceedings involving the Sierra Club and the Forest Service over proposed use of Mineral King Valley.

As indicated above, conflicts over use of natural environments may result not only from the incompatibility of a prospective extractive activity with a recreation use requiring an undisturbed natural environment, but also between a high density recreation use requiring developed facilities and a low density recreation use in which primitive conditions and solitude provide the setting. Essentially this is the situation surrounding the controversy over the prospective use of Mineral King Valley.

Mineral King Valley has been considered a prime prospect for the development of skiing and related high density recreation resort facilities by the Forest Service since 1949. Cost of access facilities apparently discouraged any positive response to the prospectus and not until a revised prospectus issued in 1965 and subsequently indicated public assumption of access road costs, were positive proposals forthcoming. In 1969 the Forest Service selected the proposal of Walt Disney Productions over five other respondents, and the prospect of a developed, high density recreation resort in the area became a lively issue. Among other things, the access road would involve traversing a part of the adjoining Sequoia National Park, which along with proposed transmission lines, was a matter of additional concern to the Sierra Club.

Since areas with appropriate slope conformation and the proper snow conditions for skiing are neither abundant nor producible with sufficient authenticity for some skiers, the advantage of analyzing alternative uses with anticipated divergent relative value over time was not available in this instance. Moreover, since the proposed facility would be an addition to an existing set of ski resorts, with some redistribution of use and displacement of benefits, the estimation of demand and benefits called for both formal and more rigorous analytical procedures than used heretofore. But aside from this change in level and complexity of analysis, the results indicate that the benefits are likely to fall short of the costs—even excluding the displaced benefits of the low density recreation activities and the environmental impacts associated with the construction of access facilities across the Sequoia National Park. In addition, it seems fair to raise the issue of the appropriateness of public assumption of transportation costs directly attributable to the need for access to a private recreation facility. The question here involves serious equity as well as economic issues, and it seems fair to suggest that it demands review and adjudication in the courts, where it is being examined.

Here again, it is interesting to note that careful, rigorous analysis of the developmental scheme—comparing both benefits and costs, including publicly assumed costs on behalf of private developers—was sufficient by itself to produce a negative judgment without having to resort to the estimated environmental amenity resource values that would be precluded by the developmental alternative.

Not all common property resources are associated with public lands and public land management decisions. The allocation of wetlands for breeding habitat of migratory waterfowl is a case in point. The resting and feeding areas are provided largely by the national wildlife refuge system, but the nesting habitat involves myriads of small ponds in the Northern Great Plains prairie potholes and in the Canadian prairie provinces. These areas are essential to the production of waterfowl that are harvested, photographed, and observed along the migratory flyways. As there is a dissociation between the costs involved in their production and the benefits of the recreational uses, it follows that the conventional market incentives for the allocation of breeding habitat to the production of migratory waterfowl are lacking. We report in this volume the results of a study by Brown and Hammack that investigates the problem and attempts to evaluate the optimum allocation of wetlands for migratory waterfowl production.

Brown and Hammack develop a bioeconomic supply and economic demand model and in this manner establish the basic functional relations that can lead to an estimate of an optimal allocation of wetlands. Although the data that are currently available are too deficient to provide, as of now, estimates in which a great deal of confidence can repose, the results are nonetheless intuitively satisfactory, i.e., seemingly correct in direction if not necessarily in magnitude. That is, since owners of wetlands incur costs, or forgo potential benefits from draining and cultivating such lands, but do not share proportionally in the benefits of the waterfowl, the amount of the wetlands that would be consciously allocated to waterfowl breeding habitat predictably would be less than the economic optimum. As to the need for refinement to obtain estimates, a virtue of the Brown–Hammack optimizing model is that it employs variables on which adequate data could be developed by a better focused collection effort. Considering the fact that there are programs in Canada and the United States looking toward public compensation to private landowners for retaining such lands as breeding areas, the study promises a means of developing a useful analytical tool for indicating the extent and cost of a program supporting allocation of private wetlands for basically public purposes. The Brown–Hammack bioeconomic model represents in this sense a departure from, and an improvement over, basic biological sustained yield models with which the results are compared and contrasted.

Quite aside from the fact that the wetlands problem addressed by Brown and Hammack differs from other environmental modifications studied in this volume in that it affects primarily private lands, it differs also from the cases previously summarized in that it affects a large region rather than a single, specific site. While it is true that the modification, say, of the natural environment associated with the remaining undeveloped portion of Hells Canyon would represent a national welfare loss of considerable magnitude, the actual environmental impact would be contained within an area on, or bordering, some 70-odd miles of the Snake River. Such localization would not be the case in connection with the continued drainage of migratory waterfowl breeding habitat because a whole physiographic region is involved as well as the migratory character of the breeding species.

The last case reported, the Trans-Alaska pipeline, while relating to a single, although interrelated overland–oceanic, transportation project, similarly has a potential environmental impact that is equally widespread and conceivably significantly more serious, thus suggesting a decision that will ultimately have some ethical or moral overtones. This being the case, the decision involving the question of the raising and transporting of North Slope oil should not have, as it has not, been based exclusively on economic analysis. It involved many imponderables and since no decision or outcome dominated all others without question, it has been reviewed by the courts, and referred to the public forum for Congressional action, thus taking an adversary and political as well as an analytic route to ultimate decision.

The ten billion barrels of oil found on Alaska's North Slope were valued at early 1973 level and constellation of prices at up to $5 billion in present worth terms, a figure that does not include the unevaluated costs of environmental damages. With more recent price gyrations in commodity markets, particularly in the case of energy commodities, it is not clear what the real net present value would be currently, but it is certain not to be less and likely to be more, even in constant (1973) dollars.

The environmental costs, on the other hand, cannot be reckoned in such quantitative terms. First, the pipeline and access road, borrow pits, and related environmental disruptions will invade the one remaining vast, authentic wilderness area in the continental United States. To many individuals who place a high value on the retention of this area in an unmodified state, the Trans-Alaska pipeline represents an unmitigated calamity. Again, the quantitative value of retaining the Alaskan wilderness in its present state will turn on the assignment of rights or priority of claims and, as we have said before, this issue is not ultimately resolved, although the courts appear to have made a start.

Quite aside from the issue of retaining a vast pristine wilderness area, the hot oil pipeline will traverse long stretches of permafrost, as well as some of the most seismically active and violent areas on the continent. Not only is the tundra ecology very fragile, but the pipeline will cross migratory wildlife routes and innumerable rivers and streams in its 780-mile length.

While fail-safe construction of the pipeline is conceivable, costs mount dramatically as the probability of failure is progressively reduced, and it is safe to assume that the construction standards will fall short of those necessary to ensure absence of failure with certainty, during the life of the project. It is not possible, given present information, to determine the probability and extent of failure, and hence to begin to estimate the environmental impact in quantitative terms. As for the actual effects of failure, a great deal will depend on federal construction stipulations and the vigor with which construction and operations are monitored, a record which to date has not been especially distinguished. The environmental damage will not be restricted to the overland route because the terminal transshipment and oceanic leg is also subject to risk of spillage from normal operation and ballast discharge. Tanker accidents are a particular hazard, given the difficult meteorological conditions, oceanic currents, and attendant navigational problems.

All the environmental hazards notwithstanding, given the uncertainty regarding many factors on which an environmental assessment depends, it is not possible to say that environmental costs exceed the value of the oil raised and delivered to market—nor, on the other hand, that they do not. But, whether owing to the difficulty in quantification of environmental costs, the intuitive judgment that environmental costs cannot exceed the range of value the oil is reckoned to have, the unequal access to the decision makers that gainers and losers from the project had, or for whatever reason, the decision to raise and deliver to market North Slope oil never seemed to be seriously in doubt.

The problem that did seem worthy of serious and widespread discussion, however, and in which economics was able to play a more important analytic role, had to do with the selection of market destination for such oil and the route and transport mode of greatest economic (and environmental) efficiency. Because the Midwest and Northeast were suffering petroleum supply shortages relative to the West Coast, and given the nature of administered pricing in the industry, petroleum delivered to the Midwest and Northeast reflected a higher value, quite apart from transport cost differentials.

In his analysis of the alternative routes and markets, Cicchetti established the superiority of the Trans-Canada route, and the Midwest and East Coast markets. The superiority was dominant. That is, not only did this route and market destination have an economic advantage over the alternative Trans-Alaska and the West Coast markets, but the environmental damages of the former route were also evaluated to be less than for the Trans-Alaska route. Accordingly, while it was not possible to determine whether the environmental damages were expected to be more or less than the value of the oil at markets, it was possible to determine that the damages associated with one route were less than those associated with the other. Since the damages were less and the net value at markets greater for the Trans-Canada pipeline, this solution dominated its alternative. A possible qualification to this conclusion relates to the question of the ease or difficulty, and hence potential difference in time, that would be involved in clearing access across Canada with the Canadian government and public. This is a matter on which economic analysis can say very little.

MANAGEMENT-RELEVANT POLICY AND RESEARCH RECOMMENDATIONS

Some of the conclusions of these analyses are rather easily come by; others may not be so crisp nor the direction from here so clear. It is readily perceived that it is very difficult to compare the value of resource commodities with the value of the environmental amenity services (or even environmental life support systems) that are destroyed by extraction. Often the evaluation of the environmental damages will defy our best efforts under any circumstances. This is certainly true of the circumstances surrounding the North Slope oil delivery system. But even in much more simple cases, for example in the Hells Canyon case, the *comprehensive* assessment of the value of environmental amenities destroyed, even without the liability assignment problem, is a very difficult problem, only parts of which we have been able to factor out and deal with effectively.

It is clear from court decisions and the environmental and amenity-oriented legislation of the past decade or so that the public is aware of the values inherent in the environment and of the need for protective legislation. It is also clear that public institutions, policies, and practices are required to give effective expression to that legislative intent. We should not violate environmental amenities frivolously or engage in trivial enterprises, with no obvious net gain in welfare for the community, which are certain to have deleterious environmental side effects.

If these values are accepted, then it is clear that all public commodity resource development or extractive projects, or even private projects of this sort requiring complementary public resource inputs, should receive careful and competent economic evaluation by disinterested personnel of an agency or institution established pursuant to the National Environmental Policy Act—or subsequent legislation with broadly similar intent. The reason for this should be obvious. Many projects will appear to have a net welfare gain, i.e., benefits exceeding costs (excluding unevaluated environmental costs), only because of the failure to account for all of the normal (nonenvironmental) costs. Two of the three proposals for the Hells Canyon development, for example, were not viable when the true opportunity cost of capital was imputed to the proposed investment.

There are several sources of spurious results in evaluation of public resource development projects. One major element of inaccurate cost representations, and hence bias in benefit–cost comparisons, on such projects is a differentially lower discount rate in these programs than required for cost-effectiveness analysis throughout the remainder of the federal government, and *a fortiori* in the private sector. Promised yields on investment in such programs can be a little over half of the capital's opportunity costs (the yields forgone in sectors from which such funds are diverted) and still show a spurious positive net benefit.[1]

A second source of cost suppression that results in biased benefit–cost comparisons for extractive undertaking or resource development projects involves the widespread incidence of preferential tax treatment accorded extractive industries. These include depletion allowances, expensing capital investments, and related practices that require the U.S. Treasury indirectly, and the general public ultimately, to defray the costs of such activities.[2]

Finally, the practice of deficit sales by the Forest Service, which permits timber to be sold on the stump at prices that will not return to the Forest Service the cost of the services it is obligated to perform as part of the sale, will lead to unwarranted resource extraction undertakings. Needless to say, the value of the timber so logged is less than its cost of logging and thus represents a net welfare loss to society independent of the environmental costs that typically are associated, in greater or lesser degree, with logging activities.

Since it is much more simple to do a competent evaluation of the true factor or resource costs of such projects than to undertake comprehensive environmental impact evaluations, many enterprises of this sort, which appear trivial when viewed in the context of larger social purposes, could be screened without need for the more difficult assessment of environmental costs. Given agency biases in matters affecting their own programs,

---

[1] An ostensible reason for the lower discount rate as suggested, for example, in the National Water Commission Report, is to "take care of the future." With average yields in these programs being only about half the returns to the capital employed elsewhere in the economy, public and private sectors alike, it is quite obvious that what is being taken care of is the public construction agencies and the members of Congress in whose districts such projects are built. If there is an honest desire to reduce consumption and increase investment, hence redistribute welfare to future members of society, an equivalent rate should be applied uniformly across all sectors of the economy. Even this does not ensure that scarce resources will be husbanded— low interest rates will stimulate investment everywhere, not discriminating between those requiring and those not requiring accelerated consumption of scarce resources. A more appropriate approach is to reflect the divergence in the relative benefits over time associated with the anticipated future relative scarcity of the resources in question, and discount all benefit streams by the same rate, as was done in the case studies in this volume. To do otherwise is to ensure perverse conservation consequences. See chapter 4; also Fisher and Krutilla, "Resource Conservation, Environmental Preservation and the Rate of Discount," *Quarterly Journal of Economics,* forthcoming.

[2] R. Talbot Page, "Economics of a Throwaway Society," manuscript in preparation.

the cost-effectiveness analyses should be entrusted to a disinterested cadre of competent professionals whose loyalties would not be subject to subversion by identification with the agencies benefiting from such activities.[3] A real gain, consistent with the recent body of environmental legislation, would likely result from simply eliminating activities of this sort which have substantial adverse effects on the environment. These projects presently survive only because of the spurious economic evaluations built into the public resources development process.

While it is true that a very large number of public and publicly related undertakings would be eliminated in this manner, many others having adverse environmental impacts would survive the screening process. And while even here the projects would benefit from a professionally competent economic evaluation, it is perhaps true that ultimately the environmental damages reckoned as economic costs will have to be assessed if the public land and related resources are to be managed consistently with the maximization of public benefits. Our studies, and those of our collaborating associates, whose work we have drawn upon in this volume, indicate that progress can be made on this methodologically difficult front. While the accomplishments may not be inconsequential in relation to the time and resources committed to the undertaking, the results are modest in the extreme in relation to the magnitude of the problem that requires attention.

With almost a third of the nation's area in public ownership, and with the call for evaluation of literally hundreds of tracts of land incumbent on the land management agencies under terms of the Wilderness Act alone, the five cases presented in this volume represent a feeble effort indeed to cope with the problem. In more optimistic terms, however, substantial theoretical and methodological advances were achieved in analyzing the five cases reported on in this volume. These are available for application to many other cases. Even so, much additional work is required on the conceptual and operational levels as well as on application to problems arising in connection with forest land allocation, mineral and energy leasing, and other resource development, including extractive undertakings on public lands and rivers. As some substantial proportion of these will have destructive consequences for irreproducible natural environments of substantial value, it is important that more sensitive and sophisticated methods of analysis be applied more widely in evaluation of alternatives by public land and resource managers than has been true of the past, and than is promised in the foreseeable future by existing institutions and processes. This poses a serious problem of logistics and communication, suggesting the need for some pertinent new institutional arrangements and efforts.

The problem to be confronted has two aspects: (1) the application of

---

[3] This suggestion is not original, of course. It was a key recommendation of the first Hoover Commission, and has surfaced from time to time in various contexts since then.

the methodology illustrated, in part, in this volume to analyses of future allocation of wild and scenic land and water resources, and (2) the extension and further development of methodology appropriate to such resource allocation decisions. The combination of budget ceilings and inflation has eroded the ranks of resource management agency personnel over the past few years. Given the resulting composition of agency priorities and staff remaining, it is unrealistic to expect the extension and development of resource allocation methodology, even if other aspects of the bureaucratic environment were propitious. Where innovative methodological and applied research is required—as it is in these circumstances—it appears that as a minimum, complementary talent for the task should be recruited from outside the resource management agencies and should operate at least partially outside the administrative framework of the federal bureaucracy.

Under normal circumstances, much of this work might eventually grow out of isolated individual scholarship at universities. However, the time required for these results to emerge from the traditional academic process exceeds the time frame within which the developed methodology should be applied if it is to be useful in assisting with the numerous irreversible land allocation and management decisions on the near horizon. It is worth noting, for example, that the Water Resources Council, while recognizing the work done on the estimation of demand in outdoor recreation spawned by the seminal work of Clawson some 15 years ago, nevertheless recommended some arbitrarily selected "interim" values for the benefits of a recreation day pending further development and refinement of the recreation demand models. Doubtless conservatism was a factor in the council's reluctance to use econometric models for demand estimation while implicitly embracing hydrologic models that provide estimates of extreme events with a larger range of variability. Nevertheless, the fact remains that research on recreation demand estimation, carried on in desultory fashion, with meager support over 15 years, has not produced cumulative results sufficiently compelling to induce their use in water resource development planning.

The work done over the past 15 years in outdoor recreation economics reveals the deficiency of uncoordinated, ill-supported efforts pursued in a young, developing field. Isolated studies by researchers unaware of similar efforts conducted elsewhere have resulted in duplication of some kinds of work, the adoption of nonuniform conventions in classification of data used in analysis, and evolution of procedures sufficiently dissimilar that the results of individual efforts cannot be integrated directly in cumulative fashion in subsequent studies, nor used widely for many planning purposes. The extent of these differences became evident during a set of workshops sponsored by the Marine Fisheries Service during July and September of 1972. It was also evident, through the mechanism of the workshop and the enlarged possibilities for communication among research scholars such interchange provides, that the differences could be identified readily, as could those issues which, because of their difficulty, deserved early, concerted attention. Unfortunately, the workshops themselves were an isolated event. Yet, if continued, they could have served the same function as did the early National Income Conferences in the development of the conceptual foundations and empirical procedures that were necessary to the development of national income accounting. This would be especially true if the mechanism were designed to include professionals from the land management agencies to assist in reducing the lag in communication between research discoveries and their diffusion within the ranks of agency personnel.

Given the quite rudimentary state of the analytical methods necessary for assisting land managers in allocation decisions affecting irreplaceable assets, the current lag in the communication of methodological advances and research findings, and the lag in the diffusion of the useful results of research among members of the resource management community, it is obvious there is a need to accelerate the rate of development and communication of such advances in knowledge within the relevant research community as well as between it and the resource management agencies. There is need for some institutional innovation that would be designed to achieve this end with a sufficiently high probability of success to warrant financial support.

It is not immediately obvious what form this institution should take. There may be various ways in which to proceed, and indeed this is a matter that is worth thoughtful attention. In any event, it may be appropriate here to sketch out one possible avenue to pursue. While not the only one possible, it may serve as a starting point.

Given the magnitude of the analytic task and the number of cases that will require study, it seems desirable to mobilize the research resources of the academic and allied research communities. Moreover, because of the widespread distribution of public lands throughout much of the country (albeit with the heaviest representation in the western United States and Alaska), several regional centers might be envisioned. The disappointing record revealed in some of the efforts undertaken by university institutes and consortia in the past suggests that careful thought should be given to the way the undertaking is organized if it is to be effective. Several desiderata are listed below:

1. The mission of the centers should be clearly defined so that there would be no misunderstanding about how the resources with which they are provided are to be used. This is necessary to ensure that the centers do not become simply havens for the pursuit of individual interests that

contribute little or nothing to the primary purpose for which they are established.

2. To assure that the centers have sufficient intellectual vitality to attract well-qualified university scholars, their mission should embrace fundamental methodological work as well as applied analyses of specific land allocation cases of immediate concern to the land management agencies.

3. Basic funding for a core staff of each center ideally should be provided from sources other than the land management agencies (e.g., foundations) in order to assure support for the methodological work and to provide a measure of independence from the immediate program and policy objectives of the land management agencies.

4. Basic funding for the core staff of each center should be for a limited term to avoid the risk of having these institutions outlive their usefulness; at the same time such funding should cover a sufficiently long period (such as 5 to 7 years) to permit initiation and completion of a significant block of research.

5. The public land management agencies should perceive a need for the centers, be prepared to use their services, and finance the services they use.

6. A strong central organization should receive and disburse funds in support of basic methodological work to ensure that the objectives of the centers are achieved; this central organization would also foster exchange of ideas among the centers through working conferences and other methods of communication.

These points outline some of the desirable attributes of an undertaking that could be responsive to the specialized research needs of improved public land management. Organizationally, the model might take the following form.

Given the locationally specific nature of the site evaluations to be made, several well-selected regional centers might be established. The locations would be subject to such considerations as the geographical distribution of university-based (and perhaps other) research talent. A university appears to be a desirable host since it would facilitate the recruitment of research talent and provide access to suitable research facilities. The center should have an independent status through special arrangements that provide for convenient access to, and services for, scholars from universities at locations other than the regional center, both from within and outside the region. In time, much of the "bread and butter" activities of the centers might be performed under research agreements for specific site evaluation studies on behalf of the contracting land management agency. Initially, however, general developmental funding would be required to undertake the necessary task of identifying the sites of regional centers and to initiate the organization of working conferences and provision of related administrative services. Throughout, in addition, general funding would be required to advance work of a general methodological nature and for the standardization of procedures that would fall outside the compass of any individual contract for a specific site evaluation.

The responsibility for organizing the undertaking and providing the administrative services for the regional centers should be assigned to a central body. The membership of this body should be independent of the universities to whom the undertaking would look for research talent. It would receive general funding for the developmental phase and for financing of functions of a general support nature, e.g., the organization of workshops, development of basic methodology that is broadly applicable to many cases, standardization of procedures, and so on.

Finally, close liaison between members of the research pools, central organization, and something like an interagency committee on standards and procedures of land and related resource management agencies should be built into the arrangement. Such liaison would facilitate the incorporation of research results and general information into agency guidelines for allocation and management of public lands. This arrangement would serve partly as a "learn-by-doing" effort to assist the land management agencies to develop the analytical capability they currently lack. However, the arrangement should be viewed as a reciprocal exchange because the members of such an interagency committee would have much to contribute to the academic community based on their practical experience, a generally good grasp of the technical details of a given problem, and access to agency scientific personnel required for scientific data inputs to analysis. The interagency committee might be likened to the original Subcommittee on Benefits and Costs of the Inter-agency River Basin Committee, which functioned during the 1940s and 1950s until establishment of the Water Resources Council. But it would be responsible for broader functions and, as explained above, would interact between both the academic research community and the respective agency practitioners.

Hopefully through the establishment of a number of regional centers, or some other alternative means whereby work of the nature suggested above could proceed at an accelerated pace and more adequate level than otherwise likely, land management agencies would have access to adequate research resources, results of competently conducted research, and the prospect of training a cadre of their own professionals better able to respond with greater sensitivity and sophistication to the problems that need to be addressed if they are to manage the public lands in a manner that maximizes public benefits.

AFTERWORD

It has been a dozen or more years since the analyses published in the first edition of *The Economics of Natural Environments* were completed. These studies were undertaken because they involved major public policy decisions. Indeed, most of the cases were argued before the Supreme Court at one stage or another in their resolution and all involved acts of government at the highest level by both the legislative and executive branches. With such a collection of cases, it seems only appropriate that this volume should carry an afterword concerning the outcomes to which these analyses contributed.

MINERAL KING VALLEY

The prospective development of Mineral King Valley for high-density, all-season recreation was the object of controversy that took a dozen years to resolve. During this time, the Sierra Club case against the development eventually reached the Supreme Court. The prospective development originated as long ago as 1949 when the Forest Service issued a development prospectus for winter sports. The prospectus did not receive an enthusiastic response. One developer withdrew after appraising the access costs. Although there was a desultory effort by the Forest Service to promote winter recreation facilities for Mineral King Valley thereafter, nothing significant happened until 1965. In that year there were a number of major developments.

The first of these was when the Forest Service requested proposals from prospective developers. The second was the award of a permit allowing Walt Disney Productions to develop the Mineral King Valley for a year-round recreational facility. The third was the signing of a bill by Governor (Pat) Brown of California that authorized a road to Mineral King Valley as part of the state highway system. The fourth was the opposition to this development by the Sierra Club. This opposition was maintained through the courts until it reached the Supreme Court for a ruling. The Supreme Court ruled in April of 1972 that the Sierra Club did not have standing to bring a class action suit, but did not rule on the merits of the club's case.

The Court let it be known in the ruling that while the club could not bring a class action suit against the prospective development, if any member or members of the club could establish that they would be injured by such a development those individuals could plead their case in court, and in July of that year the U.S. District Court allowed the Sierra Club to amend its complaint and return to litigation.

A number of things occurred that influenced the final outcome. The access to the Mineral King proposed facilities would need to cross the Sequoia National Park; indeed, the highway would disturb one of the giant sequoia groves, and Secretary of the Interior Stuart Udall, as well as the Sierra Club and the environmentally sensitive public, had some problems with that. Moreover, the road was to be provided at public expense to service a single private facility. A lot of people had problems with that. Finally, the passage of the National Environmental Policy Act (NEPA) in 1969 resulted in a protracted deferral of the development decision pending the preparation of an environmental impact statement. The final environmental impact statement did not clear all hurdles before February of 1976.

During 1976 there was a national election followed by a change in administration. A year after taking office, President Jimmy Carter was advised to recommend the extension of the boundaries of Sequoia National Park—which adjoined Mineral King Valley for much of the latter's perimeter—to include Mineral King Valley within the park. This recommendation was adopted and effectuated in Public Law 95-625 in November of 1978. In addition to the provisions for incorporating the valley into the park, the law contained a section (313-h) to the effect that the development of high-density, downhill skiing facilities (code word for Walt Disney Productions) would not be compatible with the ambiance of Mineral King Valley—to the profound dismay of golfers, bowlers, and devotees of shuffleboard and cotton candy.

HELLS CANYON

The passage of Public Law 94-199 in December of 1975 established the Hells Canyon National Recreation Area, which, among other things, added the canyon to the National Wilderness Preservation System and the Snake River in that reach to the National Wild and Scenic River System. Thus the effort to develop the Hells Canyon for its power potential, begun two decades before, was blunted with about half of the canyon preserved in its natural state.

The hydroelectric potential of the Snake River in the Hells Canyon reach commended itself to engineers from early times,[1] and actual development of

[1] "Columbia River and Tributaries, Northwestern United States," House Document No. 531, 81st cong., 2nd. sess., March 20, 1950.

the canyon began shortly after the Eisenhower Administration proclaimed its so-called "Partnership Policy." In the mid-1950s the Idaho Power Company sought to preempt a goodly portion of the Hells Canyon with a proposed five-dam development. The company hoped to get a permit to develop over an extended period of time and thus accommodate its immoderate appetite to its modest size. The Federal Power Commission (FPC) found that the proposed application for license did not conform with the efficient development of the hydroelectric potential and suggested that a proposal that would include development of some of the great storage potential of that reach of the Snake River would be required. After that, the company applied for a three-dam development, involving the Hells Canyon, Oxbow, and Brownlee sites, the latter including storage. The FPC examiner found in favor of the Idaho Power Company's development of one of the sites but found against licensing it for all of the sites on grounds that the sites that it sought to develop would exceed its needs for a very long time and thus tie up the potential for an unnecessarily long period. The FPC overruled the examiner on the latter point, and Idaho Power Company was licensed to develop all three sites. Upon completion, this "modest" undertaking trebled Idaho Power Company's capacity and is regarded by many as the crowning achievement of the Partnership Policy.

At about the same time, the Pacific Northwest Power Company (PNPC) applied for a similar development in the lower reaches of the canyon. Concern over criticism that its licensing of the Idaho Power Company development did not evidence enough rigor in pursuit of its responsibility (under the Federal Power Act) for seeing to the efficient development of the hydroelectric potential, the FPC advised the applicant to revise the application in a way to develop favorable conditions for substantial storage. There was tacit understanding that if such an application were forthcoming, the commission would have every reason to issue the applicant a license to develop the lower reach of the canyon. With this understanding, PNPC proceeded with the prerequisite "preliminary investigations" that involved a great deal of serious engineering work. These investigations ran into some millions of dollars.

When completed, consistent with all expectations, the FPC proceeded with licensing PNPC, but a hitch developed. There was another change of administrations and the new secretary of the interior, Stuart Udall, had a different vision of partnership. Given the extensive federal development of hydroelectric head on both the lower Snake and lower Columbia rivers, he asserted that the federal government had a paramount interest in the development. To demonstrate his conviction he took the matter to court where the Supreme Court found that there was no evidence in the record of the PNPC licensing hearings that this issue was addressed. So the Supreme Court remanded the case to the FPC for rehearing. Moreover, almost as an *obiter dictum*, the Court stated that it had found no evidence in the record that the alternative of not developing the remaining portion of the canyon had been considered. The statement on this issue read to the effect that it was not enough to establish that this was the least expensive way for the PNPC to obtain power, but that the question of whether or not the value of such power would compensate for the damage to the salmon and steelhead fisheries and related natural amenities should be addressed.

The case went back to the FPC for rehearing but before the hearing was completed there was again a change in administrations and the Nixon Administration withdrew the federal claim to an interest in the issue. The attorney for PNPC moved to have the FPC recognize that the issue was now moot because the federal government had withdrawn an interest in building a dam in the reach of the Snake that PNPC had applied for license to develop. The examiner demurred, however, drawing attention to the fact that the Supreme Court wanted the applicant to demonstrate that the project would indeed merit building given the impact such construction would have on the amenities of the undeveloped canyon's environment (to which numerous expert witnesses attested). This then converted the hearings to an uncomplicated case of preservation or development. Accordingly, the hearings proceeded until properly concluded.

Staff Counsel for the FPC took quite seriously the Court's instruction to weigh the value of the amenities before making the staff recommendation. And, he went about doing so very conscientiously. Indeed, on the basis of the considerations that were addressed in this undertaking he was moved to recommend against the issuance of the license.

This, of course, placed the FPC in a dilemma because the applicant had faithfully carried out all of the preliminary investigations at no small expense to itself in the belief that having acted in good faith it was entitled to receive the license. The examiner had some trying days.

When the time arrived to announce his decision, the examiner, conscious of the commitment given in good faith, arrived at the following decision. The license was to be issued to PNPC but not to take effect for a period of five years, during which the departments of agriculture and interior would have an opportunity to evaluate the Hells Canyon and environs to determine whether they qualified for inclusion in one of the national preservation systems. At that point the political forces that manifest themselves in circumstances such as these went into play, with the result that Public Law 94-199, The Hells Canyon National Recreation Act, made it through Congress and was signed by President Gerald Ford in December of 1975.

The act established immediately the Hells Canyon Wilderness, a 193, 132 acre canyon wilderness and provided for the addition of other wilderness areas beyond the canyon rim. Such wilderness area candidates were proposed for congressional action by the chief of the Forest Service, whose agency administers the Hells Canyon National Recreation Area. In addition to the wild lands and river preservation features of the legislation, a section of the lower reaches of the middle Snake was designated as a higher density recreational area. All three features were foreseen in the 1975 Hells Canyon National Recreation Act. A plan for the management of the recreation areas has been drawn up, and an environmental impact statement issued. Appeals to reconsider portions of the plan were filed with the chief of the Forest Service and reviewed by the secretary's office. The final decision regarding the details of administration was ultimately reached by the secretary of agriculture in April of 1984.

ALLOCATION OF PRAIRIE WETLANDS

The last paragraph of chapter 9 suggests that there was some ambivalence about the accuracy, or at least adequacy, of the data available to evaluate the productivity of prairie potholes for production of migratory waterfowl. The moderate ambivalence, however, was an understatement of the reservations expressed by Hammack and Brown in their monograph, *Wetlands and Waterfowl: Toward Bioeconomic Analysis*.[2] We nevertheless thought that presenting the basic model had merit, and although the quantitative results may not merit confidence because of the inadequacy of the data, the data were good enough to illustrate the application of analysis to a practical problem faced by managers of the migratory waterfowl program. This decision seems to have been vindicated by events that followed.

One of the important functions of the U.S. Fish and Wildlife Service involves the responsibility for migratory waterfowl under the several treaties with Canada, Japan, and Mexico negotiated during the first quarter of the present century. Failing to provide an operable funding method for a federal program of systematic wildlife refuge acquisitions under the Migratory Bird Conservation Act of 1929, the Congress subsequently passed the Migratory Bird Hunting Stamp Act of 1934. The funds from stamps, required of all waterfowl hunters over the age of sixteen, were supposedly to be used for acquisition of new lands. But in fact they were used mostly for operation and management of existing refuges for about the first twenty-five years of their existence.[3] Because the funds raised by this act were not used in accordance with the understanding of the sportsmen who had supported passage of this legislation, Congress amended the act in 1958 to restrict the

[2] Judd Hammack and Gardner Mallard Brown, Jr., *Waterfowl and Wetlands: Toward Bioeconomic Analysis* (Baltimore, Md., Johns Hopkins University Press for Resources for the Future, 1974).
[3] Michael J. Bean, *The Evolution of National Wildlife Law* (Washington, D.C.: Council of Environmental Quality, 1977).

funds raised for use only in the acquisition of "refuges and wildlife production areas."

While this legislation provided for a continuing stream of funds, it was soon discovered that the funds were not sufficient to preserve an adequate acreage of wetlands to achieve the Interior Department's long-range goal of 2.5 million acres. Recognizing the need for a quicker acquisition of such lands, Congress passed the Wetlands Loan Act of 1961, which authorized an advance appropriation to the fund of up to $105 million over a seven-year period. This authority was renewed in 1967 and was up for reconsideration in 1975. At that time, however, the Office of Management and Budget (OMB) questioned the justification for an extension of this legislation, holding that the request from the Fish and Wildlife Service lacked the supporting documentation OMB would require to recommend the extensions.

The Fish and Wildlife Service professionals, who largely represent the biological sciences, were unprepared and unable to respond in the way OMB directed. Faced with this reality Michael Spear, the programs and budget officer for the service, requested assistance from Robert K. Davis, assistant director of the Interior Department's Office of Policy Analysis. Davis, himself an accomplished analyst in the estimation of benefits from non-priced resource services, called attention to the Hammack and Brown monograph. Given an appropriate model with which to work, access to a great amount of relevant data, and Davis's assistance, the professionals in the Fish and Wildlife Service determined to organize and package the data in a manner understandable to OMB. That is, they undertook to evaluate the benefits and costs of an extension of the program using the Hammack-Brown analytic model. Their presentation to the OMB staff upon their return had dramatic effects. OMB not only agreed to recommend an extension of the legislation, but to do so at a higher funding level. And the Congress obliged in February of 1976.

THE WHITE CLOUD PEAKS

The disposition of the White Cloud Peaks was already known in outline at the time the first edition of this volume was published. Legislation had been passed in 1972 that made the Sawtooth Range, the Valley, and explicitly the White Cloud Peaks all parts of a national recreation area. For some period the Sawtooth Range had enjoyed recognition as an outstanding scenic area and was the object of a proposal for national park status as early as 1911. Additional bills were introduced in 1916, 1935, 1960, and 1963. The first bill promoting the Sawtooth Range and associated attractions as a national recreation area was introduced in 1965, but was amended in 1969 to include the White Cloud Peaks by the Idaho senators' responding to local reaction to the prospect of molybdenum mining there.

The Sawtooth National Recreation Area legislation, enacted in August of 1972, contained a provision that would require the National Park Service to review the area to see if it qualified as a unit of the National Park System. The National Park Service undertook a five-year, comprehensive, study of the area and did indeed identify two units (totaling 686,000 acres) of the Sawtooth National Recreation Area as a potential two-unit National Park, and a two-unit National Recreation Area of 332,220 acres. Although these areas met the criteria for national park status, in the judgment of Secretary of Interior Cecil Andrus they were too large for the National Park System to absorb. There is a suggestion in his letter to the President (February 10, 1977) that the funds available to the Park Service would be better spent ". . . in our rejuvenation effort of the existing park system." He alluded to the continued sensitive management of the National Recreation Area by the Forest Service as sufficient ". . . to protect those worthy environmental qualities."

There is one final bit of information of relevance. While the White Cloud Peaks remained within the umbrella recreation area, they have also continued to attract attention as worthy candidates for the expanding National Wilderness Preservation System. In Senator James McClure's bill for the Idaho wilderness addition, the White Cloud Peaks are prominently featured with provisions to buy out the rights of ASARCO. Although Senator Mc-Clure's bill did not come up for action, it is likely that the White Cloud Peaks will be included in whatever wilderness legislation comes out of Idaho because all of the other options are more liberal in adding *de facto* wilderness than is the McClure Bill.

TRANS-ALASKA PIPELINE

The outcome of the Trans-Alaska pipeline was clear by the time we drafted our chapter discussing the issue. The Prudhoe Bay to Valdez pipeline was authorized through a series of legal, judicial, and legislative actions by 1973 and the pipeline was built according to plan. That is history.

Still it is instructive to consider in retrospect the quality of Cicchetti's analysis. In his study he made a convincing case that the wrong oil was going to the wrong place at the wrong time. He predicted the surplus of petroleum in the California area and argued that the market for oil was in the midwest (Chicago) and New England. Indeed, in retrospect, it is exactly what the situation is. The authorities in California will not permit the oil to land there because they have no need for it domestically, no facilities to transport it across country to markets in the midwest and northeast, nor, given the atmospheric pollution problems in southern California, can they handle the crude in California refineries. The crude from Alaska eventually arrives in the Virgin Islands for refining and thereafter for transshipment to the United States. The reason for this is that it was obvious to all who participated in the debate that the original conception and justification of the oil raising and shipping on the North Slope involved Japan as the ultimate destination. And in this context the Trans-Alaska pipeline made sense. Unfortunately, there was a great deal of subterfuge necessary to enact the legislation amending the Mineral Leasing Act of 1920 to enable the secretary of the interior to issue a right-of-way permit sufficiently wide to make possible the building of the Prudhoe Bay to Valdez pipeline. Those who were aware of the subterfuge managed to get legislation that would prohibit the oil to flow to Japan, and part of the reason for this was the sincere concern about the environmental damage that would occur. Environmentalists involved in this conflict felt such hazards should not be accepted on behalf of foreign beneficiaries, and to that end, and with that argument, legislation was enacted that would prevent Prudhoe Bay crude oil to go to other than American markets.

Whatever else may be said about the current problem concerning an economic disposition of Prudhoe Bay crude, what occurs is likely to be consistent with Cicchetti's analysis of a dozen or so years ago.

INDEX

294   **Index**

Challis National Forest. *See* White Cloud
Peaks.
Chase, S. B., 61*n*, 124
China Garden project: hydroelectric
power evaluation, 103
Christy, F. T., Jr., 12*n*, 48
Cicchetti, C. J., 13*n*, 14*n*, 27, 70, 86, 93,
123, 124, 128, 133*n*, 139*n*, 140, 164,
190, 195*n*, 198*n*, 201*n*, 235, 237, 240*n*,
241*n*, 243, 244, 250*n*, 251, 252*t*, 258*n*,
261*n*
Classification and Multiple Use Act of
1964, 3, 7
Clawson, Marion, 10, 90, 124, 196, 197
Clean Air Act of 1967, 4, 35*n*
Coase, R. H., 29, 33
Coase theorem, 29–32
Common property resources, 266–67;
characteristics of public lands, 21; externalities of, 26, 27–28; methods of
assignment of rights, 33–35; optimal
allocation, 32–33; relationship with
public lands and goods, 25
Congestion costs: of jointly supplied services, 26; reciprocal nature, 27–28
Consumer's surplus: effect on property
rights assignment, 31–32; in determining the option value, 70; estimation of
recreation resources demand, 199–200;
of related ski goods and services, 208;
valuation function of prairie wetlands,
223–24
Consumption plan: for intergenerational
transfers, 66–67
Crissey, Walter, 219, 225
Cummings, Ronald, 47

D
Davis, O. A., 23
Davis, R. K., 10, 223
Deaton, A., 200*n*
Demand for amenities services, 13–14;
measurement of growth, 129–32
Demsetz, Harold, 33
Development benefits: discount rate deter-
mination, 65; equation with initial
year's preservation benefits, 126–27,
132–33, 134*t*; use in evaluation of
preservation benefits, 126–28; of Hells
Canyon hydroelectric project, 92; of
Hells Canyon reservoir recreation, 93–
97; for intergenerational transfers, 68;

of Mineral King Valley, 213*t*, 215–16;
of North Slopes oil, 240–41; in the
optimal control problem, 55
Discount rate: in conservation of exhaustible resources, 60–65; proposals
for federal projects, 167–68
Dorfman, Robert, 49*n*, 62*n*
Ducks Unlimited, 220, 227

E
Earthquakes: Trans-Alaskan pipeline
hazards, 237
Eckstein, Otto, 10*n*, 24*n*, 62, 63, 88, 100*n*,
208
Ecology: wilderness demand effect, 14
Eisner, Robert, 51*n*
Electrical World, 99*n*
Ely, R. T., 9
Environmental benefits: from smaller hy-
droelectric power projects, 105
Environmental Defense Fund, 19, 258
Environmental impact policy recommen-
dations, 277–83; of the Trans-Alaska
pipeline, 236–38, 240; Trans-Canadian
pipeline study, 256–57
Environmental impact statement: role in
public land management, 7
Environmental Law Reporter, 126*n*
Environmental opportunity costs: role in
evaluation of natural resource uses, 81
Environmental organizations: effect on
land management decisions, 19
Espey, Larry, 94
Ethical neutrality: in allocation of prop-
erty rights, 33
Exclusion of public goods, 24, 25
Existence value of economic benefits, 124
Externalities, 26–27; relationship between
public lands and public goods, 25; uni-
directional nature, 27–28
Externalities, environmental: alternative
theory, 32–33; Coase theorem applica-
tions, 30–32
Extraction of resources, alternatives, 84–
86; irreversibility of, 47–48; in the
optimal control problem, 50; White
Cloud Peaks conflict with wilderness
recreation resources, 154–56. *See also*
Mining and milling operations.

F
Federal Power Act, 87–88